# The Celebrated Captain Barclay

## Sport, Gambling and Adventure in Regency Times

### Peter Radford

review

First published in 2001
by HEADLINE BOOK PUBLISHING

First published in paperback in 2002
by REVIEW

An imprint of HEADLINE BOOK PUBLISHING

10 9 8 7 6 5 4 3 2 1

ISBN 0 7472 6490 2

Typeset by Palimpsest Book Production Limited,
Polmont, Stirlingshire

Printed and bound in Great Britain by
Clays Ltd St Ives plc.

Text design by Jane Coney

HEADLINE BOOK PUBLISHING
A division of Hodder Headline
338 Euston Road
London NW1 3BH

www.headline.co.uk
www.hodderheadline.com

Books should be returned on or before the
last date stamped below

Peter Radford is one of Britain's leading sport historians and has been fascinated by the eighteenth and nineteenth centuries for many years. He is Professor of Sport Sciences at Brunel University in west London and previously held the same title at the University of Glasgow.

As an athlete, he held the World record for the 200 metres and was a double medallist in the Olympic Games in Rome in 1960. His British record for the 100 metres remained unbeaten for twenty years.

He is married, with one daughter, and lives in Burford, Oxfordshire.

For Margaret and Lizzie with love and gratitude.

# *Contents*

# ACKNOWLEDGMENTS

Many people have helped me pursue Captain Barclay, and I wish to thank all of them. First among these is Humphrey Barclay who very generously allowed me unrestricted access to the Barclay papers. I am also grateful to Sylvia Carlyle from the Quaker Library in London for information on and access to their holdings on Captain Barclay and his family. I am particularly indebted to Kay Munro from the Glasgow University Library, who for years tracked down some of the more elusive material. Indeed, as a breed, librarians and archivists have been more generous to me with their time and expertise than I had any reason to expect. This is a heart-felt 'thank-you' to the staff of: The National Archives of Scotland in Edinburgh, Birmingham Central Library Local Studies & History Services, The London Borough of Lambeth Archives Department, Forfar Public Library, City of Dundee Libraries Department, North East of Scotland Library Service in Aberdeen, Aboyne Public Library, North Yorkshire County Library, Suffolk County Council Archives Department, Burford and Witney Public Libraries in Oxfordshire, Birmingham University Library, the Regimental Museum of the Royal Welch Fusiliers in Caernarfon, the National Portrait Gallery of Scotland in Edinburgh, and the British Library. I am grateful to the National Archive of Scotland for permission to quote from the letter from Captain Barclay on page 209. I am also grateful to David Godfrey of Antique Newspapers, Guernsey and Albert Shaw who found and supplied me with contemporary newspapers of Captain Barclay and the Fancy, and to Nick Potter of Nick Potter Ltd. in Sackville Street, London, and Brian Newbury of the Parker Gallery in Pimlico Road, London, who found and supplied me with contemporary prints and engravings of them. I am also grateful to Laurence Allan of Spink-Leger in Old Bond Street, London, for helping me to understand the scope and layout of Jackson's Rooms. Writers who have specialised in this period have also generously given me leads. These have included Leslie Gardiner (*Stage Coach to John O'Groats*), Verily Anderson (*Friends and Relations*) and Penelope Hughes-Hallett (*The Immortal Dinner*). I am also grateful to Pat Burton, Marion Colvin and Ellen Hamill who helped me prepare the manuscript at an early stage. I must also thank Bill Glad whose enthusiasm for Captain Barclay has been a great encouragement and Megan Beard in Barry, South Wales on whose table so much of Captain Barclay's story was written.

Araminta Whitley and Celia Hayley of Lucas Alexander Whitley have also earned my sincere thanks for being models of professional guidance and support. Heather Holden-Brown and her team from Headline Book Publishing, and in particular Juliana Lessa, have also been as helpful, professional and friendly as anyone could wish for. My final thanks go to Lizzie whose interest and practical support at various stages have been invaluable, and to Margaret who not only loyally accompanied me on field trips to Thistleton Gap, Coxwold, Richmond, Stonehaven, East Dean, Newmarket, Bond Street and elsewhere, but has also had to live with the celebrated Captain for years and has seldom complained. Without Margaret this book would never have been written. I am happy to acknowledge my indebtedness to all the above and countless others who have helped in some way. Any errors or omissions are, of course, mine.

# CHAPTER ONE

# *The Greatest Ever Sporting Event*

> The Captain is backed freely in London at six to four,
> although a task equally difficult was never before performed.
>
> THE LONDON CHRONICLE, 3–5 JUNE 1809

> Captain BARCLAY was pursuing his extraordinary
> undertaking yesterday, but as he proceeds, the hopes of
> accomplishing it become even more feeble.
>
> THE EDINBURGH ADVERTISER, 4 JULY 1809

> He is confident of succeeding, and he declared on Saturday, he
> would die on the road rather than give in.
>
> THE EDINBURGH EVENING COURANT, 6 JULY 1809

> CAPTAIN BARCLAY – This Gentleman on
> Wednesday completed his arduous undertaking ... One
> hundred to one, and indeed any odds whatever, were offered on
> Wednesday morning ... but no bets could be obtained.
>
> THE TIMES, 14 JULY 1809

*I*t was the afternoon of Wednesday 12 July and by now the crowds on Newmarket Heath had grown so vast that most of the men, women and children had very little possibility of seeing the action. It was hot with the midsummer sun beating down as more and more people arrived, drawn by weeks of almost incessant media coverage in *The London Chronicle*, *The St James's Chronicle* and *The Times*. Already by the previous Monday the numbers had grown so dangerously large that workmen were called in to rope off the area to keep it clear and avoid any potentially disastrous interruptions.[1] Nevertheless, among the general hubbub, the noise of enthusiastic spectators and the smells from the food stalls, the mood was of excitement and satisfaction. Just being there was enough. Just being able to tell people when you got back home that you were there at the finish. Just being able to tell your children and your grandchildren that you had been there and been part of it. Part of the greatest human feat ever attempted. That was enough.

It was the summer of 1809, and the horses alone had never attracted such crowds to Newmarket. They had come to see one man. One man who had wagered that he could walk one mile every hour of every day and every night – without a break – Sundays included, for 1,000 hours. That is just nine hours short of six weeks. His name was Captain Robert Barclay. But it was not only the extraordinary challenge of endurance that attracted national attention; it was also the size of the bet. Captain Barclay's original wager was for 1,000 guineas against James Wedderburn-Webster, but with side-bets it was rumoured that it was worth 16,000 guineas if he succeeded. At the time a farm labourer or artisan earned on average about a guinea a week,[2] and so 50 guineas, as a year's wages, was the yardstick that most of the ordinary people who made up his audience would have used to measure Barclay's potential winnings. (On this basis we should multiply Captain Barclay's bets by 400 to get a notional modern equivalent.) So, for the majority of the crowd, Captain Barclay had originally wagered over twenty years' income, but now stood to take home the equivalent of nearly 320 years' income. It was impossible to comprehend. To add to all this, another of the rumours that circulated among the crowd, and was repeated by *The Times* two days later,[3] was that the gentlemen who had betted on this event had between them wagered £100,000, or according to our calculation, £40 million today. The Prince of Wales was one of them.[4]

Clearly, this was no ordinary event. Nor was it only about money. It was not merely that extraordinary sums were at stake, as in some games of roulette, hazard or faro among the high rollers of St James's lavish gambling clubs, this was an athletic event that challenged the very limit of human capability. Many thought it impossible, and we should not imagine that they were all poor judges of physical ability. In Georgian Britain, before the internal combustion engine or electricity, more people lived by the sweat of their brow and travelled by the strength and spring in their legs than has ever been the case since. Most knew more about what a man could achieve in a day on his own two feet than we could possibly know today. The accepted wisdom when Captain Barclay began was that this feat was impossible, or dangerously close to impossible. Everyone present knew of the potentially fatal consequences of pushing the body beyond its natural limits. It was common knowledge that a man, or even a racehorse or greyhound, could die from overdoing it and overheating their blood. All the gentlemen with an education also knew from Plutarch[5] and Lucian[6] that a runner in full armour went from Marathon to Sparta (1,160 stades or 145 miles), and heated from battle had time to say nothing more than 'Rejoice!' before dropping dead on the spot. What a pity that those recording such a great act of valour and heroism could not agree whether his name was Thersippus, Eukles or Philippedes.[7] There was also the story, again from Plutarch,[8] about Euchidas, who ran 1,000 stades (125 miles) to Plataia with a flaming torch, lit at the altar at Delphi. He just had time to greet his fellow citizens and hand over the sacred torch, before he, too, fell down and died. One of the reasons these long-distance events were so attractive to the crowds was because they were so risky.

'A thousand miles in a 1,000 hours for a 1,000 guineas' was a phrase that had been on everyone's lips even before 1 June, nearly six weeks earlier, when Barclay began, and had been ever since.[9] The 1,000 hours would be up at 4 p.m. and at 2.30 he had already completed 998 of them.[10] He had two left, one for the hour leading up to three o'clock and another for the hour leading up to four o'clock. Despite all the risks over the past few weeks, everyone now was fairly certain that nothing could go wrong. In the morning 100 to 1 and even more was offered but now no odds whatsoever could be obtained.[11] It was only a case of seeing out the formalities, enjoying the atmosphere and being part of the occasion.

Like most crowds, this one was made up of a vast assortment of people. All ages and social backgrounds were there, and they had come for a variety of reasons. There were the local farmers and their wives and sturdy children, the sporting gentlemen of the Fancy, the riffraff who always hung around the edges, and numerous gentlemen and ladies who would not normally be seen dead at a sporting event. Throughout the whole of June and the first half of July fashionable ladies and gentlemen arranged to be driven out in their barouche and four to see Captain Barclay complete his hourly mile, day and night, and they shared the turf with farmers, kitchen maids, grooms, tinkers and pickpockets. They took in the hustle and bustle of the two rival groups who, with their supporters, recorders and assistants, had established two tented camps at opposite ends of the half-mile course to accommodate them and to provide hospitality to themselves and their friends. Egged on by daily reports in all the newspapers, men and women came first in their hundreds and then in their thousands, to be at an event that became not merely a sporting occasion but a major social one also. They picnicked, ran races among themselves and cheered every time Captain Barclay appeared. They took care to keep out of the way of the gentlemen of the Fancy, the fanatics who supported all the sporting events, and who, between them, had risked so much money on this one. They probably regarded this event as 'theirs', and would have been happy if the other spectators had stayed away. A sporting occasion such as this one was too important to be used by the crowd merely as entertainment. But it was far too late for that. In July 1809 there was a carnival atmosphere on Newmarket Heath and most of Britain wanted to be part of it.

During the last few nights those who had made their way there had taken every available bed in Newmarket, Cambridge or any other town or village in the vicinity.[12] Not a horse or vehicle of any description was to be had anywhere. Among the spectators, in a position befitting their social rank, just inside the ropes, those in the know could recognise the Duke of Argyle, the Duke of St Albans, Earl Grosvenor, Earl Besborough, the Earl of Jersey, Lord Foley, Lord Somerville, Sir John Lade, Sir Francis Standish, Sir James Johnston and countless more that the eye could not take in.[13] Everyone told themselves, and with some justification, that there had *never* been an occasion like this before.

Just before 2.30 p.m. there was a buzz among those nearest to the Horse and Jockey Inn[14] as Captain Barclay stepped out into the sun surrounded by a posse of supporters. He was just six weeks away from his 30th birthday, and stood an inch under 6ft.[15] He had a slightly receding hairline and his face looked drawn from six weeks of minimal, broken sleep and incessant physical effort, but many of the women present may well have described him as 'handsome'. He had lost so much weight over the past six weeks[16] that his blue flannel jacket and cream-coloured flannel breeches hung on him as they would on a skeleton. Lambswool stockings and strong shoes with thick soles completed the ensemble.[17]

In all his previous sporting exploits people had always commented on his strong, imposing physical presence, and on his muscular, well-formed arms and shoulders.[18] Boxers in the bare-knuckle Prize Ring were built like Captain Barclay, not long-distance endurance athletes. In this event, though, he had been in great pain[19] and had lost a lot of weight, and his efforts had come close to breaking him. Nevertheless, he had now taken the bandage off his right leg and seemed to be in less pain than the previous day.

He seemed in good spirits and certainly looked better than he had in the early hours of the morning. His body may have shrunk over the past few weeks, but his spirit and determination seemed to have been magnified to make up the difference. His man, William Cross,[20] now gave a final check to the Captain's shoes. The watches were scrutinized for the umpteenth time, and over the line stepped Captain Barclay to begin his 999th and penultimate mile.

What the crowd also knew about him, but was not immediately apparent that day, was that Captain Barclay was a 'gentleman', with the blood of ancient Scottish kings pulsing through his veins. A man from a famous family and with a famous name. A man educated at Trinity College, Cambridge. A man, born into money, prestige and privilege, with extensive estates not far from Aberdeen. His father had been a Member of Parliament. Here was no run-of-the-mill athlete hired by a wealthy man merely to bet on. This was no poor roughneck reduced to exhausting himself in public for the price of one or two weeks' money to keep himself in drink and his family in bread. This was a man of substance and education. This was a man whose star was definitely in the ascendance, for just two weeks into this wager his name had been put forward to the War Office as the next lieutenant colonel of his local Kincardineshire Militia.[21] No wonder he had been able to plan and execute the whole thing with the detail and precision of a military campaign. No wonder he had unheard-of physical strength and endurance, and an almost frightening determination and mental toughness. But precisely why a gentleman with education, money, land and prospects would want to expose himself to so much avoidable suffering and risk was far less clear to the thousands present.

The course that Captain Barclay was following had been measured out from his rented accommodation in a largish house adjoining Mr Parkinson's, the stone mason's, and near the Horse and Jockey. It went across the Norwich Road and in a straight line across the heath to a post half a mile away. It was beautifully smooth and even, and the grass had such a fine, cropped sward you could have rolled a sixpence 100 yards on it, or so they said.[22] Every hour he walked over this course, up to and around the post and back. Now they watched him make his way out to the post and back with stiff, aching, and tired strides in 22 minutes.[23] Everyone in the crowd started chattering and calculating. The man appointed as Captain Barclay's recorder wrote down the time, 2.52 p.m., which meant that he had completed his 999th mile eight minutes inside the deadline. James Wedderburn Webster's recorder did the same. All Captain Barclay had to do was wait the eight minutes until the next hour, the 1,000th, began and he could set out on the final leg of this 1,000 mile epic.

The immense organisation of this unprecedented sporting event had begun secretly nine months previously when Captain Barclay arranged a clandestine trial at Ury, his estate in Scotland, for George Mollison, one of his tenant farmers and loyal, family friend, to go on foot one mile every hour for eight days. Mollison was a rugged 54-year-old who stood 6ft 3 inches tall and was well built, and after eight days he reported that he could go on for six months.[24] Captain Barclay knew that he couldn't, and that the chronic effects of physical fatigue and broken sleep would be cumulative and progressive, but he learned a lot about the problems that would be encountered regarding eating, sleeping, safety, lighting, and so much more. Within the 1,000-mile wager were 1,000 deadlines to be met, 1,000 trip wires to be negotiated, and there would be an untold number of opponents willing him to fail, and in some cases plotting it too. With so much money at stake the event had not always been 'gentlemanly'.

Captain Barclay knew that in an all-night event such as this, the course would have to be illuminated, and so he had seven gas lamps erected about 100 yards apart and set up on poles on either side of the course, like street lamp-posts.[25] Newmarket Heath had never before been lit. Many towns weren't. Even in fashionable London, streets lit with gas lamps were very new.[26] In 1809 this was the cutting edge of new technology. So much so that when the various artists came to record the occasion for posterity, the lamps were almost as important a feature of their pictures as the Captain himself. The pressures of sport and big money have always been a creative crucible for innovation and experimentation.

They worked, too; at least they worked as lamps, but not as a guarantee of trouble-free night-time walking. Some of the lamps were broken, either by musket shots, or by shadowy figures in the night, who hurled stones at them to break the glass and so give them the cover of darkness they needed for their planned nefarious deeds.[27] To ensure his own safety Captain Barclay arranged for Big John Gully, ex-Champion of the Prize Ring, to act as a bodyguard and accompany him at night.[28] He also resorted to carrying in a belt around his waist, a brace of pistols,[29] presumably loaded and primed – just in case.

Three o'clock arrived and passed and Barclay showed no eagerness to set off for his final hour. It was time to savour the moment and to look back affectionately at the many incidents, some of them quite recent, which at the time seemed so close to a major crisis, but now just added extra piquancy to his imminent success. In the fourth week, when William Cross took Captain Barclay to the starting line to begin the 607th mile, it was obvious that he was asleep, despite the fact that he was standing up. William Cross had to resort to violently beating his master around his shoulders with a walking stick.[30] This not only did the trick, as no alarm clock before or since had done, it also unleashed an unprecedented deluge of curses and abuse from the Captain. But it worked and the wager was saved. William Cross was one of the few men who could have survived treating Captain Barclay in such a way, but then he was no ordinary man. He was small, tough and gnarled like a plank of old weathered oak and his manners were more like those of a groom responsible for the horses, than those of a conventional manservant, but Captain Barclay could never have found a more loyal, more vigilant or more caring attendant than William Cross.

Strained ligaments in his right knee began to give the Captain serious trouble in week three, and he developed toothache in week four. Torrential rain soaked him and his greatcoat in weeks two, four and five,[31] making it almost too heavy to wear. Typical of an English summer, this gave way to choking clouds of dust when the weather turned hot in weeks one and four.[32] So hot and dry, a water cart had to be brought in to water the course.[33] Captain Barclay's planning and professional knowledge had all but won the day. Old Dr Sandiver had been a doubtful appointment. His traditional mixture of oils and camphor, and hot cloths, had failed to relieve the pain as often as it succeeded.[34] The move to the new course and the new lodgings had definitely been the right decision in week three.[35] Strangers and friends alike had rallied round, local families providing him with home-brewed ale and Aunt Gurney knitting him 'easy slippers',[36] while his youngest brother, David, Dick Gurney and others went to Newmarket to help in whatever way they could.[37] Perhaps the most satisfaction was felt from the success of his scheme to walk one mile towards the end of one hour and then to pause briefly and walk the next mile at the start of the new hour, thus walking two miles back-to-back. The important thing about this method was that it increased his rest time to as much as an hour and a half every two hours, at least early on.

Hindsight now put some of the newspapers' exaggerated, ill-informed or alarmist stories into perspective. *The Edinburgh Advertiser* reported in the fifth week that his hopes of succeeding were 'more feeble' and that he had 'great doubts' about himself.[38] Even earlier, *The London Chronicle* had reported that all the experts believed the task impossible and confidently reported 'he will never accomplish it'.[39] All those seeing him at three o'clock in the mornings, when he seemed to go into a black slump and dragged one foot agonisingly past the other, would have been convinced, nevertheless, that the newspapers had it just about right. But the days always brought relief. Now, it all seemed so easy and old Dr Sandiver even bragged that the Captain could go on for another fortnight if needed[40] – confident, of course, that such a boast would not be put to the test. There was clearly a carnival atmosphere in the Barclay camp.

It is not hard to imagine that the mood in and around James Wedderburn Webster's tents was quite, quite different. Money was being lost, big money, and so were reputations. Webster was a small man, a well-known womaniser who, despite being married, boasted that all women were his 'lawful prize'.[41] He was only 26 years old and friends referred to him as 'Bold Webster'. He was good with horses but perhaps less good with people, and is also remembered for once, foolishly, describing his beautiful young wife, Lady Frances, as 'very like Christ', which provoked scornful laughter from Lord Byron, to whom she had made a suggestion during a game of billiards that was not Christ-like at all.[42] Later, she went on to have an affair with the Duke of Wellington, who was so enamoured with her he actually found time to write to her from the battlefield at Waterloo.[43] Bold Webster, sadly, had less judgement than boldness and now the whole world knew that he had misjudged Captain Barclay too.

Those who had bet money on Captain Barclay failing gathered together in small, glum groups. They had miscalculated and were paying a high price for it. They had also missed out on some good luck that at one stage looked as if it was coming their way. They knew that a huge fleet was waiting off the Kent coast to sail to Walcheran to take on Napoleon's forces and that Lord Huntly could have instructed Captain Barclay, his aide-de-camp, to be at Deal too. They also knew that he hadn't.

At 3.15 p.m. Captain Barclay stepped out to begin the final mile.[44] The burning heat had gone out of the sun and it was as pleasant a July day as you could ever find. The crowd was in a holiday mood and even the orange-sellers and jugglers craned their necks in expectation. Captain Barclay pulled himself up to his full height and walked with less apparent difficulty than for days. He took his time getting to the half-mile marker, and, relaxed and cheerful, turned a few seconds after 3.26. Then amid deafening cheers he strode out and walked for home.

He arrived back at 3.37, a full 23 minutes inside the deadline. The wager was won – he had done it. The crowd went wild. John Gully, the famous boxing champion, led three rousing cheers,[45] but he was now nowhere near as famous as Captain Barclay. In Newmarket the church bells rang a special peal[46] and correspondents scribbled down every detail to send off for the following day's newspapers. Captain

Barclay had dared to set himself one of the greatest sporting challenges ever, and backed with his own money and organisation had won in the full glare of public scrutiny and publicity. He was now rich and famous, and sport would never be quite the same again.

Busy, as ever, behind the scenes William Cross had prepared a bath for the Captain even before the church bells started to ring. The weary muscles relaxed in the hot water for just a few minutes, then he was taken out and dried with warm flannels.[47] By four o'clock, less than half an hour after the end of the great event, he was in bed, where he slept soundly until midnight, his first continuous night's sleep for nearly 42 days. At midnight, according to the prearranged plan, William Cross woke Captain Barclay with a light meal of water gruel, and then let him go back to sleep. It was too risky to allow an exhausted man, whose body was inured to so little rest, slip into deep, long, uninterrupted sleep. The recovery was being managed every bit as carefully as the event itself. He slept until nine o'clock in the morning and then got up and was weighed on the Newmarket scales. He was 11 stone exactly; 32 lbs less than his starting weight.[48] He claimed, nevertheless, to have fully recovered and next morning even walked the streets of Newmarket to prove it, acknowledging the crowds and accepting their congratulations.[49]

Despite his bravado, Robert Barclay knew that he had been on the receiving end of one huge slice of luck. Not related to the physical side of the task – that had in many respects proved to be the easiest part – nor to his safety – he had taken good precautions and had a good team to protect him. No, his luck lay in the fact that the largest military force that Britain had ever put together to fight overseas, and of which he should have been part, was still waiting to depart for action.[50]

Forty thousand fighting men were assembled in a huge military camp near Deal, many of them veterans of the bloody battle of Corunna at the beginning of the year. The support staff of sailors and others may have been even larger. Nearby was a huge fleet which included 400 transports and 200 men-of-war to carry them across the North Sea to the Dutch coast to destroy Napoleon's ships and supplies at Antwerp and Flushing, and to make the River Scheldt unnavigable.[51] There was a mood of impatience to get at the enemy who had cut down Sir John Moore: a week earlier Sir Walter Scott had written, 'I would to God our expedition was off'.[52] Had they left, Captain Barclay's wager would have been lost and the history of sport would have taken a different turn. It was almost as if they were waiting there in a state of suspended animation, waiting for him to finish; as if some high-ranking officer had bet his money on Captain Barclay and put his personal interests before those of the nation.

Among these fighting men was George, Marquis of Huntly, a fellow Scot whom Captain Barclay had known for years and to whom he was distantly related. He was Colonel of the 92nd Regiment of Foot and Captain Barclay was to be his aide-de-camp. The Marquis was the son of Alex, 4th Duke of Gordon, and was the more senior in every respect: he was ten years older, and he had a higher rank and a better social position. They lived close enough to each other in Scotland for Captain Barclay's hounds to go out the previous season with the Turiff Hunt under the Marquis of Huntly.[53] He, like Captain Barclay, loved a physical challenge and in the previous winter had ridden 105 miles in under seven hours to get to the Northern Meeting of which he was president, having 'eight relays of horses on the road' to get him there.[54] They were obviously good friends, but then it was easy to be friendly with the Marquis of Huntly, who was the life and soul of every party he attended. Perhaps this could be traced in part to his background and upbringing, which had often been unconventional. When he was 18 his father supervised an 'essential' part of his education by personally taking him to be initiated into the mysteries of a brothel. Most young men had to find out for themselves. He also had extrovert blood running through his veins from his mother, the Duchess's, side. She was the lovely, but racy, Jane, Duchess of Gordon, perhaps better known as Bonnie Jean who, like her rival, Georgiana Duchess of Devonshire, helped recruit men for her husband's regiment by holding the King's shilling between her lips to tempt them with the prospect of a kiss on the lips with a real, live Duchess.[55] The Marquis of Huntly was a man who, like his mother, was difficult to deny. On one occasion in the previous October, when Captain Barclay had visited him at Gordon Castle, he quickly found himself drawn into a bet laid by the Marquis that his father's runner and letter-carrier would beat him in a running race over the 19 miles of bad, hilly road to Huntly Lodge. On the spot, without training, they set out, and two hours and eight minutes later Captain Barclay won the bet, beating the letter-carrier by five miles.[56] Life around the Marquis of Huntly was always unpredictable and never dull, but Captain Barclay was neither overshadowed nor intimidated by him.

While Captain Barclay walked backwards and forwards every hour across Newmarket Heath, the 40,000 men waiting at Deal marched and drilled on the open expanses of Bramham Downs. There seemed no good reason why they were still there and by hanging around they had already lost the benefit of surprise. Week by week the political temperature rose. One week before the end of Captain Barclay's walk Napoleon defeated the Austrians at Wagram, not far from Vienna, but lost 23,000 French soldiers in the process, either killed or wounded, with another 7,000 missing.[57] Surely it was time for the fleet to leave? But still they waited. This gave time for Captain Barclay to finish his wager, recover and make his way to the Kent coast.

News of his victory reached Scotland within a couple of days, and on his way first to London and then to Ramsgate, he heard about the celebrations that were being enjoyed there, particularly around Stonehaven and Allardice Castle, where his family came from. A week later newspapers were still reporting that the toasts, the drinking and the cheering were as much about Captain Barclay's popularity as his success.[58] He was certain to receive a welcome befitting a major sporting hero from the tens of thousands of soldiers and sailors waiting off the Kent coast. It is always good to be on the winning side, and in the second half of July 1809 Captain Barclay's was definitely the winning side.

He arrived on Tuesday morning,[59] and throughout Tuesday and

Wednesday men and supplies were rowed out almost continuously to the waiting ships. At Deal, where the main force was embarking, and at Ramsgate, ten miles to the north, crowds gathered, including many ladies and gentlemen of fashion in their gigs and carriages, to see the spectacle and to wave them off, because it was clear that their departure was imminent. Emotions ran high as military bands played, and cheer after cheer rose from the small boats as the British soldiers showed their eagerness to be at the enemy at last. As they cheered, small family groups tried to look confident and composed, but many a tear was wiped from an anxious cheek as the men rowed out of earshot. Then news arrived that shots fired on the French coast had been heard at Dover,[60] and the anxiety and anticipation grew, producing those mixed emotions of wishing they would get going as soon as possible, and wishing they did not have to go at all.

Captain Barclay left from Ramsgate on Thursday 20 July,[61] only eight days after his triumph at Newmarket, with his uniform still hanging on him as if it was made for a man several sizes bigger. Later, as stories about him circulated, this period was reduced in the telling to five[62] and even to two days,[63] but the facts hardly need to be exaggerated. It was remarkable enough that so soon after 1,000 hours of physical effort and broken sleep he was able to take his place in a fighting force and go off to war.

Luck was with them, and a fresh breeze swept the vast fleet, Captain Barclay included, rapidly across the North Sea to the Dutch coast.[64] Their destination was the Island of Walcheran, which lay at the mouth of the River Scheldt, the access to Antwerp.

# CHAPTER TWO

# *A Peculiarly Vigorous Body*

*(I have had) a strong & staunch partiality from my infancy,
for general athletic exercises, which indeed, my worthy father
took every opportunity of impressing one with, by recounting
his own feats, those of my grandfather, & back even beyond
the Apologist, not to mention the many stories, with which my
infant ears, were entertained, by a certain Uncle Evan.*

LETTER FROM ROBERT BARCLAY ALLARDICE

TO JOSEPH JOHN GURNEY,

17 SEPTEMBER 1830

*Youth, high spirits, a peculiarly vigorous body, and a hereditary
bias, account very sufficiently for his earliest achievements.*

GENTLEMAN'S MAGAZINE,

JULY 1854

Robert Barclay, or Robert Barclay Allardice, as we should properly call him, was already emotionally and physically committed to being a 'serious' athlete when he was still at school and in his teens. The first real evidence of this came in August 1796, the month of his 17th birthday when he took on his first sporting wager.[1] His school was in Brixton, a rural village four miles to the south of London, probably Loughborough House School, a 'superior academy' for young noblemen and gentlemen, set in 11 acres of ground abutting Loughborough Lane.[2] He was sent there at the age of 13 and enjoyed the open-air life and the freedom that the expanse of nearby Rush Common gave him. His younger brother Jemmy was there also, but Robert missed his five other brothers and sisters and the rest of his family, and in his letters home to his father he complained if they did not write often enough. Robert Barclay Allardice had already developed a dislike of being confined indoors for too long, and preferred to be 'out in the air'; a preference that was to have a strong bearing on the way his life was to develop. He was not an outstanding scholar and was more likely to write home about the knee he had torn out of his nankeen breeches or the pigeon he had managed to hatch, than about his school work.[3]

Robert had previously been at Richmond School in Yorkshire[4] and the Barclay family were aware of the dangers of exposing him, a 13-year-old boy, to Brixton and 'the vices of the Capital'.[5] There were vices everywhere, of course, and not only those of wine, women and song that young men for centuries have been told to guard against. In the 1790s there was also gambling. Even at Brixton there was no escaping the fact that this was the golden age of gambling when the whole country seemed to lose its head, and frequently its shirt, in the dizzy whirl of speculation. The mania for gambling was not limited to Charles James Fox and Georgiana Duchess of Devonshire or their group, who lost thousands of pounds in a single sitting in fashionable St James's. All over the country people of all classes were drawn into the frenzy for gambling and would bet on almost anything. Cock-fights, donkey races, the toss of a coin or more usually the toss of three coins; everything was fair game. Gambling was simultaneously a national malaise and one of Britain's major industries.

Robert Barclay Allardice's first wager was that he could walk six miles, 'fair toe and heel' on the Brixton-to-Croydon road inside an hour. This is an interesting athletic challenge, being just too fast to walk comfortably. At this speed it is much easier, and expends less energy, to run. But the wager required strict walking; no running or jogging or even shuffling would be allowed. On every stride, the heel of the front foot must strike the ground before the toe of the rear foot left it; this was the meaning of 'fair toe and heel'. Umpires on both sides would follow every step of the way to adjudicate on the fairness of his walking. This was not simply youthful high spirits; this was a genuine test of athletic ability and discipline. Only a first-rate walker could do six miles inside an hour, fair toe and heel, even on a good road. If the walker were unfit, out of practice or unknown as a pedestrian, as Robert was, a betting man would offer 6 to 4 against the task being successfully completed.[6] On the day, however, Robert Barclay Allardice completed the task successfully and comfortably, showing that he was an accomplished athlete and not the inexperienced, delicate, pampered young gentleman, merely playing at being an athlete, that many expected.

Robert was already well known for being unusually active and athletic so it would not have come as a surprise that he was so competent, but what was surprising was the size of the wager, and that his father agreed to it. The wager was for 100 guineas. By the standards of the day, 100 guineas was a significant amount of money. It would, for example, have paid the annual salary of the surgeon in the Prince of Wales's household at Carlton House, or of the Junior Clerk.[7] It would have taken the kitchen boys at Carlton House, who were about his own age, six and a half years to earn this amount of money.[8] Yet Robert won his 100 guineas in less than 60 minutes.

Robert learned from an early age that there were big financial rewards for those who were fit and active and interested in sport. However, many Barclay family members, particularly those from some of the stricter Quaker lines, were almost certainly unhappy about the size of the wager. Apart from the money, they probably regarded the event as an expression of youthful high spirits. What do you expect from boys and young men with time on their hands and no responsibility? Particularly when so many of the forces that had shaped Robert's life so far had encouraged his athleticism. First among these was his father.

Robert Barclay senior was a much-respected Scottish laird who had always liked the sensation of hard physical labour, and although he was 48 years old when Robert was born, still liked rolling up his sleeves and feeling the trickle of sweat down his back. He was at the forefront of the agricultural revolution in Britain and was a friend of Thomas Coke, the Earl of Leicester, of Holkham Hall in Norfolk, and Lord 'Turnip' Townshend.[9] Robert Barclay's estate at Ury consisted of over 3,500 acres; 2,000 of which he cultivated as arable land and the remainder he planted as woodland.[10] In his search for new ideas on farming he claimed to have gone to every county in England, returning home on foot 'to be closer to the earth', with his servant alongside on horseback with his trunk.[11] 'A tired man,' he said, 'will struggle hard to reach home.'[12] On several occasions he had walked from Ury to London to see some of his Barclay cousins, a journey of 510 miles, which he once did in ten days.[13] Nor was he only a walker. He once wrestled a notorious Highland soldier, and twice heaved a trespassing tinker's donkey over a hedge.[14] No wonder he became known as 'The Great Master of Ury',[15] and turned every head as he walked through the streets of Stonehaven, a town he had virtually created. On these occasions he wore a red coat, a cocked hat and white breeches with gold knee bands. To the villagers who watched him walk by he was the 5th Laird of nearby Ury and their benefactor. 'I assure you,' said the old miller, 'he commanded respect'.[16] At the age of 57, he was elected unopposed as Member of Parliament for Kincardineshire, his local county, and remained their MP for nearly a decade, supporting the King, George III, William Pitt and the Tories.[17]

The Barclays were an old Scottish family who could trace their members back over 700 years even at the time of Robert's birth. Among these was another Robert Barclay, who was one of the first generation of Scottish Quakers. In 1675 he published his 'Apology For The True Christian Divinity', which contained '15 propositions', that were to be important to Quakers worldwide for generations.[18] Although Robert was no longer a Quaker himself, the influence of his old Quaker roots was still strong. Other ancestors were more war-like, such as the 16th-century Colonel David Barclay, who owned a huge sword, still kept at Ury, that few others could even lift, let alone wield aggressively.[19] The Great Master's father, another Robert Barclay, had been known as Robert the Strong.[20] So it was that the Barclay family traditions were an unusual and eccentric mixture of Quaker piety and pride in physical prowess.

Robert Barclay Allardice was born at Ury on 25 August 1779,[21] the summer in which the Derby and the Oaks were first run. His mother, Sarah Ann, was 22, 26 years younger than her husband, the Great Master, and she was his second wife. After she had given him eight children, Sarah Ann and the Great Master were divorced in 1793.[22] By then they were 36 and 62 respectively and Robert was 14.

Sarah Ann came from an even older family than the Barclays. She was an Allardice from Allardice Castle, a few miles south of Ury,[23] and she had the blood of ancient Scottish kings running through her veins. In exchange for the land that she brought with her, the Great Master agreed to assume the additional surname Allardice. In practice, however, he seldom bothered and continued to call himself simply Robert Barclay. Through her great-great-grandmother, Sarah Ann claimed to be the next in line to William, 2nd Earl of Airth and Menteith, and this gave Robert, her eldest son, an intriguing idea. Was he the Earl of Airth and Menteith in everything but name, and one day, when he was old enough, could he assume the titles?

At Ury there were lots of children for Robert to play with. When he was eight years old, he had nine-year-old Une Cameron, whom he simply called 'Cameron', the seven-year-old twins Mary and Margaret, Rodney, a girl, despite her name, who was five, James, whom Robert always called Jemmy, was nearly three, and David the baby, still at the crawling stage. An older sister named Ann had died when he was two. He also had a half-sister from the Great Master's first family, but she was grown up and had left home. She was Lucy, 26 years older than Robert, who had married Samuel Galton and had gone to live in Birmingham before Robert was even born.[24] Not surprisingly, Lucy played the role of an aunt more than a sister to the young Robert. A picture of Bonnie Prince Charlie hung on the wall in Ury, and every morning Robert and the younger children stood in front of it and saluted.[25] This was a legacy from the Great Master's mother who always supported the Stuart cause. A Quaker/Jacobite legacy was a strange one for the young Barclay Allardice children to understand. They knew, at least, that they were not like everyone else.

The society in the east of Scotland in which they grew up was strongly influenced by their history and traditions. Men were impressed by feats of strength and endurance, and told stories about them to their sons, just as their fathers had told them. It was a very old athletic tradition. The practice of challenging each other to wrestle, or to see who could lift heavy stones, or throw a weight or a blacksmith's hammer the greatest distance, was probably centuries old. For generations such feats were regarded as trials of manhood and a question of honour and prestige, rather than merely sporting activities. It was customary to have a weight lying at the gate of every Highland chieftain's house so that a visiting stranger could be asked 'as a complement' to throw it.[26] At one place in the Highlands, lifting a stone weighing 200lbs or more from the ground and placing it on top of another, four feet high, elevated a 'youth' into a 'man', regardless of his age. Each place had its own stone, and some were heavier than others. It was a culture that produced hard, competitive men who were proud of their strength. Just south of Ury there was a man of 'gigantic stature' named Captain Ferrier. He enjoyed silencing a noisy room full of boastful young men by quietly telling them that in his day he had never been considered strong, but had, nevertheless, once lifted an anchor of 70 stones (980lbs).[27] Feats of strength were a matter of personal pride but they also preserved the honour of the family or clan, and stories about them became part of folklore, a tantalising mixture of fact and fantasy.

In the long winter nights stories of strength and valour were told around the fire at Ury, as the Great Master enthralled the children with tales of his own deeds and those of his father, and other Barclays back before the days of the Apologist. There were stories about Colonel Barclay and his huge sword, of Robert the Strong and of uncles and cousins who had wrestled bulls and carried sacks of flour in their teeth. Many years later Captain Barclay recounted how from infancy he had developed a 'staunch partiality . . . for general athletic exercises' from hearing his father's tales and 'the many stories, with which my infant ears, were entertained, by a certain Uncle Evan', his father's younger brother.[28] He could hardly have failed to.

Not all the influences were Scottish or local. In 1788, when Robert was eight, his father became a Westminster MP and was re-elected at the general elections of 1790 and 1796.[29] When he came home there were stories to tell. One of the first was of the king's 'pretty smart bilious attack', which within months had developed into convulsions, coma and madness.[30] But the most colourful tales to a young boy's ears were of the encounters between the most famous athletes of the day. There was the flamboyant, yet highly 'scientific' Jewish boxer, Daniel Mendoza. Despite rampant anti-Semitism in London he became a favourite of the Prince of Wales and made public appearances at theatres around the country as well as at sports grounds, and drew fascinated crowds wherever he went.[31] His face was so well known it even sold commemorative mugs.[32] Then there was Richard Humphries and John Jackson; they were both adversaries of Mendoza, and were famed for having the manners of a 'gentleman'. Humphries was called 'The Gentleman Boxer', and the young John Jackson later became known as 'Gentleman Jackson' and both went on to become Champion of the Prize Ring.[33]

Among the fighters there was big Thomas Tring, who was the Prince of Wales's porter at Carlton House, and powerfully carried one end of the Prince's sedan chair,[34] and Benjamin Brain, known as

'Big Ben' even though he was not particularly big. He read the Bible every day.[35] Then there was the strong and determined Tom Johnson, whose real name was Jackling. He worked as a corn porter and to help a fellow porter who was too ill to work, he carried double loads, giving his extra money to his sick friend.[36] What a gallery of characters to capture the imagination of a young boy. And what amazing events they took part in. Thousands went to great pains and cheerfully put up with extraordinary inconveniences, just to see them. They went because it was the fashionable thing to do, and because there was a growing public admiration for these brave, powerful and skilful athletes. This fashion was stimulated by the young Prince of Wales and his followers, who not only went to horse races and prize fights, but even arranged their own at Brighton. The fact that prize fights were against the law gave the journey to see one an added piquancy. In 1787 the Prince of Wales went to Shepherd's Bush to see Daniel Mendoza fight Jack Martin, a butcher from Bath, only to find that the magistrates had ordered the 10th Regiment of Dragoons to break up the ring and prevent the fight from taking place.[37] The Prince of Wales and his cronies were humiliated and therefore furious. These included the hard drinking Dukes of Norfolk and Queensberry, the reckless Irish Earl of Barrymore, known as 'Hellgate', and his two brothers, who were better known as 'Newgate' and 'Cripplegate' because one was supposed to have been in every prison except Newgate, and the other was lame. Their sister, Lady Melford, had to suffer the sobriquet 'Billingsgate' because of her foul mouth.[38] Other members of the Prince's set were Colonel George Hanger, Colonel Banastre Tarleton and Sir John Lade, all described in a contemporary anonymous pamphlet, 'The Jockey Club, or Sketch of the Manners of an Age', as being the sort of 'creatures with whom men of morality or even common decency' would never associate.[39] The crowds at the prize fights seemed quite happy to be associating with them, nevertheless. A fortnight later the Prince ensured the fight did take place, this time at Barnet, in front of a crowd of 5,000.[40]

In June 1788 he and his entourage went to Croydon to watch

the young John Jackson fight Tom Fewterell. In August they were at three fights on Brighton race course, one between Tom Tyne and George Earl, in which Earl died in the ring after a blow to the temple which caused him to fall against the solid rail around the ring. The Prince of Wales was so affected by this he settled an annuity on George Earl's widow and children.[41]

Even the foot-racers and pedestrians attracted increasing attention and were cast by the newspapers and print-makers in an heroic mould. Foster Powell was first among these. A thin, mild Yorkshireman with strong legs, he had once walked the 400 miles from London to York and back in well under six days.[42] In July 1792, at the age of 58, he astonished everyone when he did it again, this time eight and three-quarter hours under the six days. Thousands lined the roads just to watch this unassuming man pass.[43] The crowd loved him. In a changing world he seemed to be dependable, a symbol that things could stay the same. The buckle-makers of Birmingham had petitioned the Prince of Wales about the hardship caused by the new fashion of wearing laces.[44] Tom Johnson was part of this new stylish set and even wore pink laces in his boxing boots,[45] but here was Foster Powell with good old-fashioned buckles on his shoes. He was as fast, if not faster, than any horse, and the papers described him as 'a wonderful old man' and 'truly a phenomenon in nature',[46] and indeed he was. Over a 28-year period he took part in events from one to 400 miles, and even went to Switzerland and France where he walked 200 miles beyond Paris and gained 'much praise'.[47]

In April 1793 the newspapers[48] carried the story of his sudden death at the age of only 59, and told of 'the very great concourse of people' who attended his funeral and followed the coffin from the New Inn, where he had lived and worked, along Fleet Street, up Ludgate Hill to his final resting place of St Paul's Cathedral.[49] They placed his body in a grave under the only tree in the churchyard, just as it was coming into new leaf. He had died following some inexpert surgery on a lump in his neck, and not, as was popularly believed, from overexertion.[50]

Foster Powell was a frugal man who never bet heavily on himself, but that was not the spirit of the age. Money was the motivation and driving force behind most sporting events, often big money. In January 1788 Frederick, Duke of York and Albany, the Prince of Wales's brother, challenged Colonel Banastre Tarleton to a six-mile walking race on the road from Hyde Park Corner to Kew Bridge, for 200 guineas.[51] Frederick was the Duke of York who, rather unfairly, is known for marching his men to the top of the hill, then marching them down again. His reputation should probably take into account the fact that as commander-in-chief of the army, he was extremely popular with his men, and founded the Royal Military College at Woolwich, and another, which later became Sandhurst.[52] He was only a year younger than the Prince of Wales and, perhaps naturally, had many of the same friends, and was drawn into the same world of sport, extravagant parties and drunken, wild, often dangerous encounters. He was nearly killed in a duel on Wimbledon Common when the ball from Colonel Charles Lennox's pistol whistled past his ear so closely it cut a curl off his wig. He then deliberately shot wide.[53] Later, in March 1791, to the dismay of the royal-watchers, he was one of the principal purchasers at Tattersall's when the Prince of Wales was forced to sell his racing stud after a public scandal at Newmarket involving the suspicious defeat of Escape, one of the Prince's best, and most expensive horses, by two inferior outsiders.[54]

Banastre Tarleton was 34, and a colonel in a regiment of Light Dragoons. He was also a friend of the Prince of Wales and was having an affair with Mrs Robinson, the Prince's 'Perdita', though he behaved much more responsibly to her than did the Prince (but then, who didn't?), and his relationship with her lasted for nearly 16 years.[55] Banastre Tarleton accompanied, or perhaps even led, the Prince of Wales and his brothers into all sorts of sporting excitement at Newmarket and at prize fights. Jon Bee, a contemporary sports reporter, lists him as one of the principal patrons of prize fighting,[56] and in October 1789 he was an umpire in a prize fight at Banbury between the Champion, Tom Johnson, and a huge, muscular Birmingham fighter called Isaac Perrins.[57] Perrins was a factory foreman and, unusually, an ex-choirmaster.[58]

On the morning of the race, Monday 28 January, however, the Duke either decided, or was persuaded, to 'decline the contest'. Instead of racing on the cold, winter streets of London, the Duke, rather ignominiously, forfeited his stake money. Royalty, lords and honourables were only a tiny tip of a very large iceberg of pedestrians and foot-racers. In the craze for gambling, the old and the young, the fat and the thin, the rich and the poor, men and women, all raced for money on the roads of Britain or on courses marked out on the downs, heaths and parks or on a horse-race course. At one extreme, in the autumn of 1789, Donald Macleod walked from Inverness to London, a distance of 560 miles, turned round and walked all the way back, and then on arriving at Inverness turned round again and walked back to London[59] – a total journey on foot of 1,680 miles. Not a bad performance, particularly as Donald Macleod was reported by the newspapers to be 100 years old at the time. He was not, apparently, an old man who dragged himself reluctantly along this long, hilly road. He did it with verve and panache. Those who saw him reported on his 'healthful appearance' and commented on 'his astonishing hilarity of disposition'.[60] Astonishing as this undoubtedly was, it was no more remarkable than his activities the following October when he was 101. One newspaper said he was 104.[61] He was engaged in a wager to go ten miles from Hyde Park Corner along the Chiswick Road to Turnham Green, when he was obstructed by road works, which the terms of the wager forbade him to go round. So he took a run and jumped over them.[62]

At the other end of the age scale, an 18-month-old girl 'ran' about half a mile down the length of the Mall in London in 23 minutes for a wager. Not one she made herself, presumably. Thousands turned out to watch.[63] This was an age of extremes.

The size of the bets depended on the depth of your purse, and the size of your need. Men and women at the bottom end of the social scale competed for money out of necessity, and not for sport or excitement. It is even possible that Robert Barclay saw one of these events when he was a boy of eight. In 1787 he was sent to his first school at Richmond in the North Riding of Yorkshire, and stayed there four years. Richmond School had the reputation of being one of the three most successful classical schools in England after Eton and Harrow,[64] but it was not particularly successful in placing much Greek and Latin into Robert's head. At this time Richmond was one of the fashionable centres for horse-racing in Yorkshire, and the race course was also used for other sporting events. In the late summer of 1788 a gruelling pedestrian wager took place there. John Batty, a poor, local pig driver in his mid-50s walked 700 miles in 14 days. This required covering, on average, more than 50 miles every day for a fortnight. He completed the task with five hours to spare, and attracted a huge number of inquisitive local inhabitants on the way. Boys from the local school must, surely, have been among them. Those who were there had an object lesson in determination and single-mindedness for he had to suffer 13 days of acute discomfort, having 'lost the skin off his feet' after the first day because of new shoes. The bet had been 20 guineas to 100, but because he only had one guinea of his own to deposit, several of those he wanted to have bets with declined and he had to join in with others to raise the stake money. To ensure any worthwhile return he also had to resort to staking a sow against ten guineas. Eventually he took home 16 guineas from his fortnight's labour. Once he had won, he bet that he could do the same again in 13 days for 100 guineas, riches indeed! But there were no takers.[65]

Just as the bets that men made depended on their wealth, or more precisely on their social position — the two were hardly separable — so the performances that the competitors achieved were split along similar lines, but in the opposite direction. In other words, the higher their social position, the more money they had to dispose of, and the poorer their performances were likely to be. For example, in the spring of 1793 two unnamed gentlemen from Lloyd's Coffee House engaged to go 30 miles in seven and a half hours for 1,000 guineas. This was a relatively easy task and they won comfortably.[66] So they should. A few weeks earlier, however, William Harris, a miller from Peterborough, had to go 42 miles also in seven and a half hours for only two guineas. He, too, won comfortably but he had to go 40 per cent further and his winnings were 500 times smaller.[67]

Although the race between the Duke of York and Colonel Tarleton did not take place, interest from such a fashionable quarter inevitably encouraged others, who followed the fashion, rather than because they needed the money. Running races became almost a cult activity and attracted a class of people who previously would have felt excluded from the village fairs and revels at which the 'lower orders' had run, wrestled, cudgelled, danced and laughed for countless generations. Running for sport was as old as the hills the young men and women of the villages ran on, but it was the women and girls who were the runners in the old rural culture, and hundreds of them ran every year for an embroidered smock and/or a guinea in gold.[68] The men and boys also ran sometimes, but they also wrestled, cudgelled, jumped in sack races tied up to their necks, and climbed greasy poles for flitches of bacon, while the crowd guffawed, shouted encouragement and drank heartily.[69] All the fun of the fair. These old rustic events were still the preserve of the lower orders but they were beginning to die out as the new industrial towns filled and the countryside emptied. Now, young men from the upper classes were following royal precedent by making their own wagers and trying their skill. In October 1790 there was a race across Kensington Gardens for a sweepstake of 100 guineas each, between Richard Barry, 7th Earl of Barrymore (alias Hellgate), Captain Grosvenor, the Hon. Mr Lamb and Lord Paget.[70] On this day they shared their newspaper coverage with stories about a 'counter revolution' in France, and more reassuring news that the eruption of Mount Vesuvius was, at last, quietening down.

On Tuesday 12 March 1793 there was a most unusual event – a run for charity. France had declared war on Britain, Holland and Spain on 1 February, and the ensuing conflict with Napoleon Bonaparte and the French Republic produced a tide of suffering across Europe and in Britain. To raise money for a fund to help the widows and children of soldiers and seamen killed in the war, Colonel the Hon. Cosmo Gordon undertook to walk five miles in under an hour. This should not be confused with the events that athletes competed in. Five miles an hour would have been a gentle Sunday stroll for them. It was the novelty that drew attention and contributions. The event was to take place along the Uxbridge Road from the first milestone beyond the Tyburn turnpike to the six-mile stone at Ealing. By the terms of the wager he had to start within a fortnight, but he chose to do it the very next day. He did it with three and a half minutes to spare, and so won the wager, with all the stakes going to the charity.[71]

Many of the events at this time were zany, even by the standards of the day. Two waiters from the Cannon Coffee House raced stark naked around St James's Park at seven o'clock on a cold November morning to the amusement of 'a great number of spectators'. Not surprisingly it amused the 'delicate nymphs of the Horse Guards' most.[72] Events became increasingly complex, as gentlemen devised ever more creative ways of challenging each other. For them the emphasis was less on the physical element of the races and more on the guile and cunning in making the match. There were the two gentlemen at White's Club in St James's who wagered to run against each other, with one running 150 yards while the other ran 100 yards backwards.[73] Some events included so many variations and complications it is difficult to imagine they could ever have been completed. Take for example the wager for 1,000 guineas, made by an unnamed Duke who lived on Piccadilly, that he could find a man who would walk the ten miles from Piccadilly to Hounslow in three hours, but having to walk backwards on every fourth step. A baronet, also unnamed, who usually risked his guineas on the horses at Newmarket, bet that such a task was impossible.[74] My money would have been with the baronet's.

The Great Master could match many of these stories. In addition to walking the 510 miles from Ury to London, he had once gone 210 miles in three days, and 81 miles in 16 hours.[75] Many pedestrians whose feats were reported in the newspapers could not match that. In all these events the gentlemen tended to race against each other and not against the lower orders and vice versa. Although sport was increasingly a great social melting pot, and people of all classes, ages and backgrounds rubbed shoulders at the big sporting events, it was not at all usual for them to face each other in direct competition. The social gulf was still too wide to be bridged easily. Admittedly it did happen in cricket. The Duke of Dorset, the Earl of Winchelsea and the Earl of Tankeville all employed men as gardeners and grooms who were really professional cricketers, and then played happily alongside them in games for high stakes.[76] Indeed, the pattern had been set even earlier when Frederick, Prince of Wales, as early as 1735 played in cricket teams with dukes, earls and commoners for stakes of £1,000.[77] He continued playing until 1751 when, at the age of 44, he died following a blow from a cricket ball.[78] This cricket ball caused the crown of England to skip a generation to George III. The course of history often hangs on small events. In 1789 the Duke of Dorset was British ambassador in Paris, and to help develop cricket in France he invited William Yaldon, one of his professionals, to take a team there. The Bastille was stormed, however, and the cricket was cancelled.[79] A case of the end of the reign stopped play. The truth was that the men such luminaries employed were the better cricketers, and wagers were more likely to be won with, than without them. Ample reason to recruit them. The social status of the dukes and earls was absolutely secure, and on the cricket field all could pretend that social divisions had evaporated in the warmth of the summer afternoons and the alchemy of sport. In truth they had not; social class is not that easily wished away. A case heard at the York Assizes in 1791 tells a truer story. It was about a horse race for 'gentlemen only' at Navesmire, which Christopher 'Kitty' Rowntree, an old man of 70, won. Kitty Rowntree was described as 'an old gentleman with one eye, dirty leather breeches and an old wig not worth eight-pence'. Was he a gentleman? Should he even have competed? The case ended up at the York Assizes.

In the course of the trial it was acknowledged that old Kitty Rowntree was a man of good character, who had never been known to do a dirty trick. All agreed that he was 'a man of good reputation', a man of his word. Yes, but was he a gentleman? A member of the Jockey Club said he was 'certainly not such a person as we intended should ride', and 'would be objected to on any race ground in England'. On the surface, this seemed to be a trial about who could call himself a 'gentleman', but it was really a trial about whether men of good birth and substantial incomes could exclude from sporting events men of lower social standing, who were likely to be fitter, stronger and more skilful, and so better at sport than they were. The prize money was £123 and had been subscribed by the gentlemen specifically to exclude those 'whose professional skill would give them an advantage, and over-match the others in point of jockeyship'. That tells it all. The gentlemen enjoyed their sport and had the time and money for it. They did not want their fun spoiled by people who were better at it than they were.

Nevertheless, the 12 good men and true of the jury decided for the old gentleman with one eye and dirty leather breeches.[80] Kitty Rowntree kept the prize money, even if it didn't make him a gentleman overnight. For most people, for most of the time, the gulf between the gentlemen and the others remained as wide and unbridgeable as it ever was. The Great Master, however, had been one of those men who had the confidence in his own ability to cross that gulf voluntarily. There were stories of him dropping in on country fairs when he was on one of his walking tours earlier in his life, and entering the wrestling ring against all comers.[81] He, of course, like the Duke of Dorset, could cross the social lines on his own terms and step back again whenever he wanted, but perhaps the examples of Daniel Mendoza, Kitty Rowntree, Richard Humphries and John Jackson, the 'gentleman' fighters, were showing that sport was ushering in new possibilities.

This is the world that shaped Robert Barclay Allardice, a world in which trials of strength and stamina, and stories about them, were woven into daily life. A world mad on sport and, at all levels, entranced by the excitement of gambling. His was a large influential family with branches in England and Scotland with a history of achievement, as well as exceptional physical prowess. But at Ury it was also a family bearing scars from disagreement and divorce. It was a family that travelled and was able to absorb influences from much further afield than most. The world was changing rapidly and the ideas and manners from all over England, the Caribbean and America quickly found their way to Ury. It was above all a safe family to grow up in, with a strong, successful and caring father at its head, who looked after everyone's welfare and made every decision.

Like an eruption of Mount Vesuvius, this world changed dramatically for Robert Barclay Allardice on Tuesday 8 April 1797, when his father died.[82]

## CHAPTER THREE

# *Rather A Disgrace*

*Our corporeal Powers are inferior to those of many animals, a
Horse is more swift, & capable of more bodily Exertion ...
the highest* probable *attainments of that nature, would still leave
us inferior in those properties to ... Powel the Pedestrian, to
Mendoza the Pugilist ... Excellence in these accomplishments
beyond a certain extent is rather a disgrace ...*

LETTER FROM SAMUEL GALTON
TO ROBERT BARCLAY ALLARDICE,
AUGUST 1798

Overnight, Robert went from being a schoolboy, cushioned by his powerful father, to being the head of a family of seven children, not one of whom was out of their teens. As Robert was still a minor, his father, prior to his death had arranged for twelve guardians – six in Scotland and six in England – to oversee Robert, his family and his affairs until he came of age at 21.[1]

Soon a dismal picture emerged. The Great Master had been very ambitious and had borrowed heavily. Money that years earlier had been put aside for the children had now been swallowed up by debts. The Scottish guardians met and decided on a hasty course of remedial action; land would have to be sold, and all but the youngest children had to be taken out of their schools and brought back to Ury. It was time to tighten the belt. Robert and Cameron would reside at Ury and would have an income of £400 a year plus use of the gardens, grazing for three horses and some cows.[2] For a labourer this would have been a fabulous amount of money, but not for a gentleman with a large house, an estate and staff. Outgoings and unavoidable costs were also high.

The timing of their father's death could hardly have been worse for Robert and his young family. There was political instability and a financial crisis in the country. The war with France was four years old, and only six weeks earlier, a minor French-inspired invasion of South Wales led to fear of more and worse to come, sparking a financial panic in England, which led to a run on the Bank of England. Reserves were so low the Bank of England was uncertain whether they could meet the cash demands. With a stroke of genius they issued £1 and £2 notes.[3] There is usually no quick fix for a financial crisis of this magnitude, and the country watched and held its breath: would this new paper money solve, delay or exacerbate the crisis?

The war with Napoleon was creating uncertainty everywhere. Then, only nine days after the Great Master's death, and with the country vulnerable to invasion as never before, news began to circulate of a mutiny among the British Navy at Spithead. It was over money. An ordinary seaman earned £11.4.0 a year and an able-bodied seaman

£14.8.0, just as their predecessors had 100 years before.[4] Prices had risen by as much as 50 per cent. These earnings put Robert's £100 wager, eight months earlier, into perspective. They also show how those from the lower orders would regard his new £400 a year allowance. The mutiny spread to Sheerness and the Nore. There was also growing unrest in Ireland. William Pitt, the Prime Minister, looked tired and unwell.[5]

This was the situation when Robert Barclay Allardice packed his trunk and prepared to leave his school at Brixton for the last time. Robert considered what his father would have done, and set off on the long journey to Ury. Five hundred and fifty-five miles, which, even by the fast mail coach, took three days and four nights, plenty of time to think. He was now the 6th Laird of Ury and the head of the family; he would take control.

Within four weeks of his father's death he had worked it all out and wrote from Ury to Samuel Galton, one of his English guardians, with his conclusions.[6] In his letter Robert said he would spend most of the summer at Ury, but first he would visit his brothers, sister and friends in England. Next winter he would continue his studies in Edinburgh, and stay there until they were complete. Then, like his father, he would travel and study farming in Norfolk. He would live economically for a few years, pay off the debts and put money aside to invest in continuing improvements at Ury. He would be both friend and 'brother' to the rest of his brothers and sisters, and they would all live together 'genteelly & comfortably'. It was a wonderfully optimistic, idyllic dream. The trouble started almost at once.

Robert knew he had six Scottish and six English guardians and was polite enough to ask for Samuel Galton's approval of his plan, but he saw the guardians as a rubber-stamping body only. Naïvely, he seemed to think that he was capable of taking over the leadership of the family and the estate and make the necessary decisions. His attitude seems to have been 'The King is dead. Long live the King.' His father, the 5th Laird of Ury, was dead. Long live the 6th Laird – himself. The guardians, of course, saw it differently. Before judging him too harshly, it must be remembered that Robert was still only 17 years old.

At Ury, despite the economies, the incoming bills still loomed larger than the income, and to help out, the guardians loyally subscribed money from their own pockets.[7] Nevertheless, Robert, either deliberately or innocently, exploited differences between them and repeatedly irritated them by telling them that he knew what his late father would have wanted better than they did.

Over the next few months the correspondence within the family reveals a mood of frustration and tetchiness beneath the civilities and surface politeness. Robert rather tactlessly complained to Samuel Galton that the English guardians, of whom he was the leader, did not understand Scottish life.[8] In turn, Lucy, his half-sister, lectured him about his behaviour. Did he expect the guardians to be blind to his faults? Did he want them to say of him that he was a rash young man who would take nobody's advice?[9]

In standing up to his guardians Robert had chosen formidable adversaries. The Scottish contingent included Lord Adam Gordon, Sir David Ogilvie and John Durno, an advocate in Aberdeen, as well as his uncle Evan, his father's only brother. In England the guardians were mostly Barclays and all successful and experienced merchants, bankers or brewers. These were considerably tougher and more practical. Not all were equally active, however, nor did they all have the same responsibility. It was Samuel Galton who was chosen as the leader of the guardians and informed Robert of their decisions. He was Robert's brother-in-law (having married Lucy, Robert's half-sister) and lived in Moseley in Birmingham. He was 44 years old, energetic, successful and articulate. He was also open-minded and had been a founding member of one of the most remarkable groups of men ever to meet socially as a group of friends. They had dinner every month in each other's homes in and around Birmingham and the west Midlands, and arranged their meetings for the nearest Monday to the full moon to ensure the best possible light to get home by. Because of this they called themselves the Lunar Society.[10] On one occasion after dinner in Samuel Galton's house, his butler was heard to ask when the 'lunatics' would be meeting again.

But what lunatics! Ten of the 14 were Fellows of the Royal Society. They had no fixed agendas for their discussions, and they kept no minutes. However, they were such radical and creative free-thinkers on topics of science, technology, politics and religion that their ideas, achievements and influence were to reverberate through the lives of millions for generations to come. There was James Watt, of steam engine and electricity fame, and Matthew Boulton, an industrialist and inventor who owned the mint in Birmingham and whose name is for ever linked with that of Watt. His button and buckle factory was socially restructured for the welfare of the workers. There was Sampson Lloyd, who laid the foundation for Lloyd's Bank, and Josiah Wedgwood, whose dishes they probably ate their dinner off, just as we do. Another member was Erasmus Darwin, the extraordinary polymath, who was a grandfather of Charles Darwin, and Joseph Priestley, whose views on religion and the French Revolution caused him to be driven out of Birmingham by the public's direct action. He had been elected an associate of the French Academy of Sciences and was a member of the Imperial Academy of Sciences in St Petersburg. The Lunatics funded his scientific research and he was in many ways their star. When he was driven out of Birmingham he went to Pennsylvania in America. William Withering was another member. He founded the Birmingham General Hospital and its botanical gardens, and experimented there with foxgloves and the digitalis he obtained from them. Thomas Day was another. He was an advocate of constitutional reform and a great follower of Rousseau (as were many of the Lunar Society) and particularly *Emile*. There was also Richard Edgeworth, an inventor poet and educator, whose daughter Maria became an important writer and educator herself. He also admired Rousseau. Samuel Galton was himself a successful industrialist, and his son later developed important ideas on inheritance and the nature of intelligence. It was men like these who plotted the course of their world out of the 18th century, and helped create the industrial, commercial and moral world of the 19th. Samuel Galton was not a lightweight for Robert to disagree with.

Robert's attempt to take on the mantle of his father suffered another blow when a personal tutor arrived. He was William Paul, and he summarised Robert's academic status somewhat starkly: Robert, he said, had never learned very much at school, and much of what he had learned he had forgotten.[11] There was not a single subject that he did not need to study more. To make matters worse, the guardians were told, Robert had 'instantly neglected his studies' since leaving school. Virtually everyone, except Robert, agreed that he needed 'improving' and must go to an English university for two or three years. He was already slipping into the athlete's stereotype – a young man with the wrong priorities in life, a young man who spent his time on the wrong things and enjoyed himself rather too much in the company of the wrong people. He also had far too high an opinion of himself.

By inclination the guardians preferred to show the route they wanted Robert to take, rather than to dictate it, to suggest rather than command. In Rousseau's way their inclination was to allow Robert to develop and grow, rather than to instruct and force him. The problem was that they also had a vision of what a landed Scottish gentleman should be, and left to his own devices Robert was not showing any sign of approaching that vision. The guardians became slowly but steadily more determined. If he was to fill his proper place in society and eventually be an effective head of his family, he must go to one of the English universities. But which one? The arguments started all over again. Robert had already declared for Edinburgh, and over the next few months Edinburgh, Oxford and Cambridge were put forward and then shelved, but no agreement was reached and Robert stayed at Ury and continued to receive his tuition from William Paul. Some of the guardians were convinced that Robert's enthusiasm for having a tutor at home was 'a mere mask to cover habits of mental indolence', and they were probably right.[12] It certainly gave him considerable freedom and it is little wonder he fought to preserve it. He was free to meet his friends and keep up with all the sporting gossip, free to walk for miles in and around the estate at Ury and go shooting on Megray Hill. He rode with the local hunt and hung out with 'the wrong sort' at the races and the local cock-pits. At the same time, as the Great Master's son and new laird, he was greeted with respect and deference by all the locals. A very flattering and seductive situation for a young man in his teens.

Meanwhile, the harsh realities of the outside world kept pushing in. The Great Master's creditors looked at the financial conditions in the country, looked at the young Barclay family, and decided they wanted their money back. More land was sold. Now the guardians had to resort to Plan B. By letting parcels of the remaining land off for grazing and to tenant farmers, the land left at Ury would now bring in less than £1,600 per annum, out of which all costs had to be met.[13] The family belt had to be tightened even further.

One of the greatest tussles between Robert and his guardians involved the Mearnshire Volunteers. The Mearns was the old name for the county of Kincardineshire. Talk of raising a local volunteer force to repel a French invasion had been going on for months, and in early 1798 William Pitt put through Parliament a Bill requiring that a list of all able-bodied men between 15 and 60 years of age be compiled in every part of Britain, with a view to setting up a network of such forces. At Ury this included Robert Barclay Allardice, who was 18. In May 1798 Lord Kintore, Lord Lieutenant of the county, wrote to the Home Office of their success in compiling their list and on 5 July the Mearnshire Volunteers came into being.[14] There were three companies, each with 50 men. One was to be led by Robert Duff of Fetteresso – he was to be a major. Another was to be led by William Nichol, a surgeon from Stonehaven – he was to be a captain. The other company was to be led by Robert Barclay Allardice, who was also to be a captain. Only landowners within the county, and their sons, with an income of £50 a year from their land, or with annual rents worth £1,000 were eligible to be officers, so it was inevitable that they would be drawn from the leading families. Nevertheless it is astonishing that they ever considered putting Robert in such a position. Surely they cannot have expected such a young man, totally lacking in any experience to mould his men into an efficient fighting force.

The new Mearnshire Volunteers were, in truth, a raggedy-taggedy outfit from the start, led as they were by a landowner with no military experience, a surgeon and a boy barely out of school – an 18th-century Dad's Army. The Steering Committee had allowed their regard for, and loyalty to the Great Master, who had been a member of their group, to cloud their judgement. On reflection they knew it. Mr Burnett, the Sheriff-deputy even put it into words and said that though the gentlemen of Kincardineshire were very willing, they were ignorant of military affairs. What they needed was additional help from someone with knowledge and experience, otherwise 'the men can be of no service', he concluded.[15]

The plan was that the men would be drilled twice a week. Robert, as a captain, would earn 9 shillings and 5 pence per day, twice a week. A short-term help in filling his pockets maybe, but it could hardly have been further away from the guardians' plans. The guardians regarded the idea that Robert was fit to exercise control over a group of men as dangerously bizarre. They were determined that he give up the pretence of being tutored at home, and at a meeting in Birmingham agreed that he should go to Oxford at once, so that he would be subject to some control and discipline. They used their influence behind the scenes, and when the first pay sheet was submitted to the War Office, to cover the period 25 July – 24 August 1798, it showed 'Captain – R. Barclay, absent on leave'.[16]

It was less than three weeks since he had originally been appointed, but already Robert was more conspicuous by his absence than his presence. Over a year had passed since the Great Master had died. The guardians were angry at Robert's procrastination. The family money was running out and they were at their wits' end to see how Robert could manage Ury and provide for the family. In only two years Robert Barclay Allardice would be on his own without their influence and backing. They knew he was not ready. The search to find a future for each of the children quickened its pace. Robert played his part in this, too. In imitation of his father he had assumed a paternalistic attitude towards his brothers and sisters, arrogantly complained that they were 'too much indulged' at their present school and suggested alternatives.[17] You can almost see the guardians smile despairingly on hearing this. Jemmy was 14, and they decided that he should be found a job, possibly as a 'writer' in India in the East India Company; the twins and Rodney would go to Birmingham to continue their education; David was too young to do anything but go to school. Only Cameron would stay at Ury. She was an amiable and well-behaved 19-year-old, and perhaps her best prospects were to marry in Scotland.[18] The family was being dispersed.

Quickly, before the Mearnshire Volunteers began a major 'inspection' at Ury, the guardians arranged a meeting for Robert in London with Henry Dundas, the great Tory grandee and friend of his father. Robert met Henry Dundas with another Robert Barclay, known as 'Black Bob', one of Robert's English guardians and a somewhat haughty, strict, 47-year-old Quaker. The purpose of the visit was to plead Jemmy's case for a job in India, but it failed. Henry Dundas thought he was too young. This was a time of national crisis, with the war with Napoleon at a critical stage.[19] News that Nelson had by the force of his own genius defeated the French Navy in the Battle of the Nile had not yet got through to Henry Dundas. Perhaps that contributed to the meeting's negative result.

After this Robert did not go on to Oxford as expected, nor did he return to Ury. Instead he shocked his family and guardians by rebelliously renting Lark Hall, a house outside Bath, and taking his tutor William Paul with him[20]. His plan was to maintain his freedom and independence and continue his 'private education' away from Ury and away from the close scrutiny of the guardians. The English guardians were based either in the south-east of London, or in Birmingham; the Scottish guardians were, of course, in Scotland. Bath was about as far away from all of them as it was possible to get. They were furious. The influence of Rousseau did not extend this far.

Robert was criticised and William Paul was on the carpet. What was he thinking about to allow it? At the very least, why had he not warned the guardians? Why had he not taken Robert to Oxford as agreed? Was he conspiring with his pupil to thwart the wishes of the guardians, or was he being deceived himself?[21] In many ways one explanation was as bad as the other. Was he fit for the job?

As pressure from the guardians grew, Robert took the additional defiant step of entering into another wager. It was a bold and rash act of self-assertion. The wager was to walk 70 miles against an experienced pedestrian by the name of Ferguson, who worked as a clerk in the city,[22] but about whom little is known. Many of the best long-distance pedestrians, including the great Foster Powell, worked for solicitors, delivering letters. They went on foot, and over a long haul were as quick as a man on horseback, but cheaper. Ferguson may have been one of these. As his father before him, Robert had decided to try his skill, strength and stamina not against another gentleman but against a worthy athletic opponent. It was never likely that the guardians would approve.

Did he do it for the sport, for the money, or was it primarily an act of bravado? Whatever the reason, he set off from Fenchurch Street in the City of London, just east of St Paul's. The route went through west London along the Bath road, and on to the tenth milestone beyond Windsor and back. No details of the size of the wager have survived; perhaps this time Robert sensibly decided to keep this information to himself. Very few other details are known either, but we do know that it was a very hot day and it must have taken about 14 hours. Robert won, with Ferguson out of sight and miles behind.

Lark Hall House was only a dozen miles from Bristol, a great sporting centre. Cricket was popular there, but it was boxing that had the greatest hold over the sporting imagination, and this was undoubtedly the hottest centre for boxing in the country. Even the young lads, many of them butcher's boys or apprentice butchers, were enthusiastic participants. The annual Lansdown Fair was one of the focal points of local boxing and other sports. In 1798, when the 19-year-old Robert arrived, there were several young athletes in and around the Bristol and Bath area, all involved in boxing. There was the 22-year-old Hen Pearce, a 17-year-old called Jem Belcher and a 15-year-old called John Gully. In 1787 Jack Martin, a butcher from Bath, had fought Daniel Mendoza at Shepherd's Bush in front of the Prince of Wales.[23] He had lost, but it was an indication that athletes from Bath were competing at the highest level, and athletes from Bristol had already made their mark. These included Ben Brain, Bill Warr and Jack Slack, all of whom were regarded as top class in their day. Bath itself had its own vibrant sporting culture, and two of its young men were taking London by storm in 1798. They were Thomas Lawrence and John Jackson, and when they were both 12 they played together in Bath. Almost inevitably, boxing, in a field and stripped to the waist like the prize-fighters, was one of their games.[24] Thomas Lawrence later achieved fame as Sir Thomas Lawrence, President of the Royal Academy, and John Jackson became 'Gentleman Jackson', Champion of the Prize Ring and the first universally respected administrator and spokesman for the sport in Britain.

Thomas Lawrence, like so many boys, 'had a fondness, an absolute passion, for pugilism'[25] and could, perhaps, have been one of the best. As it was he became a good shot, an expert courser, and was excellent at fencing and billiards. Most of all he was a genius at drawing and painting. John Jackson developed a formidably powerful physique and became one of the best sprinters and long-jumpers around, and was an outstanding boxer.[26] Bath was a highly popular centre of fashionable activity, frequented during the 'season' by those with style and money. Thomas Lawrence and John Jackson watched the fashionable scene carefully and learned its lessons. Both developed impeccable manners. Then, still in their teens, they left to try their fortunes in London. They were so successful there that, while they were still both only 19, they attracted royal attention, though for completely different reasons. In 1788 John Jackson fought a Scotsman by the name of Fewterell at Smitham Bottom, near Croydon, in front of the Prince of Wales. Jackson was the younger and smaller, and his unexpected victory in 67 minutes so impressed the Prince of Wales that he instructed Colonel Hanger to go across to the young Jackson and present him with a 'bank note.'[27] It was three and a half months before his 20th birthday.

Meanwhile, Lawrence had painted a large picture of *Homer Reciting his Poems to the Greeks* for Richard Payne Knight. An athlete, John Jackson, of course, sat in the foreground listening with rapt attention. It was a coming together of youthful optimism, high art and sport, and was hung at the Royal Academy in 1789.[28] Then, a few days before Lawrence's 20th birthday, he received a letter that started 'Sir, I am commanded by Her Majesty to desire you will come down to Windsor and bring your painting apparatus with you.' He did, and his portraits of Queen Charlotte and the seven-year-old Princess Amelia were exhibited at the Royal Academy the following year. They were excellent, even if the art critic in *The English Chronicle* wrote that the Queen's nose looked as if it was red from taking too much snuff. Perhaps it was. He was paid 60 guineas for the Queen's portrait and 15 guineas for little Amelia's.[29]

Nine years later, in 1798, when Robert was in Bath, Jackson and Lawrence were still the talk of Bath and London, and their lives with their two worlds of sport and art respectively, were still strangely intertwined. The previous year Thomas Lawrence had exhibited a most extraordinary picture at the Royal Academy, whose galleries were then in the Strand. It was a huge painting of *Satan Summoning his Legions* to illustrate the lines from *Paradise Lost* 'Awake, arise, or be forever fallen'.[30] It was in fact a full-frontal portrait of John Jackson, more than twice life size. The picture measured 14' 2" x 9'. Once the viewer got over the shock, and the towering power of Satan, there was much in the picture to interpret. There was the obvious boxing pun about having been knocked down and having to get up. Everyone knew John Jackson as the Champion of the Prize Ring, a title he had won in 1795 when he defeated the famous Daniel Mendoza at Hornchurch. There was no distinction in the 1790s between the titles

Champion of England, Britain or the World. There was only one Champion, and John Jackson was it, and there he was in all his manly splendour hanging on public display in the Royal Academy. Jackson had rooms at 13 Bond Street, a very fashionable address, only 150 yards from Piccadilly, where he gave lessons to gentlemen on the noble art of self-defence. If anyone in the Royal Academy galleries was in any doubt about who owned those huge limbs and powerful muscles, they were only minutes away from Bond Street where they could check for themselves. The face, however, was not Jackson's. It was the face of John Philip Kemble in a rage.[31] John Kemble was a famous Shakespearean actor and brother of another theatrical luminary, Mrs Sarah Siddons. Lawrence had known the Kembles ever since his boyhood in Bath. In the painting, the demon writhing upward from the pit at Satan's feet had the recognisable features of Mrs Siddons herself. At some stage Lawrence painted a cloud of smoke over the demon to conceal this, but the original painting reappeared with age and Mrs Siddons could be seen again when the light was good enough.[32]

The painting, with all its complex messages, was prompted by the fact that Thomas Lawrence, now 28, had fallen in love with Mrs Siddons' eldest daughter, Sally. Mrs Siddons attempted to impose a 'go slow' policy on their relationship and kept some of the details of it away from her brother. This was not entirely unreasonable as Sally's health was poor and Lawrence was also noticeably entranced by Sally's younger sister, Maria.[33] In 1796, when Lawrence started the picture, Sally was 21 and Maria, 17. All this seems to have created some kind of psychological storm in Lawrence, of which the Satan picture is the product. Precisely how and why Lawrence's anger and sexual frustration found its expression in a monstrously large picture of his schoolboy friend, naked, Lawrence never attempted to explain. To add to the complication of symbols, metaphors and meanings, in 1797 at the same time that Lawrence submitted his Satan picture to the Royal Academy, he also submitted a straightforward portrait of Mrs Siddons, which some members of the Academy criticised because it made her look too young.[34] She was 42. Lawrence's emotional involvement with all the Siddons women was obviously somewhat complicated. Nevertheless, Thomas Farington thought Lawrence's portrait of Mrs Siddons 'his best female head',[35] and Thomas Lawrence himself always considered his Satan picture his best work, and it stayed in his personal possession all his life.[36] Sexual tension can be a great, if mysterious, creative spur.

Thomas Lawrence's list of fashionable sitters grew just as surely as did his entanglement with the Siddonses,[37] and in Bond Street gentlemen flocked in increasing numbers to see John Jackson and to take lessons from him. Sport was becoming a matter of fashionable chit chat, and the athletes were turning into major personalities.

For Robert, returning to Bath after his successful wager, there was a buzz and excitement about sport that he could not find in the dry talk of education and family responsibilities that were his guardians' priorities. He was greeted by the local sportsmen as a fully fledged member of the athletic fraternity, that rare mixture, a genuine gentleman-athlete. He mingled with other athletes, learning about their methods, and he even had cash in his pocket from his recent winnings. His friends egged him on and bolstered his courage. The guardians, however, saw the wager as the final act of rebellion. It unleashed an angry tirade from Samuel Galton, who told him that his plans to keep a private tutor at Bath were 'improper', and that he was unimpressed by William Paul anyway as he 'has already lost all influence with You'. He lashed out against the very notion of sport having a useful purpose:

. . . It is by the improvement of your moral, intellectual Powers, that the superiority of the human Character is effected. Our corporeal powers are inferior to those of many animals, a Horse is more swift, & capable of more bodily Exertion, tho' our physical powers are not to be neglected, & in many instances are not sufficiently cultivated, yet it should be commented that the highest probable attainments of nature, would still leave us inferior in those properties to the jockeys of Hughes, to Powel the Pedestrian to Mendoza the Pugilist, and the tumblers at Sadlers Wells. Excellence in these accomplishments beyond a certain extent is rather a disgrace, because it implies a degree of Attention, which must have required the sacrifice of nobler Pursuits.

He then countered the old argument that Robert knew better than they what his father would have wanted and lectured him about 'setting up the necessary inexperience of Youth, against the mature judgement of those your father had appointed on account of that very inexperience to decide for You'. He closed with some thinly veiled comments about 'the Gratification of the Moment' and Robert's morals, and about developing his 'future Character'. To his guardians, Robert's passion for sport and his wish to be part of it were signs either of his immaturity or of his empty-headed foolishness and moral degeneracy. He was to go to Oxford 'without delay'.[38]

Despite this, Robert still did not immediately comply and stayed at Bath. A fortnight later he was even discussing with his oldest sister a plan to go to Germany.[39] He wondered whether Samuel Galton might agree. Was there no limit to his optimism? The guardians' response was to set firm dates for him to be at Oxford.[40] They held virtually all the financial and legal power over Robert, as well as controlling those sinuous tentacles of influence that all large powerful families have. Robert had spent 18 months honing his determination, obstinacy and single-mindedness against his guardians and most of the Barclay family, but within weeks he gave up his house at Bath, and formally resigned his position with the Kincardineshire Volunteers.[41] His battle with his guardians was lost, and his struggle to keep his freedom and his personal tutor was over. So was his brief military escapade. In the years to come, he may have been able to boast that he had been a captain of his own corps of Volunteers before his 19th birthday, but his military involvement had, in truth, been an embarrassing fiasco. No one would have dreamed of calling him 'Captain Barclay', except in a fit of sarcasm.

Robert finally accepted what he saw as defeat, but he did not go, as instructed, to Oxford. He went instead to Cambridge.[42] Cambridge University was considered a better seat of learning than Oxford, and less costly. Neither had much to be proud of, and both had a reputation for encouraging 'the diffusion of ignorance, vice and infidelity'. Drinking, hard drinking, was a major occupation of the students, particularly at Cambridge, but they didn't smoke. Only old men smoked.

When Robert arrived there he was not particularly impressed. It wasn't a patch on Oxford. Its streets were narrow and dirty, and so dimly lit the students used the cover of darkness to terrorise the townsfolk. One writer was unable to understand why any family would live there at all.[43] Robert went a little over the top in his disparaging of Cambridge, however, when he said there was nothing to see there except Trinity College and St Mary's Church,[44] thus dismissing at a stroke King's and all the other medieval colleges.

Cambridge, nevertheless, did massage his ego. He was admitted into Trinity College on 8 November 1798 as a Fellow Commoner. Despite the fact that he had never been an outstanding student, he was happy to boast that, as a Fellow Commoner, he was 'as high as can be here'.[45] Robert always liked to impress. Even more he liked going about dressed in 'the academical style', wearing a long purple gown with silver lace, and a cap with a large silver tassel. Like a beadle on a procession day, he said. In some quarters, such pomp attracted criticism because 'it may tend to encourage in the wearer of it a vanity, at once contemptible and unworthy'.[46] Undoubtedly it did, but it fed Robert's sense of self-importance, and he loved it. There were now only 21 months before he reached his legal majority and could be free of his governors. So he settled down to life at university to enjoy as best he could the wait. The pattern was set in the first week. He went to a couple of lectures, but decided not to begin his 'regular studies' right away. He did decide to give himself a treat, however, and arranged to go out with Lord Fitzwilliam's Stag-Hounds who were turning out a 'famous old stag'.[47] He expected 'excellent sport'. He always did.

Over the next year and a half he enjoyed all that Cambridge had to offer. His predisposition to be 'out in the air' as much as possible had some obvious consequences. It may have meant that the inside of some of the lecture halls were rather less familiar than they should have been. Despite his dislike of 'confinement' he probably got to know the interiors of the local inns, particularly the Cardinal's Cap near Pembroke College, and the two coffee-houses, one kept by Frank Smith in Bridge Street opposite the Round Church, and the other in a room set apart in the Rose Inn, facing the Market Square.[48]

At Trinity most students wore knee-breeches and white stockings. They also curled their hair. It was considered very rustic and unfashionable not to do so. Some students and nearly all the dons and heads of houses still wore wigs, fully combed, curled and powdered. But wigs and powder were rapidly going out of fashion. Dinner was at 2.15, and undergraduates, or at least the more particular ones, dressed for dinner in white waistcoats and white silk stockings which were too fine to be washed by the 'common laundress', and required special treatment. After dinner, Robert, with the rest, relaxed or took part in some sort of recreation.

They went fishing and shooting and kept their own fighting cocks. They played battledore and shuttlecock and what now seem more like children's games, tig, tag or tick, and leapfrog. They played cricket, swam and jumped (particularly hop-step-and-jump). They also swung on ropes, no doubt challenging each other to longer and longer swings and more and more complex methods of dismount. Sparring with boxing gloves was becoming popular too. Student life was boisterous, and learning to box was probably necessary for self-defence. With Newmarket just a few miles down the road, cock-fighting, horse-racing, and the betting that went with both, had a considerable hold over students, even though the university authorities strongly disapproved. Then there was chapel at 5.30 p.m.

After chapel they spent some time in their rooms, shut the outer door, took tea and 'read' for the rest of the evening. Supper was served in the hall at 9.15 but very few bothered to go. Sunday lunch was at 1.15, but they still called it 'dinner', and afterwards most went on to the afternoon university sermon at St Mary's at three o'clock. When it rained the students got wet, for there was only one umbrella, a large, clumsy thing made of oiled cloth, in Cambridge. When not in use, it was carried by a ring fastened to the top, so the handle was often dirty. It was hired out by the hour from a shop on Benet Street. Robert, however, was never one of those who queued to hire it. He obstinately refused to use any umbrella all his life. It was more manly to get wet.

Clubs at Cambridge were as popular as in London where there were clubs for almost everything. Many met in inns or coffee-houses. To stress their exclusiveness members wore specially designed uniforms consisting of coats of a characteristic colour with distinctively engraved or embossed buttons. One of the clubs at Cambridge had bright green coats lined and bound with buff silk with special buttons carrying the words 'sans souci'. The uniform also included buff-coloured breeches and a buff-coloured waistcoat decorated with frogs. The members met in each other's rooms one evening a week, when they drank and gambled at cards, often for high stakes. They also dined together once a month and could bring along a friend if they wished. These were very boozy affairs. And at the end of the year they had a big 'annual dinner'.

At Cambridge, Robert socialised, made friends and even learned something too. His tutor gave him his most glowing report yet: 'I am charmed with his disposition, and think well of his understanding, his sense is solid and he is fond of good conversation.'[49] With his 21st birthday on the horizon Robert was too impatient to get on with his life, so he did not sit his exams or take his degree. On 25 August 1799 he was 21 and had already returned to Ury to formally take over responsibility for himself, his family and the estate. Within months Robert and the rest of the Barclays ushered in a New Year and a new century, with all the optimism and trepidation that such calendar landmarks always bring. He relished the prospect to take on the world without the hindrance ever again, of guardians, or anyone else who could tell him what to do.

## CHAPTER FOUR

# The Fancy Beckons

*Fancy's a term for every blackguardism —*
*A term for favourite men, and favourite cocks —*
*A term for gentlemen who make a schism*
*Without the lobby, or within the box —*
*For the best rogues of polish'd vulgarism,*
*And those who deal in scientific knocks —*
*For bull-dog breeders, badger routers — all*
*Who live in gin and jail, or not at all.*

'THE FANCY: A SELECTION . . .'
JOHN HAMILTON REYNOLDS, 1820

On his return to Ury things were both better and worse for the new Laird of Ury than when he went off to Cambridge. Annual income had steadily risen under the guardians' plan, perhaps to as much as £4,000.[1] His sister Cameron had married John Innes of nearby Cowie,[2] and Henry Dundas had, at last, offered a 'writership' in India to Jemmy once his education was finished.[3] However, Mary, one of the twin girls had died.[2] His responsibility for four sisters and two brothers was already diminished to two sisters and soon, only one brother.

On coming of age one of Robert's first independent actions was to write to Henry Dundas to offer his 'grateful thanks' for what he had done for Jemmy, and to try a little networking.[4] Perhaps the great Henry Dundas, arguably the most powerful and influential man in Scotland, could open some doors for him. Unfortunately, in Robert's letter, smugness shone through the gratitude and earnestness: 'I arrived at age lately, I am in possession of a fine estate, greatly improved by the uncommon exertion and successful agricultural operations of my late worthy father, who I believe was well known to you.' The doors did not open. There was no offer to take his father's place in Parliament or to take up a well paid sinecure elsewhere, so Robert turned his attention to other pressing matters and within weeks wagered £2,500 that one of his sporting friends by the name of Robert Fletcher, could not walk 60 miles in 14 hours.'[5]

It is the sort of bet that comes during a boozy dinner or at the end of a long night in a tavern, when recklessness has been sharpened just as surely as judgement has been blunted. As part of the betting convention, each man deposited £2,500 with a stakeholder, who thus held £5,000 to deliver to the man who won. It was a huge sum of money, and one that Robert could not afford. He was risking nearly two-thirds of Ury's new annual income, and he wasn't even betting on his own ability, but on someone else's.

Robert seemed oblivious to the general financial climate. In the autumn of 1800 the price of wheat had risen to its highest ever, well over double that of two years earlier.[6] This had a knock-on effect. Meat was

25 per cent dearer than the year before, and cheese, butter and almost all food were expensive and scarce. The price of bread had risen out of the reach of thousands of the poorer people. People were going hungry. Food riots broke out in Birmingham, Coventry, Nottingham, Portsmouth and Sheffield. When the violence spread to London, the Riot Act had to be read, and the London Militia and the East India House Volunteers were called out to restore order. Throughout Europe the harvest had been poor and the laws of supply and demand led the landowner-farmers to ask even more for their scant supplies. The Earl of Warwick declared in Parliament that farmers were making 200 per cent profit on corn, but the lower orders were facing starvation. Such was the timing of Robert's first major sporting wager.

His adversary in this wager, Robert Fletcher, was an empty-headed young man of 19 who had more money than sense. He certainly had no thoughts for those less fortunate than himself. He lived in a mansion at Ballinshoe near Kirriemuir, about 45 miles from Ury.[7] Despite his age he was already a captain in the 17th (Leicestershire) Regiment of Foot. Robert Fletcher loved gambling but had little strength of character, and had let a huge fortune slip through his fingers, thus acquiring the title 'The Daft Laird'. He was a second son, who came into a fortune the previous year when his older brother, Thomas Fletcher, a major in the Indian Army, died unexpectedly. The rumour was that Major Fletcher had been murdered in India by the relatives of an Indian princess he had married, taken back to Scotland and then mistreated.[8] Whether the Indian princess's dowry formed part of his fortune is not known but he certainly had a lot of money. He owned Lindertis Castle, 'one of the finest seats of which the country can boast', but he chose to live in a more modern house built in the grounds of the old ruined Ballinshoe Castle.

His passion was for horse-racing and he already owned a string of racehorses. He laid bets on other people's horses, too, often for very large sums. But the Daft Laird's betting was unusual. He used it as a sort of game in which he repeatedly bet against the same person to establish a 'winner' and he was capable of turning a simple wager into a personal contest that could go on for weeks or months.

Robert knew from experience what was required to go 60 miles on foot; he had done it himself. Apart from his wager against Ferguson, when he was at Cambridge, he had walked from London to Birmingham via Cambridge in two days[9] to see Samuel Galton and Lucy, Margaret and Rodney, his three remaining sisters; 176 miles according to *Paterson's Roads*.[10] He returned to London on foot, this time going via Oxford, a distance of 'only' 113 miles, also in two days. Clearly, he knew better than most what it would take to go 60 miles in 14 hours. The Daft Laird was not up to it. He had never been particularly athletic, and he wasn't even fit. It seemed a safe bet.

Eighteenth-century sporting wagers were often complex affairs. Many events were individually created simply to bet on, by two people with opposing views; then all parties knew that they were engaged in a battle of wits. These sporting wagers were as much about thinking, and pre-event planning, as they were about muscle and sweat. The main protagonists set each other physical puzzles to solve. They were free to arrange and agree their own conditions and terms and they created their own events and agreed their own rules. The challenge was to know your event or athlete so well you could get your adversary to agree to, and sign, Articles of Agreement, having overlooked, or not properly considered, an important factor. It was not trickery, at least, not always; it was a mind game. In mid-century the master of this was the Earl of March.

The Earl of March was a Scot from a generation before Robert. He was an old man when Robert was entering the fray, but he was still active, and had a passion for fine wine, sport and women, though not necessarily in that order.[11] When he was young he won some very large stakes and side-bets in a series of remarkable wagers. When he was 23 he offered 1,000 guineas that he could produce a four-wheeled carriage drawn by four horses that would cover 19 miles in an hour. A foolhardy bet by a young man with more money than judgement was the general opinion at the time. Nearly two years later, however, after intense experimentation and development work, Wright the coach-builder in Long Acre, produced for him a 'carriage' stripped down to little more than a seat slung on leather straps. The design incorporated oilcans fixed to drip oil on to the wheel mechanisms to reduce friction. The harnesses for the horses were made of silk and whale bone. He then selected and trained racehorses that, on the day, pulled the carriage over the 19 miles in 53 minutes and 27 seconds[12] – an average speed of over 21 miles per hour.

Three years later, for another large stake, he wagered that he could convey a letter 50 miles in less than an hour. This surely was the height of madness. No man, horse or machine could do this. His knowledge of, and confidence in, the skill of cricketers however, gave the Earl of March the winning edge. He had a ball made of the same size and weight as a cricket ball, but with a letter inside. He then secretly arranged for 20 skilled cricketers to practise and perfect their throwing and catching. On the appointed day he placed them about 45 yards apart in a circle more than half a mile in circumference, and they threw the ball quickly and accurately around the circle. One hundred 'laps' of his circle equalled 50 miles, and if they were quick and accurate enough they had 60 minutes to complete the task. Imagine the arguments. Was it fair? Was this within the terms of the agreed wager? Was the distance correct? Oh yes, it was on every count. When the distance was remeasured it proved to be 'several miles' too far.[13] The Earl of March won the wager and not one cricketer seems to have dropped or misfielded the ball, even under this intense pressure.

The Earl of March's secret lay in his preparation, but this wager also tells us a lot about 18th-century cricket. We should not for a moment imagine a quiet, rustic sport on the village green. In the 18th century cricket was already tough, professional, popular and thoroughly commercial. Hambledon Cricket Club in Hampshire regularly played for stake money of as much as £500 to 1,000 guineas. They usually drew crowds as large as 20,000 to their big matches, such as when they played an England XI, and as much as 4,000 guineas would change hands on the ground in bets. It has been calculated that in the 20 years from 1770, the Hambledon Club played for stakes of over £40,000, and won £28,000.[14] Admittedly, the Hambledon Club was *the* club in 18th-century England, but it was not unique. Crowds of 20,000 could also be seen at the Artillery Ground in Finsbury Square, and elsewhere, and similar sums were played for at Goodwood, Guildford, Chertsey, Moulsey Hurst, Sevenoaks and, of course, London.[15]

For the most part, because sport had not yet been codified, controlled and regulated, it could be almost anything you wanted it to be. In some sports, such as horse-racing, cricket, boxing and cock-fighting, there were written rules of a sort, but they were very few and rudimentary; as much concerned with settling disputes related to betting, as with the detailed conduct of the event itself. These sports, plus foot-racing, wrestling, rackets, billiards and many more, provided every opportunity for a young man to test his ability, find excitement and possibly make money. All you needed in addition to money, or backers to supply it, was encyclopaedic knowledge of past wagers and the athletes' performances, an analytical mind, a steady nerve, determination and, as the Earl of March had shown, a creative imagination. It helped in these circles if you could hold your drink and not get drawn into wagers when your brain was befuddled, and if you performed your own wagers, you also needed exceptional physical ability. Without all these, it was easy to lose your money. Many did.

It was after an unsuccessful week at the Hamilton Races in October 1800 that Robert Barclay Allardice and the Daft Laird agreed their wager.[16] To Robert he must have seemed an easy target, but he had failed to make one important provision in the wager. The Articles of Agreement should have required the event to take place immediately, or within 48 hours. It was a serious omission. Robert had based his judgement on the Daft Laird's current fitness, or rather, his lack of it. To everyone's surprise and particularly Robert's, the Daft Laird, almost at once, arranged to go into training in Yorkshire under the supervision of Bill Warr, the ex-prize-fighter from Bristol.[17] Bill Warr kept the One Tun Tavern on Jermyn Street, in London's newly fashionable West End[18], a sporting inn frequented by many fashionable sportsmen who were becoming known collectively as 'The Fancy'. The two young Scottish sportsmen with a mean age of only 20, who had arranged a pedestrian wager for £5,000, were soon the talk of the Fancy in London.

Bill Warr had become well known when he lost two fights to Daniel Mendoza in 1792 and 1794. He was a somewhat rough-and-ready, untidy man, but he was now known to be a good trainer for an athlete in any sport, as well as being a successful teacher of boxing. Once he and the Daft Laird had got to Yorkshire there was little time for training. Nevertheless, it worked, and when the day came the Daft Laird completed the 60 miles inside the stipulated 14 hours and pocketed Robert Barclay Allardice's £2,500.[19] Robert had not only misjudged the Daft Laird; he had also made a fundamental error: his wager had been impetuous.

Round 1 to the Daft Laird. Perhaps he was not so daft after all!

The Fancy was the name given to the men who financed sport, wagered on it and attended the events as spectators. As the popularity of sport grew during the first 20 years of the 19th century, so did the allure of the Fancy. It became the inner sanctum of sport. It had no formal membership or structure, and was not a club, but its 'members' did have well-known meeting places, had a favourite drink, gin, and even developed their own slang and way of dressing. They carried with them an aura of excitement, daring and risk which attracted more and more followers every time a major new event was staged. The Fancy was centred on London but was also scattered around the country, and was made up of men of all ages and all social classes, though the gentlemen were given due deference because of their money and influence. They were a very unusual and complex group but they approached sport with great simplicity, and it was this simplicity which held such a large heterogeneous group together. Entertainment and excitement were part of it, and the thrill and uncertainty that major sporting events bring was also a part. The athletes risked their reputations and their health. Others risked their fortunes, or at least their dinners, when they gambled their guineas. But the sharp edge on all this excitement and uncertainty came because sport was about two things – money and the thrill of risk-taking.

The Fancy was involved with every sport, but because of the special place that pugilism was creating for itself in the sporting world, it was associated primarily with the pugilists (also known as 'prize-fighters', and sometimes even 'boxers'). During his stay in Bath, Robert had learned how important pugilism was to the Fancy. It came in several forms. There were the organised prize fights or matches, arranged like pedestrian matches, to decide bets. These may have been between the two pugilists or between their supporters, but usually they were arranged by two gentlemen of the Fancy who put up a 'purse' for them to compete for. Then, several side-bets were made on how long the fight would last, who would give the first knock-down blow, draw first blood, get his teeth knocked down his throat, need stitches over his eyes to stem the blood, or whatever any of the fans fancied putting their money on. These bruising, bare-knuckle affairs were a cross between modern boxing and wrestling, for action came in a mixture of blows and throws and lasted until one man could go on no longer. This might, occasionally, take only a few minutes but sometimes it took well over an hour. The prize fights were governed by a set of rules drawn up in 1743 by James Broughton, but in addition,[20] Articles of Agreement were drawn up for all major fights, just as for pedestrian matches, to define those points that could lead to dispute between the principal parties. As a sport, prize-fighting was further advanced than pedestrianism, not only because it had its own nationally recognised, written rules but also because it had a recognised championship, and 'The Champion' held a very special place in the nation's affections.

Pedestrianism, or foot-racing, was also part of the Fancy's domain. There were important distinctions between the sports of prize-fighting and pedestrianism. Gentlemen did not take part in prize fights, although they were almost always there to support, encourage and finance the fighters, but they might take part in pedestrian matches. Unlike pedestrian events, prize fights were against the law. This was primarily because the large and unruly crowds that gathered to watch were seen as a threat to public order. After 1789 everyone in Britain was aware of the power of the mob. It is not surprising that potential breaches of the peace made the authorities nervous. All prize fights, therefore, were arranged in semi-secrecy with only a few people being trusted with the details of time and venue until the very last moment. Despite these precautions many thousands would turn up to watch a big fight, and not infrequently a local Justice of the Peace or county magistrate also got to know and turned up to take the fighters, and sometimes the match officials, into custody. But often the JPs and magistrates went with their collars turned up, incognito, to enjoy the action.

To pursue their sport without fear of interruption, the Fancy arranged demonstration bouts at which the principal pugilists showed off their skills. These were in reality demonstrations of sparring using boxing gloves, or 'mufflers' as they were called. Often they were put on at inns and taverns to entertain the customers or at the Fives Court in Little St Martin's Street, off Jermyn Street in London, a very popular venue because it was easy to get to, dry, relatively comfortable in the winter and could accommodate up to 1,000 spectators paying from 'two bobs' (two shillings), to 'a bender' (three shillings and six pence).[21] Although they were demonstrations, they were seldom stagy or fake contests. The boxers' pride ensured most bouts were spirited, knockabout affairs that provided good entertainment and sent the audience home well satisfied and anxious for more.

Paradoxically, although gentlemen would not be seen prize-fighting, knowledge of how to fight and spar was an almost essential skill for gentlemen who wished to be considered part of the fashionable world. Pugilism was the height of fashion, and thousands of young and not-so-young men earnestly took lessons so that they could be initiated into its mysteries. The uncertainty provoked by the war with Napoleon may have played its part too, and so did the Fancy's campaign against effeminacy which they exposed and ridiculed wherever they found it. Pugilism and the Prize Ring were, almost by definition, the antithesis of effeminacy and so if you associated yourself with prize-fighting or sparring you were giving a public demonstration of your manliness, and in your own small way supporting those virtues that would save the country. Although fighting was technically against the law, by 1800 supporting it had somehow managed to become the patriotic thing to do.

The Fancy made their home wherever a sporting event was held and caroused the night away in countless sporting taverns in London, Bristol, Birmingham, Newmarket, York and any other centre where sport took place. But in the early years of the new century it was 'Jackson's Rooms' that were the fashionable epicentre of sport in Britain. They had originally been the rooms where Harry Angelo, the latest in a long line of famous fencing masters, taught. Jackson joined him after he had beaten Mendoza to become the Champion.[22] Now they were jointly owned and run on alternate days by Angelo and Jackson. John Jackson had become part of the fashionable world, partly because of his sporting success, partly because of his association with the Prince of Wales and partly because of his notoriety as a sitter for Thomas Lawrence. But in addition to that there was something about John Jackson that people liked and respected. His manners were impeccable and he seemed to possess natural dignity and gentility that made his nickname 'Gentleman' Jackson, stick. So popular were Jackson's Rooms that it was said that more than one-third of the nobility frequented them.[23] Lords of the Realm, members of the Cabinet and other dignitaries in large numbers followed the lead of the Prince of Wales and made their way there to gain instruction from Gentleman Jackson, or just to soak up the atmosphere. Six lessons constituted a course. These rooms were the focal point for the exchange of information not only on boxers and boxing, but on horse-racing, cricket, pedestrianism and all the latest sports, and remained so until he retired in 1824. Jackson himself was up to date, well informed and became virtually the national spokesman on all 'manly sports'.

Jackson and Angelo opened their rooms six days a week – never on a Sunday – and sportsmen and gentlemen of the Fancy met and mingled there on more level terms than they could on the street outside. On entering we have to imagine there were racks holding swords, foils, rapiers of various descriptions and cupboards full of boxing gloves; on the walls pictures of boxers and diagrams of fencing positions. In the large room at the back, there was a set of scales for gentlemen to weigh themselves.[24] Upstairs, in the corners and in places where they were least in the way, there were small tables where you might put down a drink, and chairs where you might sit to rest and recover for a while or just chat about your health or the next forthcoming event. There were not, apparently, any changing rooms. So we must also imagine Jackson's Rooms with jackets strewn over the chairs and tables and with the distinct smell of sweat in the air, despite the fact that the windows were thrown wide open in all but the most severe weather.

In 1800 Jackson was 32 and at the height of his fame. He was fit, athletic, strong and authoritative, and his size and proportions made an impact on all who saw him. He stood half an inch under 6' and weighed 14 stone and was said to be 'the finest formed man in Europe'.[25] He had great physical strength. In the presence of many witnesses he had once lifted from the ground ten and a quarter hundredweight. And as a special stunt he wrote his name on the wall with an 84lb weight suspended from his little finger![26]

One eyewitness described him walking down Holborn Hill towards Smithfield:

He had a scarlet coat, worked in gold at the buttonholes, ruffles, and frills of fine lace, a small white stock, no collar, a looped hat with a broad black band, buff knee-breeches, and long silk strings, striped white silk stockings, pumps, and paste buckles; his waistcoat was pale blue satin, sprigged with white. It was impossible to look on his fine ample chest, his noble shoulders, his waist (if anything too small), his large, but not too large hips, ... his limbs, his balustrade calf and beautifully turned but not over delicate ankle, his firm foot, and peculiarly small hand, without thinking that nature had sent him on earth as a model. On he went at a good five and a half miles an hour, the envy of all men, and the admiration of all women.[27]

He obviously was driven by the same fashionable forces that inspired another young man who had just joined Brooks's in St James's Street and was becoming a regular frequenter of Bond Street, George 'Beau' Brummell.[28] Following the Royal Academy exhibition in 1797, Jackson's physique was, of course, well known in every detail, and in 1800 there was something of a re-run. Once again Lawrence submitted a very large painting. Once again it included John Kemble's head on Gentleman Jackson's body. (This time, though, he did not submit a painting of Mrs Siddons, but one of her sister Frances, whom Lawrence was using as a counsellor in his ongoing emotional torment regarding the rest of the Siddons ménage.) The picture, featuring Jackson's body and Kemble's head, was of more modest proportions: a 'mere' 11' x 7'4", and Jackson was partly covered by a tunic. It was, however, skimpy enough to reveal his muscular legs and powerful arms. In his right hand he held a dagger, and in his left, a baby (for which the model was Richard Brinsley Sheridan's son, Thomas). The juxtaposition of gentleness and strength, power and protection seemed to sum up Gentleman Jackson perfectly. It is almost certain that once again some of the gentlemen who flocked to see Jackson in his rooms, popped into the Royal Academy on the Strand to check out his picture too. The subject of the painting was John Kemble playing the role of Rolla in Sheridan's *Pizzaro*. 'Rolla, the hero, the kinsman of the King ... the idol of the army; in war a tiger'.[29] And so, once again, in 1800, art, sport and the theatre became fused in this one picture.

The paintings of Jackson in the Royal Academy helped fuel the Fancy's growing preoccupation with the physical appearance of the male body. They dressed in sleek tight-fitting breeches to show their manliness, and flaunted their well-muscled arms to impress each other. They may have had a horror of effeminacy, but they embraced narcissism without a qualm.

Robert may have first met Gentleman Jackson in Bath or in Jackson's Rooms, but they did meet again in May 1800, a few months before Robert's wager with the Daft Laird, at a race meeting on Ascot Heath which they attended with their respective friends to sample the excitement and mingle with the Fancy.[30] Gentleman Jackson was the biggest celebrity there, and turned every head from the eligible daughters of the landed gentry to the stable grooms and the runny-nosed urchins. Here was the undefeated Champion of the Prize Ring. Although he had retired, he was still the Champion in the eyes of the public and had been for the past five years.

If Gentleman Jackson had an imposing physique that made men envious and women go weak at the knees, Robert Barclay was not far behind. He may have been half an inch or so shorter but he too was strongly built, with muscular arms, wide shoulders and athletic, sturdy legs. Indeed, both men were of similar build and Robert, the newcomer and Jackson's junior by 11 years, must have turned a few heads and set a few tongues wagging himself. Physical size and strength and the reputation for being willing and able to use them was a definite advantage at many of the venues where the Fancy met. The same race meeting the previous year had degenerated into a near riot. A gang that frequented race meetings with E.O. tables, cups, balls and 'other deceptive gaming tricks to entrap the unwary', found a victim in a gentleman's manservant. E.O. (even or odd) was played on small, circular tables with their edges divided into alternating even or odd sections into which a ball was rolled. The chances of winning were not 50/50, however, as the owner of the table always took a cut. The gangs of tricksters and thimbleriggers who ran these attractions were usually seven or eight strong, but sometimes bigger. The servant was enticed in by the gang for a 'sure' flutter and ended up losing all his money and his watch. A party of the Staffordshire Militia was present and intervened. Instead of solving the problem this provoked a major mêlée. The gang attacked the soldiers and 'cut and bruised them in a most shocking manner'. A message was hurriedly sent to Windsor where a party of Light Horse were persuaded to turn out to restore law and order. Eventually three of the gang were taken into custody and conveyed under escort in a coach and four to the Berkshire County Gaol. They were later sentenced to three years' hard labour with one month each year in solitary confinement.[31]

In 1800 the race meeting was more peaceful, but gentlemen of the Fancy always had to keep their wits about them. Protocol required that they looked leisurely and relaxed and wore their best sporting clothes. Robert, like all the young men making their way in the fashionable world, was very particular about what he wore. Clothes did not need to be elegant, and sometimes gentlemen deliberately dressed 'down' as if they were coachmen, but the clothes they wore were carefully selected to produce the desired effect. It was part of the cult of 'manliness'. On this occasion Robert was particularly attracted by a stylish pair of brand-new deerskin breeches that Jackson was wearing. He so admired them that he was determined to have them. A bargain was struck and Robert purchased – on the spot – the breeches off Jackson's shapely legs.[32] How the transaction was finalised is not recorded, and how John Jackson got home without his breeches we can only imagine, but certainly Robert must have had an extremely persuasive way with him to part a man like Jackson from his new breeches. Or dug very deeply into his purse.

Robert was to wear these leather breeches on suitable occasions for the rest of his life, and they consequently became his trademark. Their history was once described as unequalled in the history of breeches. After Robert had worn them for 35 years, they were said to have at least another ten years of wear in them. So enduring did they prove that people jokingly asked where the deer had come from that could produce the leather. How was it possible to kill them? They had proved so indestructible, surely their hides must have been bullet-proof. The leather breeches that once covered the impressively powerful legs so conspicuously on display in the Royal Academy were now covering Robert's. From that day, Robert Barclay Allardice and Gentleman Jackson were friends.

Because men were expected to be manly, fighting captured the spirit of the age. Men in all walks of life were expected to be physically brave and to suffer pain without flinching. Their sport reflected this. Cricketers played on rough pitches and without any protective clothing. Bruised and bleeding legs and hands were part of the game. In country fairs all over the nation, generations of men had cudgelled. A 'score' was achieved when you hit your adversary on the head and the blood ran an inch. The blow was insufficient; it was the inch of blood that counted. No one complained of the blows or the blood, and the bouts were not stopped to administer first aid. If you wished to be considered manly, it also helped if you were well muscled and physically strong. If you weren't, you had to be at least courageous and uncomplaining. Manliness, however, was not a passive thing. Men knew that they might be called on at any time to prove or defend their manliness. Both men and the women expected it. Some men seemed to revel in requiring others to demonstrate it, virtually on demand. If they did, how could you refuse? These were the prevailing attitudes that led gentlemen in particular to develop a prickly sense of honour and become touchy and indignant if they thought they had been slighted. Perhaps the nation being at war contributed to the atmosphere as well. Their concepts of 'gentlemanly conduct' and 'honour' interacted with the prevailing views on manliness, courage, fortitude and disregard for pain. Consequently the gentlemen of the Fancy lived in a world in which they had to be perpetually vigilant. Their 'honour', indeed their lives, were insecure and they dared not look too far ahead. A good example of these attitudes was Colonel Harvey Aston who, in 1788, had been the man who first introduced the young John Jackson to the Fancy, which had led to his first fight with Fewterell. In 1799 a dispute arose between three members of Colonel Aston's regiment in India while he was away: Major Picton, Major Allen and a lieutenant. On his return Colonel Aston investigated the matter and in his report wrote that the two officers had been 'illiberal' with the lieutenant. The officers objected, and two duels were fought in which the colonel had to 'satisfy' each of the majors. In the first Major Picton was given first fire. His pistol snapped but did not fire. The seconds declared that this constituted his shot. Colonel Aston then fired into the air saying that he had no quarrel with the major. The next day Major Allen fired the first shot. The colonel stood erect and motionless and the seconds believed the shot to have gone wide. It was now the colonel's turn. With great composure he raised his pistol and with a steady hand took aim. But he did not fire. He slowly drew his hand back and placed it on his heart saying, 'I am shot through the body; I believe the wound is mortal, and therefore decline returning the fire; for it never shall be said that the last act of my life was dictated by a spirit of revenge.' He sat down on the ground and was carried home where he lay in agony for several days, and then died without a murmur.[33]

The gentlemen of the Fancy lived in a world of thrills and uncertainties. They could drink to excess and gamble irresponsibly, but it was no place for the faint-hearted.

Robert Barclay Allardice was getting to know some of the bright lights of the Fancy, but the loss of a significant wager with the Daft Laird hardly gave him credibility. So he jumped eagerly at the chance to make amends, even though the Daft Laird was not willing to stake big money this time. Perhaps it was his way of showing who had the upper hand. In his 60-mile walk in 14 hours, the Daft Laird had found the last 20 miles so difficult he could not believe that Robert could cover a distance half as far again at the same speed. So he challenged Robert to a return wager. In November 1800 Robert accepted, even though the Daft Laird was willing to stake only 500 guineas. He had no choice. There was some discussion over the finer points; it was after all, seven hours longer. Some allowance would have to be made for eating and drinking and the necessary toilet arrangements and change of clothing, argued Robert. He was determined not to miss anything this time. The Articles of Agreement stated that Robert Barclay Allardice would 'make the best of his way, by walking or otherwise, on foot and undertake to go 90 miles in 21 successive hours and a half'.[34] The word 'successive' was inserted into the Articles by the Daft Laird to deny Robert a long rest. He was required to walk in *every* hour of the 21½ hours, and the event had to be completed in December. Although he could not recover his financial losses in this wager, it was a chance to restore his pride.

To complete the task successfully Robert would have to average a little over four miles an hour for over 21 hours. It was commonly known among the Fancy that they could bank on the very best pedestrians maintaining five miles an hour for ten hours. In his match against Ferguson, Robert himself may have continued at this speed for 14 hours, but that was probably approaching the limit for one day. If the rate was reduced to a modest four miles an hour the Fancy knew from experience that a good pedestrian could keep going at that speed for 12 hours a day for a month, or even longer. One expert said that apart from sickness, a good pedestrian should be able to walk 12 hours a day at that speed for the whole of his lifetime![35]

Robert's wager, however, was to average *over* four miles an hour for 21½ hours – a difficult challenge even for the very best pedestrians. Expert opinion was divided. Foster Powell had done slightly better than this 12 years earlier, but he was a phenomenon. If Robert Barclay Allardice succeeded, he would immediately move into the very top flight of pedestrians of all time. It would be some consolation for having lost his money. It was, therefore, not the speed of the walk that would test Robert, it was the length of time he would have to maintain it. His powers of endurance over such a long time had never been tested formally, so he set himself a trial.

At midnight on a cold November night, Robert Barclay Allardice set out from Ury, probably with George Mollison, who was then 46. The task that Robert had given himself was to walk to the Earl of Aberdeen's mansion at Ellon, about 32 miles away, and back again, which he did before midday.[36] This was well over five miles an hour for 12 hours – an outstanding performance. As a trial for his new wager, however, it was a waste of time. It confirmed what he already knew, that he would have no difficulty with the *speed*. But what about the 21½ hours?

To build the extra stamina Robert should have put himself into training. Training an athlete for a competition was then, and still is, an intricately balanced mixture of art, science and experience. Bill Warr, who trained the Daft Laird, had been an athlete himself, and had been giving training advice to athletes for at least ten years. Robert Barclay Allardice was just 21 and knew only what he had picked up from others. What he needed, but did not get, was expert advice from an experienced trainer.

An air of mystique surrounded training. How to train a racehorse, a man or a fighting cock to win a wager was prized information and worth good money. Those who knew most about it tended to keep their knowledge to themselves as a well-guarded secret or pass it on orally to those they chose or within their families. When Sir John Sinclair attempted a survey of training methods a few years later, he first published a series of questions about training with some preliminary answers.[37] He then sent out 'intelligent men' to collect the information he wanted. This is how it went in one case. Mr W. S. Rickwood approached a jockey and an old training groom:

> I went about my inquiry with the greatest caution, that no offence, by anything abrupt, should be conceived. The jockey had read 'the book': on requesting the favour of his opinion, as to some of the questions it contained, I met with unwilling, surly indeed rude replies; in short, I found both one and the other much indisposed to afford any information whatever; and the final result and answer from both was; 'That the man who wrote the book and asked (alias ax'd) the questions might be bl⁄ʌ⁄d; let him train himself, and be d⁄⁄⁄⁄d, if he wanted to know anything, from them he would know nothing.[38]

It was generally acknowledged that training had four essential elements:

purging, a sort of early detoxing process, which cleaned out the system before the training started; sweating, which got rid of the extra pounds of fat; diet, which was the cornerstone of training; and exercise. In the absence of any professional advice, Robert decided that he needed sweating. It was known to be a tricky process. This was where a good trainer earned his salt. Too much of it, too late, weakened your athlete. Not enough, too soon, left him overweight and breathless.

To follow current best practice Robert set himself three sweats, the last only a week before the wager. There was an early morning nip in the air. Early December mornings in eastern Scotland are often like that. When he went out after his final sweat the cold air struck at his muscles and settled in his bones, and within a couple of days he had all the signs of a chill, he was weak and his muscles ached.

The wager had been made 'p.p.' (play or pay). There could be no delay or postponement, and there was no chance that he would recover in time. Robert conceded defeat.[39]

Round 2 to the Daft Laird.

Robert was now part of a circle of friends who met wherever sporting gentlemen in eastern Scotland gathered; at various hunts, race meetings, cock-fights and fairs.[40] Among them was Fletcher Reid, who lived in a large house in Logie near Dundee. He was the Daft Laird's uncle but because of the similarity in their ages – he was 25 – they were thought to be cousins. Of all Robert's Scottish friends, Fletcher Reid was the one most closely associated with the Fancy. He lived only 35 miles from Ury and was to become not only a good friend of Robert Barclay Allardice but was to help shape the direction of his life. Only four years older than Robert, Fletcher Reid had already packed into his short life more unruly, high-spirited risk and excitement than most people ever experience. Robert and he visited sporting events together, drank and socialised.

He had been a lieutenant in the Angus Fencibles and now worked as a Customs and Excise officer. He was married but this in no way cramped his style socially. He arranged outrageous evenings at Morren's

Hotel in Dundee to which he invited all the wild, well-heeled, dissolute young men in the vicinity, who then proceeded to entertain themselves and shock almost everyone else in equal measure. Many of his 'mad adventures' were in doubtful taste, to say the least. In one notorious escapade in Logie churchyard he took a leading part in the enactment of the Day of Judgement, presiding over a mock trial in which he played God and tried all the local dignitaries, exposing their foibles for all to see and be entertained by. Then, among the respectable headstones and family vaults, he pronounced judgement, denying most of them any further progress through the pearly gates. No wonder the episode was roundly condemned locally as 'an outrage on public decency'.[41] No doubt Fletcher Reid and his friends dined out on it for months, and were spurred on by the public protestations of outrage to go one better.

Although he had a wild social life and was a lover of practical jokes, it was betting that made Fletcher Reid tick. Like his nephew the Daft Laird, he was addicted to gambling. So much so that it was said that he would rather back the losing side than no side at all, and that he considered losing the next greatest pleasure to winning. In the sporting world Fletcher Reid was something of a specialist, devoting almost all his time to prize-fighters of whom he was one of the most active and best known patrons. He exerted considerable influence on pugilistic affairs and enjoyed the friendship and confidence of almost everyone in the sport.

His interest in prize-fighting was unusual for a Scot because pugilism, at that time, was not a typically Scottish sport at all. There had only ever been one top-class pugilistic encounter in Scotland; that was in 1793 when Fewterell defeated an unnamed Highlander at Leith near Edinburgh.[42] However, Daniel Mendoza, the great Jewish boxing superstar from London, had visited Scotland on several occasions throughout the 1790s. In 1791 he had demonstrated his skills to the Gymnastic Society in Edinburgh, who presented him with a gold medal. He even took rooms in the city to demonstrate the 'pugilistic art' before moving on to Glasgow where, in one night at the Glasgow Infirmary, he took £138 at the door.[43]

A few years later, when he was still the Champion, he returned to Scotland. First of all he acted as a sergeant in the recruiting service of the Fifeshire Regiment of Fencibles and when their numbers were complete, he obtained the position of sergeant-major in the Aberdeenshire Fencibles, which he left in 1795.[44] In 1800 Mendoza was back in Scotland again giving exhibitions in Dumfries, Edinburgh, Dundee, Glasgow and Greenock,[45] and it is almost certain that Fletcher Reid and Robert Barclay Allardice took the opportunity to see the almost legendary Mendoza demonstrate his skills. His main reasons for returning to Scotland were to escape his creditors in England and to meet up again with Fletcher Reid, one of his most important backers. Anyone who could claim to know, or better still, claim to be a friend, of Daniel Mendoza, had immediate status among the Fancy. Fletcher Reid could claim even more than that. He was not only a friend of Mendoza's, he had been his backer and patron in several fights and so had considerable influence with the great boxer.

To understand the unique place that Fletcher Reid held in the boxing world it is necessary to understand the events surrounding the Championship throughout the 1790s. The great Daniel Mendoza had defeated Bill Warr in 1792 and 1794 and was the undisputed Champion of the Prize Ring, but in 1795 he was himself beaten by Gentleman Jackson. For three years Jackson remained unchallenged while he and Mendoza built up their respective businesses. Jackson had his increasingly popular rooms in Bond Street and Mendoza, who had also been a teacher, later took on a variety of jobs from sheriff's officer to actor.[46] He seems to have failed to challenge Jackson for a return fight for several reasons. Firstly, the fight game was precarious even when the financial rewards were large enough to compensate for the risks. But Mendoza's winnings even from his two victories over Bill Warr were so small they did not come near to satisfying the growing queue of creditors waiting for their money. It was the gentlemen of the Fancy who made the big money, not the athletes. What was the point in Mendoza continuing a career like that? The pugilists were also always at odds with the law, even if they were famous, or perhaps particularly if they were famous. Being a Jew in London in the 1790s was hard enough, but to draw attention to oneself by activities that the law-enforcement officers frowned on only made matters worse. Daniel Mendoza had dreams of running his own inn one day, and he would need to be law-abiding for that. Already he had been arrested several times and had been in prison for debt on more than one occasion.[47] In November 1798 he had even been on the verge of transportation out of the country.[48] It was not in Mendoza's interests to provoke the law officers any further.

In 1798 it became clear that Jackson would never be tempted to enter the ring again, and so the title became vacant. Many enthusiasts wanted Daniel Mendoza to stake his claim to the Championship once more, but he seemed reluctant. However, those who could remember his glory days still held out hope. It was at this time that a young lad appeared in London from Bristol; his name was Jem Belcher. In March 1799, still not quite 18 years old but already with an enviable reputation as a boxer in Bristol behind him, he was taken to see Bill Warr, the ex-Bristolian, at the One Tun Tavern on Jermyn Street.[49] Bill Warr took the lad upstairs to the sparring room to test his skill with the gloves on. Quite by coincidence, who should happen to stroll in with a group of his friends but Fletcher Reid.[50]

It was obvious at once that young Jem Belcher was a phenomenon, the sort of performer that comes along only once in several lifetimes. He stood half an inch under 6', and weighed less than 12 stone. A contemporary described him this way:

'There was nothing about his person that indicated bodily strength; yet when he stripped, his form was muscular and elegant. In his social hours, Jem was good-natured in the extreme; and modest and unassuming to a degree almost bordering upon bashfulness.[51]

Yet Jem Belcher was a remarkable all-round athlete. He had a quiet assurance and confidence, a cool head, natural ring sense and his boxing was well-balanced and poised. But, above all, he had unprecedented speed:

> The quickness of his hits were unparalleled, they were severely felt, but scarcely seen; and in springing backwards and forwards, his celerity was truly astonishing – and, in this particular respect, it might be justly said that Jem was without an equal.[52]

Jem Belcher was immediately popular and became known as 'The Pet of the Fancy'. A little later his friends also called him 'The Napoleon of the Ring', partly because he was so 'successful in battle', partly because they looked so alike[53] – a risky pun to employ when the whole nation was at war with Napoleon, but an indication maybe of the secret admiration for Napoleon that could be found in many corners of England. It is hard to imagine that in 1940 a young, popular boxer in England would have been affectionately called 'The Hitler of the Ring'!

Jem Belcher was quickly matched against a hard, experienced 30-year-old known as Tom 'Paddington' Jones on Old Oak Common near Wormwood Scrubs,[54] and then with Jack Bartholomew, twice.[55] Fletcher Reid was delighted, as was the rest of the Fancy; they had found a new wonder. Fletcher Reid became one of his most enthusiastic backers. In boxing circles there was a growing awareness of the importance and significance of the Championship. This was partly because of the status that Gentleman Jackson had brought to his role as Champion. Now that he had retired from the Prize Ring, in 1800 the Fancy were on the lookout for a new Champion. There was no better way to decide who should fill the vacancy than for the two best fighters in the land to meet, and this meant Daniel Mendoza and young Jem Belcher. Fletcher Reid was in an unusually privileged position: he was patron and backer of both men.

At that time patrons of sport were extremely important because they put up the money to be competed for and often paid training expenses as well. Gate money had not yet become an important factor in sports promotion, so the only income for the patrons and backers came from winning their bets, but they were frequently men of such enormous wealth that the mere winning or losing of wagers was not in itself their motive for being involved. Needless to say the fighters themselves needed something substantial to tempt them into the ring. True, a good patron would give liberal gifts to his man if the wagers were won, but these could not always be relied on. The money for which the boxers fought, the 'purse', came from the guineas deposited by backers and patrons on behalf of their chosen man. Increasingly, though, the backers, unlike the patrons, were not all lords or wealthy landowners and gentlemen; some were from the new emerging middle class, publicans, fishmongers and other tradesmen. Sometimes a 'subscription purse' was organised to which many men contributed a relatively small sum. Sometimes the boxers and their friends were responsible for putting up their own money. Nevertheless, what every fighter wanted was his own wealthy patron who could be relied on to support him, not just for one fight but for several, pay his expenses and be of sufficient influence to protect him from some of the harsher realities of life. At this time the patron was the most valued asset a fighter could have and remained so throughout this, the golden age of pugilism. But patrons wanted to get their money back if they could, so if a fighter failed to win for his patron, he could not expect continuing support.

After his second fight with Jack Bartholomew, and growing in confidence daily, Jem Belcher, still only 19, challenged Daniel Mendoza, who was by now 37 years old.[56] Mendoza was still in Scotland to escape his creditors, making money from exhibitions and a little teaching on the side, and he ignored the challenge. Disappointed but not surprised, and eager to get on with other things, Jem Belcher agreed to fight a hard-hitting Irishman called Andrew Gamble. As a great matchmaker and boxing enthusiast, Fletcher Reid wanted Mendoza and Belcher to fight, regardless of the financial implications. Because of his close association with both men, he was the only one in Britain who could bring it off. Using all his powers of persuasion, he kept working away at Mendoza. In midsummer in Edinburgh, Fletcher Reid at last persuaded the ex-Champion, who had not fought for five years, to accept Jem Belcher's challenge.

Fletcher Reid drew up the Articles of Agreement and had them signed by Daniel Mendoza on 5 August 1800 in Edinburgh. Immediately Fletcher Reid caught the coach south to London. There was no time to waste, and he arrived just in time to prevent the proposed match between Belcher and Andrew Gamble. The great fight between Mendoza and Belcher was to take place on 1 October for £600. The victorious fighter would also take the title of undisputed Champion of the Prize Ring.

The fight, however, never did take place. Mendoza arrived back in Bethnal Green on 24 September, only six days after the King had issued a proclamation forbidding all 'riots and tumults', and found his family in great distress. The bailiffs had been in, and his house had been stripped of almost every article of furniture. Talk of his fight with Jem Belcher had preceded him and had reached the ears of the magistrates. On Mendoza's second night at home, as he lay in bed in the early hours of the morning, he was arrested by two police officers. At Bow Street Police Court he was brought before Sir Richard Ford, who bound him over to keep the peace.[57]

Daniel Mendoza withdrew from the fight. Instead, Jem Belcher fought and defeated Andrew Gamble on Wimbledon Common, and so became the new Champion of the Prize Ring. The Prince of Wales and his brother the Duke of Clarence both bet on Belcher and were said to have won £3,000.[58] The excitement among the Fancy was unprecedented. Jem Belcher then successfully defended his title against Joe Berks.[59] So Fletcher Reid was patron of the Champion and at the very heart of all the fashionable and exciting action in the Prize Ring.

The fourth member of Robert Barclay's social group in Scotland was

Lord Panmure, the oldest of the group. While Robert Barclay was 21, Fletcher Reid 25 and Robert Fletcher (the Daft Laird) 19, Lord Panmure was 28 and senior to the others in several ways as well as in age. He was married, had already been a cavalry-man, raised and disbanded his own independent company of infantry, had been elected Member of Parliament supporting the Whigs and then lost his seat. He was the second son of the late George 8th Earl of Dalhousie, and at the age of 11 had inherited a vast fortune and the great Panmure estate in Forfarshire, becoming Laird of Panmure, Brechin and Navar. He lived at Brechin Castle about 30 miles from Ury.[60] As a young man he was strong-willed and ungovernable, and he became a renowned practical joker. It was only his own natural iron constitution that enabled him to survive his debauched and outrageous lifestyle.

Brechin Castle was not a residence to which mothers would take their daughters or which half-hearted friends would visit. Lord Panmure had no private life and made no attempt to conceal his bullying and womanising. He obviously had an equal disregard for public opinion and that of his long-suffering wife. If his friends attempted to correct or criticise him, he turned his violent and uncontrollable temper on them and became their sworn enemy. If they did not cross him, however, he was an outstandingly loyal and devoted friend. One writer described 'his handsome figure, his iron frame, his ready wit, his enjoyment of humour, and his boundless flow of spirits. He had scarcely entered the arena, before universal consent hailed him as the very prince of boon companions'.[61]

The dinner parties he gave at Brechin Castle, at which Robert Barclay, Fletcher Reid and Robert Fletcher were frequent guests, sometimes lasted as long as 18 hours and the consumption of claret was enormous. These dinners were humorous high-spirited affairs and it was at occasions such as this that the practical jokes that made Lord Panmure and his friends so notorious were worked out between them to be played later on unsuspecting victims at the various public gatherings and race meetings. It was at these dinners that wagers were made between them, and there was nothing within the sporting world that escaped their attention. Lord Panmure kept and raced several successful racehorses and was inevitably to be seen at race meetings big and small. But his real obsession was with cock-fighting.[62]

His nickname, 'The Glorious Savage', seems just about right, but he was also known as 'The Generous Sportsman'. This reveals a different side of him. Despite his high-profile faults, he was popular, particularly among the lower orders, probably because they had come to expect nothing better from lords and landed gentry, and because he was a benefactor as well as a despot.

Robert's wager with the Daft Laird held him in its power just as certainly as a moth is held by the fascination of a flame. Robert tried again and offered the Daft Laird the same wager as before, 90 miles in 21½ hours. It was accepted, but this time the Daft Laird agreed to quadruple the previous stakes. He was on to a good thing. This time the bet was 2,000 guineas a side, and they agreed neutral territory on the road between Brechin, Lord Panmure's home town, and Forfar.[63] They were known to be a little under 13 miles apart so the road did not require remeasuring. Robert would walk from Brechin to Forfar and back seven times. The event took place in February 1801 and probably started from Brechin so that on finishing he would be nearer home.

The general opinion on the day was that Robert would win. Encouraged by the crowd, and accompanied on horseback by several friends and hangers-on, Robert set out at a brisk pace. It is always difficult in these circumstances not to get carried away by the enthusiasm and excitement of the start. But 90 miles on foot is a long way, and he realised too late that he had set off much too quickly. Nevertheless, by slowing considerably, he managed to keep going all day, and after 13 hours had completed four lengths, or about 67 miles, and was at Brechin. Feeling unusually weary and weak he took a good rest. The Daft Laird's insistence on the term 'successive hours' now became significant. The umpires on both sides consulted their watches to ensure that the rest was not too long. There is no record of who Robert and the Daft Laird appointed as their respective umpires, but it is most likely that they chose Lord Panmure as the deciding referee: the man the two umpires 'referred' their decisions to if they could not agree.

The distance covered so far was similar to the trial to Ellon the previous November, but then, with no crowd, the early pace had been much less ambitious. He had already been going for 13 hours, and he still had 26 miles to go. He felt weak and unsure. Psychologically, the task was made more difficult by having to set off and walk away from the finish. Even if he kept up his previous pace there was still another five and a half hours of walking ahead before he got back to where he was. It was a daunting prospect.

To give himself strength and confidence he followed the practice of Foster Powell and took a draught of brandy and water, and then set off again to Forfar. Unlike Powell, however, it made Robert physically sick. He managed to struggle on for another half an hour or so racked by sickness, but it was obvious he would have to rest properly, and so break the 'successive hours' requirement. When they saw Robert's condition, there must have been many who were reminded of the advice in The Sporting Magazine the previous year: ' . . .we recollect more instances than one of Gentlemen having lost their lives by breaking a blood-vessel, from too great exertion'.[64] The following month the same magazine reported on a wager by a 20-year-old by the name of Denison from Thirsk, to walk 50 miles in ten hours. Although he won his wager by 12 minutes he 'exerted himself to such a degree, that he dropped down, and was taken home in a chaise as a dying man'.[65]

The old fears were only just beneath the surface. Had not Philippedes proved that a man with sufficient willpower, could push his body beyond the limits of his own endurance and die from his efforts? Once more Robert conceded defeat, and the officials awarded the wager and the combined purse of 4,000 guineas to the Daft Laird. Robert rested for about two hours until the sickness subsided and he felt stronger. Then, when there was no necessity to continue, he felt capable of going on. Six hours still remained of the 21½ and there were only about 23 miles to go. Even now, he could have completed the distance in the required time, but not in 'successive hours'. He was only a year older than Denison. Had he lost his wager, or saved his own life? Was his resignation a sign of weakness, or the wisest thing he had ever done? When the event was over, Robert suspected it was the former.

Round 3 to the Daft Laird.

The annoyance and frustration of losing an event you could and should have won is something that most athletes have to bear at some time. For Robert, what made it worse was that *The Edinburgh Advertiser* trumpeted his defeat all over Scotland:

> The bet between Mr BARCLAY, of Ury, and Mr FLETCHER, of Ballinshoe, so much talked of, was decided . . . having exerted himself too much at first, he (Mr Barclay) became so much fatigued, that he was obliged to give it up – of course, he lost the wager.[66]

What humiliation! Then *The Sporting Magazine* told the same story for all the Fancy around Britain to read.[67] He was certainly being talked about by the Fancy, but for all the wrong reasons.

Although the papers did not report it, Robert and his circle knew that this was his third consecutive loss to the Daft Laird. Robert's irritation and impatience to get his own back led him into another quickly made bet. We can only guess at the circumstances, but Robert wagered the Daft Laird 1,000 guineas that he, the Daft Laird, could not walk 60 miles in 21 hours. On Doncaster race course, in the first week in March, the Daft Laird proved him wrong.[68] It was so easy the observers lost interest well before the end; some reports say he finished three and a half and some four and a half hours inside the time. The previous autumn the Daft Laird had won his wager to go 60 miles in 14 hours, so why now was he given half as long again? Had the Daft Laird allowed himself over the winter to get fat and unfit? Had Robert been so taunted by the Daft Laird's boasting that he snapped up a bet without thinking about it first? Was he drunk? It was a ridiculous wager, and one that Robert should have had the sense to avoid.

Round 4 to the Daft Laird.

At this rate, the only place that Robert would find in the Fancy would be as a butt for their humour. In less than five months he had lost four wagers with the Daft Laird, and £6,175, which was more than four times his family's total income over the same period. Shocking as this was, it seemed more or less normal in the circles in which he moved. Later in the year a correspondent to *The Sporting Magazine*[69] pointed out that the Daft Laird had placed three separate bets of 1,000 guineas each (less than half his winnings from Robert), on three separate horse races. The total time taken to decide the three bets was a second under eight minutes. Yet this sum and the interest from it, they calculated, would have supported 150 labouring men's families for a whole year.

Reckless extravagance fuels more. The pace did not slacken. The friends followed their own interests and indulged their personal passions as they chose. The Daft Laird continued to bet and in March even arranged a 100-mile horse race.[70] Fletcher Reid supported and promoted Jem Belcher to become Champion of the Prize Ring and at Hallion's Tennis Court in Edinburgh, Lord Panmure won a cock-fighting match that lasted six days and involved 41 pairs of birds.[71] Not to be outdone, Robert bought race horses and began to race them. In May he entered one of his horses, Tally Ho, in a two-race match which even by the standards of the day was described as 'extraordinary'.[72] The wager was that Tally Ho would beat Wirly at Hamilton and Rollicker at Montrose, both the races to be over 10 miles, and all the horses to carry 12 stone. The bet was 400 guineas against Wirly's owner, Charles Graham, an ex-pedestrian, and 1,000 guineas against Rollicker's owner, Robert Fletcher, the Daft Laird.

Robert and the Daft Laird were engaged in what had the increasing appearance of a dance of death. One would have to succumb. One would be destroyed. It looked like being Robert Barclay Allardice. Anxiety ran high in the Barclay household.

# CHAPTER FIVE

# *The Largest Sum*

*Mr Barclay ... makes the bet 5000L, each side, with Mr
Fletcher, a Gentleman of fortune ... Mr Barclay will
therefore walk for 10,000L.*

THE ENGLISH CHRONICLE, 5–7 NOVEMBER 1801

*The whole sporting world was deeply interested in the event,
and upwards of* One Hundred Thousand Pounds *were lost
and won on this Bet.*

THE EDINBURGH ADVERTISER, 10–13 NOVEMBER 1801

R. BARCLAY, ESQ. OF URY
TIME MATCH 10,000L – p.p.
*This match against time ... being the largest sum of any time
match ever attempted in this kingdom.*

THE EDINBURGH ADVERTISER, 13–17 NOVEMBER 1801

*L*ord Panmure persuaded Robert to go and see Jackey Smith who was 'very knowing in all sporting science'. He, and probably he alone, could see that Robert's defeats were not signs of incompetence, but rather that he needed the services of an expert trainer.[1] Jackey Smith was a Yorkshireman who lived at Oulston in the North Riding as a tenant farmer on Lord Fauconburg's estate. He had acquired a national reputation as an expert on training and had made a good living in and around sport for well over 30 years. In the 1750s his father, also John Smith, had a stud at Oulston where he bred racehorses.[2]

Among Jackey Smith's great strengths were his enthusiasm and his ability to make his athletes believe in themselves. He was a tough taskmaster with some extreme methods and expected his athletes to work hard. He even resented the time they spent asleep in bed, limiting it to five hours a night in bed and a further two in a hammock. In practice his athletes probably got little more than a total of six hours sleep a night – in line with the old advice, 'Six hours for a man, seven for a woman and eight for a fool'. Just over 18 months earlier Charles Graham, the owner of the racehorse Wirly, had gone to Jackey Smith to be trained for a pedestrian wager, but he could not take the severity of the regime and gave up.[3]

Robert Barclay Allardice agreed to see Jackey Smith in June, and to impress him walked the 300 miles to Oulston.[4] It was one of those hot, humid spells of weather that come so unexpectedly and infrequently to Scotland and the north of England. Young boys rushed to the nearest shallow stream and jumped in enthusiastically to splash around, old men sought the deepest, darkest shade to drink their long refreshing draughts of ale, and young ladies tilted their broad-brimmed hats a few degrees lower to stop their noses turning bright red. To everyone's relief the hot weather looked like producing the best harvest for years. For a 300-mile walk, however, clear blue skies and direct constant sun are less welcome and Robert walked in a top hat to keep the sun off his head and neck. The plan was to cover 60 miles a day and be in Oulston after five days. His father had walked 50 miles a day for ten days; surely, he could walk 60 miles a day for five. But 60 miles a day meant 15 hours of walking a day, every day, excluding breaks for meals.

Robert's journey took him along Scotland's east coast road over the River Tay at Dundee, and on the ferry across the River Forth at Queensferry, along the coast road to Berwick to avoid the hills, and on to Newcastle and Durham. On the fifth day, with weary legs, his route took him from Durham through the morning into Darlington and along the lonely road with long featureless stretches into Northallerton. And then the flat or gently undulating stretch of road into Boroughbridge, a busy, energetic country town with coaches and travellers who had taken the easy route, bustling around the Crown and the Greyhounds.

In the autumn Robert contacted the Daft Laird again to renew the bet. This time they decided on 5,000 guineas a side. The Articles of Agreement were written up and each deposited 5,000 guineas with the stakeholder, a total of 10,000 guineas (£10,500). It was a prodigious sum for 1801. *The Edinburgh Advertiser* described it as 'the largest sum of any time match ever attempted in this kingdom'.[5]

The Daft Laird insisted on two additional clauses. Robert must give eight days' notice and complete the wager in November. He did not say why. The newspapers in Scotland and England first began reporting the wager in the last week in August. They also reported his previous loss of 2,000 guineas (£2,100). *The Edinburgh Evening Courant* carried the story on 3 September alongside news of a sermon preached by Dr Jamieson in Nicholson Street, Edinburgh 'for the benefit of the destitute sick'. The collection amounted to £23.[6] There was deep poverty everywhere. Everyone could see that the harvest would be an exceptional one, and they hoped the price of food would soon fall. It certainly needed to. The size of the harvest was itself a problem, however. There were reports that some farms were producing double their yield of the previous year. So anxious were people to take advantage of this, the best opportunity they had had for years, that they worked themselves into the ground to get the harvest in. *The Edinburgh*

*Evening Courant* told of one young woman in Cumberland who died in the harvest field from the 'excessive heat and violent exertion'.[7] She wasn't the only one. For many of the lower orders the hot summer and huge harvest only added to their problems. It was probably no coincidence that *The Edinburgh Advertiser* carried the story of Robert's wager on the same page and in the same column as the story that Lord Panmure had 'generously' given £40 to the Kirk Session of Monikie and 12 guineas to the Kirk Session of Monifieth – all for 'the benefit of their parochial poor'. Every other parish that came within his land was to receive a proportional share 'of his well-timed bounty' too.[8] The readers did their sums and drew their own conclusions.

Lord Panmure's public relations were obviously much better than Robert's. Although Lord Panmure's contribution did not break the bank, his reputation as 'the Generous Sportsman' was enhanced. Robert's was not. Traditionally, gentlemen had always involved themselves in sport. Racing and hunting and sometimes games took up a lot of their time. It might have seemed frivolous but it was generally agreed they had to occupy themselves with something. What else could they do with their time? They squandered their money, but they were expected to show some charitable concern for those less fortunate than themselves. When they did, their other extravagances and weaknesses were often excused. Lord Panmure was continuing this long tradition. Those were times of great national hardship, and Robert's father, too, would undoubtedly have made some gesture towards the poor of Stonehaven. Robert's image after a year as head of his family was different. Even though he was a gentleman, philanthropy did not seem to be on his mind. Even worse, the interests of his family, who relied on him almost exclusively, did not seem to concern him either. His only interest appears to have been himself, and his sole priority was his own sporting performance. It was a questionable agenda for a gentleman.

The hardship of the common people had grown ever since 1793 when the war with France had begun. Thousands had died, food had become scarce and expensive, and large sections of the country had gone hungry. The much hoped for relief from the exceptional harvest in 1801 did not materialise. One of the problems was 'forestalling'. Joseph Farington, who travelled through England and Scotland during the late summer and early autumn of 1801, described in his diary how prices were kept high. Speculators bought up stocks of wheat, corn and barley and then kept them off the market until they could command the price they wanted. In addition:

a spirit of monopoly has arisen in a few years and is increasing daily ... there are persons who make it a business to go about among the farmers & Cottagers in the adjoining country, and purchase from them Fowls, – Eggs, – &c&c even Garden stuff is included. These the Dealer brings to Market & having the Monopoly demands his own Price. ... The consequence is grievous to the people at large ... I fear there is no remedy.[9]

This was the atmosphere that produced conflicting responses to the big spenders of the Fancy and to sport in general. Some admired the athletes and loved the excitement and the spectacle of their sport. Others despised it because of the money and excesses, and set themselves against it.

Robert arrived back in Oulston to start his training at the beginning of September. There were eight weeks before November and training usually lasted no more than six weeks, but Jackey Smith was taking no chances. Step one was to take 8 ozs of blood from Robert's arm. Then he had to swallow quickly a concoction made of ipecacuanah and emetic tartar to the ratio of 10 to 1, so that, as planned, Robert began his training by being violently sick.[10] Before the sweating and the serious work could start, it was important to cleanse the system. Robert experienced the age-old method of purifying and detoxification.

In week one the rhythm of training was established. Jackey Smith's regime required the athlete to be woken at 4 a.m. and placed in a hammock for the rest of the short night.[11] Training began at 6 a.m. Up to now, Robert had been a walker, even at times a lifter and thrower of weights, but he had never been a runner. Jackey Smith believed running to be essential. At first, speed was unimportant; it was the rhythm that mattered. Even that was difficult with the clothes Robert had to wear – two pairs of breeches, two waistcoats and a greatcoat – all designed to make him sweat. This was followed by massage and a sweat for half an hour or so. A blanket was thrown over his shoulders and he lay on a bed, covered with more blankets and 'a feather bed'.[12] The bed had even been pre-heated with a bedpan filled with red-hot coals. This process wasn't called a 'sweat', for nothing. A tankard of strong malt liquor followed, and then he was taken outside again for an hour of relaxed walking in warm dry clothing and another warming greatcoat.

In the afternoons running was augmented with general labouring around the farm and went on relentlessly throughout the first week. Jackey Smith also worked on Robert's technique. He was taught to lean forward, to shorten his steps and keep his feet close to the ground at all times. Leaning forward meant that his body weight was taken on the knees and saved his back from fatigue and injury. As well as being a hard trainer Jackey Smith was observant and meticulous. His style was also to withhold praise. Stories circulated that Robert had been sent to Easingwold and back, a round trip of 20 miles, with a heavy load of cheese and butter on his shoulders, with the instruction to be back in 90 minutes.[13] Later, Robert denied the story, but there can be no doubt that Jackey Smith was a persistent, attentive and inventive trainer whose methods tested every aspect of Robert's strength, skill and endurance.

He settled into his role as obedient athlete, and loved it. Perhaps being away from Ury and the daily reminders of his responsibilities, and taking orders unquestioningly from an older man, gave him a sense of child-like security. Perhaps it was the impending crisis at Ury following his huge financial losses, and the public loss of face from his repeated defeats, that led Robert to accept Lord Panmure's advice and succumb so willingly to Jackey Smith's total dominance. Jackey Smith became for a while a substitute father-figure. Whatever the cause, the trainer's influence came at the right time and would shape the rest of Robert's life. Jackey Smith had a son of 19 – Robert was now 22 – who sometimes joined in the training. A training partner is often a priceless asset.

The relationship between athlete and coach is often mysterious, and when it works it is better left unanalysed, but this relationship between Robert and Jackey Smith was particularly strange. There was a clear and unbridgeable class difference between the two men. Robert was a landowner and a gentleman in every traditional sense. He even believed himself to be the heir to the Earldoms of Airth and Menteith. Jackey Smith was an old farmer who did not even own his own land, and who had no titles and no social graces; he could not have been passed off as a gentleman in any circles. Their relationship scandalised many of the Yorkshire gentry because it seemed to threaten the natural order of things. It was gentlemen who ordered their social inferiors around, not the reverse. A writer to *The Times* commented in a tone of high moral indignation that 'Smith made him [Robert Barclay Allardice] live upon raw meat and hard food and do all sorts of hard work ... and ordered him about just as if he had been a spaniel'.[14] Robert, of course, saw it differently and later wrote to the press expressing his gratitude to Jackey Smith for his 'generous attention'.[15] He knew, as the correspondents to the newspapers did not, that the rapport that develops during training between an athlete and his coach has never had anything to do with social class. It is mutual respect that makes it work.

The comments in *The Times* about the food were closer to the target. There were raw eggs and the beef and mutton were always underdone. No sauces, spices or condiments were allowed to brighten up the monotonous meals. The food may have been dull but at least there was plenty of it, and a glass of 'white Lisbon' was allowed morning and evening.[16] Gentlemen had to be given some concessions.

In week three, the speed of the early morning runs increased. The exercise was hard and unremitting, but all physical effort brings its own rewards, of sorts. The purges were unpleasant but soon over. It was the sweats that were the challenge. But Robert knew, as did everyone else in sport, that the sweats were the key to successful training. And Yorkshire was the home of the sweat. When applied to racehorses it was even known as a 'Yorkshire sweat'. This involved a three- or four-mile gallop with the horse under heavy blankets until it was in a white lather, dripping with perspiration. Yorkshiremen called it a 'muck sweat'. These sweating gallops were as essential for racehorses as their equivalent was for men. It reduced their fat and cleansed the pores of dirt. After such a gallop horses were pulled up at a stable or rubbing house where the sweat was scraped off with 'sweat slippers'.[17] Men were rubbed down with dry flannel.

No competitor in serious sport could escape the sweat but it was acknowledged to be a most tricky business and handled wrongly sweats could be very weakening. Fortunately Jackey Smith was one of the preeminent experts on sweating, a man of vast experience, whose methods deserved to be studied. Robert was fascinated by the training processes, and became a keen student as well as an athlete.

In Oulston the weeks slipped by. September came and went. Robert absorbed himself in his training and concentrated on the wager, cocooned from the troubles of the rest of the world. Thoughts of the Daft Laird taking his money again strengthened his resolve whenever he felt like giving up or rebelling. He knew that this was the most important period of his life so far. It would make him, or as with Charles Graham, it would break him. On Sunday 4 October, however, unexpected news arrived.

Britain had just agreed the preliminaries of peace with France. The news had arrived on the streets in London late on Friday 2nd. There was instant, unbridled jubilation, particularly among the lower orders. They were war-weary, poor and hungry. Eight years of war had taken their toll. Londoners traditionally marked such important events by illuminating the city. They fixed tallow candles on to wooden triangles and put them in their windows. Shops and larger windows were often illuminated with oil lamps fixed on a black board and arranged in the form of a crown with 'G.R.' on either side. On Friday the news had come too suddenly for there to be much illumination, but on Saturday night 3 October the masses that began to gather expected to see illumination everywhere. The crowd believed that if a house was not illuminated the people inside were not celebrating the peace, and by the same token they decided that if you were not celebrating the peace, you were opposed to it.

The masses sensed their political power and made for fashionable New Bond Street where the toffs lived, to ensure that those with money and influence were doing the right thing. Less than 400 yards from Jackson's Rooms, an ugly crowd began to gather in front of a house in darkness. It was number 148 in which the Hon. Thomas Lord Camelford had rooms. He was an eccentric 26-year-old who had a deserved reputation for quarrelsome, violent and unpredictable behaviour. He stood a shade under 6'2", weighed nearly 14 stone and was an important member of the Fancy.[18] By temperament and physique he was not the sort of man to pick a quarrel with.

He ran away to sea at 14, and on one occasion, while still in his teens, he was put in irons and flogged, twice, by his senior officer, Captain George Vancouver, for insubordination. The young Camelford insisted that Captain Vancouver address him as My Lord. Captain Vancouver refused.

Punishment failed to subdue Lord Camelford, and, in desperation, the other officers put him ashore in Hawaii to make his own way home. Four years later, on board *The Perdrix*, he shot and killed a junior officer, Lieutenant Peterson, over a dispute about seniority. Lord Camelford was court martialled and acquitted. Later, an iceberg in the Antarctic struck a ship on which he was serving. He survived that, too. In May 1800 in the Court of the King's Bench he had to face a charge of physical assault against a man named Humphries. The case was heard before Lord Kenyon and a Special Jury. In his summing-up Lord Kenyon warned all the hot-heads of the Fancy, 'Young men of high rank and hasty tempers ought to have such a lesson read to them' – and awarded £500 damages against Lord Camelford.[19]

There is little doubt that Lord Camelford needed the warning, but little chance of him heeding it. He was a regular visitor at sporting events around London and he particularly liked the company of the prize-fighters. When he heard that Daniel Mendoza was back in London and looking for paying pupils, he approached Mendoza for lessons. But he was not one of the run-of-the-mill students that John Jackson, Bill Warr and the other boxing 'professors' were used to, as the following episode, in Daniel Mendoza's own words, shows:

When I attended his lordship, he requested me to spar with him which I accordingly did, and he professed to feel highly gratified at my exertions, and intimated that he would show me an original attitude of his own, in which he had attained a degree of perfection that would counteract any assault that could be made on him. At his request, therefore, I aimed several blows at him, one of which took place, and in consequence of his lordship's throwing back his head with great violence, he thrust it through the glazed door of a book-case. This accident irritated him greatly, and as soon as he was extricated, which was not done without great difficulty, he asked whether I had ever played at the game of single stick? On my answering I was not entirely unacquainted with the sport, he insisted on my engaging with him; and having procured a pair of weapons from an adjoining room, we set to. At this game I found his lordship a better proficient than myself; he stuck with great force as well as skill, and I speedily received a violent blow over the ear, which caused great pain at the time. However, I resolved not to yield, and therefore continued till he was tired, when he again proposed to change the amusement to fencing, and though I candidly told him, I knew nothing of this art, he insisted upon my engaging with him, to which I was with reluctance induced to consent. On one of my foils happening to break, he very coolly observed, we might as well change them for a pair of small swords, with which, he said, if we took proper care, we could not possibly injure each other. To this proposal I at first strongly objected, and declared my determination not to engage with weapons of such a dangerous nature: upon which my noble antagonist appeared highly irritated, and I began to apprehend the violent effects of his anger: therefore with the view of appeasing his wrath, I pretended to assent to his proposal, merely expressing a wish that he would take care of my family, in case of any accident happening to me. This he promised to do, and left me for the purpose of fetching the swords. As soon as the coast was clear, I rushed out of the room, and flew down stairs, with all the rapidity in my power: such was my impatience to depart, that I never stopped till I had reached the bottom of the staircase, when I found I had descended too low, and had got to the cellar door; consequently I was obliged to return, and having, at last, reached the street door, departed abruptly from the house, and, as may be readily imagined, never felt the least inclination to re-enter it.[20]

This, you might imagine, would have been the end of their relationship, but not so. Lord Camelford continued to put work Mendoza's way and Mendoza continued to accept it.

On Monday 13 July 1801, a hot, dusty summer day, only weeks before the unexpected peace celebrations, Lord Camelford was on Wimbledon Common to see a fight between Tom Jones and Isaac Bitton. The fight was for 40 guineas and attracted a good turnout. Among the gentlemen in the crowd was Sir Wheeler Cuffe in his bright yellow curricle, and the Hon. Thomas Coventry in a rather grand tilbury. Only the week before, Coventry had lost £8,000 in a single game of billiards at Margate. Then there were the stalwarts, Sir Henry Vane Tempest, Sir Richard Heathcote, little Lord 'Tommy' Onslow and Sir John Lade, not this time with his wife Lady Letitia, who was believed to be as good at driving a coach and four as he was, and even better at boxing and swearing. Fletcher Reid was there and many fighters or ex-fighters and boxing professors also attended: Gentleman Jackson, Bill Warr,

Daniel Mendoza, Harry Lee and Jem Belcher, who worked as Tom Jones's second.[21]

Lord Camelford, as usual on Fancy occasions, took along his dog Trusty, a famous fighting bulldog, and his 'man' Bill Richmond, a black 'fixer', originally from Staten Island. They watched the fight from the top of his carriage in the outer ring. Jones was an experienced 32-year-old from Paddington, and Isaac Bitton was a bigger, stronger and much younger Jewish fighter, who was a newcomer to the Prize Ring. How good was Bitton? It took him 22 minutes to deliver the answer, and to hit 'Paddington' Jones senseless.[22] During the fight a well-muscled, powerfully built drunk tried to force his way into the ring, but the other pugilists who were on duty as 'whippers', coped with such nuisances as a matter of routine. Whippers were an early version of bouncers but they had whips to clear a space when they needed to, and used them with gusto. After the fight and before the crowd had a chance to disperse, the drunk pushed forward again shouting, 'Where's young Jem Belcher? Where's your champion?' Jem Belcher came forward to see what all the commotion was about. Once he was in range the drunk, whose name was Joe Berks and who came from Shropshire, lashed out with his fists. Jem Belcher ducked and then in return slapped the drunk on the cheek. This should have been the end of the matter, but the whippers failed to get rid of him and he pursued Jem Belcher and went on the attack again. In self-defence Jem Belcher was forced to fight and the crowd cleared a small space as the new Champion of the Prize Ring scrapped with a drunk. This was most unseemly and Gentleman Jackson and Bill Warr rushed in to restore order. But the fight continued in the recently vacated ring for another 19 minutes. The crowd were enthralled. Here was real excitement. Fletcher Reid and Jem Belcher's other supporters were dismayed, but Lord Camelford was intrigued. Would a sober and properly trained Joe Berks be the man to take the title of Champion of the Prize Ring away from Jem Belcher? It was too good a story for the newspapers to miss. *The Oracle* reported that Joe Berk's nose and half his lip had been torn away, and *The Morning Post* asserted that he was 'so dangerously ill that his life was despaired of'.[23] It wasn't true. The papers were hyping up the story. Nevertheless, Joe Berks did pay a price for his audacity. He left Wimbledon badly battered and bleeding; the wound across his nose, where Jem Belcher's knuckles had dug deep, left a scar that he carried all his life. But he had been noticed by the gentlemen of the Fancy and he must surely have earned himself the right to fight Jem Belcher for the Championship. So, while the public were reading in their morning newspapers of Joe Berk's imminent death, Lord Camelford was actually taking him to see Daniel Mendoza to talk about starting a training programme.[24]

Lord Camelford's plan was for Daniel Mendoza to train Joe Berks secretly in readiness for a properly organised and recognised fight with Jem Belcher that would ensure him the best odds. Fletcher Reid was Jem Belcher's patron and there was little doubt that he would agree to the fight. The secret, however, was soon out. So, at the beginning of September, while Robert Barclay Allardice was in training with Jackey Smith for his huge wager with the Daft Laird, Joe Berks was in training with Daniel Mendoza for an attack on Jem Belcher's title. The whole of the Fancy and much of the country followed their training in the daily and sporting press. Mendoza paid special attention to Joe Berks's diet, just as Jackey Smith and the other trainers did with their athletes, giving him 'raw eggs to improve his wind and raw beef to make him savage'.[25] *The Times* poked fun at training as if it was nothing more than magical potions and superstitious clap-trap,[26] but Robert Barclay Allardice and Joe Berks knew better. In the modern sporting world of 1801, no athlete facing a major contest could survive without rigorous and skilful training.

Lord Camelford and Fletcher Reid arranged the Belcher–Berks fight for 19 September, for a purse of 100 guineas, but the magistrates issued a warrant to stop it and it had to be postponed. It was rearranged for Monday 12 October. As the mob gathered outside Lord Camelford's house, the big fight was just over a week away.[27]

Behind the dark windows of his house Lord Camelford quietly eyed the noisy mob, a heavy bludgeon in his hands. When they started to throw stones and brick-ends at his windows his temper snapped. He rushed out into the street wielding his bludgeon with such violence that a dozen people staggered back stunned and bleeding. In his frenzy he lost his grip and quickly drew his sword, swiping out at those nearest him. In the mayhem that followed the mob scattered and ran for their lives. As they retreated they threw a hail of bricks, one of which levelled Lord Camelford. He was helped back into his house, and all went quiet again, but not for long.[28]

Lord Camelford was on good terms with the prize-fighters, another example of the blurring of the social barriers between the classes that sport made possible. One contemporary writer put it this way:

> The pugilists respected His Lordship, partly because he knew everything about their science and was no mean practitioner of it himself, and partly because he was always ready to open his purse to them. In consequence these fellows were very proud to boast of his friendship. But it must be appreciated that the relationship was absolutely correct; Camelford never forgot his rank even in the lowest society. He always received the respect due to his position, and if a coal-heaver or meatporter of his acquaintance attempted any insolence he was swiftly paid in his own coin. In good society, with his sister Lady Grenville, his mother and his friends, he was the best-bred and finest gentleman you could imagine.[29]

Among those who helped him back into the house was Mungo, a second-rate black fighter about whom very little is known, and probably Bill Richmond, another black fighter who was with Lord Camelford at Wimbledon. Neither Mungo nor Bill Richmond had ever appeared in the Prize Ring, but both could 'look after themselves'. Bill Richmond was 38 and weighed only 10 stone 12 lbs, so was too light to be successful in the Prize Ring. He was, however, an all-round sportsman and was well known and respected as a sparrer, cricketer and long-jumper. He was talkative, witty and good-natured and had been brought to Britain at the age of 14 by General Earl Percy. His mother had been a slave in New York. Quite remarkably he received an education and learned the trade of cabinet-maker, but colour prejudice was an ever-present fact of life for Bill Richmond, though he combated it with a mixture of pugnacity, humour, intelligence and tact.[30] It was said that 'he wore his sable colours meekly', but we should not imagine him as mild and subservient. Certainly the lords and gentlemen would expect him to know his place just as they knew theirs, but this was expected of every labourer, servant, shopkeeper and clerk, anyway. Bill Richmond never allowed his strong and sunny personality to be submerged beneath diffidence and artificial good manners. At least in sport and among the Fancy black athletes could find a respected niche which allowed them to mix with those of different social classes and ethnic groups.[31]

The calm outside Lord Camelford's house did not last long. Later that night the mob, now enlarged, returned and hurled every object they could lay their hands on, breaking every window and causing extensive damage. This was the politics of direct action. A first-floor window was pushed in, revealing the dark figure of Lord Camelford foaming with rage and clutching in each hand loaded pistols pointing straight at the crowd. He was not a man to bluff; he would fire at them if necessary. At that moment the lives of several of the mob, and eventually his life too, were in the balance, but two of his men overpowered him and dragged him away, locked him in a back room and somehow managed to persuade the crowd to disperse.[32]

Lord Camelford versus a London mob was an unequal battle, even for Lord Camelford, and he was convinced they would return. So he decided to enlist support. Bill Richmond was dispatched to the Peahen Tavern, the Admiral Nelson and the other haunts in Field Lane off Holborn where many of the pugilists used to hang out. The inducement of five shillings a night and a good supper ensured that on Sunday evening Lord Camelford had his own private company of security guards made up of 40 tough and experienced fighters under the direction of Bill Richmond. Their presence alone was enough to keep the mob at bay that night and then, in the fickle way of mobs, they moved on looking for new targets.

Lord Camelford's security force provoked indignation among the authorities. This time he had gone too far. If wealthy and powerful men could raise their own private force would anyone ever be safe again? Did this contribute to public law and order, or threaten it? Instead of lying low and waiting for the fuss to die down, Lord Camelford fanned the flames and prosecuted the authorities for not providing adequate protection for him. This was too much for the Bow Street police. They hit Lord Camelford where it hurt most, and in a way that made it impossible for him to publicly object or retaliate. The night before the Belcher–Berks fight was due to take place on Tuesday 12 October, they stopped it.

Lord Camelford's house was so badly damaged he was staying at the Cocoa Tree Club on the corner of Pall Mall. His house, however, was not empty. Some pugilists were staying there, probably to protect it, and Jem Belcher was among them.[33] Illumination had gone on in the city night after night and the mob continued to prowl the streets trying to enforce it. William Cobbett described the crowds that supported the peace as a 'foolish mob' and 'vile miscreants'. For Cobbett, Saturday 10th, exactly one week after the fracas outside Lord Camelford's house, was 'the most shameful, the most infamous that England ever saw'. Events centred around General Laureston, Napoleon's first aide-de-camp, who arrived in London to ratify the preliminaries of peace:

A set of brutes in the shape of men, took the horses from the carriage of this Frenchman ... and drew him in triumph from Bond street down St. James's street, along Pall Mall, to the admiralty, to Downing street, through the horse guards, along the royal road in the mall, &c&c&c. It was a day of sorrow to every man, except the foolish mob and the miserable ministers, who, by making the peace, preserved places, which they never ought to have filled.[34]

It was not surprising that the Bow Street Runners decided to stop the Belcher–Berks fight. The general mood in London was becoming too volatile. On Monday night Townsend, the most famous of the Runners, gained access to Lord Camelford's house, arrested Jem Belcher and took him into custody. As Champion of the Prize Ring he was a bigger fish to catch than Joe Berks. In other circumstances it might have seemed odd that a fighter on the eve of a big fight was spending the night in the house of his rival's patron, but these were exceptional times and no one seems to have been suspicious. At lunchtime the next day Jem Belcher was released on his own recognisance, but the fight could not go on and the crowd that had gathered at Enfield to see it dispersed in a mood of anger and resentment.[35] But the Fancy were not to be defeated so easily. They were determined that the Belcher–Berks fight would go ahead. The responsibility for ensuring this fell to Fletcher Reid, as a few days later Lord Camelford disappeared mysteriously from the streets of London. No one knew that, in disguise and under an assumed name, he had slipped out of Britain into France with an elaborate plot to assassinate Napoleon Bonaparte single-handed.[36] He distrusted the peace just as much as William Cobbett did and had decided to take matters into his own hands. But it would be a long time before anyone penetrated the mystery of Lord Camelford's disappearance.

In elaborate secrecy Fletcher Reid rearranged the fight for 25 November, six weeks away. Time for the dust to settle.

Meanwhile, at Oulston, Robert's daily grind of training continued. In mid-October, at about the same time as Jem Belcher was released from custody, Jackey Smith made a critical decision. He examined Robert's hand in the dark against the light of a candle, studied the diffusion of light through the fingers and decided that Robert was ready for the final time trial. The weather was changeable with a hint of frost in the air. Twice a gill of 'mountain wine' was produced; this was proof indeed that the strict training was nearing its end.[37]

The date of the trial was finalised and the course within Lord

Fauconburg's park at Newborough Priory decided on. Robert was to go 110 miles against the watch. The trial was designed to test his endurance well beyond the 21½ hours of his wager. Only the very best walkers could cover 100 miles in 24 hours. Foster Powell had managed 100 miles in 21 hours 20 minutes. A Jewish peddler and a man named Waite had both claimed to have gone 100 miles in 18 hours or less, but no one paid any credence to these claims. It was generally agreed that the best time ever was by Wills, a famous Shropshire pedestrian, who in 1789 had walked 100 miles on Blackheath under controlled conditions in 20 hours and 35 minutes.[38]

As the day of Robert's trial arrived low clouds gathered, grey and continuous as far as the eye could see. It was going to rain. And rain it did, starting just before midnight when the trial began. It poured all night and all day. The course was marked out experimentally with oil lamps but with the dense low cloud there was no other light. Robert had to keep close to the roped line of the path to see where he was going. Within a few hours and before daybreak he had worn a path of mud as he circled the same route over and over again. By the time the pale, grey dawn crept in he was up to his ankles in mud.

Jackey Smith, relieved occasionally by his son, notched each completed lap on a stick, and checked each notch with his large watch. Robert Barclay Allardice pressed on relentlessly. Three times in the course of the day Jackey Smith stopped him and led him into a nearby cottage. The shutters were closed to keep the room dark and to deaden any sounds from outside. As far as rest was concerned it was quality not quantity that counted and Jackey Smith ordered quiet to produce the best conditions for rest. Only a few minutes' quiet could work wonders and he allowed Robert just ten. Once he was through the door dry clothes were produced and the old wet ones quickly discarded. Warm, dry flannel cloths were used to rub him dry. On a simple table in the corner there were chicken legs, a little stale bread (because it was easier to digest) and a jug of old ale. There was a general bustle. Everything was done quickly to get Robert dry, refreshed and lying down quietly for a few minutes. And then out again into the rain and the mud to take on the next few hours of concentrated effort.

By midday it was becoming clear that an exceptional performance was unfolding. He must have completed 100 miles well inside 18 hours, but Jackey Smith let him go on. He did another 10 miles and at 7.27 in the evening Jackey Smith stepped forward and stopped the trial. Robert had covered 110 miles in 19 hours and 27 minutes. This was the greatest long-distance pedestrian performance ever recorded. Over five and a half miles an hour for nearly 19½ hours, and in atrocious conditions.[39] At that rate he would win his wager with the Daft Laird by five and three quarter hours. In the words of one writer: 'this performace may be deemed the greatest upon record, being at the rate of upwards of one hundred and thirty-five miles in twenty-four hours'.[40]

Robert was now ready, and the eight days' notice required by the Articles of Agreement was given to the Daft Laird. The date was fixed for Tuesday 10 November 1801. For the venue Jackey Smith suggested a strip of the old Roman road across Barmby Moor going from York to Hull, and about 25 miles from Oulston. They eventually selected a one-mile stretch starting from the New Inn, near Pocklington, about 12 miles from York. The road was straight and almost flat with two very minor, short uphill slopes.

The Daft Laird had insisted on the wager taking place in November for two reasons. Firstly, he estimated that in November there was the greatest chance of high winds, heavy rain or thick fog. As usual, the wager had been made p.p. (play or pay), so once the date had been fixed eight days in advance, it could not be changed, regardless of the weather. Secondly the Daft Laird believed that in November the human frame was at its most relaxed and weak.[41] He was betting on a 'November effect'. Round Five of their battle was about to begin. It would be decisive. Were the Daft Laird's calculations correct? At the start of November and only a few days before the event, severe gales struck the Hull coast and many boats were driven ashore by high winds, with 14 being reported lost between Hull and Harwich.[42] The omens were not good for Robert.

The buzz around the New Inn began on Monday 9 November. Workmen started digging deep holes to hold the poles on which the gas lamps with reflectors were to be fixed. The old Roman road was getting its first lamp-posts. This alone was enough to draw the curious from the nearby villages of Pocklington, Hayton, Allerthorpe and Wilberfoss. Street lighting was unknown here. Indeed it was unknown virtually anywhere in Britain. While this was going on marquees and tents were erected and Robert and the Daft Laird supervised the exact positioning of the poles at each end of the measured mile. There was some discussion about whether the poles should be exactly one mile apart, in which case Robert would have to walk further than one mile on each lap to walk around them, or whether the poles should be slightly closer together to allow for this. He calculated that if the poles were exactly one mile apart he would have to walk an extra stride and a half each mile, a total of 135 extra strides.[43] He walked the extra distance. Better this than lose his wager over a dispute.

In November it gets dark early in Yorkshire, and as the afternoon wore on and the light failed, this illuminated stretch of road and the twinkling lights from the inn and the tents attracted a large crowd. Hundreds of locals were tempted from the comfort of their beds that night, but many of the Fancy, who arrived by coach or post horse throughout the day, knew long since that they would not sleep that night. Nor the next. Halfway along the course was a farmhouse belonging to Mr Winter, a respectable farmer.[44] This had been taken over by the Barclay team and was well lit. It was to be Robert's base for refreshments and for the surgeon from Edinburgh he had sent for just in case. This would keep him away from the crush of the inn and be warmer and safer than the tents.

The arrangement was that Robert would walk to and fro across the same one-mile stretch of Roman road 90 times within 21½ hours. Observers were stationed at each post to record each lap and to see that everything was fair. Late on Monday night the buzz of the spectators rose to a roar as Robert Barclay Allardice, Jackey Smith, his son, the surgeon and several friends arrived at the starting post. Then came the Daft Laird and his friends. It was late at night but *The English Chronicle* reported that the size of the crowd was already 'amazing'.[45] With the people pressing forward to get a better look, Robert and the Daft Laird each appointed an umpire, who in turn agreed on a referee to whom they would refer their decision if they could not agree. The umpires examined and accepted six stop-watches. There was a roar as Robert took off his voluminous greatcoat. *The Edinburgh Advertiser* stated that he was in high spirits and wore a tight flannel shirt, flannel trousers, lambswool stockings, thick-soled shoes and a night-cap.[46] It was a cold November night and a lot of heat is lost out of the top of the head. A warm night-cap might help nullify the 'November effect'. Precisely at midnight, under the watchful eye of the two umpires and the referee, the six stop-watches were set and put into a sturdy mahogany box at the finishing post, and the box was sealed. A hush settled over the crowd and Robert Barclay Allardice, Master of Ury, was off.

The required speed per mile was well known. If in the course of the day he allowed himself a total of one and a half hours to rest, he had to complete each mile inside 14 minutes and 20 seconds; 28.40 for each two miles. Everyone was calculating. To lay your bets as contests like this progressed you needed to be a mathematician.

Robert arrived back from his first two-mile leg in 25 minutes and 10 seconds, well within schedule. After 16 miles and just after 3.20 in the morning Jackey Smith stopped him and took him into Mr Winter's farmhouse. Here the refreshments and the fresh, dry clothes were already laid out. There was no need for the surgeon. The knowing ones passed on the word – he was still ahead of schedule. Even after the ten-minute break he had 15 minutes in hand. Not surprisingly, betting was already 2 to 1 on Robert being successful. The raucous but well-behaved crowd lit bonfires to keep warm and drank as if it was a public holiday. Betting was brisk throughout the night, and it was said that 100,000 guineas changed hands. No one recorded how much ale and gin were consumed. Robert continued, following the same pattern on each lap. Mostly he walked but broke into an easy run each time he came to one of the slightly uphill sections.

A few minutes before seven in the morning Jackey Smith stopped him again. Seven hours into the wager and with 32 miles completed, Robert's walking, for the first time, seemed heavy and laboured. Perhaps he was affected by the weather, which had become increasingly hazy over the past three hours or so. Was this the 'November effect'? He went into Mr Winter's for his ten minutes' rest with the betting 7 to 4 in his favour. After the break he still had over 20 minutes in hand, but he had not enjoyed the past three hours and hoped the haze would not settle and become fog. Those recording the time reported that his pace had slowed by about five seconds a mile. The Daft Laird watched critically. The wager was in the balance. Who would the November weather favour? The answer came about an hour later when daybreak took hold and drove the haze away. Robert's spirits rose simultaneously and he emerged looking stronger than ever. Perhaps the Daft Laird had miscalculated.

With the daylight came even more people, and the crowd was now huge. *The Sun* described them as a 'great concourse',[47] and *The English Chronicle* reported that 'thousands of foot and horse attended'.[48] Such a large crowd can bring its own hazards, especially as many had too much to drink. To protect Robert, horsemen were arranged to go in front and behind, forming a circle that advanced up and down the road around him. But this was the main York to Hull road and people going about their normal business had to get through too. Wagons, carriages and even the mail coaches had to pass. The noisy spectators ushered them all to the side of the road to give Robert and his circle of horsemen as much room as possible. Even the West Yorkshire Militia, who were marching to York, were halted by their commanding officer and formed into single file on either side of the road so as not to interrupt him. They also entered into the spirit of the occasion and shouted, 'we wish you may win' or words to that effect, as Robert went by, producing, according to one eyewitness, 'a most beautiful effect'.[49] For a tired athlete the most beautiful effect of all is knowing you are ahead and have the crowd on your side, and as the event progressed towards its inevitable conclusion people abandoned any neutrality and shouted and encouraged him on. Many who had gathered merely to watch the spectacle ended up as his fans. By 11 a.m. and with 50 miles completed he was a whole hour ahead of schedule and the odds rose to 4 to 1 and then 5 to 1. After 60 miles, according to plan, Jackey Smith's son was sent out to walk with Robert over the last 30 miles. But he wasn't needed. The "November effect" had not materialised. Robert knew now that he would win and was 'in high spirits, with much cheerfulness'.

He walked through all the hours of daylight and once again the November night fell. The oil lamps and candles were lit and Robert continued on his way. Not once was the Edinburgh surgeon called upon, and four seconds after 8.22 p.m. Robert completed his 90th mile. He had won comfortably by almost an hour and eight minutes. The spectators cheered and hats and scarves were thrown joyfully in the air. In the style of those in London who had taken the horses out of the shafts of General Laureston's coach and drawn him down the Mall, so this jubilant crowd tried to do the same and draw Robert in a coach up and down the road. He modestly refused them so they carried him off on their shoulders instead. He had won the wager and captured the hearts of the watchers. No wonder the papers reported that he seemed 'highly satisfied', 'strong and hearty', and 'much affected' by it all. 'I could have gone 20 miles further,' he said.[50]

So affected was he by everyone's help, consideration and support that he effusively and publicly thanked the inhabitants of Pocklington for their 'handsome treatment', thanked Jackey Smith for his 'generous attention', and expressed his gratitude to 'all ranks' for their 'polite and attentive behaviour'. They 'have left on my memory an impression of such grateful sentiments, as death only can erase'.[51]

He had won 5,000 guineas of the Daft Laird's money and retained his own 5,000-guinea stake, thus recovering all but £925 of his earlier losses to the Daft Laird. He may not have wiped the slate totally clean, but it was a wonderful reversal of fortune. Ury was no longer under threat, and all those who lived there or whose livings depended on it, could relax, smile and admire the judgement of the new laird. Equally important, perhaps, was the way in which the experience changed him. From Jackey Smith he learned discipline. He also learned that no matter how self-reliant you are, there are times when you must rely on others. They were important lessons.

Round Five to Robert Barclay Allardice.

At Ury and the surrounding neighbourhood the news was greeted with jubilation. At Stonehaven they built and lit a large bonfire in the middle of the square and drank Robert's health with a hogshead of porter and partied for days. The papers reported on the 'brilliant' illuminations in the town and the country houses for miles around. At Inverbervie people made for the Head Inn, decorated and illuminated it and lit a bonfire there too, just as if there was news of a major victory.[52] For the people around Ury it was precisely that.

For Robert there were now two priorities. One was to get back to Ury to settle financial problems with his new cash, and the other was to go to London to see the Belcher–Berks fight. It was scheduled for the 25th, only a fortnight away. To do both meant travelling a total of 769 miles. Some idea of the magnitude of the undertaking can be got from Lord Campbell, who travelled part of the same road only three years earlier when he went by mail coach from Edinburgh to London (391 miles):

> A journey to London was ... considered a very formidable undertaking. I was to perform it by mail coach ... taking only three nights and two days ... But this speed was thought to be highly dangerous to the head, independently of all the perils of an overturn, and stories were told of men and women, who having reached London with such celerity, died suddenly of an affection of the brain.[53]

At that rate Robert's journey would have taken at least five days and five nights and brought him into London in a useless state. But he did it. He went by coach to Ury, delivered his money and received his accolades and then packed a fresh trunk and caught the coach to the south again. First to Dundee and over the River Tay by ferry, then to Edinburgh, and after paying his £7.10.0, from Drysdale's at 4 p.m. on the mail coach for London. Already, stories about his physical indestructibility were circulating.

Only ten days after Robert's great performance at Pocklington he was in London and was taken by Fletcher Reid to Jem Belcher's training venue. It was just a matter of days before the fight and Belcher was trim and hard. He was about a year and a half younger than Robert and about the same weight, but half an inch taller, which gave him the appearance of being slimmer. His build and appearance were deceptive. Observers were frequently surprised that such a slight-looking man could produce such power in the ring. His power came from phenomenal speed that no one had ever seen in the ring before. The two famous young athletes eyed each other up and Robert quickly came to the conclusion that the stories of Belcher's speed, power and all-round athleticism must be exaggerations. To prove the point Robert wagered £10 on the spot that Jem Belcher could not throw a stone over 100 yards with each hand, a good test of speed, power and athletic skill. The usual practice in throwing wagers was that the stipulated distance had to be achieved twice. Once in each direction. That way any influence of wind or sloping ground would be neutralised. It is not known how large a stone they agreed upon, but it is likely to have been small enough to fit comfortably into the hand and smaller than a cricket ball. To Robert's astonishment Jem Belcher peeled off his jacket and threw the stone an extraordinary 140 yards with his right hand, and then 120 yards in the opposite direction with his left.[54] Whatever the size and weight of the stone, this was a formidable achievement. He was fast, powerful and skilful and, almost uniquely, he had two great throwing arms.

A few days later on Wednesday 25 November, despite giving

away the advantage of weight and strength to Joe Berks, Jem Belcher successfully defended his title at Cockpool Green, about seven miles from Maidenhead, winning in 18 minutes. *The English Chronicle* reported how 'amazingly active' he was, 'throwing his blows with both hands', and attributed his success to his 'quickness of arm' and his 'activity of body'.[55] Jem Belcher was still the Champion of the Prize Ring, and for many of the Fancy there was already talk about whether Robert Barclay Allardice had done enough to be considered Champion of the Pedestrians.

# CHAPTER SIX

# Remarkable For Thy Heels

*Thy ancestor, Robert, was remarkable for his head; and thou
art remarkable for thy heels.*

'A QUAKER KINSMAN', QUOTED IN

*A JOURNAL OF A TOUR IN SCOTLAND*

ROBERT SOUTHEY, 1819

*... the waiter just whispers 'Barclay and Chicken', and they
waits to hear no more.*

*SILK AND SCARLET*

THE DRUID, 1862

*I*f the death of his father was the first turning point in Robert's life, his public triumph on Barmby Moor was undeniably the second, for it was there that he discovered his private and public identity. He returned to Ury with the respect and stature befitting the Laird of Ury and he played the role to the full.

But it was in walking, and the weariness that went with it, that he found who he was. In the open air, buffeted by the weather, he felt alive and powerful, and he found it irresistible. Pushing himself to his physical limit became a challenge, almost a daily temptation, which each time seemed to redefine him uniquely, and reinforced his sense of identity. If he could go by horse or by coach, he often found himself going on foot. If he could stay overnight in a local inn, he would spurn the opportunity, muttering something about how miserable such inns were, and set out to walk through the night instead. This was not the usual way of gentlemen.

Stories circulated about his extraordinary endurance. In August 1802 he walked for two and a half days over rough, steep Scottish roads, covering 180 miles, without once going to bed. His journey was to see old Dr Grant at Kirkmichael about 80 miles away and he decided, of course, to go on foot, taking the trusty 48-year-old George Mollison with him. They probably set off from Ury at three o'clock in the morning and travelled south-east along the 'easy' lowland route past Glamis Castle, arriving at Kirkmichael 19 hours later, at about ten o'clock in the evening. After supper they talked and drank the night away. They probably stayed with Dr Grant until after lunch. Instead of going back the way they came, Robert decided on the longer and vastly more difficult route through the Grampian Mountains.[1] It was about 100 miles. First they walked east a couple of miles across the Strathardle Hills and then joined the old military road north into the mountains. Up to the Spittal of Glenshee and on to the Devil's Elbow at 2,199 feet, and then on through the night to Glen Clunie Lodge and Braemar. Even then there was still the best part of 60 miles to go, past Balmoral and Crathie village, on to Ballater, Aboyne, Banchory and then home to Ury, arriving around 3 p.m. There were easier ways of getting to and from Kirkmichael.

As people told and retold the story of this journey it got stretched in the telling, so that when Captain Clias, a Swiss army officer, heard of it years later, it had become a 180-mile walk 'without rest'.[2] But the way Robert's performances were exaggerated showed how impressed, sometimes even overawed, people were with what he did. His performances seemed to find a chord in people that they could relate to. On Barmby Moor, for example, the crowd that pressed in on him wanted him to succeed. They wanted him to be amazing. It was as if he was doing things that they all would like to have done, almost as if they felt he was doing them on their behalf.

While Robert was performing his prodigious walking feats, so too were William Wordsworth, Samuel Taylor Coleridge and their circle. They walked not only to discover nature or the picturesque; they walked to discover themselves.[3] Wordsworth often walked for hours, sometimes all day. Coleridge once walked 90 miles in two days in the Quantock Hills, and walked and climbed to exhaustion in the Lakeland fells. Nor was this only a male thing. Walking was such a regular and important part of Dorothy Wordsworth's life that when she didn't, she specifically recorded in her diary, 'did not walk'. Indeed, when she and William were at Alfoxden, there were days when there was very little else, apparently, worth recording.[4] It was an age that discovered human dignity in the simple task of walking, a new grandeur in long and tiring physical effort and nobility in experiencing and resisting fatigue. Walking was not merely a backdrop to the self-searching and self-discovery that were a prelude to the creative process. It was part of it. William Hazlitt, another inveterate walker and part-time member of the Fancy, put it this way:

> Coleridge has told me that he himself liked to compose in walking over uneven ground; or breaking through the straggling branches of a copse-wood; whereas Wordsworth always wrote (if he could) walking up and down a straight gravel walk . . .[5]

Physical effort, and walking in particular, was essential to this, the Romantic Age, and Robert was rapidly becoming a symbol of the age.

A person walking to exhaustion inescapably becomes aware of the sensations of their own body and is forced to face their own limitations. Even when they are walking with others, the focus of attention is themselves. Such self-absorption is not always easy to live with. It tends to exclude others, except as spectators, as Sara, Coleridge's young wife, could testify. In Robert's case, self-absorption was not linked to self-analysis or even self-awareness, and he had no idea how to make his own feelings accessible to others. He did not have the lyrical powers to transpose his experiences into poetry as did Wordsworth, nor Coleridge's metaphysical turn of mind to translate them into experiences that could be shared. How Robert felt, therefore, was likely to be misunderstood. He did have sport, however, and it was through his sport that others could vicariously share in the effort and the fatigue, the successes and the failures. He also had Fletcher Reid and the Daft Laird to ensure he had plenty of sporting challenges to tempt him.

In 1803 when he was back in London Robert took part in three wagers in six months over distances of 440 yards, one mile and 64 miles. All had been set up by his friends. The first was with Joe Berks, the prize-fighter whose nose still bore the scars of Jem Belcher's knuckles. Belcher and Berks had fought each other nine times, and every time Belcher had won. In their last fight in August 1802 Joe Berks got a terrible beating and after 14 rounds could no longer stand; his friends had to place him in a carriage and send him to his home near Grosvenor Square. Fletcher Reid, as Jem Belcher's patron, arranged the fight, but no one came forward to support Joe Berks. Lord Camelford was not in town. Four days later Fletcher Reid gave a dinner for his pugilist friends at Bill Warr's One Tun Tavern, where the young Jem Belcher had first been introduced to the Fancy. There was a big turnout of the Fancy, and Joe Berks, showing all the signs of a man who had just had a mauling from a very effective fighter, made an appearance, probably for the free meal. Jem Belcher turned up later. Bill Warr's son Jack was also there. He had not yet tried to emulate his father in the ring, but he was young and fit and was acknowledged to be one of the fastest young runners around.

At the end of the dinner the gentlemen of the Fancy looked around for a little more sport before settling into a night of drinking and sporting songs. They decided to honour Bill Warr by testing young Jack's running ability. One hundred yards was marked out in the field behind the tavern and all trooped out to see the lad run. What they wanted was a race, so two guineas was put up as an inducement. Imagine the astonishment of the Fancy when the bruised and battered Joe Berks stepped forward to take on the challenge. No one could doubt Joe Berks's spirit. And imagine the looks of incredulity on their faces as Joe Berks romped home five yards ahead of the youngster and pocketed the two guineas.[6] Perhaps Joe Berks was a better runner than boxer. Fletcher Reid seized the opportunity and later tried him out further and backed him with 20 guineas to run from the One Tun to Chalk Farm and back in an hour. It was less than three miles each way and well within the compass of most athletes, but Joe Berks was nearly 13 stone and not built like a runner at all. The Daft Laird bet against him and lost his money again when Joe Berks arrived back 14 minutes before the deadline.[7]

Robert loved London and left Ury to enjoy himself there as often as he could. He was now close to the description given to generations of Barclay men – 'six feet high and remarkably handsome' – and London gave him every opportunity to exploit his looks and popularity to the full. When he was in Scotland he attended fashionable events such as the Northern Shooting Club Meeting, to which 'the most elegant and eligible ladies of the north' also went,[8] but Robert seemed far too preoccupied with himself to form any meaningful relationships. This was true of the Fancy as a whole. They were so driven by their own manly concerns they had little time for anything else. The most important relationships seemed to be with their sport, the bottle, each other, and short-term liaisons with women who did not expect anything else. In the winter, during the hunting season, the gentlemen of the Fancy were as well known for 'riding' the country girls at the local inns, as for riding to hounds.[9] And when they were in London there was certainly no shortage of girls who walked the streets, day and night, hanging around the taverns, just as much as they did around the theatres. On a Saturday in September 1804 no fewer than 30 'girls of the town' were taken into custody on Fleet Street alone.[10]

When in London, with an eye to convenience rather than style, Robert took rooms in Great Suffolk Street behind the Haymarket Theatre. This was a seedy, run-down area of tumbledown buildings, overcrowded with disreputable characters, and known as 'Porridge Island'. But it was well placed for the taverns in St James's and must have been relatively easy on the pocket, and he seemed to like it.[11] Economy, however, was not the driving force behind his decision to make Porridge Island his London base. In everything he did he seemed to enjoy parting with his money, and it slipped through his fingers like ale through a colander. It was as if he did not want to acknowledge any limitations, even financial ones, on what he could do. Robert's deep, baritone voice became a familiar part of the post-dinner singsongs as the gin and ale flowed and the next round of sporting wagers was made. He drank a lot at Bill Warr's One Tun, where so many west-country men from Bath and Bristol drank. He also ate a lot and developed a reputation for having a huge appetite. This was a period in Robert's life when he enjoyed himself unscrupulously. He was the life-and-soul of many a party. Fletcher Reid and the Daft Laird also spent a lot of time in London and between them pushed up the wagers and stake-money to new heights. In 1802, for example, they had wagered 200 guineas a side against each other over a fight between Belcher and Berks, which by the time the fight took place, they had pushed up to £1,450 a side.[12] This trio of young men – Robert Barclay Allardice, Fletcher Reid and the Daft Laird from within a radius of 20 miles in Scotland, were the prime movers in the London Fancy. Men with Scottish accents were, at least for the time being, taking over sport in the capital, and enjoying every moment of it.

The one mile race between Robert Barclay Allardice and Joe Berks took place in June 1803. Predictably, Fletcher Reid and the Daft Laird were behind it. Fletcher Reid bet heavily on Joe Berks and against Robert, and the Daft Laird, having learned his lesson about betting against Robert, bet on him winning. This time he won as Robert defeated Joe Berks with great ease.[13] A month later, on one of the hottest days of the year Robert won another wager to walk from his rooms in Porridge Island to Newmarket in 12 hours.[14] The distance was believed to be 64 miles, and three years earlier he had taken 12 hours to go the same distance between Ury and Ellon. He won in ten hours, two hours within the time – a remarkable achievement, which so strengthened his confidence he was even tempted to accept a bet from Fletcher Reid to run 440 yards against Jack Warr in the highly public and fashionable venue of Hyde Park. Robert's form over such a short distance was unknown and the betting was 2 to 1 against him. Nevertheless he won again, beating young Jack Warr by ten yards.[15] Robert had now proved himself to be the complete all round pedestrian. He was the toast of the Fancy.

His friendship with Fletcher Reid and his penchant for sporting dinners and the company of the Fancy led him deeper into the world of the prize fighters. He preferred their rough and ready ways and in their company he could slip out of his gentlemanly coat with ease. Perhaps a bigger problem for him now was slipping his gentleman's coat back on again when he needed to. At 5'11" in height and nearly 13 stone in weight, Robert Barclay Allardice was a natural in Jackson's Rooms, where he went to practise sparring and to learn from Gentleman Jackson the skills necessary to be a star in the pugilistic world. He developed his strength, and it was said of him that 'the deltoid muscle of his arm is uncommonly large, and expanded in a manner that indicates great strength'.[16]

In June the blackest gloom descended over the Fancy and particularly the One Tun. Jem Belcher was playing rackets in the court in Little St Martin's Lane a few hundred yards away, with a gentleman named

Edwin Stuart. Jem had the speed, touch and power to be a very good player. After one of the points, he allowed his concentration to slip just as the marker returned the ball with unusual force, and it hit Jem in the left eye. Those who saw the incident said the ball almost took his eye from the socket. At the age of only 22 and at the peak of his fame and powers, Jem Belcher was blind in one eye.[17]

Fletcher Reid and his other patrons came to the rescue with speed. They used their influence to get Jem installed as the landlord of the Two Brewers in Wardour Street, which would at least provide him with a living. Lord Camelford, back in London from a spell in a French gaol, not only contributed in characteristic fashion to Jem Belcher's new career, he also gave him his favourite fighting dog, Trusty, which he had earlier rechristened Belcher in Jem's honour. Trusty, a squat, powerful, battle-scarred bull terrier, was originally owned by Harry Mellish, from Blyth in Yorkshire, a young member of the Fancy with a noticeably pale complexion and dark hair. He had agreed to sell Trusty to Lord Camelford for two guineas a pound. When eventually they weighed him and found him to be 42 lbs, they agreed that it was an insult to sell him for mere money, and so he went to Lord Camelford in exchange for a favourite gun and a case of pistols, and became Belcher. One great fighter named after another. Belcher had already fought and won 50 battles and Lord Camelford loved to be seen out with him. He swore that money would never part him from Belcher. He was as good as his word. On hearing of Jem Belcher's tragic accident he made Jem a gift of his namesake. Jem once more reinstated the old name and took Trusty with him to the Two Brewers.[18]

Sport never stands still, and soon the talk at the One Tun and the Two Brewers was of the need for new blood to try for the Championship. Bristol was the obvious hunting ground, and within weeks a new Bristol fighter was on the coach to London, and Robert was sent to Holborn to meet him.

Off the coach stepped a man only 5'8" tall and weighing about 11½ stone. He had a mop of sandy hair and looked pale and weary.

Not a likely looking candidate for the title 'Champion of the Prize Ring', except for his barrel 43" chest. His name was Hen Pearce.[19] He always resisted the nickname 'Harry', insisting he was christened Hen and not Henry. When he fought he was as courageous and ruthless as a fighting cock, and the Fancy soon nicknamed him 'The Game Chicken'. He was described as 'quite an uncultivated man' and 'remarkably illiterate', but he and Robert became very close friends. They drank together, sparred together in Jackson's Rooms and trained together. Robert even became something of a bore talking endlessly about his new friend and rising star in the pugilistic world. The Fancy encouraged the friendship. Robert was known to be cheerful good company and a free spender, and they wanted him to keep the Game Chicken's spirits up when he got homesick for Bristol. Perhaps Robert did the job too well for the Game Chicken developed a reputation not only for hard training, but also for enthusiastically pursuing wine, women and song.

Life for a young boxer was hard, and the fights and the training weren't the only challenges. To get on you had to please the influential gentlemen of the Fancy. Almost as soon as the Game Chicken arrived in London, Gentleman Jackson summoned him from his bed one night to demonstrate his abilities for a few influential gentlemen of the Fancy in a tiny 10'x10' room at the Horse and Dolphin in Windmill Street. His opponent was the veteran Jack Firby. After several rounds, the walls and the gentlemen's waistcoats were splattered with blood and Jack Firby was in such a bad way the landlord thought he might not recover. So he got a cleaning woman to wash down the walls overnight to remove the evidence. Before leaving, Jackson told the Game Chicken to report to his rooms on Bond Street at midday, which he did, despite getting back to his lodgings near the Strand too late to get in and having to walk the streets till morning.[20]

The Game Chicken followed up his bout with Jack Firby (who fortunately did survive his mauling) with another one with Joe Berks. Fletcher Reid was delighted with his new find.

Even for sportsmen there is a limit to how much they can insulate themselves from and ignore the world that others call the 'real' one. By the spring of 1803 the peace with France that Lord Camelford had so mistrusted, was recognised as a sham, and in May Britain declared war on France. Napoleon assembled thousands of flat-bottomed boats and an army of hundreds of thousands of men along the coast facing Britain. Once again, the nation was gripped with anti-French fever and the fear of an invasion. Men rushed to enlist in the army or with the volunteers. How long could a patriotic young gentleman look the other way and spend his time on sport and socialising?

Robert returned to Ury to put the estate under the legal trusteeship of his brother-in-law, John Innes, and on 3 February 1804 was commissioned as second lieutenant in the 23rd Regiment of Foot, The Royal Welch Fusiliers[21] – an event that he celebrated perhaps too enthusiastically with Fletcher Reid, the Daft Laird and others. Under the influence of drink he agreed a wager to go from Hoddeston to the Royal Exchange in three hours and within ten days. It was 23 miles and the bet was for 200 guineas. Robert had been living in London since before Christmas. His usual exercise regime had been broken and the habit of dropping into Bill Warr's One Tun Tavern had its effect. For once he was unfit and Fletcher Reid seized his chance.

Robert left London for the clean air of Hertfordshire for a few days' training. His previous successes had been based on hard training and good preparation. Now he had neither. What he needed was an excuse, or at least a face-saving story. Luck was with him, for on the date agreed, Sunday 13 February, he went out at 5 a.m. to find the roads icy. *The Times* reported the event the following Tuesday:

> . . . several gentlemen left town on Sunday to see the pedestrian start, and accompany him to town on horseback; the crowd that went to meet him was immense; while many of the Gentleman's friends waited for him at 8 o'clock at the Royal Exchange, where they expected to meet him according to appointment.

Their surprise, however, was great in the extreme, when they waited several hours beyond the time without seeing or hearing from him. Many of the equestrians went several miles on the Edmonton road but saw no more than those who remained in town.[22]

Rumour and speculation began to fly. Perhaps he was ill. Perhaps Fletcher Reid had conceded defeat before the start. Later they heard Robert's version. The wet road had frozen into a solid sheet of ice about three miles from the start and he could not get past.[23] It was a feeble excuse but it seems to have been accepted. Everyone concluded that the wager had been put off by mutual agreement and would take place at a later date, but it never did. Perhaps they accepted that a wager 'agreed' when one or both parties were too drunk to be responsible, was no wager at all. It was also a Sunday. There would have been fierce criticism for taking part in such a public wager on a Sunday. The event must have been a huge embarrassment to Robert because he took the opportunity for the rest of the spring to ease up on the socialising and returned to his habit of regular long walks.

Invasion was expected 'every day, and almost every hour' and in May Robert was sent with his regiment to Eastbourne to prepare for the defence of Britain. Many other regular and volunteer regiments were assembled along the south coast. At Langley Camp, just outside Eastbourne, several regiments were camped throughout the summer and the autumn in clay huts. They were engaged, day and night in digging an enormously long ditch, ten feet deep, to stop the progress of the enemy's artillery when they landed.[24]

They were still there waiting in the autumn. Thousands of soldiers in one place for months on end have to find some way of lightening the mood. They drank and sang and challenged each other with trials of strength and skill. Often the mood was playful. On one occasion, for example, Robert was out walking in the fields with a friend, when they came upon a pond. 'For a guinea I jump over and land in the adjoining field.' 'Done,' came the reply, and Robert took one huge leap and landed up to his neck in the water.[25] At Eastbourne his life again became one long training session. Whenever he was off duty he covered countless miles along the South Downs and was often so far from his barracks that he got into the habit of taking a large satchel with him packed with food to satisfy his enormous appetite. Samuel Taylor Coleridge, too, was still walking, almost compulsively. The previous autumn he had walked 263 miles from Inverness to Perth in eight days, leaving his wife and family behind. In January, after being ill in bed nursed by Dorothy Wordsworth, he 'revived by a sudden Frost' and got up and walked 19 miles over the fells in four hours and 35 minutes.[26] There were no rewards or even praise for these efforts. He, like Robert, did it for himself.

Days and weeks turned into months, and when it was obvious that the troops could be in for a long wait, Robert sent for Fletcher Reid to arrange some more serious competitions for him and for Bill Warr to help him train. Under his guidance, Robert ran three wagers in the eight weeks between mid-August and mid-October, and won them all. The first was to run two miles in 12 minutes, which he did with two and a half seconds to spare, on ground wet from days of rain and with high winds blowing in his face.[27] The next was a mile race for 200 guineas against Captain Molineux Marston of the 48th (Northamptonshire) Regiment. He won this in five minutes and seven seconds.[28] The third, on Friday 12 October, was for 500 guineas against John Ireland, specially brought down from Manchester. Robert won in four minutes and 50 seconds. Ireland dropped out with a quarter of the race still to run – a most surprising let-down from such an experienced professional.[29]

Robert was always fussy about his accommodation. On Monday 1 October he packed his deal trunk and moved into new lodgings suggested to him by his barrack-sergeant, James Gearing – the small front sitting room of his mother's drug shop at Hailsham. It was an old family business in which the knowledge of the drugs, salves and ointments had passed down by word of mouth from earlier generations.

Mrs Gearing, a little, dark-eyed, precise woman, was part of this long line. A solitary small bottle of blue liquid was on display in the window, but the shop was hidden from the road behind a brick wall. The front door creaked and and the old floorboards sagged. On view inside were lots of simple jars, pots, and bottles; so many, in fact, that it was thought some of them must have been fakes. 'Poison', 'Paregoric' and 'Soothing Syrup' could be read in faded gold letters on some of the labels. There was a counter, and at the end nearest the window three slots in which the three ointment knives of different sizes and lengths were kept. Mrs Gearing's Drug Shop was a gold mine for anyone interested in pills and potions to help an athlete prepare for his wagers. Robert was not one to waste such an opportunity.[30]

At Hailsham, with Fletcher Reid and Bill Warr nearby, Robert was on good form. He was remembered as a good tenant and a churchgoer, with a manly presence and a gentlemanly demeanour. He was promoted to first lieutenant.[31] Some of his exploits with Fletcher Reid, nevertheless, were too wild to be retold. Fletcher Reid's company and his penchant for practical jokes, seems to have left its mark in Sussex as it did in Scotland.

At the age of 25, the pattern of Robert's life was more or less established. He was an incessant walker, a free-spending laird, and an officer in His Majesty's Army. He enjoyed his freedom, but it was not complete freedom; as an officer and a gentleman, certain standards of behaviour were not only expected, they were required. For example, in April 1804 two lieutenants in the 7th Battalion of Reserves were drummed out of their regiment in disgrace for using bad language and making indecent comments to the wives of two other officers.[32] Because Robert tended to choose the company of men who were rough and uncultivated, who had neither the manners nor the conversation of gentlemen – illiterate prize-fighters and others who hung out in London's sporting taverns – he needed to be something of a chameleon. He needed two styles of behaviour and two styles of language and conversation. He also needed two styles of dress and appearance. There were times, after hours on the road in heavy rain or hot, dusty weather, when he looked more like a vagabond than an army officer. He was living with a foot in two parallel worlds.

Robert Barclay was not alone in this. There was a fascination among the fashionable young gentlemen for 'living low'. Wealthy young gentlemen liked to be seen out with their fighting dogs because they were associated with the lower orders. Young gentlemen, to the horror of their parents, liked to be seen in sleazy taverns and dressed as coachmen. Tommy Onslow, later Lord Cranley, perhaps went too far. He dressed and spoke like a coachman and even had his front teeth filed to a V so he could whistle like a coachman through them.[33] Almost inevitably Lord Camelford took it to the extreme. At night he frequently dressed as a down-and-out and prowled incognito around those areas of London where few would dare go alone, even in broad daylight, befriending the lowest of the low. When he found someone there in particular distress he pressed money into their hands on the strict understanding that they told no one where it had come from. He was said to have distributed thousands of pounds in this way.[34] Infiltrating this world unrecognised may not have been as difficult as it sounds. A contemporary survey suggested that there were 15,000 beggars in London, although this figure also included their children.[35] Despite the suggestion in the same survey that the beggars in the city collected no less than £100,000 a year from the public, there was abject poverty in the dark, foul alleyways.

Generally, however, people knew where they belonged in the social strata, and behaved and dressed accordingly. When gentlemen deliberately dressed to be unrecognisable as gentlemen, it was socially disruptive – which was why they did it. They liked the way it caught people off-balance. Sometimes they were driven by curiosity: temporarily they could become almost invisible and sample another life. Sometimes it was sinister when they used it to confuse and disorientate people and then take advantage of them.

Stories were told of Lord Camelford who was sitting in a 'box' in a coffee-house in Conduit Street and 'meanly attired, as he often was'.[36] A 'dashing fellow' came in and called for a pint of Madeira and two candles, which eventually arrived in the adjoining box. Lord Camelford then called out 'in a mimic' tone for two candle snuffers, snuffed out the 'dashing fellow's' candles and leisurely returned to his own box. 'Waiter, waiter, who the d⁄⁄l is this fellow who dares thus to insult a Gentleman?' 'Lord Camelford, Sir.' 'Horror struck' and 'almost doubting he was still in existence', the dashing fellow crept silently away without ever touching his Madeira.

Lord Camelford lived and behaved as he pleased. He, too, lived in two worlds. In March, in the coffee room of the Prince of Wales Hotel in London, he was in gentleman mode and went up to Captain Best, an officer in a West Indian regiment, and said: 'Mr Best, I understand you have been traducing my character, and insulting my girl Fanny, in a most ungentleman⁄like manner. Such conduct, Sir, is infamous, and you must be a damned scoundrel.'[37] This was language another gentleman could not ignore. The dispute was described as being over 'a favourite woman' of theirs, Fanny Simmons, who at different times had lived with each of them, although married to someone else. The gentlemen of the Fancy had turned wagering into a form of sport, but they also considered women and short⁄term affairs as sport. A competitive sport at that. Next morning the two men met again in a field on the Uxbridge Road, behind Holland House. Captain Best tried to get Lord Camelford to retract, but to no avail. The next step was inevitable. Their seconds measured the ground, and the matter was settled with pistols. It was agreed they should fire together, but Lord Camelford's shot was marginally first. He missed, but Captain Best's shot hit Lord Camelford below his right shoulder as he stood sideways on, pistol hand extended. The lead ball went between the second and third ribs, passed through his right lung, through his spinal cord and came to rest in the left⁄hand side of his spine. He fell instantly. Captain Best ran up saying, 'Camelford, I hope you are not seriously hurt.' To which Lord Camelford replied, as he lay on the ground, 'Best, I am a dead man, you have killed me, but I freely forgive you.' Captain Best was described, understandably, as being 'much agitated'. He left the ground in a post-chaise and fled the country.[38] Lord Camelford was taken to a house in a nearby lane and his family and a surgeon were called for. The ball could not be removed and paralysis slowly crept up his body. It was his sister, Lady Greville, who took it worst. She

> . . . was in deep distress; her attachment to her brother being very strong from their infancy. On her Ladyship's entering the house, she nearly fainted away, in consequence of which it was not deemed proper for her to see her brother in his present state.[39]

He died the following Saturday.

The gentlemen of the Fancy took enormous risks by the very lifestyle they chose, over and above the risks posed by Napoleon. Such was their self-absorption, they seemed unaware of the effect their lifestyle had on their families.

Neither Lieutenant Barclay nor any other of the thousands of soldiers along the south coast saw any military action there. The threat was removed when Napoleon withdrew his massed invasion troops to cover his eastern flank against Austria. Robert went back to Ury briefly to pick up the threads of his old life. John Innes, his brother-in-law, was still legally in charge of business at Ury, so Robert had the pleasure of returning as the head of the family, but without any real responsibility. He took a leaf out of Lord Camelford's book and dressed up as a tramp to visit, incognito, some of the new tenant farmers. How they treated him determined how he would treat them in the coming year.[40]

Even back in London he began to develop a reputation for being somewhat boorish and heavy-handed. He continued to hang out socially with the Game Chicken and they became a notoriously uncouth duo whose company was avoided by the more refined gentlemen, and all the respectable ladies. One story tells how they were out training one morning, and enjoying breakfast: 'Once two officers at an inn were pitching into 'em because they'd got their breakfast-table; the waiter just whispers "Barclay and Chicken", and they waits to hear no more.'[41]

The other stories of Lieutenant Barclay continued to be mainly about his walks that turned what could have been mundane journeys into major endurance exercises. In March, after he had visited his sister and Samuel Galton in Birmingham, he walked the 72 miles to Wrexham in North Wales, where his regiment was stationed. He went via Shrewsbury, and probably took less than 12 hours. He boasted that he did it between breakfast and dinner.[42]

In June he was the centre of attention on Epsom race course, where he was due to run a half-mile race against Captain George Cooke of the 1st Regiment of Foot Guards. It was scheduled for midday on Thursday 13 June and was to be his first race for eight months. Consequently, it attracted an enormous crowd including 'many fashionable females' who 'graced the ground'. Betting was brisk and when Robert appeared he was 'greeted amidst the acclamations of the whole assemblage'. Expectation was high, but George Cooke did not turn up and Robert ran over the course alone, to claim all the bets.[43] What was the explanation? Was George Cooke so conscious of Robert's superiority he saw no point in humiliating himself? Was he too ill to race? If so, why had he not sent a message? Had they agreed, after a throw of the dice, that he would withdraw? It was done in horse-racing. This was Robert's second opponent in eight months to either drop out or not show up. There was never an explanation.

In July he walked from his rooms in London's Porridge Island to Seaford, only a few miles beyond Hailsham – 64 miles in ten hours.[44] Equal to the best he had ever done but not in competition, for this was not for a wager but just for the pleasure of pushing himself. Meanwhile, his friend the Game Chicken was having unambiguous success in his fights. He followed up his early victories against Jack Firby and Joe Berks with wins against Elias Spray at Moulsey Hurst, and Stephen Carte on Shepperton Common. On a Tuesday at the beginning of October 1805, the Fancy came to Hailsham to see the Game Chicken defeat another Bristolian, John Gully, in a classic fight lasting an hour and ten minutes. Fletcher Reid got John Gully out of gaol specially for the fight. It was the first time Robert had helped Fletcher Reid in the organisation of a title fight. An 'immense' and fashionable crowd gathered around a green above the village where a 24ft ring had been erected. Beau Brummell and William, Duke of Clarence, one of the Prince of Wales's younger brothers, were among them.[45]

Three weeks later Robert and the rest of Lt Gen. Lord Cathcart's army left from Ramsgate for Cuxhaven, arriving there, after 19 days at sea, on 17 November.[46] They had a long severe march to the banks of the River Weser and set up camp. There was still a day's march to Bremen, and most of the foot soldiers were exhausted. Their services were not needed at Bremen for a while, so they had a chance to recover. But days turned to weeks and they did not move on until early January. Then they went on to occupy Bremen and Verden, fulfilling their part of the plan to protect Hanover. Again they were destined to be militarily idle, and for over a month they remained waiting for more active duties. They were almost certainly not physically idle. A makeshift military camp in Germany in the middle of winter cannot be much fun, and the officers knew enough about their men to keep them fully occupied physically. By the middle of February they were fitter than when they arrived, but it became clear that events had overtaken them and that they were now in the wrong place, so they struck camp and marched back to Cuxhaven to sail home to Harwich.[47]

Meanwhile, in Britain the people reeled in shock when they heard that William Pitt, the Prime Minister, and probably the most important man in England for the past 23 years, had died. His final words were believed to be 'Oh my country! How I leave my country!' His death had come not long after the news of Lord Nelson's death at the Battle of Trafalgar. Even Charles James Fox felt so low after Nelson's funeral that he said that he, too, would be dead by the summer.

While he was away Robert had missed the Game Chicken's successful defence of his title against the one-eyed Jem Belcher, which brought him universal recognition as the Champion. Despite the distinct mood of gloom and despondency in the country, Robert was full of the cheerfulness and bonhomie of a young man in his prime. Having disembarked at Harwich, he and his regiment were stationed at Woodbridge Garrison in Suffolk and they entertained themselves as usual with drinking and wagers. In the mess room, on one notable evening in March, someone offered to wager against anyone walking one mile every hour for 100 hours – four days and nights, plus four hours. Robert would not be drawn and declared it impossible. So confident was he that he offered 1,000 guineas against any man in England completing such a feat if each mile was started on the hour. On the topic of long-distance walking Robert was the preeminent expert, and his view went unchallenged. The man who offered the bet was almost certainly Fletcher Reid's nephew, James Wedderburn Webster, who was stationed at Woodbridge Garrison with the 11th Regiment of Light Dragoons.[48] No one knew then that this unaccepted wager would later be the basis of one of the most talked about events of the century.

So convivial was the company that evening that it was memorable for other reasons too. Robert followed up his 1,000-guinea wager with another. He bet 1,000 guineas that he could lift half a ton (10cwt/1,120 lbs) from the ground. He was now so confident in his ability he wanted to show off his fitness and strength as well as his undoubted endurance. There were no takers, so just for their entertainment Robert proved his point by tying together a number of weights (1,204 lbs in total) and lifted them from the ground. This was even better than Gentleman Jackson. Robert then placed his right hand on the floor, palm upwards, and asked the heaviest man in the room to stand on it. The man was the regimental paymaster, William Keith, who weighed 18 stone. Merely steadying Keith with his left hand, Robert picked him up one-handed and placed him on the table. In Scotland, Robert was also known to be a good discus thrower. The gathered party went outside and Robert demonstrated his versatility by throwing a 56lb weight 24 feet, using a straight-arm technique, perhaps in a hammer-throwing style but without any turns. Then, in true Scottish style, he threw the same weight overhead, a distance of 15 feet.[49]

Such feats called for repetition, and within weeks he repeated his 'I'll lift you with one hand' trick on Colonel Charles Lennox, whom the whole country knew as the man who, in a duel, had shot off a curl of the Duke of York's wig. He was 42, stood 6' 3" tall and weighed close to 16 stone.[50] The Fancy also knew him as a cricketer who once hit a cricket ball 240 yards, 200 yards on the first bounce.[51]

Robert was now 26 and in his prime as an athlete. Physically, there seemed to be nothing he could not do. Among the boxers and the soldiers he was in his element. He enjoyed their company and basked in their adulation. There were, however, some storm clouds gathering. The world in which he was a gentleman had expectations too. In a time of national crisis, was this not all a little frivolous for a gentleman from a respectable family who had other responsibilities? Some members of his family definitely thought so. According to Robert Southey, the Poet Laureate, one of them even said to him, somewhat boldly, 'Thy ancestor, Robert, was remarkable for his head; and thou art remarkable for your heels.'[52]

It was not a compliment. No matter how extraordinary his achievements, a gentleman would find it hard to get respect for being only an athlete.

## CHAPTER SEVEN

# *Hocus Pocus*

to 'Hocus' a man is to put something into his drink of a narcotic
quality, that renders him unfit for action.'

*PUGILISTICA: THE HISTORY OF BRITISH BOXING*

H.D. MILES, 1878

... a prepared liquid was administered to Wood after he had
gone 22 miles.

*THE ST JAMES'S CHRONICLE,*

17–20 OCTOBER 1807

On 10 June 1806 Robert Barclay Allardice parted from the 1st Battalion of the 23rd Regiment of Foot and became a captain in the Nova Scotia Fencible Infantry.[1] From now on he was 'Captain Barclay'. Almost before the ink was dry on the agreement, however, he put on his walking shoes and set off early and without breakfast, from his house in London's Porridge Island to Colchester. Not, of course, the easy way by coach following the road out of the capital north of the Thames, but on foot, 22 miles, south of the river to Gravesend. He then rowed across the River Thames to Tilbury Fort, and walked the remaining 33 miles to the garrison at Colchester where his old battalion was stationed.[2] By the time he left to start the same journey in reverse, he had decided to resign his commission in the Nova Scotia Fencibles, and on 13 July, only 33 days after leaving his old battalion, he became a captain in the 2nd Battalion of his old regiment.[3]

The following day at Doncaster race course, 150 miles away, two Lancashire weavers raced each other over nearly nine and a half miles for 400 guineas. They attracted a lot of local interest. One report stated that 'a prodigious concourse of people' gathered to watch them,[4] and *The Edinburgh Evening Courant* said the crowd was 'immense' and included 'many *Lancashire witches*' (their italics).[5] The winner, by nearly a minute, was Abraham Wood. He had started the race as 2 to 1 favourite despite the fact that he had one foot strapped up, having dislocated a small bone in it two weeks earlier. So impressive was he that after the race he offered to rest an hour and then race a mile against anyone, for a further 50 guineas. No one took up the challenge. Abraham Wood was a tall, slim 29-year-old, with 'little flesh', who stood an inch below 6', and had a 'remarkably fine' build for running.[6] Originally he came from the Rochdale area but had moved to Manchester where he had been racing successfully since he was a teenager and probably earned more from running than from weaving. The loser was Jonathan Pollard, a neat runner, but not in Wood's class. Nevertheless, he so impressed the sporting press that after the race they speculated that 'no man in the kingdom, Wood excepted, can beat him' and reported provocatively that Abraham Wood had 'challenged to run any man in the world, for any sum'.

It did not take long for the news to get to Captain Barclay in London. He ignored the challenge, and instead agreed to run a 440-yard race against the talented and controversial Edward Goulburn.[7] Every officer and gentleman in the country knew of the infamous Cornet Edward Goulburn. A few months before the race he was sued for libel in the Court of King's Bench by three of his senior officers. Edward Goulburn was a lowly cornet in the Royal Horse Guards when he wrote and published 'The Blueviad', a poem in which his senior officers appeared in the guise of Bluster, Lothario, Macsycophant, Numscull, Pomposo, Sir Peter Absolute and Slipslop. In the style of Alexander Pope's 'Dunciad', he wrote beautifully constructed rhyming couplets dipped in vitriol, that were all too easy to understand and whose subjects were all too easy to identify. One, he accused of womanising:

Wife, Maid or Virgin, are to him the same
And each at his desire, must yield their fame.

Another of flashing:

What yields him most supreme delight
By showing parts obscene, disgust your sight.

And another, the overweight Captain John Horsley, alias Bluster, of debauchery:

With looks ill temper'd, fraught with gloomy pride,
Bluster next rears, his gross & pamper'd hide;
The face bespeaks the man, at once we see,
The bloated remnants of a Debauchee.[8]

He accused others of being drunk, foul-mouthed and violent, or worse.

It must have been a surprise when only three sued him for libel since the reputation and dignity of all of them was seriously damaged, probably for ever. Although the officers won their case, they were awarded only £50 damages, and the moral victory probably went to Goulburn. He was, of course, forced to leave the Royal Horse Guards. How could he have stayed? After he left, he was insulted (perhaps not surprisingly) by Captain Horsley.

Goulburn, now a private citizen, responded by challenging Captain Horsley to a duel. Captain Horsley ignored it, on the grounds that 'Mr Goulburn's character did not entitle him to be met as a gentleman'. Edward Goulburn was not the man to be trifled with, and he immediately made public Captain Horsley's refusal. Honour demanded to be satisfied. Captain Horsley's fellow officers, fearing that they would be further damaged if he did not act as a gentleman and meet his challenger, forced him to resign from the regiment. Disgraced for not acting like a gentleman and by a non-gentleman, too.

Edward Goulburn was a provocative and controversial man. He was also multi-talented. In addition to his poetic and satirical skills he was a spirited runner, particularly over short distances. So good was he, and his determination to get his own way so notorious, that he started his race against Captain Barclay as 6 to 4 favourite. They met in front of a large partisan crowd on Lord's Cricket Ground, on what later would become Dorset Square. William Lord charged spectators 6d a head, to keep undesirables out, but it did not always work.[9] Emotions on all sides ran high when the two men lined up against each other. The officers and gentlemen of the Fancy believed Edward Goulburn needed to be taught a lesson. At the start, Captain Barclay rushed into the lead with the notorious Goulburn tucked in behind him. For 300 yards they ran stride for stride, locked in a test of strength and speed and a battle of wills. The spectators roared their approval, but then Goulburn ran out of steam and Captain Barclay eventually came in a comfortable winner in 60 seconds.[10] He had won an important moral victory for the officers and gentlemen, and had taught the clever, obnoxious upstart a lesson.

Captain Barclay continued to ignore Wood's challenge, but instead, issued his own, to 'any man in England to walk from one mile to a hundred, giving two months' notice, for their own sum'.[11] The two challenges had important differences. Abraham Wood's was for running and Captain Barclay's was for walking. There had always been a grey area between these and the Fancy were usually careful to specify whether the race was to be 'fair toe and heel' or merely 'on foot' when negotiating Articles of Agreement. Nevertheless, in September 1806 there was a court case over the issue.[12] Despite the difficulties, there was a growing feeling that there should be a champion pedestrian, just as there was a champion boxer, though there was little agreement about how to do it. In boxing it was relatively easy to decide who was the Champion. The two best men fought each other, and the winner took the title. But how could the champion pedestrian be decided? What should the distance be? Different distances might produce different champions. Should they run or walk? Despite these imponderables, most agreed that Abraham Wood and Captain Barclay had to meet head-on in competition at some suitable, agreed distance.

Captain Barclay was fit and strong and able to select his races, but the Game Chicken's lifestyle had finally caught up with him. Drink, and 'the fond caresses of the softer sex, among whom he was a most distinguished favourite', impaired his health and he was forced to retire as Champion.[13] An athlete's hold on their sport's biggest prize is often tenuous and frequently brief. The boxing title was, therefore, vacant again and there was widespread talk about who might be the next Champion. The most likely claimant to the vacant title was John Gully, but he had not fought since he lost to the Game Chicken at Hailsham.

In October with no one coming forward to accept his challenge to 'any man in the world', Abraham Wood accepted a wager to run 20 miles in two and a quarter hours on Brighton race course, and won by ten minutes.[14] A few days later he accepted a wager to run 440 yards in a minute, and won it, 'with apparent ease', one second inside the time. Captain Barclay's challenge 'to any man in England' lay on the table unanswered, but he kept himself physically and mentally alert in readiness.

Meanwhile, Captain Barclay's new battalion had moved from Colchester to Wrexham, uncomfortably far from the London sporting scene. It proved, however, just another spur to Captain Barclay to demonstrate once again that he could achieve virtually any physical challenge he set his mind to. So, undeterred by the 400 miles and the fact that it was winter, he slipped away from Wrexham one dark night to see a fight in London. To provide a cover story he got permission from his commanding officer to go to Liverpool 50 miles away, to visit his brother David whom he had not seen since coming back from Germany.[15]

Not to arouse suspicion he left empty-handed, even without a greatcoat. He walked two hours to Chester, and then mounted the unsprung and uncomfortable box seat of the London mail coach. It was raining and cold enough to suggest snow as the Royal Mail drawn by four horses sped and rattled its way to Nantwich. Sitting outside on a coach in winter was a severe test for anyone. *Tom Brown's School Days* tells of what it was like when half an hour of bitter cold robbed the legs of all their sensation, and how the guard had to physically lift passengers off the top of the coach because their legs were too lifeless to move.[16] Winter travellers would describe how the cold numbed them into semi-consciousness, causing outside passengers to fall off. The cold-induced sleep was irresistible. One coach arrived at Chippenham from Bath with two of its passengers frozen to death and a third dying, while one more fortunate traveller said it was as if he had taken a draught of laudanum at the last coach stop, rather than his customary rum and milk. Even in the best of weather a tired passenger on top of a coach had to guard against 'dropping off'. The coach driver, wrapped in his voluminous coat, cape, scarf and hat, would jab his elbow in the ribs of any passenger alongside him to keep him alert.

Before they got to Lichfield the icy rain turned to sleet. Though he was very cold and soaked to the skin, the discipline of the road permitted only ten minutes at The Swan, before he had to climb back on board. As the four fresh horses rushed them on to Watling Street and London via Woburn and St Albans, the rain and sleet stopped and the cold air dried Captain Barclay's clothes on his back. Once in London he learned that the secret venue for the fight was Wormwood Scrubs north of London and made his way there as quickly as possible. After the fight he returned to his rooms on Great Suffolk Street, and only then was he able to climb into a hot tub, hoping that pneumonia had not already set in. Even then there was time for only two hours in bed, before he had to be off again to catch the night mail, this time to Shrewsbury. The coach left promptly at 7.30 p.m. as part of the great cavalcade of mail coaches that left London every weekday evening, destined for all corners of Britain.

The first three hours took Captain Barclay along the familiar road to St Albans and Redbourne, where they were allowed the luxury of 20 minutes for breakfast. Then back on the road to Dunstable, before branching off with horns blowing, to Daventry, Coventry and Birmingham. Here he got off, even though the coach continued on to Chester. It gave him the opportunity to visit his sister, Lucy, at Moseley. Then, to give himself the appearance of a man who had just walked from Liverpool, he walked the remaining 72 miles to Wrexham, via Shifnal, Shrewsbury and Chester. He eventually arrived back in his mess room at Wrexham in time for a late dinner 'on the fifth night', having covered nearly 400 miles in the round trip and spending only two hours in bed the whole time. Charles Apperley, alias Nimrod, the great contemporary expert on coach travel, believed that the hardships endured by Captain Barclay on this expedition would have been unendurable by any other man.[17] Stories of Captain Barclay's indestructibility were retold with even greater gusto after this. It seemed almost impertinent that anyone would challenge him for the title of Champion.

In December 1806 Captain Barclay returned to Ury for his usual couple of winter months of hunting, and this time he took Jem Belcher's dog, Trusty, with him. Trusty was the most famous dog in the country and when Jem Belcher was arrested and put in gaol for debt, he gave Trusty to Captain Barclay, who swore that Trusty would never fight again as long as he lived.[18] Captain Barclay's other companion on the journey north was a new groom-cum-manservant named William Cross, a tough, active, weather-hardened man about 5'8" tall who claimed to be more comfortable outdoors than in. He looked like it, too.

Once back at Ury, Captain Barclay took William Cross out with him to walk to Crathie, deep in the Grampian Mountains, near Balmoral – a round trip of about 100 miles along roads that were described as 'the worst in the Kingdom'. They arrived back at Ury 19 hours after they started, 17½ of which were spent walking.[19] William Cross had passed muster, and he stayed with Captain Barclay for the next 30 years.

The winter visit to Ury was short that year, and by early January 1807 Captain Barclay and William Cross were on their way back to London in readiness for the new season. The first dramatic development was on Tuesday 22 January when Fletcher Reid received news at Shepperton that his mother had died and that he had inherited her money and estates in Scotland. It called for a celebration. In the morning after the drunken party, Fletcher Reid's manservant went in to rouse him and found him dead. He had died in a drunken stupor. The news stunned the Fancy and the newspapers carried a poetic tribute to him written in boxing slang:

In the still of night Death to Shepperton went,
And there catching poor Fletcher asleep,
He into his wind such a finisher sent,
That no longer 'the time' could he keep.

Thus forced to give in, we his fate must lament,
While the coward grim Death must we blame:
For if in the morn he to Shepperton went,
He feared Fletcher's true science and game.

Then repose to his ashes, soft rest to his soul,
For harmless was he through life's span,
With the friend of his bosom enjoying the bowl,
And wishing no evil to man.[20]

While Captain Barclay had been doing his best to prove his indestructibility, many of his close friends were doing the reverse. Fletcher Reid was dead at the age of 32; Lord Camelford had died in a duel at the age of 29. The Daft Laird had gambled away his entire fortune and was locked away in the debtors' prison in Liverpool. He was 25. When he finally signed away all his claims to his land and property, he thanked God he was no longer responsible for them. He died in this gaol 12 years later never having shaved his beard from the day he went in.[21] Jem Belcher had lost an eye at the age of 22, and the Game Chicken his health at 29.

It was a turning point in Captain Barclay's life, and also in the history of boxing. The Prize Ring title was vacant; its two great recent superstars were probably out of contention; the principal fight promoter and leading patron was dead. It was time for a new beginning.

All the boxing enthusiasts were on the lookout for new talent. John Gully from Bristol was the favourite to be the next Champion, but there were others. John Gully was 23, intelligent, level-headed and a good technical boxer. Gentleman Jackson told Captain Barclay that a 25-year-old unfashionable boxer named Tom Cribb also had promise. Admittedly he was slow, but he could take a blow well and could absorb unusual amounts of physical punishment without flinching. Originally he had come from Hanham on the outskirts of Bristol — another good omen — but he had lived in London for the past 12 years. So far his boxing career had been undistinguished. He had his first fight when he was 23, beating a 49-year-old called George Maddox. After that he beat Tom Blake, and a Jewish fighter named Isaac Pick, who, rather insultingly, was known by the gentiles as Ikey Pig. Then Tom Cribb was beaten in 52 rounds by George

Nichols — a defeat that some attributed to Cribb being drunk before the fight. Afterwards came a peculiar fight against Bill Richmond, Lord Camelford's black minder. Bill Richmond was only a few weeks away from his 42nd birthday and was much the lighter man. Quite sensibly, Bill Richmond's strategy was to avoid being hit and to tire his opponent out. He did it so successfully that no blow of any kind was landed for 20 minutes, and Tom Cribb seemed unable to go in and finish him off. Tom Cribb never liked Bill Richmond after this; it had been too humiliating, even though he had eventually won after an hour and a half.[22]

Captain Barclay decided to take control of Tom Cribb, and within weeks of Fletcher Reid's death had offered 200 guineas for Tom Cribb to fight Jem Belcher.[23] In March he took the unprecedented step of taking Cribb to Kent to train him personally. Never before had a patron and gentleman of the Fancy rolled up his sleeves and trained his own athlete. It was not a championship fight, however. Jem Belcher was no longer the Champion and Tom Cribb wasn't even a leading contender. Jem Belcher, out of gaol again, agreed to the fight because he knew he had to rediscover his winning ways if he ever expected to regain the title. He was, nevertheless, incensed that he had been matched against such a lacklustre fighter as Tom Cribb.[24]

The fight took place on Tuesday 8 April 1807 at Moulsey Hurst. Captain Barclay's new position in the Fancy was sealed when he took the Duke of Clarence to the fight in his drag.[25] The Duke of Clarence was very popular among the Fancy, partly because he was the King's third son and partly because his house at nearby Bushey Park was near to Moulsey Hurst, and so gave a measure of protection against over-zealous law-enforcement officers. He was also popular because of, or despite, his coarse language, a huge fund of dirty stories, uncouth behaviour and his liaison with Mrs Jordan, the best known actress in England, who two weeks before the fight, gave birth to Amelia, their tenth child.[26]

Tom Cribb, the heavier of the two fighters by 30 lbs, astonished the experts with his new technique and ring sense and he won the fight in 41 minutes. Jem Belcher damaged his right hand in the 16th round, and thereafter fought not only one-eyed, but one-handed.[27] It was a day when strength, endurance and doggedness overcame speed, skill and flair, but it was a close thing. Both men were almost too exhausted to stand at the end.

The solution to the Barclay/Wood stand-off emerged soon after the Belcher–Cribb fight. It was agreed that the ultimate test to decide the pedestrian championship would be a 24-hour race.[28] Captain Barclay's reluctance to agree a wager with Wood was well known, but his status in the Fancy required him to settle the matter between Wood and himself, just as they would have expected mutual challenges to a duel to be settled. But there were difficulties. Abraham Wood was not a fellow gentleman, and, surprisingly, no gentleman came forward to back him or to guarantee his money.

Captain Barclay was now at the centre of the Fancy's affairs and was as much involved in the Prize Ring as with his own pedestrian events. At the end of July he acted as an umpire to Tom Belcher, Jem Belcher's youngest brother, in a fight against Dutch Sam, whose umpire was the Hon. Keppel Berkeley Craven. The deciding 'referee was the great eccentric and famous epicure Twistleton Fiennes, known more formally as Lord Say and Sele. This was a major celebrity event, even though it was between two relative lightweights who would never be heavy enough to fight for the Championship. Once again it was held at Moulsey Hurst, and was patronised by the Duke of Clarence. *The Sporting Magazine* reported that 'one-fifth of the court calendar' were present.[29]

In round 34, well behind in the fight already, Tom Belcher lost balance and fell to his knees as he delivered a blow. At that moment Dutch Sam's return punch struck him. Cries of 'foul' filled the air. It was generally acknowledged that Dutch Sam had intended to hit his opponent while he was still standing. Gentleman Jackson, in his usual way, advised the umpires that it was fair. His judgement was that Tom Belcher was not 'down' when Dutch Sam's blow struck, only 'on his way down'. To be truly 'down', his knees and at least one hand would have to be on the floor. Ninety-nine times out of 100 the umpires would have accepted this interpretation, but there was a difficulty. James Broughton's 1743 rules stated that 'no person is to hit his adversary when he is down' and that 'a man on his knees to be reckoned down'. It seemed clear enough. Berkeley Craven accepted Gentleman Jackson's recommendation based on his judgement; Captain Barclay would accept only the letter of Broughton's rules. This was a very unusual situation. It was very rare for the umpires not to agree. Agreeing in such circumstances was part of their gentlemanly code.

The difficulty arose because the original Broughton rules were based on an assumption that as a matter of honour and manly pride no boxer would ever go down voluntarily. Going down in the ring was a sign that you had been overcome and had, at least temporarily, succumbed to your opponent. But after Broughton's time, men with a different personal and moral code came into the ring. They were willing to go down strategically. It was called 'dropping'. A round ended when a man went down, and by dropping they could bring the round to an end whenever they needed a breather, or if they had delivered a blow and wanted to avoid a return punch. When winning was more important than personal pride or honour, any tactic could be justified. This had been a problem for years. Even Mendoza and Bill Warr had introduced an additional Article of Agreement for their Championship fight in 1792 to cover it. Over the years fight officials and rule interpreters such as Gentleman Jackson were forced to a far stricter interpretation of what was 'down' than Broughton had ever envisaged in his rules.

The final say was given to Twistleton Fiennes, the deciding referee. He made matters worse by declining to make a decision, so Archibald Duke of Hamilton was called on to decide. It was his view that the role of the referee was to bring the two umpires to a decision that both could accept, not to overrule one of them. Captain Barclay, however, would not budge, so the Duke of Hamilton, too, refused to make a decision.[30] So, for almost the first time in Prize Ring history, he had to declare a drawn fight. All bets were void and the two men would have to do it all over again.

Less than a fortnight later, on Friday 7 August, the Fancy gathered again at Brighton Races for four days of racing and festivities to celebrate the Prince of Wales's birthday. The Prince of Wales rode to the races on horseback, and the Duke of Clarence watched them from the Hill, not this time in Captain Barclay's carriage, but in Mrs Fitzherbert's. In the evening the Princes entertained 'a numerous party' in the Pavilion. The racing was a prelude to a celebratory grand review on the race course. At midday precisely the Prince of Wales and the Duke of Clarence reviewed the 1st, 3rd and three troops of 14th Light Dragoons, the Berkshire and 2nd Somerset, Cheshire and South Gloucester Militias, and the Horse and Foot Artillery, who had been gathered there for three hours in readiness for the colourful affair.[31] Among all this activity Captain Barclay had meetings about the proposed 24-hour event with Abraham Wood with a publican from Spitalfields, who was the token gentleman appointed to agree the money and terms on Abraham Wood's behalf.[32] The size of the wager was not disclosed, but was variously described by people who claimed to know, as for 200, 300, 500 and 600 guineas a side. The other details were clearer. The event would take place on Monday 12 October at Newmarket on the first day of the Second October Race Meeting. They were both to go on foot for 24 hours, and the winner would be the one who covered the greatest distance. But there was an unexpected clause in the agreement: Abraham Wood was to give Captain Barclay a 20-mile start.

Another major sporting event was arranged to take place two days later at Newmarket. It was the fight to fill the vacant Championship of the Prize Ring. So the Fancy had put in place an unprecedented mid-October sporting festival of three major events at Newmarket. The Second October Race Meeting, Captain Barclay *v.* Abraham Wood to decide the Pedestrian Championship, and a Championship Fight. The fight was to be between John Gully and Bob Gregson, a huge, powerful newcomer from Lancashire, coming in as a substitute for the Game Chicken, now that it was obvious he was no longer in condition to fight again.

This was the most important wager of Captain Barclay's life so far, and there were only eight weeks to go. It was time to abandon the bad air and endless temptations of London and move to a more remote training venue. He decided on an area on the South Downs that he had criss-crossed on foot many times when he lived at Mrs Gearing's drug shop, Eastdean, about eight miles away, and just inland from Beachy Head. The air was the best in the country, and the downs would be springy under foot and easy on the legs for all that training.[33] It was also ideally placed for some sea bathing, an important new ingredient of training he intended to try.

Captain Barclay took Bill Warr to Eastdean to help him with his training, and John Gully joined them to prepare for his fight with Gregson. Tom Belcher came for a week or two to finish his preparation for his re-match with Dutch Sam. Captain Barclay enlisted Tom Cribb to help the other fighters with their sparring. William Cross was also there, of course, to look after Captain Barclay. This had now become a fully fledged athletes' training camp, one of the first of its kind anywhere. It was partly financed by Captain Barclay and partly by the Hon. Berkeley Craven and the Marquis of Tweedale. Not to be outdone, the opposition set up an athletes' training camp of their own, 17 miles away at Brighton. Here, there was Abraham Wood, Bob Gregson, Harry Lee, a well-known trainer and boxing second, and Bill Richmond. They were financed by rival Fancy members, Major Morgan and Captain Harry Mellish.[34] There was a strong regional flavour to these impending events: both Wood and Gregson were Lancastrians, Bill Richmond had links with York and Harry Mellish was from Yorkshire. In Captain Barclay's camp, the other four athletes were all Bristolians. The two forthcoming events were virtually the North v. the South. It added extra spice to the occasion, and the whole country took sides.

From early in the morning Captain Barclay, John Gully and Tom Cribb could be seen running, walking and sparring on the downs.

They were all big men with huge appetites. Every day Captain Barclay ate two or three pounds of beef steak for breakfast alone. Keeping them supplied with food was a major job, and business at Smith's Shop increased greatly. The Barclay training camp made a big impact and at first the locals came out to watch them. But, as August slipped into September the locals learned that these London-based athletes could be loud and high-spirited and liked throwing their weight around and so gave them a wide berth.

One morning, John Gully and Tom Cribb were out training, dressed in country smocks, when they came across a couple of well-built local farm labourers. Tom Cribb picked a fight with one of them and sent him running with a sore head and a bloody nose, followed closely by his friend. The pretext was that the local man was 'mistreating a pig' and needed to be taught a lesson.[35] A more likely explanation was that the two trained prize-fighters liked to take advantage of their skill and fitness to lord it over the locals. Even the act of dressing up in smocks was suspicious. The local farmers commonly wore smocks but they were not normal wear for such city-dwellers as John Gully and Tom Cribb.

Those who were anxious to put money on the event looked for clues to the athletes' current form, but the training camps deliberately suppressed or distorted information to manipulate the betting. Nevertheless it was reported that Captain Barclay's race fitness was so good he could jog 84 miles in 12 hours. Even allowing for rests, this must have meant he could complete 130 miles in 24 hours. And the news from the Abraham Wood camp was that he had recently run 50 miles in only seven hours and looked relaxed and impressive.[36] There was another story that he had also completed a 100-mile time trial and felt so fresh he wanted to go on and do another 50.[37] Most of the gossip suggested that Abraham Wood should win, but there was a general nervousness about betting against Captain Barclay.

In the middle of September the betting was:

Evens:          on Captain Barclay going 130 miles

| Evens: | on Captain Barclay going more than 100 miles in the first 19 hours |
|---|---|
| 6 to 4: | on Abraham Wood being the favourite during the first 5 hours of the race |
| 100 to 90: | on Abraham Wood winning and covering more than 20 miles further than Captain Barclay.[38] |

Could Abraham Wood really complete 150 miles on foot in 24 hours?

With a little over a fortnight to go Captain Barclay and Bill Warr left their training camp and walked the 115 miles to Newmarket. On walks like this Captain Barclay always kept to the main coaching roads, or 'the great and direct roads', as they were called. They had better surfaces to walk on and had a choice of good inns, and he especially appreciated their well-stocked larders and cellars. On his walk to Newmarket he and Bill Warr stopped at the Coach and Horses at Newport, just past Stansted in Essex. To keep his strength up Captain Barclay ordered an 8 lb leg of underdone mutton which he devoured, to the bone, in only ten minutes.[39] They arrived at Newmarket, tired but not hungry, on Thursday 1 October, one week ahead of Abraham Wood.

The crowds were already gathering, and even a week before the races, the town was so full that new arrivals had to look for accommodation ten miles away. In the days before the race, newcomers, whatever their rank, had to pay handsomely to get a space to sleep in a hay loft. The newspapers reminded their readers that Abraham Wood was 'acknowledged the first goer of a long distance ever known, his performances having by far exceeded what was ever done by the noted Powell'.[40] With one week to go Abraham Wood was still favourite and was backed to go 100 miles in 16 hours.

In the days before the match, however, Captain Barclay's friends put such large sums on him that the betting began to turn around. Thousands of pounds changed hands in the Newmarket streets and taverns and most of it for Captain Barclay. How could his supporters be so certain of success? What did they know? Was the race fixed?

Even *The Times* reported that there was 'a suspicion that there would not be fair play' and on the eve of the race 10 to 1 was offered that it would be called off because of it.[41]

But still the people came, men and women of all ranks and all ages. Newmarket was used to crowds, but not like this. 'Such was the anxiety caused by the wonderful undertaking of the pedestrians, that the company poured into the town in a manner that can be only compared to Brentford at an election.'[42] Harry Angelo, the fencing master, aged 51, in his anxiety to be there, decided to walk the 50 miles from London. The 19-year-old Lord Byron, still smug from seeing his *Hours of Idleness* in all the London bookshops, came over with friends in a barouche-and-four from Cambridge. One of his companions was Theodore Hook, also 19, who within a few years would run the *John Bull*, the most popular and sometimes outrageous Sunday newspaper of its time.[43] 'No fair was ever more crowded,' said *The Morning Herald*.[44]

Fortunately for the assembled masses, those who had bet that the race would not take place, lost their money, for at 8 a.m. precisely on Monday 12 October Captain Barclay and Abraham Wood set off.[45] It had, however, been touch and go. As late as the day before, there was no agreement even about where the course would be. When Captain Barclay had arrived in Newmarket two weeks before, he set about finalising his plans, just as he had six years earlier on Barmby Moor. The course he decided on was a one-mile stretch of turf on Newmarket race course on the Beacon Course. Once again he organised lighting, and even went further, arranging for the course to be covered with a mile-long awning to keep him dry. When Abraham Wood arrived, he decided on a different course, a three-mile stretch of turf about a mile away.[46] Up to the final day, the wager was planned to take place on two courses, both lit up, both lined with tents, booths and flags, but separate and independent of each other. In more senses than one it was an indication of how far apart the two rival camps were, how little they communicated and how little common ground they shared. Fortunately, there were last-minute negotiations behind the scenes and a compromise was reached whereby neither man used his chosen course. Instead, they agreed to a measured mile of gently sloping grass alongside the London Road and on the opposite side to the race course. It was rolled and lined and roped off to keep the spectators at bay. A sturdy post marked the start, and there were marquees on either side, each with a sofa, one marquee for Captain Barclay and one for Abraham Wood.[47] At the alloted time, the marshals, recorders and two timekeepers were also in their places. They were given the two watches that Mr Bramble, the watchmaker from Oxford Street, had specially selected and regulated.

Surprisingly, the athletes were dressed alike in white flannel jackets, flannel shorts down to the knee, flannel socks, a small handkerchief tied loosely round the neck and light shoes on their feet. On the command 'Time', they set off. The betting ranged from 3 to 1, to 5 to 2 on Captain Barclay. There were whispers, however, that he was *certain* to win, and so very few people would take any odds.

Wood went off 'with considerable velocity'. After five minutes, he was nearly 300 yards ahead. After half an hour, a mile ahead, and after an hour, two miles. Captain Barclay settled into a steady rhythm covering six miles in the hour. At 11 a.m. Captain Barclay completed 18 miles and went to his marquee for some warm fowl. Sixteen minutes later Wood went into his tent for five minutes for his refreshment. He had completed 22 miles and was four miles ahead. The whispers that the race was fixed and that Captain Barclay was certain to win began to subside. Wood was gaining ground on Captain Barclay at the rate of one mile every hour. At this rate he would win by five miles. The odds in favour of Captain Barclay reduced to 7 to 4. After four hours Captain Barclay went in for his second refreshment. He was still covering his six miles every hour, but since his break Abraham Wood had begun to look sluggish and to slow down. A mile and a half later he went back to his marquee and lay down on the sofa for ten minutes, looking exhausted. Captain Barclay continued with the metronome regularity he started with. One mile every ten minutes with no variation. The crowd began to buzz. Men rushed up and down passing on the news and trying to get the full story. Meanwhile, there was consternation in Abraham Wood's marquee. Harry Lee rubbed Wood's feet and ankles and sent him out again, this time without his shoes. He often ran bare-footed, but it was a mistake and he cut his feet and had to return to put his shoes on again. After five hours he was gaining no ground on Captain Barclay, and after six, was actually losing it. Rumour and counter-rumour surged through the crowd. Twenty minutes later. Wood returned again to his marquee and two surgeons were called. Then came the announcement: 'Abraham Wood has resigned the match.'[48]

Those who went to collect their winnings were greeted with anger and indignation. The bets would not be paid. There had been trickery. It was unfair. Someone was to blame. Wild rumours flew around: Wood had been taken ill – he had complained of sickness and spasms in his stomach – doctors had been called and had bled him – on Wednesday morning his life was in great danger, and in the evening Captain Barclay went 'and spoke to him with great feeling' – Wood smiled and the two athletes shook hands – shortly after, at 9 p.m., Abraham Wood died – the post-mortem was due on Thursday.[49] All these stories had to be revised when, two days later, he turned up at the Championship fight between Gully and Gregson, looking well.[50] The people were confused and angry. They had been cheated out of their race and they needed a culprit. They decided that it should be Abraham Wood, and in the words of the *Sporting Magazine*, he 'received rough usage' from the crowd.[51] Later, at a public house at Cambridge, drinkers put out the lights when they discovered he was there, and after a scuffle, kicked him out. Captain Barclay fared better and was received as the injured party.

In the Championship fight, John Gully won a desperate contest and was confirmed as the Champion of the Prize Ring. Both Gully and Gregson had fought to the limit of their endurance and were so battered and damaged that there was serious concern about both of them. Jem Belcher 'cried like a child' at John Gully's condition, and he was the winner! After the fight, as Gully lay almost lifeless in Captain Barclay's carriage, Bob Gregson was brought over so the two men could shake hands.[52] Honour demanded that animosity was not maintained to death.

The following day at the races, Captain Barclay drove John Gully and Bob Gregson round the course to receive the applause of the crowd, but Gregson was not well enough to stay long. For these few days at Newmarket Captain Barclay played the role of the all-conquering hero. He had defeated Wood and had been on the winning side against the northerners, twice.

Fortunately for Bob Gregson, he had a good constitution and healed quickly. In less than six weeks he was posing naked alongside the newly arrived Elgin Marbles. Artists and gentlemen of the Fancy paid up to a guinea each to see first hand how well the physiques of the best British athletes compared with those of Classical antiquity.[53]

But the controversy about the Barclay–Wood race raged on. At Newmarket, virtually everyone, and particularly Captain Barclay's fellow gentlemen of the Fancy, blamed Abraham Wood and the publican from Spitalfields for the fiasco. The papers were quick to point out that the publican had personally stood £150 of Wood's stake money, but had never before risked more than £20 on anything uncertain.[54] The consensus at Newmarket was that Wood had deliberately 'thrown over' the race. In London, however, the gentlemen were unconvinced and most refused to pay. Why would Wood's supporters knobble their own man? Was it not Captain Barclay and his followers who stood to gain the most? How could the rumours before the race be explained? Something had clearly been planned and known of long before the event began. Such an episode was a threat to sport itself. They referred the matter to Tattersall's at Hyde Park Corner, the London headquarters of the Jockey Club, a mixture of gentleman's club, coffee room and tavern, which managed to retain an air of elegance, and where ungentlemanly conduct was never tolerated. Merely 'smoking in the room', or making a noise or disturbance was enough to get the miscreant expelled.[55] It was common for bets to be laid and fortunes to change hands at Tattersall's and controversies were also decided there.

They better than anyone knew the racing and gambling business. It was there that the gentlemen of the Jockey Club went to consider the evidence.

Their conclusion, which was final and binding, gave a new slant to things. The bets, they ruled, ought not to be paid. Wood was exonerated; he was the victim not the culprit. An eyewitness reported that when Wood left his marquee after 22 miles he 'wasn't worth a farthing'. Someone had slipped 'a prepared liquid, alias laudanum' into his drink.[56] But who? One of Wood's 'friends'? One of Captain Barclay's friends? Did Captain Barclay know? Who knew about drugs? Who would act in such an ungentlemanly manner? The episode caused bad blood within the Fancy and there were complaints that it led to a loss of confidence in their system and brought sport into disrepute. The newspapers, however, were quick to state that there was no collusion between Captain Barclay and Abraham Wood, and that Captain Barclay was personally blameless.

The gentlemen of the Fancy were, nevertheless, acutely dissatisfied, and it did not take long for the tide of opinion to turn against Captain Barclay. How could he be considered the champion pedestrian? Had he not already admitted his inferiority to Abraham Wood by accepting a 20-mile start? The *Sporting Magazine* put it this way: 'the laurel of England is not to be won by the Captain without winning it at a dearer rate'.[57]

So, Captain Barclay lost his preeminence in the Fancy and was not the Champion pedestrian. Some of the aggrieved Northern gentlemen looked round for another candidate. They found a man with the perfect name, Lieutenant Fairman of the Royal Lancashire Militia. Fairman was a small man, only 5'4" tall and weighing 9 stone. Almost at once he turned the tables on Captain Barclay. If Captain Barclay wanted to be considered the Champion pedestrian he should give his opponent 20 miles start – particularly as his opponent was as small and wiry as Captain Barclay was big and strong. Captain Barclay travelled back to Ury in a surly mood. No, he did not agree to give Fairman a 20-mile start. Correspondence between them went back and forth for three months. If Captain Barclay would not agree to a 24-hour race giving away 20 miles, perhaps he would agree to a 500-mile race? He didn't. Instead Captain Barclay proposed a race at Ury over any distance from 50 to 100 miles for a stake that he would nominate. As expected, Fairman rejected such a one-sided proposal. Fairman stipulated that the race must be midway between Scotland and London. York perhaps? The sum to be between £500 and £5,000. Captain Barclay did not agree. Then, as an inducement, Fairman promised that if he beat Captain Barclay with a 20-mile start he would race him again over 24 hours on even terms.[58] Still stalemate.

Bold Webster reentered the scene and offered to back Lieutenant Fairman for 1,000 guineas against any gentleman, with an additional side-bet that whoever stopped first to refresh himself would lose half his stake.[59] Captain Barclay was known to like his refreshment. Still no agreement. While Captain Barclay was still away at Ury, the frustrated Northern camp arranged for Lieutenant Fairman to perform a very public 20-mile match from Marble Arch to Harrow and back. Captain Barclay had generated so much publicity for pedestrians that, even without him, the event attracted huge crowds. From Oxford Street to Paddington they packed in, stood on carts and carriages and hung out of windows to get a glimpse. Ladies waved their handkerchiefs and the men cheered. A crowd of horsemen surrounded Fairman, as earlier they had surrounded Captain Barclay, and they and Big Bob Gregson, now fully recovered, tried to keep the way clear.[60] After winning by four minutes, Lieutenant Fairman, backed by Bold Webster, delivered the *coup de grâce*. He offered to run:

1. Any man in the kingdom – on the same terms as Barclay had Wood;
2. Any gentleman of his own stature – 100 miles, for 1,000 guineas;
3. Any man in the world – the winner being the one who went the furthest without refreshment.[61]

Captain Barclay had been upstaged, outmanoeuvred and overshadowed. He ignored the challenge, but instead proposed to go 1,000 miles at the rate of 50 miles a day for 20 successive days. Bold Webster believed that achievable, so he ignored it. Another Lancastrian pedestrian, Lieutenant Halifax, then caught the eye of the Fancy with two winning results: 600 miles at the rate of 30 miles a day for 20 days, and in March 1808, a most unusual event: 200 miles at the rate of two miles an hour for 100 hours.[62]

This then, was how the 1,000 miles in 1,000 hours idea was born in the spring of 1808. It was the search for the ultimate test. A thousand miles was that; combined with Bold Webster's challenge two years earlier for someone to attempt a mile an hour for 100 hours. The greatest test of all, over which, surely, there could be no dispute, would be a mile an hour for 1,000 hours.

In the autumn of that year Captain Barclay arranged for George Mollison to walk a mile an hour for eight days in secret at Ury.[63] The event would be so important to Captain Barclay's reputation and his purse that he resigned his commission with the Royal Welch Fusiliers to give himself the time and freedom he needed to prepare. The difficult part was to know how to train for it. George Mollison's walk had shown that the limiting factor was not speed or strength – it was broken sleep. Before finally deciding on the event Captain Barclay gave himself a trial. He was staying with Murray Farquarson, lieutenant colonel of the neighbouring Aberdeen Militia, at his house at Allannore, beyond Braemar. It was August with very long days and short nights. By 5 a.m. Captain Barclay was up and out for a day of grouse-shooting which did not finish till 5 p.m. He estimated that he covered 30 miles. After dinner he set out for Ury, walking all night. It was close to 60 miles and took him eleven hours, arriving home in the morning. With no sleep, he spent the next day walking around Ury and Stonehaven conducting his normal business, and in the afternoon walked to a ball in Laurencekirk, 16 miles away. The dancing and festivities did not let up till 3.30 a.m. when he set off once more to walk home. He arrived at Ury about 7 a.m. He had had no sleep for two nights. He then took a gun into the fields and spent the third day shooting partridges. In total he spent three days in continual activity and had two nights without sleep.[64] Almost incidentally he calculated that he must have covered at least 130 miles, but that was the least important part of it. He confirmed to himself that he could manage without sleep – that was what mattered.

In October he agreed the bet with Bold Webster. He would go on foot 1,000 miles in 1,000 successive hours for 1,000 guineas. The whole country waited impatiently for nearly eight months. Then they made their way, once again in their thousands, to Newmarket in the summer of 1809 to witness the drama.

Captain Barclay's overwhelming success there secured his reputation and fame for ever.

# CHAPTER EIGHT

# Bravo — Barclay For Ever

*He [Captain Barclay] suffered no injury ... and returned home in perfect health.*

WALTER THOM, *PEDESTRIANISM*, 1813

*Capt Barclay, by a science of training peculiar to himself, had reduced Crib ... by Scots living; but ... kept his stamina pure.*

*THE ST JAMES'S CHRONICLE*, 28 SEPT – 1 OCT 1811

*Bravo — Barclay for ever.*
*Bravo, Cap'n — Hurra.*
*Crib and Barclay for ever.*

THOMAS TEGG, 1811

*T*here cannot have been a single soldier among the 40,000 that left for Walcheran who did not know of Captain Barclay's exploits. Not one who did not know he was rich and famous. Nor can there have been a single one who did not know that their expedition had lost time and the benefit of surprise — most of the country knew it. They would have been shocked however, to know that within two months the force would return, having failed ignominiously. On their return to the ports of Ramsgate and Deal the cemeteries were piled high with bodies, and makeshift reception centres and hospitals were set up to take the tide of sick and disabled soldiers, many of whom were carried in by colleagues little better than themselves. Six months later, the official returns (less one battalion that had not submitted), showed that of the 40,000 men that set sail 11,513 were still sick, 3,960 were dead (but not from action), 106 were killed in action, 84 had deserted and 25 were discharged.[1] A loss to the British army of nearly 40 per cent of the force.

The consequences of this failure were as far-ranging and spectacular as the failure itself. The War Minister, Lord Castlereagh, resigned and challenged the Foreign Secretary, George Canning, to a duel on Putney Heath, in which the War Minister wounded the Foreign Secretary in the thigh with his second shot. The Prime Minister, the Duke of Portland, resigned, and Spencer Percival, a small, easy-going, polite man, became Prime Minister to lead Britain against the increasingly dominant Napoleon Bonaparte.

The expedition had been doomed from the start, partly because of a clash of ambition and a split in the Cabinet in Westminster. Lord Castlereagh was responsible for planning the expedition, and George Canning had some responsibility for assembling and staffing it, but because of their personal rivalry there was little meaningful co-operation between them. In addition, the expedition's commanding officer was Major General John Pitt, Earl of Chatham, a leisurely 52-year-old with gentlemanly manners and an undistinguished military career. His time-keeping was so notoriously bad he was known as 'the late Lord Chatham'. On one occasion at Walcheran, when the

Marquis of Huntly sent to him for further orders, he had to wait a week for a reply.

Delay and procrastination played into the hands of two enemies – the second was fever and disease. Walcheran Island was low-lying with a maze of open draining trenches and ditches, and the French had time to breach the sea walls to let sea water in to swamp the land. The weather was hot, humid and rainy, and the combination of heat, humidity, rotting vegetation and stagnant water sent up a thick, evil-smelling mist everywhere. Very quickly miasmatic fever struck the troops, followed by a combination of malaria, dysentery, typhoid and typhus. 'Walcheran fever,' a form of malaria that continually recurred, struck down the men. It was so widespread that Wellington later requested that no battalions from the Walcheran expedition be sent to fight in the Peninsular Wars.[2] Captain Barclay, however, claimed to be 'in perfect health', when he returned to Britain in September 1809, and to have 'suffered no injury from the climate of Walcheran'.[3]

Claiming to have survived the expedition unscathed was perhaps the only boast that anyone could make on return from Walcheran. Sympathy for being the victims of others' incompetence was reserved for the rank and file. There was little or none of that for the officers. Captain Barclay did not return in disgrace personally, but he needed to put it behind him, and he decided to restrict himself in future to nothing more than his local militia. His military career was effectively over, and he had never once had the opportunity to use his famed determination, or his great physical strength and fitness in action.

Captain Barclay returned to London, where he lingered for several weeks picking up the threads of his old sporting life. He heard for the first time of the fever of imitation that had followed his 1,000 miles in 1,000 hours, before he had even left for Walcheran. Within days of his success at Newmarket, the newspapers had reported at least two new attempts, one by a fat man from Bond Street that was destined to fail even before it started. Others followed rapidly. An ambitious attempt by a man from Somerset, known as John Bull, to go one and a half miles an hour for 1,000 hours was announced.[4] Not to be outdone, a Scottish clergyman attempted to read six chapters of the Bible every hour for 1,000 hours,[5] and another member of the non-athletic fraternity set out on the daunting task of eating a sausage every hour for 1,000 hours.[6] All failed, and some didn't even begin. The sausage wager failed by 997 hours.

When Captain Barclay eventually felt ready to go home to Ury in the late autumn of 1809, he did so by driving the mail coach on every stage of the journey from London to Dundee, a distance of over 400 miles. Then he walked the remaining 17 miles to Ury.[7] The message was clear: he had returned unaffected by Walcheran fever and was as fit and strong as ever. Sadly, this was not true of everyone. In his absence, his sister Cameron had died at the age of 31. The Game Chicken had succumbed to consumption, also aged 31, and his old sporting friend and ex-Bristolian, Bill Warr, had also died.

Captain Barclay stayed at Ury for nine months, longer than for many years, and long enough to re-establish himself among the local landowners as a respectable gentleman farmer. He played the part of Laird of Ury well, for the first time in years paying attention to the business of the estate and to local affairs. There was even a rare happy family occasion when his sister Mag married the wealthy Hudson Gurney from Norwich.[8] In November 1809 S. W. Fores published a coloured engraving of him by Williams, to add to the others by Robert Dighton and Thomas Rowlandson. He was a regular churchgoer, was elected to membership of the Highland and Agricultural Society of Scotland,[9] sold some of his Allardice land and arranged to hire fields at Ury for the Kincardineshire Militia's 22 days of permanent training.[10] As lieutenant colonel he oversaw this training and earned £350.00.2 in the process.

London and the sporting life of the Fancy, were never far from Captain Barclay's thoughts, though, and in the early summer of 1810 he returned to the capital. One of the items of gossip was the arrival of the 'American Champion', who was staying at the Horse and Dolphin, south of Leicester Square, where Bill Richmond was the landlord. His name was Tom Molineux, a 26-year-old black fighter who stood 5'9" tall and was well muscled, weighing about 13 ½ stone. The story was that he had gained his freedom from slavery by winning a fight that saved his owner, Mr Algernon Molineux of Virginia, a large sum of money wagered, potentially injudiciously, under the influence of drink. His grateful owner gave him not only his freedom but $500 with which Tom Molineux made his way to London.[11]

It was arranged for him to exhibit his skills in Jackson's Rooms, and for Captain Barclay to try him out. The encounter with the newcomer was looked forward to with unusual interest. It became the talk of London and the subject of rumour and counter-rumour for years. Apparently, on the day of their meeting Captain Barclay arrived at Jackson's Rooms somewhat late, to find Tom Molineux already changed and wearing Captain Barclay's own mufflers or boxing gloves, a special thinly padded pair of gloves that delivered a harder blow than properly padded mufflers would allow. Someone must have put Tom Molineux up to it. With the aid of Captain Barclay's less-than-legal gloves Tom Molineux floored Captain Barclay with a powerful body blow that broke his ribs.[12] Maybe Captain Barclay was rusty after a year's inactivity, maybe Walcheran had left its mark after all. Or maybe Tom Molineux was a very tough customer indeed.

The story was at least founded on fact. Captain Barclay did spar with Tom Molineux in Jackson's Rooms, and he almost certainly kept a pair of battered and battle-scarred gloves there. Perhaps he should have been more scrupulous when he realised the padding was getting thin. But everyone knew that Gentleman Jackson would never have permitted a deliberately illegal pair of gloves to be kept in his rooms and certainly not a pair so blatantly dishonest as the rumourmongers were describing. They said that the gloves contained a horseshoe or some other piece of iron.

This was the second time that rumour and innuendo had associated Captain Barclay with cheating on a serious scale. He clearly had his enemies. His single-minded determination to succeed was sometimes difficult for people to understand, and was not a characteristic that made everyone warm to him. Was he so ruthless he would stoop to any underhand trick? Would he really stop at nothing? Some clearly thought so. All the versions of the story of Captain Barclay's encounter with Tom Molineux in Jackson's Rooms agreed that Captain Barclay left there with broken ribs. Tom Molineux and his mentor Bill Richmond had added to the embarrassment and humiliation of Walcheran.

It was not in Captain Barclay's nature to disregard such things, and he left London uncharacteristically swiftly afterwards. Not, however, before he had instructed Tom Cribb to keep an eye on the newcomer. John Gully had retired from fighting, and Tom Cribb was now recognised as the Champion. It was obvious after this showing that Molineux would find backers in London and that he might challenge for the Championship.

Back in Scotland, Captain Barclay got the news of Tom Molineux's first official fight. It was against Burrows of Bristol; no one ever did know his first name. Bill Richmond raised the £50 stake and was Molineux's second in the ring. Tom Cribb seconded Burrows. It was one of the conventions of the Prize Ring that the second conceded defeat on behalf of the fighter when he could not get him back to scratch to start a new round. This doubtful honour fell to Tom Cribb after 65 minutes. There was never any real doubt that Molineux would win, but Tom Cribb lost his composure after the fight and picked a quarrel with Bill Richmond over an alleged foul punch during the fight. The two men quickly came to blows.[13] Undignified behaviour indeed, but Cribb had disliked Richmond ever since Richmond had humiliated him by dancing around him in the ring for 20 minutes in their fight in 1805, defying Cribb to land a punch. Captain Barclay and Tom Cribb both had a score to settle.

In August, news made its way to Ury of Molineux's second fight, this time against Tom Blake, known, at least before the fight, as 'Tom Tough', but perhaps not afterwards. Molineux won easily in eight rounds. Once again Bill Richmond seconded Molineux, and once again it fell to Tom Cribb as his opponent's second, to concede defeat.[14]

It was, of course, not merely that a stranger had entered the arena and innocently been drawn into the camp of the 'enemy'. Tom Molineux was black. After Molineux's victory over Tom Blake, Blake turned to Tom Cribb, his second, and said, 'Tom, I don't mind being licked by you, but to think that I should have been beaten by that black thief!'[15] (Cribb had defeated Tom Blake in 1805.) He knew these sentiments were guaranteed a good reception from Tom Cribb. Whether Tom Cribb had a prejudice against all black fighters or whether he simply transferred his personal dislike of Bill Richmond to his new protégé is impossible to tell, but Tom Molineux had walked into the centre of other people's animosity.

While all this was going on, and the Fancy talked of Tom Molineux challenging for the Championship, technically there was no champion at all. After John Gully had retired in May 1808, the title descended to Tom Cribb. Under Captain Barclay's guidance he defended his title successfully in a second fight against the one-eyed Jem Belcher on Epsom Downs in February 1809, but immediately after it announced his own retirement from the ring. In recognition of his year as champion, he was presented with a flamboyant belt made of lion's skin and with silver claws.[16] Bill Richmond knew that Tom Molineux could now seize the initiative. So, a few weeks after Molineux's victory over Tom Blake, Molineux issued a challenge to any man in England to fight for the Championship. This was too much for Tom Cribb and Captain Barclay. Neither was able to stand back and watch Bill Richmond and Tom Molineux succeed. An angry and indignant Tom Cribb came out of retirement. One newspaper put it this way:

Some persons feel alarmed at the bare idea that a black man and a foreigner should seize the championship of England, and decorate his sable brow with the hard-earned laurels of Cribb. He must, however, have his fair chance, though Tom swears that, for the honour of old England 'He'll be d///d if he will relinquish a single sprig except with his life.'[17]

This was in September 1810, and Captain Barclay was still in Scotland 500 miles away from all this commotion, caught in a situation where honour demanded he should stay: the Marquis of Huntly had asked him to take over as Master of the Turriff Hunt. A request from the Marquis of Huntly was an honour not to be turned down.[18] So, from mid-October 1810 to early April 1811, Captain Barclay, Master of the Turriff Hunt, could not return to London.

The risks and hazards of following the fox-hounds suited the Fancy perfectly. A long run tested the wind and resolve, and high fences and open streams tested nerve and mettle of horse and rider for all to see. For those approaching a daunting barrier, the advice was to throw your heart over first and the rest would follow. Wellington believed that men who hunted regularly made the best soldiers. Twice a week that winter Captain Barclay got up very early to ride the 51 miles from Ury to Turriff in the dark before breakfast. On a typical day, he attended the hounds to cover, often 15 miles from their kennels, and then followed the hounds for 20 to 25 miles. Afterwards, he returned the pack of hounds to their kennels with his huntsman John Craik (pronounced Crack by the locals). He then had dinner and rode the 51 miles back to Ury, again in the dark, arriving, if he was lucky, about 11 o'clock at night. On average he must have ridden 150 miles and been away from Ury for 21 hours at a stretch. It was a tough physical regime. There are always those who are willing to embellish a story, and they said he *walked* to Turriff twice a week, but this would have been impossible, even for Captain Barclay.

In the week before Christmas 1810 news arrived at Ury of the fight for the Championship between Tom Cribb and Tom Molineux. It took place in torrential rain on Copthall Common near East Grinstead. In Captain Barclay and Bill Warr's absence, Tom Cribb had been supported by Paul Methuen and Lord Stradbroke, and John Gully had helped with his training. But under their benign regime without the firm hand of Captain Barclay, Tom Cribb was overweight and underdisciplined, and swaggered around declaring that Tom Molineux was 'a novice' and that fighting him would be 'child's play'. Even the usually wary Fancy allowed the rhetoric and their prejudice to cloud their judgement and odds were freely laid that Tom Molineux would not last 15 minutes.[19] Ironically, Tom Cribb had often been referred to as 'the black diamond' from the days when he was a coal porter working for Mr Sant, and now his nickname became more popular. Men who bet that Molineux would still be standing against the 'black diamond' after half an hour were considered light-headed.

The day turned out to be awful. It was cold and it rained in torrents. Nevertheless, a good-natured crowd of around 5,000 braved the weather. One eyewitness wrote that the thousands who waded knee-deep in mud for five miles along a clayey road, somehow managed to keep as cheerful as if the fight had been arranged on a bowling green.[20] Lord Hamilton, Lord Stradbroke, Sir Thomas Ap Rhys, Colonel Barton, Daniel Mendoza and John Gully were among the large crowd, and the Prince of Wales sent his man, Jack Radford, to take down a full account. To protect the boxers from the worst of the driving rain John Jackson arranged for the ring to be set up on a stage at the foot of a small hill, but to no avail. Almost as soon as they had stripped, the fighters were soaked to the skin and bitterly cold.

After 15 minutes, Tom Molineux had drawn first blood. At 30 minutes he had a clear advantage. Twenty-five minutes later, however, Bill Richmond, his second, had to concede defeat. But only after some disgraceful scenes that brought no credit on the spectators or the fight officials. The fight on Copthall Common proved to be one of the darkest chapters in the history of British sport.

The problem arose just before the half-hour was up. Tom Molineux was gaining the upper hand and the betting was 6 to 4 in his favour. Cribb was in a vulnerable position. Molineux was on the attack with Cribb trapped on the ropes and in no position to protect himself. The mood of the initially good-natured crowd began to turn. Just before the 30-minute signal, a group of about 200 of Tom Cribb's fans — probably those who had bet that Tom Molineux would not last half an hour — surged forward, broke through the whippers and got on to the stage. With the ring overrun with hostile spectators, the fight came to an immediate halt. In a mêlée such as this no information is reliable, and it is impossible to be certain about the harm that the invading crowd did to Tom Molineux but some versions of the story claimed that one of his fingers was broken. At the very least, it was a terrifying experience. Somehow the fight was restarted. Fifteen minutes later, at the end of the 28th round, both men were carried to their corner. Tom Cribb, as was the custom, sat on John Gully's knee, while old Joe Ward worked to get him ready for round 29. When Sir Thomas Ap Rhys, the referee, called 'Time' after the regulation 30 seconds, Tom Cribb was too exhausted to move. At this moment the fight should have been declared over and victory gone to Tom Molineux. But as a diversionary tactic, Joe Ward rushed across to Bill Richmond and accused him of putting lead bullets in Molineux's fists. Molineux stood, bewildered, in the middle of the ring ready to fight, and was prevailed upon to open his fists to disprove the accusation. Needless to say, there were no lead bullets. But the ruse worked. Tom Cribb had a little more time to recover and Molineux lost his concentration. It was all that was needed to tip the balance. Sir Thomas Ap Rhys had called 'Time' twice more while all this commotion was going on in the ring, but he should have declared the fight over and Tom Molineux the winner. He didn't and Tom Cribb went on to 'win' in just over an hour.[21]

Three days later, a letter addressed to Tom Cribb appeared in the London papers. It was from Tom Molineux and signed with his mark. Its tact, tolerance and generosity were remarkable and put Tom Cribb, Joe Ward and the vast majority of British fight fans to shame.

Sir,
My friends think that had the weather on last Tuesday, the day on which I contended with you, not been so unfavourable, I should have won the battle; I therefore challenge you to a second meeting, at any time within two months, for such a

sum as those gentlemen who place confidence in me may be pleased to arrange.

As it is possible this letter may meet the public eye, I cannot omit the opportunity of expressing a confident hope that the circumstance of my being a different colour to that of a people amongst whom I have sought protection, will not in any way operate to my prejudice.

I am, sir,

Your most obedient humble servant,

T. MOLINEUX

Witness,

J. Schofield.[22]

The Fancy knew that the fight had been unfair and a guilty conscience worried some of them for years. Even ten years later, Daniel Mendoza who was there and saw for himself, wrote: 'In the battle between Cribb and Molineux, it is well known the latter had won three times. Some who had backed Cribb for hundreds, would have taken five pounds, before the battle was decided, for their money; but favouritism prevailed.'[23] And John Wilson, Professor of Moral Philosophy at Edinburgh University, but also, in his youth, a good long jumper and an expert in all things athletic, and known to the public as Christopher North, his pen name when he wrote for Blackwood's Magazine, also wrote years later: 'What Briton will dare say Molineux did not win the first battle with the Champion (Cribb)?'[24]

Tom Cribb, uncertain about winning a rematch, set the minimum purse he was willing to fight for at 500 guineas (250 guineas a side) and so put it out of reach of Richmond and Molineux, who had lost all their cash at Copthall Common. No one from the Fancy came forward to fund them. Tom Cribb 'accepted' Tom Molineux's challenge, knowing that he and Richmond could probably not raise the stake. It worked, and Bill Richmond was forced to look for another fight. It was for 100 guineas, with a newcomer named Heskin Rimmer from Lancashire.[25]

The fight took place on 21 May at Moulsey Hurst, in front of a crowd of 10,000, including, of course, Captain Barclay. In round 16, Tom Molineux hit Rimmer with a tremendous blow to his stomach, which doubled him up and sent him senseless to the floor. The spectators surged forward in such numbers that they overwhelmed the fighters and their seconds. Pierce Egan, the most celebrated of the contemporary sports reporters, wrote: '. . . the ring was broken, owing, it is said, from the antipathy felt against a man of colour proving the conqueror'.[26] But a visiting Frenchman, Louis Simond, saw it differently:

> '. . . A pleasing reflection softened the brutality of this sight; it was the impartiality with which the populace observed the loi de combat, and saw one of their own people thus mauled and bruised by a foreigner and a negro, suffering him to enjoy his triumph unmolested; for the interruption had been a mere ebullition of curiosity and enthusiastic admiration for the art – not ill-will or unfair interference. When I call this collection of people populace, I do not mean that they were all low people; there were no ragged coats in sight, and half the mob were gentlemen.[27]

Whether it was due to 'antipathy' or 'enthusiastic admiration', the interruption lasted 20 minutes, an unnerving delay for any fighter. This time Tom Molineux seemed to benefit by it, as Louis Simond describes:

> . . . The white man seemed still able and stout, but fell like an ox under the club of the butcher at the first round – at the second – and so on, from bad to worse, rising each time with more difficulty. It became a shocking sight. Victory was out of the question, and had been almost from the beginning. His better wind might have afforded him a chance – he had lost it by the interruption. The black was now fresh – . . .[28]

There was no avoiding a rematch now, but Tom Cribb had no enthusiasm for it. He had won £900 from his doubtful victory at Copthall Common and had used it to invest in a new life. He got married, told his wife he would never fight again and bought his own coal business in White Lion Street, Seven Dials, just off Shaftesbury Avenue. He set his price at 600 guineas (300 guineas a side) to push the fight even further beyond Molineux's and Richmond's means. The Fancy disapproved, believing that Cribb must either fight or resign his title. To Captain Barclay and others this was unthinkable. It would mean that Tom Molineux, as the first contender, would almost automatically assume the title of Champion. So, a few days after the Molineux–Rimmer fight, a meeting was organised by Gentleman Jackson at the Horse and Dolphin. Such was the interest that the meeting was attended not only by Cribb, Molineux, Captain Barclay and Bill Richmond, but also by the Marquis of Queensberry, the Earl of Sefton, Lord Archibald Hamilton, Lord Yarmouth, Lord Pomfret, Lord Barrymore, Sir Henry Smyth, Sir Clement Brigg, Sir Bellingham Graham, Sir Francis Baynton, the Hon. Berkeley Craven, General Grosvenor, General Barton, Mr Paul Methuen, Mr Thirlwell Harrison, Mr J. Schofield, and many more. Gentleman Jackson was in the chair.[29]

The compromise they reached was that Tom Cribb and Tom Molineux would fight for 300 guineas a side but only 100 guineas would be deposited with Gentleman Jackson that evening. The remaining 200 guineas a side could wait for another two months. Whereupon Captain Barclay and Bill Richmond each placed 100 guineas on the table for their respective men. Bill Richmond's finances were so low, however, he was forced to borrow most of this from Mr Schofield, the fishmonger from Bond Street. The fight would take place within four months, and not less than 100 miles from London on the Great North Road. The Articles were agreed and signed by Tom Cribb. Tom Molineux gave his mark.[30]

Captain Barclay now took control and decided to train Tom Cribb himself, in Scotland. Tom Cribb had a month to sort out the management of his new coal business and make his peace with his wife. Of the outstanding 200 guineas, 100 guineas was paid by Tom Cribb from his own money, and the remainder was made up by Captain Barclay with contributions from Sir Henry Smyth, Mr Thirlwell Harrison and others. Tom Cribb therefore had a one-third stake in the forthcoming fight, Captain Barclay's share was about 50 per cent and the others had a minor interest. This, of course, was before the betting started. For the fight Captain Barclay again appointed John Gully and old Joe Ward as Cribb's second and bottle-holder. Joe Ward was also detailed to look after their interests in the final negotiations with Bill Richmond over the precise location for the fight, while Captain Barclay was away training Cribb.

Captain Barclay and Tom Cribb's journey north started on Friday 21 June 1811, by easy stages along the Great North Road. They took their time and spent two weeks getting to Ury, visiting friends on the way – a deliberately contrived calm before the storm.[31] They were the two most famous athletes in the country and attracted excitement wherever they went. They were not merely sporting curiosities – they were heroes, and there was an extra bustle at every coaching inn they turned into. Wellington was struggling to establish his superiority in Spain, and Britain had been at war almost without a break for 18 years. Cribb and Barclay were welcomed as much needed proof that British manhood was still the best in the world, and they were greeted with a mixture of curiosity, enthusiasm and awe.

Any calming effects that their leisurely journey north might have produced disappeared once they got to Ury. To Captain Barclay's surprise, he found it was also the home, albeit temporarily, of 900 men of the Kincardineshire Militia who were there for their annual 'permanent' training. Their commandant, Lieutenant Colonel George Harley Drummond, had paid for an area about a mile away to be cleared and levelled to avoid the necessity of hiring fields at Ury, but after it was finished, it was found to be 'totally unfit for the purpose of drilling' and so, at the last minute, two fields at Ury had to be used after all.[32]

Member of Parliament, friend of William Pitt, landowner, agricultural innovator, wrestler and walker, Captain Barclay's father commanded so much respect locally that he became known as the Great Master of Ury.

Robert Barclay Allardice at the age of 19 when he was admitted as a Fellow Commoner to Trinity College, Cambridge. He had already won good money in two successful sporting wagers.

Ury, near Stonehaven in eastern Scotland, was the Barclay family home. Although it looked like an over-large dovecote it was originally built like a fortress and had no front door. The only way in was to be hoisted up to the first floor by rope or in a basket.

Foster Powell's long-distance walking exploits continued into his 50s and he drew large, appreciative crowds wherever he went. Samuel Galton quoted him to the young Robert Barclay Allardice as an example of unattainable sporting excellence.

Daniel Mendoza, the charismatic Jewish fighter who attracted the admiring attention of the Prince of Wales and his circle of fashionable friends. He brought a new level of science and analysis to his sport.

The man with the best physique in Regency Britain, Gentleman John Jackson was the friend and personal trainer of Lord Byron and was a respected spokesman on all the manly sports for over 20 years. The size, proportion and definition of his body became well known through Thomas Lawrence's paintings of him.

After retiring as Champion, Gentleman Jackson joined Harry Angelo, the fencing master, in his rooms at 13 Old Bond Street. The rooms became even more popular and the Prince of Wales, Lord Byron and one third of the peerage flocked there to take lessons from him.

Jem Belcher was a phenomenal athlete with unprecedented speed and a mild and gentle personality. At the age of 22 he lost the sight in one eye and slumped into depression and ill health. He died at the age of 30.

A somewhat untidy man, Bill Warr fought three times for the Championship, all unsuccessfully. He became a good trainer whose services were in demand by athletes in many sports.

'Remarkably illiterate' and remarkably successful, Hen Pearce, better known as The Game Chicken, was a popular fighter who was never beaten in competition. He and Captain Barclay trained and socialised together, but 'the fond caresses of the opposite sex' and consumption brought him to a premature end. He died at the age of 32.

A physically strong but turbulent character, Lord Camelford was ruthless and quarrelsome but charitable to those less fortunate than himself and was an important member of the Fancy. He died in a duel at the age of 29.

A successful boxer, cricketer and long jumper, Bill Richmond supervised Tom Molineux's two attempts to win the Championship. He became a popular publican and a respected member of the Fancy.

Captain Barclay and his unmistakable Scottishness are caricatured in this print that was available in the London print shops soon after the second Cribb/Molineux fight. Here, he is the dominant figure controlling Tom Cribb's every movement.

A freed slave from Virginia, Molineux fought twice for the Championship, almost certainly 'winning' the first, although not given the decision. His fights with Tom Cribb had the whole nation sitting on the edge of their seats in nervous anticipation.

Another print that was on sale in London shortly after the second Cribb/Molineux fight shows Cribb in the foreground uncorking a bottle of port (Molineux) that was known as 'blackstrap'. Behind Cribb, the crowd shouts out its appreciation of Barclay's skills as a trainer.

After his success in the ring Cribb became a popular publican. Here, he is showing off the silver cup that was presented to him in 1811 after his second victory over Molineux.

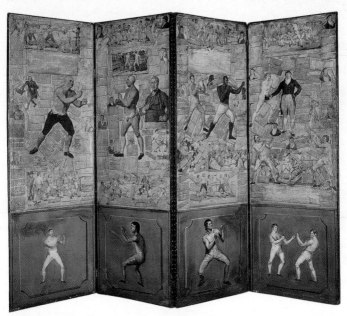

Even with the help of Gentleman John Jackson and Harry Angelo, it took Lord Byron three years of cutting and pasting to finish this six-foot-high folding screen. It was a labour of love, with one side covered with cuttings of boxers taken from newspapers, magazines and *Boxiana*. The world of the theatre was featured on the other side. (*Alex Ramsay/The World of Interiors*)

James Giles's portrait is a detailed essay on Captain Barclay's life. It shows him at the age of 64, carrying his walking stick (perhaps the one with a lead-lined handle) and sporting a Belcher necktie. Ury, the little Quaker Meeting House and his herd of Short Horn cattle are in the background.

Tom Cribb was 16 stone when he arrived at Ury, 'corpulent, big-bellied, full of gross humours, and short breathed'.[33] In a couple of weeks he would be 30 and he faced a training regime in which Captain Barclay would control virtually every aspect of his life for eleven weeks: what he ate, when he slept, how he exercised and almost who he spoke to. Life at Ury was simple and Spartan. The necessities of life were there, but no comforts. Captain Barclay and his sister Rodney usually lived this way, and it was also an ideal environment for temptation-free training. Captain Barclay started by administering a purgative to Tom Cribb, a 2 oz dose of phosphate of soda, a salt suggested by George Pearson, a distinguished doctor whose offices were in Golden Square in London's Soho.[34] Captain Barclay tried it out instead of the traditional Glauber's salt because so many athletes objected to the taste of the latter. Two further doses of 'salts' were administered, at four days' interval. These purges were an essential overture to the training process. Tom Cribb was then given a sporting gun, made by the famous gun-maker Joe Manton, to take pot shots at magpies and wood pigeons in the hills around Ury. The men in the militia, who were engaged in the serious business of drilling, did so as 'the reports of his musquet resounded everywhere'.[35] When they left at the end of their annual training, Tom Cribb was still there, kept outside all morning, afternoon and evening by Captain Barclay as the city ways were worked out of his legs.

Captain Barclay arranged occasional trips for Tom Cribb to see different faces and to socialise, but this could bring problems, as they found in the pages of the *Edinburgh Star*, and later, in the London papers.

On Sunday last, Cribb, the celebrated pugilist, arrived at Aberdeen, on a visit to a gentleman there. He is at present in training at Ury, the seat of Captain Barclay, preparatory to the great battle to be fought with Molineux on 27th September, near Doncaster. When the amount of money collected for the relief of British prisoners in France, now suffering for the cause of their country, scarcely amounts to £49,000, there is – Blush, O Britain! – there is £50,000 depending upon a boxing match! The Champion Cribb's arrival, and on a Sunday too! On a visit to a gentleman of Aberdeen (we should be glad to know what kind of gentleman he is) on his way to Captain Barclay's seat, where he is to go into training. This must be announced, forsooth, as if he, the meritorious Cribb, did honour to the City of Aberdeen by his presence! What will the starving manufacturers of Scotland say, when they read this? Shame! Shame upon it![36]

It was the old story, an echo of Samuel Galton admonishing him as a schoolboy about what a disgrace it was to spend too much time on sport. Sport was not respectable and even less so for a gentleman.

On the 28 July a reply was sent to the editor of the *Edinburgh Star*:

Mr. Cribb presents his respects to the Editor of the Edinburgh Star. – Mr Cribb saw (with what satisfaction the Editor may suppose) the paragraph relating to him in the late paper, and will take the opportunity of soon passing through Edinburgh, to make due personal acknowledgements for the favour done him.[37]

It was almost certainly written by Captain Barclay. His irritation at having to defend, yet again, his involvement in sport, led him to ignore any rational argument or respond to the points that had been made. His reply was simply a thinly veiled threat. But the letter was sent over Tom Cribb's name and did him no favours at all. It is never wise to take on an editor in the columns of his own newspaper – he holds too many advantages. The editor replied, claiming sarcastically that he had no knowledge of 'the noble science of boxing' and asking for the sake of fairness for time to find himself a champion to put into training.[38] He must have had many more supporters among the genteel readers of the paper than did Tom Cribb. It was a distraction that Captain

Barclay and Tom Cribb did not need, and fortunately the episode fizzled out, but it was evidence of the strange twilight world that the prize-fighters lived in, poised somewhere between public adulation and official condemnation. If Cribb lost his fight with Molineux, the condemnation would surface everywhere.

For Tom Cribb there were annoyances everywhere and even training was an irritant. His fluid intake was limited to a maximum of three pints a day, and so he had to endure almost continuous thirst. He was allowed to drink old home-brewed beer with breakfast and dinner, but he was never allowed to exceed the limit.[39] As the volume of exercise increased and he sweated and his thirst became intolerable, he was allowed to plunge his arms up to the elbows into a barrel of cold water. It was better than nothing.

Captain Barclay increased both the duration and the toughness of his training and accompanied him as they walked 10 to 12 miles a day. Tom Cribb, however, was a very reluctant runner, particularly up hills. Stories circulated that to encourage Tom Cribb to run Captain Barclay filled his pockets with sharp pebbles and threw them at Tom Cribb's shins as he ran away up a hill, forcing Cribb to follow to get his revenge.[40] If Captain Barclay did use such an extraordinary tactic to get Cribb to run, it was no more extraordinary than another story told about a later phase of the training. When he was refining Cribb's technique and working on his boxing stance, it was rumoured that Captain Barclay tied Cribb's leading hand to the back of a cart so that Cribb could 'feel' the new position and remember to keep his guard up. He then got William Cross to put a horse into the shafts and drive it 30 miles, with Cribb forced to follow, his leading hand held in the desired position for several exhausting hours. A brutally practical lesson that would have been hard to forget.

One of the essential elements of Captain Barclay's training discipline for Tom Cribb was his diet. A strict meat diet consisting of lean, underdone beefsteaks with broiled mutton and chicken legs for variety. There was no veal, lamb or pork – they acted as a laxative. No fat or grease – they created bile. No fish – it was too watery. No turnips, carrots and potatoes – they were also too watery. No butter – it was indigestible. No cheese – it tended to turn rancid in the stomach. No eggs, except for the raw yolk taken in the morning. Spices and dressings were banned, except vinegar which aided digestion, and salt was used very sparingly. Biscuits and stale bread, however, were permitted in almost any quantity, and were the staples that kept Tom Cribb from being hungry.[41]

It was not the monotony of the diet that made Tom Cribb complain. It was the volume of physical work. After the first couple of weeks, in addition to the daily 10 to 12 miles, he was also given general labouring work – filling dung carts, felling trees, digging trenches and carrying sacks of grain. Occasionally on a Thursday, the local market day, Captain Barclay sent Cribb into nearby Stonehaven to give lessons in sparring to those who could pay. It had the effect of keeping him sharp, and was a welcome diversion as well as securing some pocket money.[42]

The image of prize-fighting still relied on the personal status and reputation of Gentleman Jackson. He was now 40, but as impressive as ever. Louis Simond called him in 1810 'the finest figure of a man I ever saw; all muscle; I could not clasp with my two hands the upper part of his arm, when the biceps were swollen by the contraction of the limb'.[43] Simond described his rooms on Bond Street as 'a school for the fashionables of London', which seemed to transcend sport and, because of Jackson's personal good manners and reputation for honesty, had become the focal point of sporting honour and good behaviour. Jackson was universally respected and admired and was the model that others aspired to follow. Even the illiterate Game Chicken had managed to promote a positive image of prize-fighters when he risked his life to save a helpless girl from a house fire.[44] Tom Cribb, however, had a different image. He was seen as a dull, ponderous man and John Cam Hobhouse, one of Lord Byron's friends, went as far as to call him the 'stupid beast'.[45] As a counterbalance to this Captain Barclay tried to promote a more positive picture by telling a story about one of Cribb's rare evenings off from training. Cribb was walking along Union Street in Aberdeen when a woman, apparently in great distress, approached him. The story she told so affected him that 'the emotions of his heart became evident in the muscles of his face', and he gave her all the silver in his pocket. 'God bless your honour,' she said, 'ye' are surely not an or'nary man.'[46]

By the end of the first five weeks Tom Cribb had lost 19 lbs, was running a fast 440 yards every morning and evening and walking 18 to 20 miles in between, as well as labouring around the Ury estate and practising his boxing skills. She was right, Tom Cribb was not an 'or'nary man'.

Meanwhile, old Joe Ward and John Gully were at work finalising the arrangements for the venue. On 29 July *The St. James's Chronicle* unwisely publicised their decision that the fight would take place at Doncaster, either on the race course or in the huge yard behind the Rose and Crown where Daniel Mendoza and Richard Humphries had fought 21 years earlier. (It was unwise because the more notice the public authorities had of the date and venue, the more likely they were to stop it.) All the stakes, they said, had now been made good and were in the hands of Gentleman Jackson, and the betting was 6 to 4 on Cribb, and evens that the fight would not last 45 minutes.[47]

This, sadly, was not the only topic of conversation among the Fancy in London and elsewhere. On 30 July Jem Belcher died at the absurdly young age of 30. At his funeral on Sunday 4 August, so many followers went to Marylebone cemetery that the principal mourners could scarcely reach the graveside. Even such apparently hardened men as Bill Richmond, Bob Gregson, Bill Wood and Jack Powers cried openly. Bill Richmond travelled especially back for the funeral from the West Country where he and Tom Molineux were touring to raise money for the fight.[48]

At Ury the death of Jem Belcher cast a long shadow. It reminded Captain Barclay and Tom Cribb what a risky game they were in and how frail men are, even the strongest and the fittest. But they pressed on with the training. For variety Captain Barclay arranged to train for a week at Blackhall Castle in the Highlands, a beautiful estate reached by a two-mile avenue running alongside the River Dee. Blackhall was the home of his friend Archibald Farquarson and was near Banchory, about 18 miles from Ury, while to the south lay the slopes of Scolty where Captain Barclay took Cribb for much of his training. Archibald Farquarson was a young man cast in a similar mould to the Daft Laird. He bet heavily on the turf and was easily influenced, particularly by Captain Barclay, who was such a hero of his that he even copied some of his brusque, hard-man manners. He joined in with some of Tom Cribb's training.[49] Captain Barclay, Tom Cribb and William Cross travelled to Blackhall and back on foot, of course.

Back at Ury in the middle of August, Captain Barclay began the sweats. A sweating day started, like any other, at 6 a.m. First came a four-mile time-trial run in warm flannel clothes. This was followed by the well-named 'sweating-liquor'. Its recipe was:

1 oz. caraway seed
1 oz. root liquorice
½ oz. coriander seed
½ oz. sugar candy
2 pints cider
Mix spices with cider and boil down to half volume.
Pour into tankard and serve hot.[50]

Still in his flannels, Tom Cribb was put to bed under six to eight blankets and a 'feather bed', and was required to stay there sweating for 25 to 30 minutes. He was then rubbed dry, weighed and given warm, dry flannels to wear. After that he was taken outside again for a gentle walk of a couple of miles before being called in for a breakfast of roast fowl.

The sweat was repeated one week later, and then another trip was arranged to the Highlands. This time to Mar Lodge, beyond

Braemar, about 60 miles away. It took them two days to walk there, staying overnight at Aboyne, and arriving at Mar Lodge in time for dinner on the second day. Captain Barclay noted with considerable satisfaction how easily Tom Cribb could walk 30 miles a day, in comparison with his fitness at the start of training eight weeks earlier, when he could not even walk 10. Again they stayed about a week, shooting, stalking, climbing and walking. All the indicators were good. Tom Cribb's wind was excellent; he could keep going all day. His weight was stable, his flesh firm and the candle test showed his skin to be smooth, elastic and transparent. The weekly one-mile time-trials proved he was nimble and that his breathing recovered quickly. Time for the third and final sweat, after which he was recorded as 13 stone 5 lbs. It was the end of the first week in September, only three weeks before the fight. He had lost 37 lbs and was nearly ready.[51]

One week later they set out for the fight. The first leg of their journey was to Easingwold in Yorkshire, about 300 miles away, where they were to rendezvous with old Joe Ward and John Gully. Captain Barclay decided that they would walk it. It took just over a week and attracted so much attention it was even reported in *The Times*.[52]

Negotiations over the precise venue for the fight, however, ran into difficulties, spluttered and eventually stalled. The Richmond camp still wanted to fight at Doncaster or at least in Yorkshire where Bill Richmond was well known and where they were relatively popular. Captain Barclay feared interference from the magistrates there, because the newspapers had given them so much notice. Neither side would budge and eventually the toss of a coin had to decide it. Captain Barclay won, and the fight was switched to Lincolnshire just west of Melton Mowbray, at the point where three counties – Lincolnshire, Rutland and Leicestershire – meet. It was, of course, still a closely guarded secret.[53]

The fight was to take place on Saturday 28 September 1811. On the previous Monday, Captain Barclay, Tom Cribb and their entire entourage left Easingwold, took the Great North Road south and put up at the Red Lion at Sleaford. This was his permanent base, but on the night before the fight he moved even closer and stayed at the Black Bull at North Witham.[54] The frugality of Ury had so focussed Cribb on the need to be spartan that he turned up his nose at the refinements of the inns, particularly the towels smelling of lavender.

All those who were looking for clues as to the fight venue watched and followed closely, and a crowd began to gather around them. On Wednesday 25th Tom Molineux and Bill Richmond arrived at Stamford, before moving on to the New Inn at Greetham. The two fighters were now only five miles apart. The papers reported all this action, and the Fancy and all the curious took to the roads. The great and direct roads, the cross roads and the lanes, all were clogged with people. By Friday night there was not a bed to be had for 20 miles.

The fight was due to start at noon the next day but by 6 a.m. hundreds were already on the move. They needed to be. The lowest contemporary estimates put the crowd at 15,000 and the largest at 25,000, with the most common figure being 20,000. This was the greatest sporting event of the Regency, and the papers reported that a quarter of the spectators were 'Nobility and Gentry'. They included the Marquis of Queensberry, Lord Yarmouth, Lord Pomfret, Sir Francis Baynton, Sir Charles Aston, Sir Henry Smyth, the Hon. Berkeley Craven, General Grosvenor and Major Harry Mellish.[55] The Prince Regent did not attend but he was said to be on tenterhooks waiting to hear the outcome.

For Captain Barclay it was the culmination of months of work and he was involved in every part of the preparations. On the night before the fight he negotiated the hire of a field at Thistleton Gap from a farmer. The fee was high – £50. When Captain Barclay handed him a cheque, the farmer refused to accept it until George Marriot, a good-hearted, jovial man whom he knew from Melton Mowbray, came forward to guarantee it. On the big day Captain Barclay was up before first light and went to Thistleton Gap to ensure the ring was erected correctly. Then he returned to the Black Bull to supervise Tom Cribb's breakfast – just two boiled eggs.[56]

It was a fine day and the crowd gathered very early. Many had not been to bed even if they had found a bed to go to. A member of the crowd described it this way:

> The stage, which was twenty-five foot square, was erected in a stubble field surrounded first by a roped ring in order to prevent any interruptions by the crowd, and secondly by as well-framed, and supported a circle of pedestrians as were, perhaps ever witnessed, notwithstanding the great distance from the metropolis. The first row of these, as usual upon these occasions laying down, the second kneeling, and the rest standing up. Outside these again were numerous horsemen, some seated, while others more eager stood circus-like on their saddles. These were intermixed with every description of carriage, gig, barouche, buggy, cart, and wagon. The display of sporting men, from the peer on the box of the four in hand to the rustic in clarted shoes, made as fitting a picture as the Fancy can well conceive. Every fighting man of note, every pugilistic amateur, was to be seen there.[57]

Betting at the ringside was 3 to 1 on a Cribb victory, and 6 to 4 he would deliver the first knock-down blow. Huge sums changed hands, and Captain Barclay had such confidence in the outcome he bet over £3,000 on the result. No wonder he supervised every aspect of Cribb's preparation, and the fight itself. If Cribb lost they would all be ruined.

Shortly after 12 o'clock, Tom Cribb jumped on to the stage followed by Joe Ward and John Gully. The greeting they received was tumultuous. For the past three months Tom Cribb had been under Captain Barclay's direct supervision. Now he was on his own, and Captain Barclay made his way to the nearest circle of supporters containing the highest ranked members of the Fancy. All eyes were on Tom Cribb. At only 13 stone 6 lbs he looked less square than usual and his arms seemed longer. Then, up stepped Tom Molineux, who 'jumped over the railing with considerable spirit, bowing'.[58] The Bills, Richmond and Gibbons, followed him. Their reception was much more muted. For the first time the crowd could weigh up the two men. Cribb was obviously the bigger — 2¼ inches taller, a few pounds heavier and with a longer reach. He also looked confident. Molineux was visibly nervous and paced around with short, quick steps. Bill Richmond and Bill Gibbons went over to say something to him and he forced a broad smile. Then Joe Ward tied Cribb's colours to his corner post; the old blue bird's-eye, often adopted by the Bristolians and favoured by Jem Belcher in particular: a blue background, with black dots in small white circles. In the other corner Bill Gibbons tied Molineux's colours, a crimson and orange handkerchief.[59]

The two men were brought forward by their seconds and bottle-holders. They met eyeball to eyeball in the centre of the ring and, as was the custom, shook hands. An eerie hush fell on Thistleton Gap. Twenty thousand heads craned to get the best view. Eighteen minutes had been taken up with these preliminaries but now the fighters were ready.

For a good minute they sized each other up looking for an opening, and then Molineux went down from a blow to the throat. The roar was heard miles away. In round 2, however, Molineux was the first to draw blood and Cribb was thrown. When Gully and Ward got him back to the corner they found his right eye closing from a swelling under it as big as a goose's egg. John Gully quickly lanced it with a sharp knife. Betting was 5 to 2 on Cribb. Round 3 began with Tom Cribb's right eye nearly closed, but the fighting started at a break-neck pace, with ferocious hitting on both sides. Molineux fought to the head and Cribb to the body. Tom Cribb was bleeding from his nose and mouth and now his left eye began to swell up too. His fighting spirit, however, was never in doubt and he planted a fierce blow to Molineux's stomach, but it failed to stop him. Molineux closed the round by holding Cribb with one hand, and then supporting himself on the ground with the other, threw Cribb across the ring with a perfectly executed cross-buttock. Even the most partisan Cribb supporter marvelled at Molineux's strength and skill. There was only a 30-second break between rounds and Captain Barclay, not liking what was unfolding in front of him, made his way hurriedly to Cribb's corner. As Joe Ward attempted to stem the bleeding from Tom Cribb's mouth with slugs of brandy, Captain Barclay quickly gave Tom Cribb new instructions. He was to fight on the retreat and make Molineux come to him. It was a strategy designed to test his opponent's wind, and to keep himself out of reach, so he could not so easily be thrown. Once he had drawn his man forward, he was to work on Molineux's body – another strategy to test the wind of an unfit man. Meanwhile, the betting had slipped to 7 to 4 on Cribb, and was only in his favour because of his reputation for bottomless courage.

Round 4 continued in much the same vein, with one eyewitness describing how Cribb bled 'from every organ' but continued to smile. Perhaps he was the first to see that Molineux's breathing was getting laboured. Nevertheless Molineux continued fighting to the head and Cribb to the body, but Molineux still came out of it the best and Tom Cribb fell looking tired.

There was more intense action in round 5, and eventually Tom Cribb fell again from a blow, but in falling received another. Memories of the Dutch Sam–Tom Belcher fight four years earlier that Captain Barclay had umpired. Screams of 'foul' from thousands of hoarse voices filled the air, but the deciding referee was Gentleman Jackson and his interpretation of the rules was well known. As long as Tom Cribb's hands were free and had not touched the ground he was not to be considered 'down'. No foul. End of round 5.[60]

Tens of thousands of pounds, and months of work lay in the balance. Cribb was still bleeding profusely and his head was badly swollen and disfigured. Both men looked battle-weary but it was Molineux who was winning most of the exchanges. The pattern continued into round 6. And then it happened. Molineux showed great skill in stopping a good right from Tom Cribb, who, undaunted, produced another right that for weight, timing and distance was as good a punch as he ever delivered, or would ever need to. 'It not only appeared to roll him [Molineux] up, but seemed as if it completely knocked the wind out of him, which issued so strong from his mouth like smoke from a pipe, that he was literally gasping for breath.'[61]

Five to 1 on Cribb. That one blow changed the fight and from that moment Molineux was a beaten man. He managed bravely to struggle on without any semblance of hope for five more rounds, but in round 9 he rushed in, more in desperation than hope, and was met by another thunderous blow, this time to the chin. Tom Molineux fell as if dead, his jaw broken in two places.[62]

After half a minute, when it was obvious that Molineux could not be brought up to scratch again, Joe Ward rushed across the ring and untied Molineux's crimson and orange colours, and claiming them for Tom Cribb. Meanwhile, Cribb and Gully embraced ecstatically and danced 'a sort of Scotch reel', a tribute no doubt to Captain Barclay.[63] Tom Molineux was unaware of the jubilation as he was carried away unconscious by Bill Richmond and Bill Gibbons. In the Prize Ring defeat could be total. Surgeons were called and he was taken to the Royal Oak at Grantham where he could get proper treatment. He was found to have several broken ribs as well as the broken jaw.

Everyone in the crowd was talking excitedly to everyone else. To entertain the spectators a second fight was arranged: a mediocre, lacklustre affair between Tom Cribb's brother George and a boxing nonentity whom no one knew. George Cribb lost in half an hour.[64] But nobody was really interested. They were still talking about the fight, its high points, the amazing skill, the courage, the resounding victory. Before they dispersed Gentleman Jackson made a collection for Tom Molineux, which was five shillings short of £50.[65]

Tom Cribb's rewards were his one-third of the 600-guinea stake money plus about £400 in bets. Those who knew Tom Cribb the best had bet the most, and had big winnings. They knew he was determined and single-minded and would never give in. They bet on him with confidence. His father-in-law mortgaged his house and put the cash on Cribb. His faith in his son-in-law earned him over £3,000.[66] Mr Sant, the coal merchant, who was Cribb's ex-boss, won over £2,000. Bob Gregson, who had fought Cribb three years earlier, won a complete suit of clothes with a guinea in every pocket, plus a shirt, cravat, gloves and walking stick. The guinea in every pocket was a clever ruse. In September 1811 there was an acute shortage of gold and silver coins in Britain, so acute, the Duke of Norfolk had complained at a meeting of the Bank of England's General Court on 19 September, that business was difficult to conduct in the north of England. No problem, he was told, £½ million had been issued in tokens, and more would follow. Betting with tokens was too thin-blooded for the Fancy, however.[67] The problem was that the value of gold and silver had risen to the point where the coins were worth more than their face value. On 10 September the newspapers reported that the Mint had set the price of gold at £3.17.10½ per ounce, but that the market price was £4.13.6 – nearly 25 per cent greater.[68] The market price of silver was 44 per cent higher than the Mint's. It was illegal to sell gold guineas for more than their face value, but it was commonly done. How could you stop it? One person advertised for a reward. 'Lost – Eight Guineas – Whoever may have found the same, and will bring them shall receive ten pounds reward.'[69]

Confidence in cheques and paper money was even worse, which was one reason why, on the eve of the fight, Captain Barclay's cheque had not at first been accepted.

The biggest winner, by far, was Captain Barclay. He had risked the most too. Nevertheless his winnings of £10,000 were colossal, even taking into consideration that he was effectively the trainer and fight promoter as well.

Captain Barclay's day was not yet quite over. Despite the rejoicing Tom Cribb too was the worse for wear. His head was hideously bruised and misshapen, he had cut his hands severely in delivering his blows, but it was his eyes that had suffered most and he was temporarily blind. Captain Barclay made sure he got back to the carriage and was taken to the Red Lion at Sleaford and put to bed. Despite the terrible state he was in Tom Cribb managed to joke that the fight had been hard, but had not been as bad as Captain Barclay's training.[70]

Tom Cribb recovered quickly and next morning he, Captain Barclay and Joe Ward left the Red Lion and drove the 14 miles to the Royal Oak in Grantham in a carriage drawn by four horses and decorated with Cribb's blue bird's-eye colours to pay their respects to Tom Molineux.[71] He was not well enough to get out of bed to receive them and still could not speak. Magnanimity in victory was part of the sporting routine of which the British and the Fancy in particular were so proud, and Tom Cribb played the role to the full. At Tom Molineux's bedside he held out his hand to him and spoke words of sympathy and kindness. Duty done, Captain Barclay, Tom Cribb and Joe Ward climbed back on their beribboned carriage and began their triumphant journey south to London along the Great North Road, the main trunk road between the capital and York and the busiest long-distance coaching road in Britain. They left Grantham and travelled through Witham Common, Stamford, Norman Cross, Alconbury, Huntingdon, Caxton, Royston, Puckeridge, Ware, Waltham Abbey to north London. It was a day to savour.

> He was cheered through all the towns he passed, after the manner of an officer bearing dispatches of a victory, so much was it felt by the people of England: and upon the approach to his house in White Lion Street, Seven Dials, the crowd had assembled in such numbers as to render it impassable.[72]

In the post-fight analysis the experts and enthusiasts reached a fairly uniform conclusion. Tom Molineux had gained skill but lacked confidence – He was strong but his wind was bad – It was hardly his fault; he had been forced to tour round the country raising money – He did not have the benefit of Captain Barclay's training – Tom Cribb had delivered blows that no man living could withstand – His wind was good and his courage or 'bottom' was extraordinary – Tom Molineux had been a worthy opponent – But, in comparison with their first fight, the difference was Captain Barclay's training.

Two heroes emerged from the battle at Thistleton Gap: Tom Cribb and Captain Barclay, his trainer. The victorious journey to London was as much Captain Barclay's as it was Tom Cribb's. What satisfaction to read in all the newspapers of his reception 'after the manner of an officer bearing dispatches of a victory'.

There had never been excitement like it. All the Fancy taverns were the centre of long boozy parties. The climax came a week later when Tom Cribb, Captain Barclay and 60 of the Fancy sat down to a splendid celebratory dinner at Bob Gregson's Castle Tavern in Holborn. Eight weeks later they had another celebratory dinner at the Castle, with Tom Cribb in the chair, and they presented him with an engraved silver cup valued at 80 guineas. After dinner, in their usual custom, they sang long into the night. One song, written by Frederick Lawson and sung by John Emery, one of Covent Garden's best actors, sums up the role of hero played by both Tom Cribb and Captain Barclay, and how symbolic the victory had become as the country continued to struggle with Napoleon. After ten verses celebrating the boxers of the past, it finished:

England's champion now behold,
In him who fills the chair, sirs,
Who never yet a battle sold,
Nor lost one in despair, sirs,
For in each contest, or set-to,
Brave Tom bore off the laurel,
Which proudly planted on his brow,
Says, 'touch me at your peril'.

Now fill your glasses to the brim,
And honour well my toast, sirs,
May we be found in fighting trim
When Boney treads our coast, sirs,

The gallant Barclay shall lead on,
The fancy lads adore him,
And Devil or Napoleon,
Leave us alone to floor him.[73]

Pictures linked Tom Cribb and Captain Barclay as joint heroes. A set of hand-coloured engravings was published very soon after the fight by Thomas Tegg in Cheapside. In one, *Scotch Training for a Milling Match*, Captain Barclay is the central caricatured figure with a huge Scottish thistle in his hat. Tom Cribb is in the background sitting with his trousers round his knees, on a bucket. 'Oh – my guts Cap'n,' he says, 'don't you think I am reduced enough?'[74] In another, *Crib Uncorking Blackstrap*, Tom Cribb is pulling the cork, while in the background a member of the Fancy offers a toast, 'Gentlemen – the Milling Champion at Thistleton Gap'. The rest of the crowd shout enthusiastically:

Bravo, Cap'n – Hurra.
Crib and Barclay for ever.
Bravo, Cap'n.
Bravo – Bravo – Scotch Training for ever.
Bravo – Barclay for ever.[75]

In a little over two years Captain Barclay had achieved undreamed of fame and earned more than one fortune – all from sport. No one could say now that he was only remarkable for his heels. No one could tell him now that excellence in sport was rather a disgrace. The world would now have to take Captain Barclay on his own terms.

# CHAPTER NINE

# Of Gentlemen and Mad Dogs

*In private and public life, Captain Barclay has ever evidenced inflexible adherence to those strict principles of honour and integrity which characterise a gentleman.'*

PEDESTRIANISM

WALTER THOM, 1813

*Though Barclay was a great patron of Jackson, the latter could not resist the impulse to cry out 'For shame, Captain, shame!'*

SPORTASCRAPIANA

C. A. WHEELER, 1868

*... his [Captain Barclay's] society was to be avoided ... as much as a mad dog's.*

H. STURT, 1814 (PAMPHLET)

*I*n the autumn of 1811 the Fancy were in their pomp. For months, in Jackson's Rooms and every sporting tavern in London, they told and retold every story of the fight. Tom Cribb was now famous, but, having earned his rewards, he resolved never to go into the Prize Ring again. He remained the Champion and he did not formally retire, but he went back to his wife and his coal business and slipped easily into a comfortable life of bonhomie. The Fancy held on to the belief that one day he would be back, but he seemed gradually to take on the persona of the archetypal John Bull: good-natured and convivial, but firm and resolute if crossed; solid and reliable; a little slow perhaps, but a man who looked his adversaries in the face, and stood up to them openly and without malice or deceit. Any animosity that Tom Cribb may have felt towards Tom Molineux was now gone, and they even went to the theatre together.[1] The Fancy, too, embraced Tom Molineux. It made Tom Cribb's victory even more significant to acknowledge Molineux as a formidable opponent. But they went even further, accepting Tom Molineux as one of them and including him in their songs. 'A Boxing We Will Go' was perhaps the most popular of them and was sung countless times in the multitude of sporting taverns. It was obviously a boxing and a drinking song, but it was also a national song, full of self-pride, and it was a battle-song against Napoleon. In verse seven, Mendoza, Gully and Molineux join Cribb and stand defiantly against Napoleon. A more heterogeneous group would be hard to imagine: a 48-year-old Jewish fighter from London's East End, a Bristolian who had to be freed from prison to fight for the Championship, and a black American and freed slave who had been in Britain for only about 18 months.

## A BOXING WE WILL GO

Come move the song, and stir the glass,
For why should we be sad;
Let's drink to some free-hearted lass,
And Cribb, the boxing lad.

And a boxing we will go, will go, will go,
And a boxing we will go.

Italians stab their friends behind,
In darkest shades of night;
But Britons they are bold and kind,
And box their friends by light.

And a boxing we will go . . . etc.

The sons of France their pistols use,
Pop, pop and they have done;
But Britons with their hands will bruise,
And scorn away to run.

And a boxing we will go . . . etc.

Throw pistols, poinards, swords aside,
And all such deadly tools;
Let boxing be the Britons' pride,
The Science of their Schools!

And a boxing we will go . . . etc.

Since boxing is a manly game
And Britons' recreation;
By boxing we will raise our fame
'Bove any other nation.

And a boxing we will go . . . etc.

If Boney doubt it, let him come,
And try with Cribb a round;
And Cribb shall beat him like a drum
And make his carcass sound.

And a boxing we will go . . . etc.

Mendoza, Gully, Molineux,
Each nature's weapon wield;
Who each at Boney would stand true,
And never to him yield.

And a boxing we will go . . . etc.

We've many more would like to floor,
The little upstart king;
And soon for mercy make him roar,
Within a spacious ring.

And a boxing we will go . . . etc.

A fig for Boney – let's have done,
With that ungracious name;
We'll drink and pass our days in fun,
And box to raise our fame.

And a boxing we will go, will go, will go,
And a boxing we will go.[2]

For a boxer to be given a starring role in one of the Fancy's songs, as Cribb, Mendoza, Gully and Molineux were here, was the ultimate sign of acceptance and recognition. The Fancy were an odd group in many ways. They could be touchy, boisterous, obstinate and insensitive. They were reckless with their money and looked coldly on other people's suffering, but they could, on occasions, be extraordinarily warm-hearted and embraced outsiders with enthusiasm.

As the Fancy's songs made clear, every activity in Britain was carried on against the backdrop of fear of Napoleon and the hope and belief that in Spain Lord Wellington and his generals had at last got the measure of him. Four days before the Cribb–Molineux fight Lt Gen. Sir Thomas Picton and his troops were successful at El Bodon. On 28 October Lt Gen. Lord Roland Hill (alias Daddy Hill because of his fatherly concern for his men) was successful at

Arroya dos Molinos. There was the sense that perhaps the tide was turning and that Lord Wellington was getting the upper hand.[3] If British manhood could take a leaf out of Tom Cribb's and Tom Molineux's book, Napoleon would have to succumb.

At the very heart of the Fancy, Captain Barclay drank with the rest and sang the latest songs in his deep unmistakably Scottish voice, but unlike Cribb he wasn't yet content to merely receive the accolades for his past glories and slide into a mellow middle age. Everyone knew him for his great strength and endurance, so why should he not carry on demonstrating his superiority? Jackson's Rooms were his regular haunt, and he donned his new gloves (after the uproar over his gloves when he sparred with Molineux, he had to have new gloves), and 'set to' with many a gentleman, grateful for his few minutes of fame, sparring with the famous Captain Barclay.

So successful had the Fancy been over the past twenty years in financing events and raising the profile of sport, there was now a whole new generation of enthusiastic, young sporting talent waiting for their time in the sun. Among them was John Shaw, a 22-year-old from Wollaton near Nottingham, who as a youngster, had been encouraged by Jem Belcher. He was a corporal in the élite 2nd Life Guards, and at 6'½" tall, stood out, even among them, the tallest force in the British Army. In the country as a whole there were only two men in 1,000 over 6'.[4] His physique matched his height, and systematic training with dumb-bells and the broad sword had produced a formidable, well-disciplined fighting machine weighing nearly 15 stone, with great strength and 'elasticity' in his wrists and shoulders. He also had an 'excellent temper'. Pierce Egan described him 'like Hercules in appearance, with arms like two Maypoles, assisted with proportionate strength'.[5] His only weakness may have been that, like Tom Cribb, he was a little slow. 'John' or 'Jack' was far too commonplace for such an impressive man, so the Fancy decided he should be known as 'Life Guardsman Shaw'. He was taken to Jackson's Rooms to show his paces. It would be a brave, perhaps foolhardy, gentleman who stood against him.

Captain Barclay was 32, and so gave away the advantage of age as well as of height, weight and reach. In their fight in Jackson's Rooms Life Guardsman Shaw delivered such a well-timed, damaging blow to Captain Barclay's mouth that he dislodged some of his teeth and sent him hurrying to the dentist.[6] It was a bruised and thoughtful Captain Barclay that made his way back to Ury afterwards. A year later they set to again, in the Bedford Rooms in Covent Garden.[7] This time Captain Barclay managed to keep his teeth, but Life Guardsman Shaw was clearly the better man. He was talked about openly as the next Champion in the making, but it was not to be. In 1815 the 2nd Life Guards were called to the plains of Waterloo, and Sir Walter Scott tells the story of how, on the first day of the battle, Life Guardsman Shaw was engaged, like so many others, in hand-to-hand fighting with the French. Shaw killed or disabled ten of them before being wounded in the chest. On the second day with his wound dressed, but contrary to advice, he went out again to face the enemy, but was hit by gunshot and died the day after the battle.[8]

After his encounter with Life Guardsman Shaw, Captain Barclay's journey from London to Ury in December 1811 had an additional hazard. His route along the Great North Road ran through part of Nottinghamshire, not far from Thistleton Gap, where according to the newspapers, riots were taking place. Men, and maybe women too, carrying guns were breaking and destroying the new frames that had been introduced to make stockings and the famous Nottingham lace. The trouble had started only a few days after the Cribb–Molineux fight and had been going on for weeks. Lives were being lost and the local Militia and the Scots Greys had been called out. It was a violent reaction to low wages and lost jobs brought on by the introduction of new technology, that made it possible to manufacture stockings and lace at a fraction of the previous price and with fewer workers. The activists claimed to be following 'Ned Ludd' (later, Captain and eventually, General Ludd), and so became known as Luddites. Unemployment rose, and even those in work, watched their incomes plummet because so many others were competing for their jobs. The solution? Smash the new machines! One employer, attempting to justify his lowering of workers' wages, blamed it on the unemployed who, he said, had asked for work 'at any price'. He had merely done as he was asked![9] In London, the government's response was to rush through a Bill that added frame-breaking to the list of capital crimes. Many MPs with no sympathy whatsoever for the Luddites, nevertheless argued that surely the list of capital crimes was long enough already.

In December 1811 there was violence, serious, shocking violence, in London, too, but unrelated to the Luddites. In the space of 12 days, seven people, including a baby, were either clubbed to death or had their throats slit, all in the same small area in the east end, near Ratcliffe Highway.[10] An atmosphere of such neurotic fear spread through the city that the House of Commons was forced to set up a committee of enquiry, and there were renewed cries for an improved police force. First the blame fell on the Portuguese and then on the Irish, but what if one or more Britons were to blame? What would that say about the British character? Fear and self-doubt spread through the country. Robert Southey, the Poet Laureate, wrote from the Lake District,

> We in the country here are thinking of nothing but the dreadful murders, which seem to bring a stigma, not merely on the police, but on the land we live in, and even our human nature. No circumstance which did not concern myself ever disturbed me so much. I have been more affected, more agitated, but never had so mingled a feeling of horror, and indignation, and astonishment, with a sense of insecurity too, which no man in this state of society ever felt before, and a feeling that the national character was disgraced.[11]

Another correspondent, writing to John Beckett, the Under-Secretary at the Home Office, wrote, 'The late acts of atrocity stamp our character nationally as a most barbarous set of savages.'[12] It was all a far cry from the songs that the Fancy were singing boasting of the simple innocence of Britons who settled their disputes sensibly with their fists and, unlike foreigners, did not resort to knives or guns. The Britain that Captain Barclay travelled through on his way to Ury was already different from the one he had crossed with Tom Cribb on their way to the Big Fight, only three months before. Instead of expectation, optimism and sport, there was fear, self-doubt and unrest in the air.

In the New Year there were parliamentary elections in Kincardineshire. To Captain Barclay they seemed like a heaven-sent opportunity to capitalise on his post-fight popularity and to achieve even greater status and recognition by emulating his father. Even though he had no strong political affiliations he decided to stand for his native Kincardineshire. It was not merely opportunism. The Ratcliffe Highway murders and the Luddites made the whole country think about their national character and their security. From his vantage point at the pinnacle of the Fancy, Captain Barclay had opinions about both. The country needed men to be taught to obey the rules, to settle their differences openly and in accordance with those rules.

For its national defence, and to ensure success against Napoleon, Britain needed its men to be strong and brave and not flinch from pain and hardship. In short, at home and abroad, Britain needed the values and practices of the Fancy. Had the Fancy been a political party, he would have been their parliamentary candidate. As it was, he presented himself as a tolerant, free-thinking independent and banked heavily on his own personal popularity. This is how his parliamentary candidacy was described:

> . . . in his [Captain Barclay's] political sentiments he is moderate and independent. As far from violently censuring those whose political conduct he does not approve, as from blindly following the opinions of those with whom he publicly acts or personally esteems – he thinks for himself, and judges of measures by their efficacy, or tries them by the legitimate deductions of rational probability.

... as a public character, responsible for his opinions and conduct at the shrine of his country, he has always proved his sincere respect for the rights of others, and his unfeigned attachment to the British constitution.[13]

His adversary was George Harley Drummond, his old commanding officer from the Kincardineshire Volunteers and Militia and one of the Drummond banking family whose headquarters were in Charing Cross in London. He also had an estate in the lovely Drumtochty glen, south-west of Ury, where he built a splendid Gothic castle, on the steps of which the ghost of a green lady appeared every May.[14]

The electorate was a small, select group of local gentlemen landowners, and it became clear fairly early in the campaign that they had a somewhat ambiguous view of Captain Barclay and whether they wanted him to represent them. What sort of gentleman was he? Had he not been, in effect, an absentee Laird of Ury for years, leaving the running of the estate to his brother-in-law? Had he not compromised his position as a gentleman by mixing socially, on more or less equal terms, with prize-fighters from the lower orders, and had he not invited them to stay with him in his house at Ury? Had he not risked his family's wealth recklessly on sporting wagers?

The 26 February was set as the day when everything would be decided, but in the event the contest did not take place. Although it was a blow to his ego and his pride, Captain Barclay judiciously withdrew and George Harley Drummond was unanimously elected as Member of Parliament for Kincardineshire.[15] Captain Barclay tried to put it behind him and occupied himself for the rest of the winter hunting with his hounds three times a week. But it was a humiliation and an affront to his position in society. It forced him to recognise, perhaps for the first time, that fame and notoriety may not have been enough. He was a gentleman by birth and an athlete from choice and he had always assumed that he could live in both worlds, slipping from one to the other at will, and welcomed in both. It was a tough lesson that he had to work hard at being a gentleman too and that perhaps he had not worked hard enough at it. It was a jolt that came at the same time as his greatest sporting fame, and it unnerved and unsettled him.

As events turned out he would soon have another chance of contesting the seat. In the afternoon of 11 May, Spencer Percival, the Tory Prime Minister and Chancellor of the Exchequer, was shot through the heart in the lobby of the House of Commons. His assassin was John Bellingham, a tall, thin, failed commercial agent from Liverpool, who blamed the Prime Minister personally, for his bankruptcy. In May 1812 the green lady had good reason to make her annual appearance on the steps of Drumtochty Castle.

Samuel Taylor Coleridge was in Fleet Street when he heard the news. Shocked and tearful he went into a tavern frequented by the lower orders and found 50 men and women openly celebrating and drinking toasts to the downfall of the government.[16] In the Midlands and north of England the Luddites, encouraged by this blow at the heart of government renewed their attacks, and not only smashed machinery, but now, banding together in to large armed groups, terrorised, injured and even killed their opponents. Their activities spread from Nottinghamshire into Derbyshire, Lancashire and the West Riding of Yorkshire. Food riots in Bristol, Chester, Truro, Falmouth and Plymouth followed.

The government was, quite naturally, fearful of the growing mood of alarm in the country. John Bellingham was quickly rushed through a trial at the Old Bailey and hanged at Newgate only seven days after the assassination. The authorities were nervous and had arranged for mounted troops to be stationed strategically throughout London to act if needed, but early in the morning of the day of the hanging it poured with rain, soaking those that gathered at Newgate to see the drama and deterring many more from attending. Crowds at Newgate were notoriously dangerous, as people surging forward for a better view could so easily crush those in front of them. Warning notices were held on poles by the constables: 'BEWARE OF ENTERING THE CROWD! REMEMBER THAT THIRTY POOR CREATURES WERE PRESSED TO DEATH

WHEN HOLLOWAY AND HAGGERTY WERE EXECUTED!'[17] Holloway and Haggerty had been hanged at Newgate in 1807 in front of a crowd of 40,000. Some put the number of dead at closer to 100 than 30. For those who wanted a good view of Bellingham's execution in safety the houses opposite offered seats in their windows for prices ranging from two shillings and sixpence to two guineas. Lord Byron, well known for his Luddite sympathies, was among them.[18]

In the last hours before his own execution many things, big and small, must crowd into a man's mind. One of John Bellingham's troubles was caused by the authorities, who, to prevent him from taking his own life, denied him a razor. He complained that, unshaven, he would not appear as a gentleman. If the wet and bedraggled masses noticed, they forgave him this lapse. In his final minutes, as the black hood was fixed around his head on the scaffold, voices in the crowd began to chant 'God Bless You!' and 'God Save You!' But on the stroke of 8 a.m. when he dropped, 'the most perfect and awful silence prevailed' and not a single sound was made by anyone. At first Bellingham was still, then he struggled a little, and the executioner pulled on his heels to hasten the end. He was cut down after an hour and placed in a cart, covered with a sack. The executioner, his assistant and a boy climbed in the cart and accompanied him along Newgate Street, down St Martin's Le Grand, up Little Britain to Smithfield and on to the Surgeon's College in Duke Street, where they delivered the corpse to the Beadle. The bodies of the executed were a useful resource for those involved in medical research. On this, Bellingham's final journey, he was preceded by the City Marshall and followed closely by the crowd, while every window along the route was thronged with people anxious to get a glimpse. To oblige them, the executioner removed the sack from time to time so they could see the corpse. When the surgeon opened his body, he found Bellingham's heart still beating. It continued to beat until one o'clock in the afternoon, five hours after the hanging.[19]

After Percival's assassination, the Earl of Liverpool was appointed Prime Minister, but within a matter of days lost a vote of confidence and was forced to resign. New elections were called. This time, however, Captain Barclay took no part. He was still nursing the mental wounds from having to withdraw from the earlier contest, but he had no intention of making any concessions to the local gentlemen and turned his back on politics for good.

Throughout this period of political and social turmoil the Fancy were quite understandably subdued. The London Prize Ring was at a low ebb and there was no attempt to promote any more Championship fights, and few major pedestrian matches were organised. Gentlemen, however, were as touchy and hot-headed as ever. General Thornton and Theodore Hook fought a duel that ended with them exchanging shots, merely because General Thornton was enthusiastic about the waltz and Theodore Hook thought it would lead to licentiousness and lax morals.[20] At Ury Captain Barclay read the news in the papers, entered into local affairs and socialised with the neighbours. Once again he was appointed lieutenant colonel in his local Kincardineshire Militia during their period of annual training.

The conviviality of the large gathering of local officers and men led to Captain Barclay agreeing to an odd, double-headed wager with one of his junior officers referred to as Captain D. There were two Captain Ds in the Kincardineshire Militia, Captain Alexander Duthie and Captain Robert Davidson. Captain Barclay was to run 9 miles in an hour, and Captain D was to drive his gig loaded with 476 lbs, 16 miles in an hour. Both wagers to be completed on the Stonehaven Road and on the same day. Nine miles in an hour is not in itself difficult. Abraham Wood had run about 11 miles in an hour in 1800. Captain Barclay, however, had not competed in a wager since his 1,000-mile event three years before. It was for an undeclared, but 'considerable' sum and had all the hallmarks of his wagers with the Daft Laird when he was a young man; wagers accepted in the heat of the moment, spurred on by poor judgement, ego or whisky. To make the wager immeasurably more difficult, he also accepted to complete it within 48 hours. He was still as active as ever and probably walked at least 20 miles every day as part of his regular routine, spurning horses and carriages except for long journeys when time was short. But it was only background fitness not the specifically targeted fitness needed to race in a wager. He was fit, Captain Barclay was always fit, but was he sharp enough?

Without the benefit of training, therefore, he donned his flannel jacket and knee-length shorts, put on his 'thin' shoes and stepped out, bare-calfed on Tuesday 7 July 1812, to face the spectators gathered along the agreed course, a measured mile on the Aberdeen to Stonehaven Road. This was just along the road from Ury and so was the closest he had ever come to performing in front of a home crowd. The first three-quarters of an hour of running was uneventful and unimpressive. His pace lagged behind the necessary schedule but he could do little about it. After 49 minutes he stopped and took a cup of wine and vinegar. Refreshed and invigorated he set out to increase his pace − or so he hoped, but his untrained legs did not agree, and when the time-keeper called out the hour, Captain Barclay was only half way down the final stretch. He lost by half a mile. Nevertheless, *The Edinburgh Advertiser*'s reporter was so overawed by seeing this famous athlete in person, he wrote flatteringly that 'this wonderful effort was witnessed with astonishment' by the spectators, and that 'several horses on the road were unable to keep up with him'.[21] But there was in truth very little that was wonderful about it, and Captain Barclay must have regretted that he had allowed himself to be drawn into it. Captain D then went on to lose the second half of the wager too. His overloaded cart broke down.

Later in the year when Captain Barclay was back in London and going through his paces as usual at Jackson's Rooms, he found himself facing a young sporting gentleman named Edward Budd who worked in the War Office. He stood 5'10" tall and weighed 12 stone, and was a natural athlete who packed great skill, timing and enthusiasm into his compact frame. It was hard to find a sport he did not excel at. He was a particularly good cricketer, and probably Britain's best sprinter, having beaten the other two claimants to this title, Lord Frederick Beauclerc and Curley, the Brighton Shepherd. This time, unlike in his bouts with Life Guardsman Shaw, Captain Barclay had the advantage of height, weight and reach. The account of their meeting is best told in Edward Budd's own words.

I occasionally sparred with him [Captain Barclay] at Jackson's rooms in Bond Street, and on one of those occasions, soon after the commencement of our 'set-to', Barclay fell from a blow I gave him, and on rising attributed his fall to the slipperiness of the floor, through having too much water sprinkled on it, when I jocularly remarked, striking the back of one glove in the palm of the other, 'No, no old friend, 'twas this did it.' He then rushed at me in a most savage manner, and, getting me into a corner of the room, he forced my head backward through a little cupboard door. Our arrangement had been, that the Captain, who was a stone and a half heavier than I, should not take advantage of his weight in a corner. Though Barclay was a great patron of Jackson, the latter could not resist the impulse to cry out, 'For shame, Captain, shame!'[22]

Captain Barclay was obviously rattled. He had never been a genteel sparrer but he now had to resort to ever more desperate tactics to keep intact his reputation as Britain's best athlete. Perhaps that reputation was already slipping away. All great athletes when they reach their thirties have to face the thought, however abhorrent, that one day they must yield to the next generation. They have to accept the irritation that their rare defeats are as memorable to others as their victories. Captain Barclay's latest defeat and short temper were soon a topic of tavern conversation. Edward Budd continued telling the story until he was an old man.

His recent defeats were a major setback to Captain Barclay, though to the public and to the Fancy he was still the athlete extraordinary – the man who walked a mile every hour for 1,000 hours, and the great trainer responsible for Cribb's famous victory over

Molineux. The public are often unwilling to let a major sporting hero leave the stage, even in the face of evidence that it is time to do so.

On Friday 17 July 1812, the first monthly part of a new publication arrived on the streets of London. It was called *Boxiana, or Sketches of Ancient and Modern Pugilism* and was dedicated to Captain Barclay, 'that distinguished patron of the Old English Sports'. Its author was described as 'One of the Fancy', but for years the identity of the author remained a mystery to the ordinary reader. He was Pierce Egan, a sporting journalist of Irish extraction, who fittingly was known as the 'Xenophon of the Ring' and became the Fancy's mouthpiece. No one could have imagined then how popular and how influential *Boxiana* would become. It came out in monthly parts for the next 10 months, and was then published as a full-length book. It started off with the history of boxing, but as the readers snatched up each new monthly issue its author's confidence grew and he made reference to some of the most respected names of the age, including the Lord Mayor of London and the Secretary of War and the Colonies as supporters of boxing. *Boxiana* became, in effect, a campaign to promote the virtues of old English sports and of pugilism in particular. By popular demand *Boxiana* was reissued in its entirety in 1818 and that was followed in the 1820s by volumes two, three, four and five, then by the *Second Series* plus several imitations.[23]

*Boxiana* was not the first book on boxing. The previous year had seen the publication of two others: one by John Badcock, alias Jon Bee, and the other by Bill Oxberry, a well-known comic actor.[24] But the reading public immediately singled out *Boxiana* as being different. It was modern and used the latest scientific analysis. It was racy and intimate, telling personal stories of the boxers and all the leading personalities of the past three generations. It mixed italics, capitals and bold text into a unique cocktail that gave the reader the stresses and emphasis for the words just as the Fancy spoke them and it used the Fancy's own slang. It was almost as if you were standing shoulder to shoulder with them at the ring side, hearing them speak. Above all, *Boxiana* told its readers what they wanted to hear, that there was a moral purpose to it all. Boxing and all the old British sports should be encouraged as the best way to inculcate the right physical, mental and moral values into young men. Without these sports Britons might slither down the slippery pole and become no better than the French or Italians. Its legion of readers could not get enough of it, and *Boxiana* became a Regency publishing phenomenon.

On the very first page, the dedication to Captain Barclay laid out the key messages:

In viewing you, Sir, as a LOVER AND PATRON OF THOSE SPORTS that tend to invigorate the human frame, and inculcate those principles of generosity and true courage, by which the inhabitants of the English Nation are so eminently distinguished above every other country, is the unsophisticated reason in dedicating to the attention of Captain BARCLAY – **BOXIANA**, or, SKETCHES OF ANCIENT AND MODERN PUGILISM.

. . . to those persons who feel that Englishmen are not automatons; and however necessary discipline may be for the precision and movement of great bodies, . . . it would ultimately be of non-effect, were it not animated by a native spirit, producing that love of country, which has been found principally to originate from, what the fastidious term – *vulgar Sports!*

. . . those brilliant victories which have reflected so much honour to the English Nation – may be traced from something like these sources: sources which give generosity to the mind, and humanity to the heart, by instilling those unalterable principles into the breast of every Briton, not to take an unfair advantage of his antagonist; and which cannot be more *nationally* illustrated, than in the recollection of a British Sailor, at the taking of Fort Omoa, who being in possession of two swords, and suddenly meeting an enemy destitute of any weapon of defence, with unparalleled manliness and generosity *divided* the instruments of death with him, that he might have a fair chance for his life!

SPORTS, Sir, which can produce *thorough-bred* actions like the above, will outlive all the sneers of the fastidious, and cant of the hyper-critics!!!

I remain, SIR,
With every consideration
and manly respect,
Your humble Servant,
ONE OF THE FANCY

While *Boxiana* was still appearing in monthly parts, its popularity brought about a complementary text on pedestrianism. This, too, had Captain Barclay on the title page. Not, as in *Boxiana*, because it was dedicated to him but because it was, in part, about him. Intended at first as a tribute to Captain Barclay, it grew in the writing to include notes on dozens of pedestrians, as *Boxiana* had included notes on dozens of pugilists. Its themes were familiar too and its preface sets them out:

The author has considered Exercise in a military point of view, and thinks he cannot too strongly urge the necessity of adopting such measures for training our troops preparatory to actual service as would fit them for undergoing the hardships of the campaign. . . .

But as exercise conduces so much to the strength and soundness of both body and mind, the subjects treated in this volume, may be deemed, he presumes of sufficient moment to deserve the attention of all classes.[25]

But who was the author, described simply on the title page as 'The Author of the History of Aberdeen'? It was Walter Thom, a man in his fifties, who knew little or nothing about pedestrianism, who produced it in Aberdeen 'at the suggestion of a few friends'. Many of the entries, in the style of the age, were borrowed and adapted from reports in newspapers and *The Sporting Magazine*, but with significant additions. Walter Thom got over the shortcomings of his own knowledge of pedestrianism by going to the very best source: 'To Capt. Barclay, in particular, he is much indebted, for having not only furnished the chapter on training, but also for having taken the trouble to revise the greater part of the work.'[26]

Although it was Walter Thom's book, of the 286 pages nearly two-thirds were either written by Captain Barclay or were specifically about him or his family. Not surprisingly, it became known as *Barclay's Pedestrianism*. The importance of pedestrianism for the army is stressed over and over again but Thom makes no reference to its character-building properties. Captain Barclay, however, at the end of his chapter on training could not resist telling the story of Tom Cribb giving a poor woman in Aberdeen all the silver in his pocket.[27] Here was compassion and concern alongside strength and manliness. He also retold *Boxiana*'s story of William Windham, Secretary of War and the Colonies in Greville's Ministry of All the Talents. William Windham had died in 1810, but had been one of the Fancy's brightest stars, attending prize fights for many years. William Windham presented to Gentleman Jackson, as a mark of his esteem, a print showing in one section, a Roman scene with 'an *Italian* darting his stiletto at his victim', while on the other, 'the combat of two *Englishmen* in a ring'.

> For this celebrated genius [William Windham] was always of the opinion, that nothing tended more to preserve among the English peasantry those sentiments of good faith and honour which have ever distinguished them from the natives of Italy and Spain, than the frequent practice of fair and open BOXING.[28]

The writing skills of Walter Thom and Captain Barclay, however, were no match for Pierce Egan's and despite their similarities *Pedestrianism* was no *Boxiana*. *Pedestrianism* turned out to be little more than a catalogue of results and reports, and with the exception of Captain Barclay, failed to breathe life into its characters as *Boxiana* did. Although it could be bought in London, in Paternoster Row, Leadenhall Street and Berkeley Square, it had something of a 'local' east-coast-of-Scotland feel to it. It was printed in Aberdeen, was written in the area, and focused on a local hero. After its first edition in 1813 it was never printed again. For a brief time however, it gave Walter Thom and Captain Barclay a platform for their views and a rare opportunity to put the record straight.

In *Pedestrianism* Captain Barclay finally lays to rest the rebuke he received when he was 18 from Samuel Galton and which irked him all his life. That he, Captain Barclay, would always be inferior to 'Powel the Pedestrian' and 'Mendoza the Pugilist'. *Pedestrianism* shows that, in his way, Captain Barclay was every bit as good and maybe better than either of them. Samuel Galton's assertion that horses were faster or stronger than men was at last answered. *Pedestrianism* points out that pound for pound horses were weaker. It was not 'rather a disgrace' to achieve 'excellence in these accomplishments', it was laudable, or as *Pedestrianism* clearly states, 'It is only the thoughtless and inconsiderate part of the community that does not discover the benefits resulting from the exploits of such celebrated professors (as Captain Barclay).'

But in setting the record straight, there was a new message, and as Captain Barclay had 'taken the trouble to revise the greater part' of it, it has to be assumed that it was Captain Barclay's message too – delivered specifically to the gentlemen of Kincardineshire. Despite Captain Barclay's sporting exploits being highlighted and celebrated, *Pedestrianism* for the first time relegates them to second place. Repeatedly, it stresses that Captain Barclay was not primarily an athlete. He was a gentleman and a farmer.

His favourite pursuits have ever been the art of agriculture, as the serious business of his life, and the manly sports, as his amusement or recreation.[29]
  . . . his predilection for the manly sports has never interfered

with his important business, or in any manner, retarded the improvement of his estate.[30]

His gentlemanly characteristics are stressed:

He is well acquainted with general history, the Greek and Latin classics, and converses fluently on most subjects that are introduced in company as topics of discussion.[31]

In private and public life, Capt. Barclay has ever evidenced inflexible adherence to those strict principles of honour and integrity which characterise a gentleman . . .[32]

It also gave a potted history of the Scottish Barclays and pointed out to the readers that Captain Barclay was of royal blood and that he was the Earl of Airth, Menteith and Stratherene in everything but name. Despite the words of praise and admiration however, the tone is often defensive, even on occasions verging on the apologetic, particularly about the pack of foxhounds he kept at Ury.

The life of a country gentleman, . . . especially in Scotland produces little variety, and unless he shall occupy himself with rural affairs, or entertain a passion for literary pursuits, he possesses no means of relieving the vacuity of his situation, but such as arise from field sports. . . . But having engaged deeply in the improvements of his estate, he renounced his pack for more serious concerns, to which, for several years, he wholly devoted his attention.[33]

In the post-Thistleton Gap years, Captain Barclay's life seemed to become a series of living contradictions. He was a famous athlete who began to lose most of his competitions, though he continued to be celebrated and honoured. Two new engravings of him appeared and were sold in the London print shops, but he had to withdraw from local parliamentary elections through lack of support. To gain respect he had gone along with statements that seemed to trivialise the very activity he had been most committed to. At this time of contradiction and conflict, his instinct was to immerse himself again in sport and the affairs of the Fancy.

In the spring of 1813 as *Pedestrianism* was telling its readers that he had given up his pack of foxhounds at Ury for more 'serious' things, he took a house at Fritwell. It was north of Oxford between Banbury and Bicester, and he used it as a hunting lodge, and as a base to go to other sporting events nearby. Still wearing Gentleman Jackson's leather breeches he went out regularly with Sir Thomas Mostyn's hounds and in April went to the Mostyn Hunt Races on Cottisford Heath and, more fashionably dressed, attended the dinner afterwards.[34] He also went to nearby Sherington to see Tom Molineux fight again. Poor Tom Molineux was unfit and unprepared and did not want to fight anyway. Only the need for money forced him into the ring. His opponent was a 23-year-old whom the gentlemen from the south of England rather sniffily called 'a Lancashire rough'. This particular Lancashire rough, however, was not only an all-round athlete but was good fun and probably the best company of any of the prize-fighters. He was renowned for the way he danced the clog hornpipe and he could drink a glass of wine while standing on his head. His name was Jack Carter and he first came to notice when he went with some friends to see a 4-mile race between a horse and a jackass. When the jackass failed to turn up his friends entered him as the jackass. He ran and won the race to the great hilarity of everyone present. Jack Carter was a jackass, so why not? He was a runner and a boxer too but not a noticeably successful one, having fought only twice, winning the first and losing the second. He lost this one against Tom Molineux too when he fainted at the very moment that Tom Molineux was about to give in.[35] A more unsatisfactory fight was never fought in the Prize Ring.

Also in the spring of 1813, Captain Barclay spent six weeks training his manservant William Cross.[36] The newspapers always called Cross his 'groom', and he was that as well. The event was a 100-mile wager against Ned Rayner, the Kentish pedestrian. Cross had accompanied Captain Barclay on foot on countless journeys for the past five and a half years and so his background fitness was probably as good as anyone's in the country, even before he began any specific training. In May on Sunbury Common, not far from Hampton Court, Captain Barclay accompanied Cross for the first eight miles of the 100-mile wager. Though the pace he set was too fast, it was in fact achilles-tendon problems that eventually forced Cross to give in. He was treated with a mixture of camphor and Florence Oil, but to no effect. William Cross could not go on.[37] Ned Rayner however, won by his own merits and not merely because Cross was forced to withdraw. Even Captain Barclay recognised that. He told Rayner afterwards that he was the best runner he had ever seen and gave him 20 guineas,[38] a generous gesture considering that Rayner had already won the 200 guinea-a-side wager and that most of William Cross's money had come from Captain Barclay. He would not have said such a thing five years earlier about any rival pedestrian. However, he was not willing yet to accept that he would not be challenging and competing against the new generation of athletes.

The buzz of the event and the discipline of daily training lured Captain Barclay back again. In June 1813 he agreed to run a two-mile wager for 100 guineas against Lieutenant Needham of the 7th Dragoons.[39] The race was in Hyde Park, one mile from the beginning of the Promenade to Kensington Gardens and back again. Kensington Gardens and the Promenade were fashionable venues, places in which to see and be seen, especially on Sundays. On the Sunday before the race the most fashionable ladies in London had shown off the new season's lemon and straw-coloured silk dresses to those who still wore last year's azure blue,[40] and to the fashionable gentlemen who were parading themselves and their skills with their well-groomed horses and neat carriages. With the usual thoroughness that he employed when making the practical arrangements for his wagers, Captain Barclay secured in advance the cottage at the weight-house by Hyde Park Gate to use as a base before and after the wager.[41]

Captain Barclay and Captain Needham had arranged their race to start at seven o'clock on a Tuesday morning. On the appointed day the weather was chilly and the crowd was thin but they watched attentively as the two captains ran shoulder to shoulder for the first, outward mile to Kensington Gardens. They kept together at the turn, and were still together halfway along the return mile. Then Captain Needham simply ran away from the leaden Captain Barclay and won by anything from 40 to 100 yards, depending on which account you trust most. Captain Barclay, outrun and exhausted, threw himself on the bed in the cottage to recover.[42]

Despite his run of defeats, there was no question of Captain Barclay retiring from sport. He certainly could never retire from the daily routine of walking and exercise. When he walked he was always an athlete, and that was all there was to it.

By mid-summer of 1813 the nervous and self-critical mood of the country had changed. Under Lord Liverpool the Tory government was relatively strong and stable. A man had been hanged at Newgate for the Ratcliffe Highway murders and they had dimmed in the memory. Colonel Peter Hawker complained that on 12 August the Yorkshire Moors 'swarmed' with 'the disciples of General Ludd'[43] who had given themselves a holiday from ludding to watch the grouse-shooting, but the truth was that the militant activities of the Luddites had reached their peak in 1812 and had virtually stopped after their leaders were hanged at York in 1813. Suddenly at the beginning of July 1813 the nation's mood was lifted even further.

Dispatches arrived in London of Wellington's spectacular rout of 60,000 French troops at Vittoria in northern Spain. So complete was his victory that the French fled, leaving behind their baggage, provisions, ammunition and even their treasury. Out of 138 field guns they abandoned all but one, and a howitzer.[44] The British troops then disgraced themselves by looting the captured baggage rather than pursuing the retreating enemy.[45] Casualties on both sides were heavy and the names of the dead and wounded British officers were listed in *The Courier* and *The Gazette*, though the names of the dead and wounded ordinary soldiers were not given. Despite the casualties it was accurately described in the newspapers as 'the most complete defeat of the enemy yet experienced in the peninsula'.[46] The diplomat Sir George Jackson wrote that everyone in London was 'wild with joy' and that people were 'in the very highest spirits'. Celebrations lasted for days. The streets were illuminated, and the words WELLINGTON and VICTORY were picked out in lights in streets and squares, while firework displays blazed across the skies and victory parties sprang up everywhere. Everyone sensed that this at last was real victory and that Napoleon was on the run.[47] The Prince of Wales gave a grand ball and supper at Carlton House, followed a few days later by another extravagant party for 400 guests including most of the royal family. It started in the middle of the afternoon and did not finish until four in the morning.[48]

Despite the national jubilation Captain Barclay was touchy and volatile. He was still coming to terms with the fact that his days as an athlete were probably over and those around him knew better than to cross him. He continued to walk of course, sometimes, it seemed, obsessively. Even then, the outside world sometimes encroached in ways that irritated him. One day he was as usual striding out along the road when a horse and cart passed him. As he went by, the driver turned and offered him a lift, to which Captain Barclay replied, 'Do you think I would?' In reply the driver must have said something insulting or off-hand. It was too much for Captain Barclay, who set off after the horse and cart, caught up with them on a long hill and challenged the driver to a fight. Using the skills he practised in Jackson's Rooms, he got the better of him and 'taught him a lesson'.[49] His irritability and bad temper were now more conspicuous than his athletic prowess. Worse was to follow.

It all started on Thursday 30 September 1813. Captain Barclay, just past his 34th birthday, was enjoying a convivial social evening in Stonehaven, drinking wine and playing whist. Among his group was Archibald Farquarson, who had joined in with Tom Cribb's training when Captain Barclay had taken Cribb to visit him in the Highlands. There was also a Dutch gentleman of about 60 years of age by the name of Mr H. Sturt, who was temporarily living in the area with his wife and brother, Captain Sturt.[50] The war with Napoleon made it impossible for them to return to Holland. There were about 10,000 Dutch men and women in Britain all of whom were held, virtually prisoners of war, waiting for the war to end.

It was late in the evening when the quarrel broke out. A lot of wine had been drunk and as is often the case, later no one was sure who had started it. It appears that Captain Barclay in the course of play, accused Mr Sturt of cheating, to which Mr Sturt replied that he had not. What else Mr Sturt might have said is uncertain, but stung by the serious accusation of cheating he may well have made some comments to the effect that he, Captain Barclay, was a fine one to talk. What sort of gentleman was he, choosing to surround himself, as he did, with such social high-flyers as prize-fighters and occupying his time with such gentlemanly activities as pugilism, etc.? It struck a raw nerve and Captain Barclay's response was simple, he hit Mr Sturt, thus, apparently, proving Mr Sturt's point for him. Not surprisingly, Mr Sturt became more angry and indignant. He had been insulted and hurt. More words were exchanged, even less temperate than the previous, and Archibald Farquarson leapt to Captain Barclay's defence, although he hardly needed it. The evening came to an abrupt end in a cloud of mutual animosity with Mr Sturt pointing out that he was nearly twice Captain Barclay's age. Matters, as you can imagine, did not stop there.

The events of the evening preyed on Mr Sturt's mind all night, and immediately after breakfast he wrote a note to Captain Barclay asking him to acknowledge his 'error', adding, as if to give Captain Barclay a let-out, that he did not believe he would have committed such an outrage had he not been 'heated by liquor'. Before the incident the Sturts had invited Captain Barclay to dinner the following evening at Inchmarlo, a mansion about two miles west of Banchory, and Mr

Sturt probably intended to hand his note to Captain Barclay then. It would have been a somewhat strained evening at best and Captain Barclay, perhaps sensibly, did not turn up. When Captain Barclay failed to arrive for dinner, Mr Sturt's brother, Captain Sturt, took a post-chaise to Ury and delivered the note himself. If Mr Sturt had hoped for an apology he was disappointed. Captain Barclay's reply was unambiguous.

Ury, Oct 1, 1813
Sir,
I have only to say, that, in reply to your letter, that I was not heated by wine, and perfectly cool and collected in regard to everything that passed last night; under that impression, you cannot suppose for a moment that I will make any apology whatever. I am, etc.
Allardice Barclay
To H. Sturt.[51]

For Mr Sturt the whole episode now became a matter of honour and nothing short of a 'meeting' (that is, a duel) would settle it. There was a frenzy of anxious activity by both sides over the weekend and at 4.30 a.m. on Monday Mr Sturt, accompanied by his brother, who was to act as his second, set out with duelling pistols for the meeting. It was always advisable to be accompanied by a physician on such occasions so Dr Kerr travelled with them. From Ury Captain Barclay also set out accompanied by his second, General William Burnett, a respected gentleman in his early 50s from Banchory Lodge. Neither of the seconds was convinced that the duel was inevitable or even necessary, and at the traditional meeting between them prior to the event they agreed that a mutual apology should satisfy all parties. Mr Sturt was to apologise for his language and Captain Barclay was to apologise for the blow.

The 'apology' however, when it happened some moments later, was such a half-hearted thing that later in the day Captain Barclay was able to claim that he had not apologised at all and that the only apology had come from the Dutch man. This led to another dispute. Captain Barclay was in an ugly mood when he sat down to write to Mr Sturt on the following Saturday.

Ury, Oct 9th, 1813
Sir,
On my return home just now from Turriff I found yours – you never for a moment would have conceived that I made any Apology to you last Monday. I said nothing that would by any chance be twisted into one – and positively refused to shake hands with you, this to most men would have been sufficient, to make them proceed to the Business, you on the contrary left the ground satisfied – I have only to say now that your conduct in the first instance was infamous, afterwards that of a coward, and I am strongly advised by my friends to meet you with no other weapon but a Horse Whip, however as I know you only want an excuse to shelter your Cowardice, I shall give you the meeting you demand, on Monday morning next, at the 8th Mile Stone on the Slug Road at 7 o'clock –
I am etc. etc.
Barclay Allardice

Read the above carefully as you may mistake it for an Apology. – R.B.A.[52]

Of the two antagonists and their respective seconds only Captain Barclay believed he had not apologised. When word got back to Mr Sturt that Captain Barclay was boasting of having received but not given an apology he became even more annoyed and indignant, and the second 'meeting' now became all but inevitable.

To add further insult to injury Mr Sturt also heard reports that Archibald Farquarson was boasting that he too, had struck him. Later, Farquarson confirmed this in writing, stating that he struck Mr Sturt because of his abusive language about his friend Captain Barclay when he was out of the room. Matters rapidly went from bad to worse and Mr Douglas, the sheriff, visited the Sturt brothers and bound them over to keep the peace – but at whose instigation he did not say. This prevented Mr Sturt from fighting his duel with Captain Barclay. By now the two Sturt brothers, Captain Barclay and Archibald Farquarson were all so angry that they were probably out of control. Mr Sturt challenged Archibald Farquarson to 'meet' him at 8 a.m. at the 22nd mile stone on the road from Aberdeen to Braemar and Captain Barclay set up a joint 'meeting' at the original venue at the 8th mile stone on the Slug Road.

Mr Sturt was now caught up in a most perilously dangerous business. He was committed to fight two duels with two men on the same day, and he stood little chance of surviving both uninjured, or even alive. He was also bound over to keep the peace whereas his antagonists apparently were not. Even if he survived, the consequences for Mr Sturt were very serious indeed. Stringent precautions had to be taken. Dr Kerr could not be persuaded to turn out a second time, so Mr Sturt sent to Aberdeen for Dr Williamson, who reached Inchmarlo at one hour after midnight on the appointed morning. On arrival he was packed off to bed to get a few hours' sleep. It was important for the doctor to be as fresh as possible. There was little prospect of any sleep that night however, for Mr Sturt and his wife. At 5 a.m. they all had to be up.

At 3 a.m. a messenger, probably William Cross, arrived at Inchmarlo with a letter from Captain Barclay and Archibald Farquarson. They too had been bound over to keep the peace so the duels were off, but not before they issued some further insults to Mr Sturt. They blamed him for sending the sheriff and finally warned him against making any improper use of their names in future. Both sides continued to throw fresh kindling on the blazing fire. Mr Sturt told each of them separately that had they not been cowards they could have evaded the sheriff, as he had been prepared to do. And he again challenged them to a 'meeting', this time in another county where the sheriff had no jurisdiction. This was a well-known strategy to everyone in the Fancy. It was why the Cribb–Molineux fight had been at the junction of three counties. Captain Barclay and Archibald Farquarson did not take him up on his offer. Like many hotheads, Archibald had no stomach for the real action and hid behind Captain Barclay. He would take on Mr Sturt after Captain Barclay had finished with him, he said.

On Monday 11 October, Mr Sturt sent a letter to Captain Barclay demanding a meeting in another county.[53] The servant delivering it returned to Mr Sturt telling him that Captain Barclay would send an answer, but he never did. The episode had been going on for 12 days and no part of it could be kept secret any longer. A silly, undisciplined incident at the whist table was now so public that the entire fashionable world in Kincardineshire, Aberdeen and Deeside knew about it – and presumably most of the unfashionable world too. Friends and relatives applied pressure on Captain Barclay to bring the matter to an end. This was no way to prove his gentlemanly credentials or to gain respect. As he tried to find a way to extricate himself, Captain Barclay had a stroke of luck. At the same time as this bad-tempered trivia was being played out in eastern Scotland, more momentous events in Europe continued. Within a few days of Mr Sturt's final letter, Napoleon was defeated at Leipzig,[54] in November a people's revolution in Holland helped force the French out, and on 21 November a Dutch delegation arrived in London to invite the Prince of Orange back. Once the Netherlands was no longer under the control of the French, the Dutch in Britain were free to go back. Within weeks of their final exchange of letters Mr Sturt, his wife and his brother returned to Holland – but not with happy memories of Scotland.[55]

# CHAPTER TEN

# A Superior System

*Captain Barclay's desire to establish a regular system of manly
corporeal exercises ... is a laudable and patriotic ambition.*

THE SPORTING MAGAZINE, 1813

*It is astonishing what confidence men are taught to feel, from
the superior system of training pursued by Captain Barclay.*

PIERCE EGAN, 1818

*T*en days after the final inconclusive exchange of letters and insults, Captain Barclay travelled to the Salutation Inn in Perth to see a pugilistic show by a young man named Bill Fuller, who stood 5′ 10″ tall and weighed 12 stone, starting out on the ladder to pugilistic fame.[1] He was a Norfolk man, one of Bill Richmond's protégés, and so to Captain Barclay, he was automatically one of the 'opposition'.[2] The traditional travelling pugilistic show consisted of demonstrations of the various attacking and defensive positions of the champions – Cribb, Belcher, Mendoza, etc. – followed by some of the pugilist's own positions and moves. After that came sparring matches with any local yokels ennobled by ambition and drink, who wanted to try their luck. Then, after the Master of Ceremonies had brought the entertainment to a close, the gentlemen were invited to reserve a slot or two in the pugilist's appointment book over the next day or so, and take public or private lessons in the noble art of self-defence. There was a steady demand for shows like this all over the country and they were a source of regular income for the pugilists. Going from town to town giving demonstrations and lessons in taverns and local halls was hard and bruising work, but less risky and more regular than fights in the Prize Ring. Virtually all the pugilists did it; some turned it into a lucrative business, as Daniel Mendoza had when he started it about 40 years earlier.

As the evening in the Salutation Inn was coming to a close and Bill Fuller had satisfied the local braves, Captain Barclay stepped forward and offered to spar with him. This was a significant break with convention. Apart from Captain Barclay, gentlemen did not fight the pugilists in public and for fun. Twelve months before, Captain Barclay had done the same thing, taking on, and being beaten for the second time, by Life Guardsman Shaw in a public show in the Bedford Rooms in Covent Garden.[3] But, apart from that, it was virtually unknown. Gentlemen had no qualms about taking lessons from the pugilists, and even sparred with them with the mufflers on in the controlled environment of Jackson's Rooms. Occasionally, they would even invite them into their own homes for lessons and some bemuffled sparring, but their social status and rank made it unthinkable that they would ever choose to meet a pugilist toe-to-toe in public, even wearing mufflers. Coming so soon after the Sturt affair, it was a clear demonstration that Captain Barclay would make no concessions to convention, or to his fellow gentlemen. He belonged with the Fancy who understood and admired him. Their respect was all he now wanted or expected.

Afterwards, *The Perth Courier* wrote of the contest that Captain Barclay 'was decidedly superior to his opponent, who received a pretty smart drubbing'. It was a good story and was soon picked up by the other papers, and the news quickly spread round Britain that Captain Barclay had defeated 'a famous bruiser from London'.[4]

Bill Fuller wasn't exactly 'famous', but he was unusual in many ways. He had had only two fights, both within the past year, and both against Bill Jay, another young and inexperienced fighter. Jay won the first in 15 minutes and Fuller the second, in 42 minutes. He would only ever enter the Prize Ring once again, to face Tom Molineux in the following May.[5] After that he was to make his reputation as a teacher, modelling himself on Gentleman Jackson. Within a few years Bill Fuller left Britain for America and became known as the 'American Gentleman Jackson', a man of good manners and with good business sense. Pierce Egan said of him then that he was 'admired in England, France and America for his civility, politeness and attention to all ranks of society in teaching the Art of Self Defence'.[6]

On that October evening in the Salutation Inn, everyone knew that once Captain Barclay had committed himself publicly to spar with Bill Fuller, he would stop at nothing to win. Bill Fuller, on the other hand, realised that it would not be good sense or business to publicly humiliate a prominent gentleman, especially in his own neighbourhood – particularly, if the gentleman happened to be Captain Barclay. So, as Captain Barclay fought with all the aggression, skill and strength he possessed, Bill Fuller fought to contain Captain Barclay. No one recorded the details of the bout, but it is hardly surprising that Captain Barclay came out on top.

A correspondent to *The Sporting Magazine* saw it as greatly significant: 'It is generally thought among the fighters, as well as the fanciers, that if Captain Barclay would so condescend, he would Crib the honours of the championship itself from the black diamond, the present holder.'[7] It was wonderfully flattering for Captain Barclay, but it is extremely unlikely that any of the fighters or the 'fanciers' thought the same. Tom Cribb was overweight and unfit, and in no shape to defend his title; that was true. But it was ridiculous to suggest that Captain Barclay was in any position to challenge for his title. When Tom Cribb, the Champion, had returned to his coal business, his celebrity status attracted many new customers, gentlemen who ordered their coal from him for the first time; unfortunately, many more than were willing to pay their bills promptly. His business collapsed. Nevertheless, so many still wanted to meet him and shake his hand that he decided to become the landlord at the Union Arms where he could cash in on his popularity. The Union Arms was on the corner of Panton Street and Oxendon Street in Haymarket and just round the corner from Captain Barclay's London rooms in Porridge Island. He was a great success and quickly established himself as a traditionally genial 'mine host'. The Union Arms became one of the most popular hangouts of the Fancy.[8]

No gentleman of the Fancy, however, seemed to have any stomach for challenging the boxing status quo. They liked the stability of having Cribb as the Champion, and so the fights they arranged were minor ones to bring on the younger talent. These were good to wager on and good entertainment, but not serious championship events. Top of the young crop of contenders for Cribb's title were Life Guardsman Shaw, Tom Oliver, Ned Painter and George Cooper, all about ten years younger than Tom Cribb and Captain Barclay, all hungry for success. Captain Barclay's two defeats at the hands of the huge and powerful Life Guardsman Shaw were enough to put into perspective *The Sporting Magazine*'s empty claims. His defeat by Edward Budd, a fellow gentleman who was a stone and a half lighter than himself, rendered the remarks nothing short of ludicrous.[9] *The Sporting Magazine* was the Fancy's magazine. Most would have read it with a smile; they knew how inaccurate and unreliable newspapers were. But Captain Barclay was still a hero to the Fancy, and it would take more than a few defeats to dislodge his superman image. To *The Sporting Magazine*'s correspondent he was 'incredible'. The writer continued with his flattery:

> Captain Barclay, by means of continued training, and a system of living, which combines the full exercise of every organ with the most nutritious and least burthensome diet, and only what is absolutely necessary in the way of repose, has improved the strength of his naturally robust frame to such a degree that it is impossible to conceive anything in the capacity of the human muscles beyond what he can execute in point of exertion and perseverance. Indeed, his performances are absolutely incredible to those who have not had opportunity of learning to what an extent the powers of the human body may be carried by proper management.[10]

All of this may have been true in the summer of 1809, but not in October 1813.

*The Sporting Magazine*'s correspondent also found a link between Captain Barclay's performance against Bill Fuller and the war. He took *Boxiana and Pedestrianism*'s message that the old British sports produced strong, valiant and honourable men, and gave it a new twist. Captain Barclay had been involved in sport all these years, he said, only to be an example to others.

> Captain Barclay's object in pursuing this course of living and devoting himself so much to corporeal exercises, is to render them fashionable, not only among young men of the higher ranks, as they were among the Nobility of Greece and Rome, and all the most polished, as well as most warlike nations of antiquity;

but to make them familiar among the people, always prone to take example by their superiors, but in matters of this kind particularly, whence a hope may be reasonably entertained of restoring the hardihood and martial spirit of our famed ancestors, with that once far famed robustness of frame of which so few traces are to be found in the degenerate race of our time. We freely avow, that we think Captain Barclay's desire to establish a regular system of manly corporeal exercises, similar to those of the Palaestrae and Gymnasia of the Greeks, and of the Circus and the Campus Martius of the Romans, is a laudable and patriotic ambition.[11]

The piece was written after the allies' successes at Vittoria and Leipzig when almost everyone saw everything in military terms. Lady Bessborough described the prevailing mood in the country as one of 'military mania'. Even women's fashions adopted epaulettes and short, military-style jackets.[12] The end of the long war with Napoleon was in sight. Europe was on the brink of peace negotiations. Britain was in a mood of self-congratulation and was looking for heroes everywhere. Now, the Fancy's own magazine was crediting Captain Barclay with a system for ensuring the future 'hardihood and martial spirit of our famed ancestors', and linking them with the nobility of ancient Greece and Rome and patriotism.

So, in the winter of 1813–14, Captain Barclay's public role was redefined. He had been the most famous athlete of his age, then one of its most successful trainers, and now his 'system of manly corporeal exercises' was to be the model for making the next generation 'robust', 'hardy' and with a 'martial spirit'. What this system was, was never actually defined, but it was based on the training given to Tom Cribb, blended with Captain Barclay's own well-known Spartan routine. The system included regular sweating, daily exercise, minimal sleep and a simple, nutritious diet. None of this was new of course. He had learned most of it under Jackey Smith's guidance. What Captain Barclay did was to give it prominence by his own incessant, high-profile example. Many talked of early rising, sweating and tough, regular, exercise, but Captain Barclay had lived it for well over a decade.

Throughout the cold, hard winter of 1813–14, Captain Barclay stayed in Scotland, walking prodigious distances whenever the weather would allow. The military news continued to be good. Marshal Blucher's Prussian troops defeated Napoleon at La Rothière on 1 February and there were victories for the allies at Laon, Bordeaux, Arcis-sur-Aube and La Fère-Champenoise in March. On the last day of March the allies entered Paris in triumph and Napoleon abdicated unconditionally on 11 April.

Captain Barclay took the coach south to London looking forward to a good summer's sport ahead. He soon became involved with one of Tom Cribb's friends, Tom Oliver. He had originally been known as the 'Battersea Gardener', but the name didn't stick, partly because he wasn't from Battersea, but mainly because the word 'gardener' didn't seem an adequate description of a man with such a remarkable body. He was 25 years old and his physique was so close to perfection that he became greatly prized by painters and sculptors as a model. 'His skin was as white as a duchess', his arms as corded as a blacksmith's – a more beautiful and symmetrical frame and more splendidly developed muscular limbs no one could ever wish to see.'[13] Throughout April and early May Captain Barclay prepared Tom Oliver to fight a new 30-year-old Lancastrian named Ned Painter. Painter was well known as a strong man, and was one of the best throwers of a 56lb weight in England. At first, Tom Oliver's training didn't go well. He seemed to be ill and was constantly exhausted. The truth was that Captain Barclay's approach to everything was extreme. He required more running, more sparring, less recovery and less sleep. More than Tom Oliver could recover from, and Captain Barclay had to learn the hard way that systems cannot be imposed on everyone in the same way, and that training is as much an art as a science. This was no grossly overweight Tom Cribb who needed to be knocked into shape the hard way. This was a lithe, young man at the peak of his powers who needed fine-tuning for his forthcoming fight. Tom Oliver was being over-trained. Fortunately Captain Barclay sized up the situation correctly and reduced the volume and intensity of training. It did the trick, and under this new, benign regime Tom Oliver flourished. Captain Barclay then received even more credit for the flexibility of his system.

> When his [Tom Oliver's] pitch was correctly ascertained, his constitution was so finely and vigorously tempered, so much spirit, lightness, and sound stamina were infused into his frame, that it was thought he could have fought an hour without much difficulty. It is astonishing what confidence men are taught to feel, from the superior system of training pursued by Captain Barclay.[14]

As it turned out, he didn't need to fight for an hour. He beat Ned Painter in 26 minutes, although he was 'much punished' in the process. At the end, Tom Cribb, his second, was so jubilant, he took Tom Oliver in his arms and, to the delight of the crowd, carried him round the ring in triumph.[15]

The correspondent to *The Sporting Magazine* was right about at least one thing. Captain Barclay's 'system of manly corporeal exercises', and other similar systems, were fashionable. The interest in sound, physical health based on training for sport did not necessarily mean that those who took it up had any interest in competing. Most did not. Most of the Fancy who trained at Jackson's Rooms never expected to take part in a sporting event. For example, while Tom Oliver was following Captain Barclay's system in preparation for his fight with Painter, Lord Byron was recording in his journal his own training programme, supervised by Gentleman Jackson.

Thursday, March 17
I have been sparring with Jackson for exercise this morning; and mean to continue and renew my acquaintance with the mufflers.

My chest, and arms, and wind are in very good plight, and I am not in flesh. I used to be a hard hitter, and my arms are very long for my height. At any rate, exercise is good, and this the severest of all; fencing and the broad-sword never fatigued me half so much. . . .[16]

Sunday, March 20

. . . Sparred with Jackson again yesterday morning, and shall tomorrow. I feel all the better for it, in spirits, though my arms and shoulders are very stiff from it. Mem. To attend the pugilistic dinner: Marquess Huntly is in the chair. . . .[17]

Albany, March 28

This night got into my new apartments, rented from Lord Althorpe, on a lease of seven years. Spacious, and room for my books and sabres. *In* the *house*, too, another advantage. The last few days, or whole week, have been very abstemious, regular in exercise, and yet very *un*well. Yesterday, dined *tête-à-tête* at the Cocao with Scrope Davies — sat from six till midnight — drank between us one bottle of champagne and six of claret . . . No headache, nor sickness, that night nor to-day. Got up, if anything, earlier than usual — sparred with Jackson *ad sudorem*, and have been much better in health than for many days. . . .[18]

April 10

. . . I have not stirred out of these rooms for these four days past: but I have sparred for exercise (windows open) with Jackson an hour daily, to attenuate and keep up the ethereal part of me. The more violent the fatigue, the better my spirits for the rest of the day; and then, my evenings have that calm nothingness of languor, which I most delight in. To-day I have boxed an hour — written an ode to Napoleon — copied it — eaten six biscuits — drunk four bottles of soda water — redde away the rest of my time . . . .[19]

Byron was not training for sport. It simply made him feel better. He was, nevertheless, a great boxing enthusiast and was nearing the end of a three-year project decorating a 6′ high folding screen with pictures and cuttings of boxers.[20] Gentleman Jackson and Harry Angelo helped him.

The 'pugilistic dinner' that Byron referred to, with the Marquis of Huntly in the chair, was to set up a Pugilistic Club to regulate boxing in the same way that the Jockey Club had been regulating horse-racing for years. The idea that there should be such a club was a sign of how far the sport had come. Preliminary meetings were held in Jackson's Rooms, at which the club's objectives were agreed and its rules and regulations adopted. They purchased the ropes and timber for a ring and appointed their first 'commissary', Bill Gibbons, who was to keep and be responsible for constructing the ring at approved fights. Officers were appointed and a uniform agreed – blue coats and yellow kerseymere waistcoats, with the letters PC engraved on the buttons. All members had to wear the uniform on the club's public occasions. On 21 May at the Thatched House Tavern on St James's Street, 45 members and their guests, among them Tom Cribb, John Gully, Tom Belcher and Gentleman Jackson, sat down to the Pugilistic Club's inaugural dinner. Captain Barclay, of course, was prominent among them, and this time Sir Henry Smyth was in the chair. Tom Oliver was there too, sporting two black eyes from his fight with Ned Painter only five days earlier. It was, in effect, a dinner of the Fancy. After the meal and a speech by Francis, Earl of Yarmouth about sportsmanship and 'the national utility of the pugilistic art', Captain Barclay set the wheels in motion for another fight between Oliver and Painter.[21] Although it did not take place for years, Captain Barclay had set the pattern: the Pugilistic Club intended to be a working club and not just a dinner club. It was to be the governing body of boxing.

On 7 June more dignitaries than had ever assembled in London arrived to celebrate the peace. The main guests were Alexander I, Tsar of all the Russias, and Frederick William III, King of Prussia, their retinues and their respective military commanders, Prince Matvei

Platov, 'the hetman of all the Cossacks', and Field Marshal Gebhard von Blucher. In addition, there was Prince Clemens Metternich and Prince Hardenburg, the Austrian and Prussian Chancellors, respectively. The Russian party stayed at the Pultney Hotel on Piccadilly and also included the Tsar's brother, Prince Constantine, and his sister, the Grand Duchess of Oldenburg. The Prussian party stayed at Carlton House and also included the Prince Royal, Prince Frederick, and Prince William. Work stopped everywhere while Londoners went mad, celebrity spotting. Nor was it only Londoners. It was calculated that 100,000 people from outside the capital flocked in to try to catch a glimpse of them. Colonel Peter Hawker moved his family from Hampshire to London for three weeks so as not to miss anything.[22] The city was clogged. You could not get bread or milk, or even have your clothes cleaned.[23]

Londoners reserved their special accolade for the silver-haired, well-built and stately Marshal Blucher, the victor of Leipzig. They released his horses from their shafts and drew his carriage themselves through the streets. Indeed they would hardly stop. Lady Frances Shelley wrote in her diary: 'Blucher came to the door to please the mob, who had been drawing him around all morning. . . . it was all they could do to get Blucher safe into the house as he was nearly crushed to death.'[24]

'It is quite ridiculous how wild London is,' wrote James Frampton to his mother.[25] There were illuminations and fireworks, a magnificent ball at White's, and a grand fête hosted at Carlton House by the Prince Regent. The visitors walked and rode in Hyde Park and Kensington Gardens and attended dinner parties, the theatre and the opera. They went to the races at Ascot and Oxford and reviewed the troops in Hyde Park and the Fleet at Portsmouth. Joseph Turner sketched the scene. As an additional mark of respect, the Prince Regent also commissioned Thomas Lawrence, Gentleman Jackson's oldest friend, to paint the portraits of the Tsar of Russia and the King of Prussia, Marshal Blucher and General Platov.

On Wednesday 15 June Lord Lowther laid on a special treat at his house on Pall Mall for Tsar Alexander of Russia, General Platov and Marshal Blucher. Lord Lowther had arranged with the Pugilistic Club for some of the leading fighters to give an exhibition of sparring, so that the foreign visitors could see the British art of self-defence and the system of fighting that made British men skilful, brave and honourable. The show was an immediate hit. So much so, that they asked for it to be repeated for the rest of the party. So, two days later, on Friday 17 June, another exhibition was arranged, also in Lord Lowther's house. This time the Tsar of Russia, General Platov and Marshal Blucher were joined by King Frederick William of Prussia, the Prince Royal of Prussia, Prince Frederick, Prince William, Prince Mecklenburgh, General D'York and many others.[26]

William, Viscount Lowther (later to become the Earl of Lonsdale) was an attendant to the Prince Regent and a keen follower of the Fancy. The second show he played host to was even more impressive than the first. It included demonstration bouts by the stars of the past and the future – the Champion Tom Cribb, Tom Belcher, Bill Richmond, Tom Oliver, Ned Painter and the great Gentleman Jackson himself. Jackson's performances were a particular and rare treat. He was now 46 years old and almost never sparred in public, and didn't even spar with the prize-fighters in his own rooms. Bill Richmond was 51. Pierce Egan, after his campaign for pugilism and the old British sports, in the pages of *Boxiana*, was understandably smug.

'The *set-to's*, in general, were excellent; but the *sparring* of JACKSON was particularly admired. The elegance of his positions, the celerity of his attack, the fortitude of his manner, and the superior mode he developed of guarding his frame from the attacks of his adversaries, created a lively interest among the royal warriors. ... The Champion of England (CRIB) occasioned a general *stare* among the spectators, and the veteran Blucher eyed him with more than common attention. The royal guests expressed their satisfaction at the treat they had experienced;

and . . . complimented his lordship as the patron of so manly and characteristic a trait of his country.'[27]

At one stroke, sport had moved on. The most powerful men in Europe had seen and admired it and complimented a lord on his patronage of it. It hardly mattered now what other gentlemen thought. Pugilism, and indeed all the old British sports, had a future, an international future at that.

At the end of the summer, when all the festivities were over, it was a self-satisfied Captain Barclay who took the road north once again to Ury.

# CHAPTER ELEVEN

# *Feather Beds Revisited*

*At first he made his address to her without any view of marriage but she did not yield to his embrace till he made a solemn promise ...*

FRANCIS JEFFREY, 1820

*We always regarded Mrs Barclay as Captain Barclay's wife, & the Captain always spoke of her as such.*

JANE WYSE, 1871

*Mrs Barclay ... [was] extremely uneasy and distressed on account of the Connection which had taken place ... without any regular marriage.*

FRANCIS JEFFREY, 1820

Only Rodney lived at Ury on a permanent basis. Her older sister Mag had married the wealthy Hudson Gurney and had been living partly in Norwich and partly in London for years. David, her youngest brother, was a captain in the 42nd Highland Regiment and was seldom at home. Captain Barclay tended to spend most of the winters there, but even then he spent as much time away hunting as he did in residence. Rodney was now 33 years old and unmarried and her life at Ury was simple and uncluttered. The house itself was unchanged since the Great Master's time, except that there were even fewer comforts and virtually no luxuries. Visitors saw at a glance that the master of the house prided himself on his harsh, Spartan lifestyle. Rodney had little choice but to comply. Captain Barclay's absence for most of each year had made her self-reliant and independent. There was little money to handle. Captain Barclay's income from Ury was about £7,000 a year,[1] a respectable income, but by no means a fortune by the standards of the sporting gentlemen he hunted and sparred with and very little of this was available to Rodney. For most of the active members of the Fancy £10,000 was regarded as a basic minimum.[2] It was only Captain Barclay's accumulated winnings from his 1,000-mile wager at Newmarket and at Thistleton Gap that allowed him to indulge his sporting interests so enthusiastically, and to spend so extravagantly. His costs were high, and a pack of hounds and a stable of hunters for the hunting season wore holes in the pockets of even the very wealthy. His huge bet at Thistleton Gap also showed he was still willing to take enormous risks with his money. His attitude to money was odd. He spent almost none of it on personal luxury or on comfort. Indeed, he made a point of living as frugally as possible. Nevertheless, he gambled freely and socialised extravagantly, and had as little sense of the value of money as many other gentlemen of the Fancy.

The staff at Ury was always small, but Rodney did have a young maid. Her name was Mary Dalgarno and she was 17. Mary was a bright, intelligent, dark-haired girl, from a poor family in Aberdeen. She was described as being of 'low extraction' and her father, Alexander Dalgarno, as 'a man in an obscure position of life' who lived on Water Street near the harbour. To be fair to him however, he was also described as 'a person of excellent and irreproachable character'.[3] A poor but respectable family such as the Dalgarnos was always glad to have a daughter in service in the big house.

On Captain Barclay's return from London in the autumn of 1814, he took an immediate fancy to Mary Dalgarno and tried to get her into bed. He was now 36 years old and used to getting his own way, and there were few that could, or dared refuse him anything. Nevertheless, Mary resisted him and she stuck to her principles long enough to frustrate and annoy Captain Barclay and push him to his limit, as few before had ever dared to.

Throughout the winter of 1814 and the spring and summer of 1815, while the whole of Britain followed the exploits of Napoleon as he escaped from Elba and was eventually stopped by Wellington and Blucher at Waterloo, Captain Barclay was possessed by his desire for his sister's young maid. Eventually, to weaken her resolve he told her that he wanted to marry her. How many poor servant girls in the past have heard such a promise from the lord and master of the house? And how many have succumbed? Mary did too, but only after she had entered into a sort of solemn pact with him whereby they each agreed that they would, one day, marry each other. When, was apparently not part of the pact.

It cannot have taken long for Rodney to find out that her brother was having sex at Ury with her young maid, but there is no record of what was said about it. It may have been Rodney's discovery of the affair that led to Captain Barclay taking Mary away from Ury. It may, on the other hand, have been Mary herself. She was proving herself to be a determined and spirited young woman, and she was unwilling to forget their promises. It may have been Mary who refused to live at Ury as the laird's mistress one minute, and his sister's maid, the next. Whatever the reason, they left Ury together in the autumn of 1815 and drove south to his 'hunting seat' at Fritwell, just north of Oxford. It was 450 miles away, and they could live there with fewer prying eyes and fewer questions asked. The hunting seat was no ordinary one; it was the old Manor House at Fritwell, opposite the church.[4]

Whatever story Mary told her father about why she was leaving Scotland for England, she gave no hint to him that the real reason was that she was going to live with Captain Barclay as his mistress. On arrival at Fritwell, Captain Barclay added a dramatic new twist to the saga. He introduced Mary to the local vicar, as his wife.

Their arrival was a big event in the village, and to mark the occasion the church bells rang a welcome for them.[5] In the first few days all was happy bustle and excitement as the trunks were unpacked and Mary engaged her own servants. Renovation began and Mary went with her 'husband' to the carpenter's shop to talk to the men about what needed to be done at the Manor House for its new mistress.[6] Then they settled down to 'married' life together. Captain Barclay introduced her to his friends and began to live the life of a country gentleman, socialising and going out with the hunt as often as he could. Life was not quite 'normal', however. Mary refused to live contentedly at Fritwell, or anywhere else, as Captain Barclay's mistress, only as his wife. She would not forget their pact.

No one can be certain whether Captain Barclay ever intended to marry Mary. If he had been serious in his intention to do so, why did he not do it in Scotland? There was a steady flow of young couples going from England to Gretna Green precisely because the lower age of consent made it easier to marry in Scotland. In England Mary was underage and would require her father's permission. Why had Captain Barclay taken her to England? If he had wanted to avoid the disapproving looks and comments of his fellow gentlemen and their wives around Ury, why had he not gone to Inverness or somewhere else in Scotland? Taking her to England made it even more difficult for them to realise their promises. Perhaps that is why he did it.

Under pressure from Mary and to prove he was still committed to his promise, Captain Barclay applied for a licence to marry her. He must have known, however, that as Mary was a minor, it would not be granted without her father's permission, and of course it was not. Captain Barclay was still unwilling to make his arrangement with Mary public in Scotland, and so could not ask her father. That is always assuming he did intend to marry her. The greatest likelihood was that the application was a ruse simply to satisfy Mary. He also made the application for a license to marry at a parish some distance away so that none of the Fritwell villagers ever knew it had been made. As far as the Fritwell folk were concerned, they were already husband and wife.

Throughout the winter of 1815–16, Captain Barclay and Mary lived at Fritwell. Wearing his famous Gentleman Jackson leather breeches, he spent his time following some of the most famous hunts in England, often at Melton Mowbray, considered by many to be the capital of the hunting world, and only about ten miles from Thistleton Gap. Here he renewed his friendship with Charles Apperley, alias 'Nimrod', the great authority on coach travel, and George Osbaldeston, known as 'Squire' to all his contemporaries, who was a famous gambler, rider and master of foxhounds.[7] Both Nimrod and the Squire were in tune with Captain Barclay and the Fancy, and their friendships were to last all his life. He also met up again with Beau Brummell, who had been at the Game Chicken–John Gully fight at Hailsham nine years earlier.[8] They were an unlikely pair, but they did have several friends in common. One was Alderman Harvey Christian Coombe, who was once Lord Mayor of London. He was also a brewer and so was known to his friends as 'Mash-tub'. Mash-tub was an important and influential member of the Fancy and was one of the high rollers at the various London gambling clubs which Brummell, to his cost, also frequented. Beau Brummell owed £10,000 to Mash-tub and others. He had already fallen out with the Prince Regent over his 'fat friend' remark at the Argyll Rooms in 1812 and his star had been in decline ever since.[9] His excessive gambling and extravagant tastes made his end predictable and inevitable. He fled to France May 1816 to escape arrest for debt, leaving his porcelain, plate, port, table linen, books and guns to be sold by Christie's.

Mary, meanwhile, was proving herself a to be a young woman of exceptional talents. In public, she played the role of Captain Barclay's wife brilliantly. Her manners, speech and deportment were so clearly those of a lady that all the servants, villagers and local dignitaries were taken in completely. She even fooled her own maid. In private, things were different. Mary was now pregnant and she became increasingly distressed that they were not yet married.

On 4 July 1816 Mary gave birth to a daughter, who was baptised Margaret, after Captain Barclay's favourite sister Mag, at Fritwell on 12 October.[10] Captain Barclay and his 'wife' were now a stable part of village life and played the role of lord and lady of the Manor. Less than three weeks after Margaret was born, Fritwell, like villages all over the country, celebrated the first anniversary of Wellington's victory at Waterloo. When 'Captain and Mrs Barclay' attended Fritwell's 'Waterloo Feast' as guests of honour, they gave everyone a reason for a triple celebration. They celebrated Wellington's great victory, drank the health of their new baby, and they told everyone that this was also their first wedding anniversary! Captain Barclay was not entirely satisfied however, and added a toast hoping that 'the next (child) might be a son and heir'.[11] For a while the Manor House was the scene of domestic contentment. A nursemaid was appointed for the new baby and all the women in the house loved taking a turn holding and rocking little Margaret in their arms. Even Captain Barclay seemed to be enjoying life with Mary and behaved, at least in public, as if this situation could go on for ever. Mary, however, was a determined woman.

For him there was any number of diversions. His status in the Fancy was undiminished, as a famous ex-athlete, a successful trainer, and now as the architect of his famous 'system', and there were almost endless demands to attend events and functions, demands that he was unable to refuse, so he spent less and less time at Fritwell. Over the Christmas period in 1815 he had travelled to Blackheath, south of Greenwich, to see Josiah Eaton, a baker, complete one mile every hour for 1,100 hours – more than four days longer than his own great effort.[12] Captain Barclay, however, was unimpressed, even though Eaton was more than ten years older than he was. He suspected some trickery or that someone had let slip their vigilance and so allowed the athlete to miss a few miles or at least a longer recovery now and then. He would never accept that anyone had beaten his 1,000-mile performance.

It was certainly true that over the years many had attempted it and failed, but not all. The first reported success was in 1811 when it was claimed that Thomas Standen had completed 1,100 miles on the 'Barclay Plan', that is one mile every hour with two miles back-to-back.[13] Captain Barclay was unconvinced by this, too. Instead, he preferred to list those who had failed. Mr Howe on Cliffe Common in Somerset, who lasted only 15 days.[14] Mr Blackie who resigned on the 23rd day having lost 48 lbs.[15] Mr Martindale who completed only 30 days and lost 20 lbs.[16] In the summer of 1816, however, Josiah Eaton settled any dispute about his ability when he once again completed 1,100 miles in 1,100 hours at Blackheath, but this time reduced his recovery period by starting each mile within 20 minutes of the start of each hour, a vastly more difficult undertaking than the 'Barclay Plan'.[17] Twice he had out-Barclayed Barclay. The third occasion was even more extraordinary. Three months later he set out on Brixton Causeway to walk 2,000 half-miles in 2,000 successive half-hours, thus reducing the longest possible rest period to little more than 40 minutes, even if he followed the 'Barclay Plan'. He eventually had to give up after completing 1,998 half-miles.[18]

The other great new endurance star among the pedestrians was George Wilson, a poor, thin man who was even older than Josiah Eaton.[19] George Wilson, however, had a flair for showmanship, and in September 1815, also at Blackheath, he set out at 6 a.m. to go 1,000 miles in 20 days. He wore either a large, broad-brimmed Chinese hat or a green, silk hunting cap on his head, which he held slightly to one side as he walked. He attracted such vast crowds that Blackheath turned into a cross between a fair and a carnival. Men had to go in front of him with whips to cut a way through the spectators, and men with 10ft staves followed behind to stop them closing in and treading on his heels. Tents and booths were erected everywhere. The largest ones were put up by wine and liquor sellers and caterers who arranged chairs inside, facing out towards the action. They also provided musicians to entertain their guests. Waiters served drinks and food – oysters, lobsters, hams, sirloin and cold rounds of beef. A 'celebrated elephant' was stationed at George Wilson's headquarters and trumpeted at the end of every mile, and Saunders arrived with his Equestrian Theatre.[20] There were menageries, jugglers, fire-eaters and a Scottish piper. The local inn, the Hare and Billet, served more than 2,500 pints of beer alone, every day. For those seeking mementoes copperplate presses were at work producing portraits and a different action picture of George Wilson every day. The event made him so famous, he became known afterwards as 'The Blackheath Pedestrian'.

The Blackheath Pedestrian had been inspired by Captain Barclay and in the past had gone to see him in action. With his poor background he felt he couldn't rival Captain Barclay's fashionable appeal, but he hadn't bargained for the public's interest. To restore peace and quiet to Blackheath some magistrates issued a warrant for his arrest on the morning of the 16th day. He had gone 751¼ miles. This had never been a Fancy event. No wealthy gentlemen had put up money for it or placed bets on its outcome. Only 100 guineas were at stake and that was raised by subscription.[21] This was a new sort of pedestrian event and was promoted and funded by an emerging commercial, or 'middle-class'. Sport was changing.

During this time at Fritwell, Captain Barclay also travelled to see other pedestrians in action, including Old Tom Jenkins,[22] Ned Rayner[23] and Daniel Crisp,[24] and attended fights involving Jack Carter,[25] Tom Oliver,[26] Jack Scroggins,[27] Harry Holt,[28] Jack Randall,[29] Tom Spring,[30] Jack Stringer,[31] Bill Neat,[32] Jack Church[33] and others. He was even appointed umpire for Tom Oliver in his fight with Jack Carter at Gretna Green, in October 1816, just eight days before baby Margaret was christened at Fritwell.[34] The Marquis of Queensberry was the umpire for Carter. The irony of a visit to Gretna Green without Mary, who would have given anything to have accompanied him to the blacksmith's shop there, cannot have been lost on either of them.

Captain Barclay's trips became longer and longer, and often he returned to Ury leaving Mary alone at Fritwell with the baby and the servants. Eventually he was spending more time at Ury than Fritwell. Mary waited, sometimes patiently and sometimes not, for her man to return. She had pictures of him. Her favourites were two miniatures he had given her, one in his walking dress and one in a boxing attitude,[35] but she would rather he was there in person. There was no sign that he was making any preparations for their marriage. Even Captain Barclay had to admit that Mary was 'uneasy and distressed'.[36] In early September after they had been at Fritwell for two years, Captain Barclay set off for the fight between Tom Spring and Jack Stringer at Molesey Hurst.[37] Afterwards he returned to Ury, not Fritwell. It was too much for Mary and she left the Manor House and made her way back with little Margaret to Aberdeen, to her father's modest house.

It was the autumn of 1817. Radical voices had begun to make themselves heard as victory euphoria had turned to post-war discontent. In December 1816 the meeting of the radical Spenceans at Spa Fields had attracted thousands and the government had become convinced that there was 'a plot to seize London'. In March 1817 Habeas Corpus had been suspended, and radical activity had largely been driven underground. William Cobbett had fled to America but continued to write there. Also in March, the Blanket March from Lancashire to London had held the threat of violence. In June Jeremiah Brandreth had attempted to whip up revolutionary feelings on the Nottingham – Derbyshire borders, adding to the mood of confrontation between a people and their government, and demanding major reforms. Bills had been rushed through Parliament to prohibit the holding of seditious meetings and men who might once have been tried as rioters were now tried for treason.[38] Such was the atmosphere in the north of England as Mary and her baby made their risky journey from Fritwell to Aberdeen. No records survive of how they got there or who, if anyone, accompanied them.

To add to Mary's concerns, she must have wondered what would greet her when she got back home. She had left deceitfully, was unmarried, but returned with a baby. When Captain Barclay heard that Mary and the baby had returned to Aberdeen, only a handful of miles away, he sped over there. When he arrived in Aberdeen he had to do something urgently to calm the distressed but determined Mary. He may have had an irate father and an indignant family to contend with, and he had his own conscience to satisfy. There were two possible courses of action. One was to marry Mary. This would almost certainly have satisfied Mary and her father. Alternatively, he could have made it clear that he wasn't going to marry her, and made provision for her future and the baby's. Captain Barclay took neither option and created a third. He went to Aberdeen University to seek the advice of Professor William Paul, who 20 years earlier had been his tutor at Ury. The man whom Samuel Galton had criticised so strongly for failing to guide or control the young Robert Barclay Allardice properly was now Professor of Philosophy at King's College. William Paul arranged for David Hutcheon, an advocate from Aberdeen, to prepare a 'deed', which was completed and delivered in November. While he waited for it, Captain Barclay stayed at Ury and Mary at Water Street in Aberdeen with her father.[39]

The deed was a legal document, which acknowledged:

a) Captain Barclay and Mary Dalgarno had in the past accepted each other as lawful spouses, and
b) this had been done in contemplation of their future marriage.
c) Captain Barclay would pay her £300 a year for life, and a share of his estate.

Captain Barclay called it a 'contract of marriage'. It wasn't that, but it was a legal recognition of their earlier promises to each other and it did give her financial security. Had he intended to marry her, it would have been much easier to do so than to go to the trouble and cost of having such a strange document drawn up. Was he trying to find a way of keeping Mary without actually marrying her? Was this an act of defiance to prove to Mary that he could not be pushed faster than he wanted to go? There is no doubt that he was intent on delaying their marriage, at the very least. Whatever his motives, however, the 'contract' worked. Captain Barclay and Mary Dalgarno both signed it, so did their witnesses, Alexander Dalgarno, her father, Professor Paul and David Hutcheon. For Mary it was at least a step forward, but only a small step. She had been in Aberdeen for three months, but now she had her 'contract' she agreed to go back to Fritwell. Captain Barclay, however, would not be prevailed upon to go with her. He followed later.

There were some other beneficiaries of this episode. Having been forced to see first-hand the suffering and hardship of the local poor, Captain Barclay did what any self-respecting laird would have done. He acted to alleviate their misery and donated 50 bolls of coal to the poor of Stonehaven to help them keep warm in the winter, a gesture he repeated for several years.[40]

In the winter of 1817–18 he returned to Fritwell and immediately immersed himself in the local hunting scene again, this time with such a single-minded intensity that the hunting fraternity still talked about it twenty years later. He had only four hunters, one of which was a 'fine Scottish mare', and yet he managed to go out with the hunt that season on at least 82 days.[41] This was typical Barclay behaviour. He was a man with an almost insatiable appetite – and need – for hard, physical work.

The following summer Captain Barclay turned his attention to the pedestrian and boxing scenes. He was now a regular, almost full-time trainer, whose 'sound judgement' the sporting world was coming increasingly to respect. He trained Daniel Crisp the pedestrian,[42] and Bill Neat the pugilist,[43] for various contests. George Cooper, another pugilist, however, seemed to 'train off'.[44] In other words he seemed to get worse with training. Presumably he was doing enough physical work already, and the additional training was an unwelcome overload.

When the winter came round again he showed all the signs of settling once more into his now familiar all-absorbing hunting routine. He made no move that suggested he ever intended to convert the 'contract of marriage' into an actual one, and the mood of happy reconciliation with Mary slipped away. Once again she was pregnant. Over a year had passed since she had returned to Fritwell, happy in the knowledge that she had her contract, but the contract had the hallmark of an empty document and she could hardly escape the conclusion that Captain Barclay had no intention of marrying her. After her 21st birthday she became depressed, distraught and quite ill. Perhaps she had convinced herself that the barrier to them marrying was that she was still legally a minor in England.

Mary's distressed mental state forced Captain Barclay to reconsider his attitudes and his behaviour towards her, for in the spring of 1819 he had a change of heart. He put Mary and little Margaret in his carriage and drove them to his rooms in London. They lived there together, long enough to provide the necessary six months' qualifying residence within the Parish of St George's, where Captain Barclay applied for, and was granted, a marriage licence.[45]

On 19 July 1819 Mary Dalgarno walked down the aisle of the fashionable St George's Church in Hanover Square and married Captain Barclay.[46] It was only a long stone's throw from Bond Street and Jackson's Rooms. Almost everyone, it seemed, married in St George's. In 1816 there were 1,063 weddings there, including nine on Christmas Day alone. It was such a popular marriage venue that it became known as 'the London Temple of Hymen'. Percy Byshe Shelley and Harriet Westbrook married there in 1814, and three months after Captain Barclay and Mary Dalgarno's ceremony, Augustus Frederick Fitzclarence, the eldest son of the Duke of Clarence and Mrs Jordan, married Mary Wyndham Fox there.[47] Ten days after their wedding, Mary gave birth to their second daughter, whom they named Mary after her mother and after one of Captain Barclay's twin sisters, who had died at the age of 19.[48]

Even by the anything-goes moral standards of the Regency, it was a daring thing to do to walk down the aisle nearly nine months pregnant, even in London's Temple of Hymen. One thing was certain; as they had convinced everyone at Fritwell that they were already husband and wife, they could not return there and acknowledge the deceit. Nor could they go back to Ury. They could not be sure whether Mary, an ex-servant girl of 'low extraction', would be accepted into polite society. There was also the delicate matter of Rodney, Captain Barclay's sister. What would she feel about welcoming her servant girl back as the lady of the house? Instead, Captain Barclay acquired another hunting lodge in the village of Old in Northamptonshire, and Captain and Mrs Barclay and their two children went to live there.[49]

They were settled in Old in time for the winter and it was probably the first time in their four-year relationship that Mary had a clear, untroubled mind. Nevertheless, a marriage ceremony cannot in itself solve everything. There were still many scars to heal and a new future to create. Mag Gurney made a start. She held out an olive branch by travelling to Old to meet the new Mrs Barclay Allardice, the headstrong three-year-old little Margaret and the baby.[50] This was the first sign that Mary might be accepted into the Barclay family.

Despite this promising move, Captain Barclay and Mary could not stay for ever in the hunting lodge at Old. Sooner or later plans would have to be made for the family to return to Ury. What sort of life would Mary have back in Scotland? It would not be easy for her to be integrated into 'polite society'. The social gulf was so large she could be isolated: the laird's wife who received no invitations and whom no one visited. Captain Barclay wrote to Mrs Duff of Fetteresso, the nearest neighbour to Ury, explaining the situation. Mrs Duff deserves an affectionate footnote in the history of compassion. She wrote back promising that whenever Mary returned to Ury, she would call on her and treat her in a manner fitting the laird's wife.[51] Things were looking better for Mary.

In the spring of 1820 she was pregnant again. She was 23 and Captain Barclay 40. The spring and summer of 1820 must have been a happy time for Mary. Her husband had swallowed his pride and was trying to ease her way into his family and into the social scene in Scotland. As she was pregnant, however, they did not make the long journey north. On Sunday 27 August 1820 Mary gave birth to a son but he died within a few minutes. Three days later, on Wednesday 30th, Mary died too.[52]

On Friday, while Mary's body still lay in the house, Captain Barclay solemnly began to write on the title page of a new family Bible.[53] First, his name, R. Barclay Allardice and the date, 1st September 1820. Then the dates of the birth of his first daughter, Margaret; the birth of his second daughter, Mary; and the death of his wife, Mary. He did not mention his son. He took the miniature of himself in boxing attitude that he had given to Mary, and which was her favourite, and hung it on his watch chain.

On the following Tuesday Mary was buried in the churchyard of the parish church of Old, and her small son was buried with her.[54] Her headstone read:

*Sacred*
*To the memory of*
*Mary, wife*
*of Robert Barclay Allardice, Esqr*
*of Ury*
*in Kincardineshire,*
*North Britain,*
*who died August 30, 1820,*
*Aged 23 years.*

She had been Mrs Barclay Allardice for a little over one year.

When their mother died, Margaret was four and something of a handful, and Mary was 13 months old. Captain Barclay 'adored' Mary but he knew that he had a particular responsibility to Margaret, who had been born three years before he and Mary were married and so was illegitimate. Once back at Ury he began to make arrangements for her future and wrote to Lord George Cranston and Francis Jeffrey, legal counsels in Edinburgh, seeking their advice. This was the same Francis, Lord Jeffrey who, with Sydney Smith and Henry Brougham, had founded *The Edinburgh Review* and was its powerful editor. He was

remembered for his famous put-down in 1814 – 'This will never do' –
when reviewing Wordsworth's *'Excursion'*.[55] He also held well-known
views on the importance to society of property and inherited rank, and
the privilege and power that went with them.[56] Captain Barclay posed
Cranston and Jeffrey a series of questions, and expressed the wish that
Margaret, his elder daughter should:

1. be considered 'legitimate', and
2. inherit Ury on his death, even though earlier deeds (1722) specified
that inheritance could be by males only.

Only if Margaret was legitimate could she inherit Ury, or one day
become the Countess of Airth and Menteith. Captain Barclay had
known virtually all his life that when his mother died he could make a
claim to the title '2nd Earl of Airth and Menteith', but as she remained
in good health the claim to the earldoms had lain dormant since he was
a boy. It had, however, never been forgotten. When the time came to
advance his claim it would establish for ever his status and that of
his family.

The obvious way for Captain Barclay to legitimise Margaret
was to claim that he and Mary were married before Margaret was
born. He went back to the 'contract of marriage' drawn up to
entice Margaret back to Fritwell after she had run away. The
wording that they had 'accepted each other for lawful spouses'
now took on a new significance. Could their mutual promises
to each other at Ury be considered a marriage? If not, could the
contract of marriage be used retrospectively to legitimise Margaret?
The legal issues were complex. The contract would not have had
any validity in England, but what did Scottish law say on these
matters?

In an attempt to win legitimacy for Margaret, Captain Barclay
exposed with great candour and honesty, the whole of his relationship
with Mary Dalgarno.[57] One striking thing about the 24-page document
that resulted was that he never seems to have considered that he might

one day have a son who would inherit Ury. He had decided never to marry again.

The legal men wanted to probe further. Francis Jeffrey dismissed the promises the Captain and Mary had made to each other. 'I do not think that the original promise . . . can be proved,' he wrote. The written 'contract' was a different matter. It was obviously a formal promise, and his reading of Scottish law was that if Captain Barclay and Mary had sex in Scotland after the 'contract' had been agreed, it would have the effect of making 'a complete Scottish marriage', and would have 'the effect of legitimising the existing progeny'. 'If there is evidence of the copula in Scotland subsequent to the marriage contract I am of the opinion that a Declaration of Legitimacy should be brought in the name of the Eldest Daughter . . .'[58] Evidence that they had sex in Scotland would obviously be hard to come by. She was dead, and even Captain Barclay had to admit that during the three months that the 'contract' was being drawn up, Mary lived in Aberdeen and he lived at Ury.

George Cranstoun's opinion was more promising: 'I am of the opinion that the . . . contract of marriage . . . entered into when the parties were cohabiting in Scotland . . . constituted a legal marriage, and had the effect of legitimising the children previously born of the connection . . .'[59] Even this view, however, was based on their 'cohabiting in Scotland' during the critical three months. Both lawyers agreed that the 'contract' followed by sex in Scotland would have legitimised Margaret retrospectively under Scottish law, and this seems to have satisfied Captain Barclay. Everyone assumed they had sex.

For all practical purposes Margaret could now be considered legitimate, and the last two years of anxiety and distress that Mary experienced when Captain Barclay delayed marrying may well have been unnecessary. Perhaps she had been his lawful wife all this time.

Captain Barclay had been out of the mainstream of the Fancy in London for so long that rumours began circulating about him. One was that he was engaged in a wager to go from London to Edinburgh without money, supporting himself by begging all the way. The story wasn't true. Captain Barclay wasn't begging, or living in barns, or walking to London, but someone was. It turned out to be a much younger and smaller man.[60]

But although Captain Barclay was absent from the main activities of the Fancy, his interest hadn't waned, and at the end of the year there was a big enough event to tempt him to Berkshire. It was a fight between Tom Hickman and the Bristolian Bill Neat, who stood a little less than 6' in height, and 'hits from the shoulder with an astonishing and peculiar force'. Hickman was a Black Countryman whose fists possessed 'the knocking-down force of a forge-hammer', and who was 'ferocious in the fight, even to bull-dog fierceness'. He was known as 'The Gas Light Man', or simply 'Gas'. Captain Barclay was among the 30,000 fight fans who crowded on to Hungerford Downs on 11 December 1821 and saw Bill Neat defeat Gas in less than 25 minutes. It was one of the greatest fights for years.[61]

The Fancy that Captain Barclay came back to had changed, however. Those with a nostalgia for the past continued to celebrate the old Prize Ring and its heroes. In March 1819, Gentleman Jackson had arranged a show for Archduke Maximilian, who had expressed a wish to see a demonstration of the 'national and manly sports' during his visit to London. It had been a great success, the Archduke particularly admiring the 'manly and fine appearance' of Tom Cribb and the 'muscular arm of Tom Oliver', and giving praise to 'the manliness of the English character'. The pugilists had become a tourist attraction.[62] In 1820, aware that Gentleman Jackson might soon be coming to the end of his career, the Fancy had presented him with a magnificent service of silver plate worth 300 guineas in recognition of his past services.[63]

The most splendid and prestigious occasion in which they were involved was the Prince Regent's coronation. Following the dangerous events of 'Peterloo' in 1819 and the Cato Street plot in 1820, Lord Liverpool's government had a fear of revolution and civil disorder.

Lord Gwydyr, the Deputy Great Chamberlain of England, who was responsible for the coronation arrangements, was also concerned about Queen Caroline, who seemed to be as popular with the ordinary people as she was hated by her husband, the Prince Regent. He ignored her at every turn and planned to exclude her from his coronation at Westminster Hall. How would the people react? To be on the safe side if things turned ugly, Lord Gwydyr, apparently at the Prince Regent's suggestion, approached Gentleman Jackson to select a band of pugilists to act as a special security force at the doors of Westminster Hall. With the help of a Mr Watson, a member of the Fancy, Gentleman Jackson selected 18 pugilists:

| | | |
|---|---|---|
| Tom Cribb | Harry Harmer | Peter Crawley |
| Tom Spring | Harry Lee | Dick Curtis |
| Tom Belcher | Tom Owen | Ben Medley |
| Jack Carter | Josh Hudson | Bob Purcell |
| Bill Richmond | Tom Oliver | Phil Sampson |
| Ben Burn | Harry Holt | Bill Eales. |

They were splendidly dressed as royal pages and stationed with a gatekeeper at different entrances. At the great doors were Gentleman Jackson, Tom Cribb and Tom Spring. As he entered the Hall on the great day, the Prince Regent 'cast a pleasing glance' on Gentleman Jackson 'by way of recognition'.[64] As feared, however, Queen Caroline followed him to the Hall in her state coach drawn by six bay horses. Lady Hood, her Lady of the Bedchamber, and Lady Anne Hamilton, her Mistress of the Robes, accompanied her. Behind, in another carriage, came Lord Hood, her Chamberlain, and the Hon. Keppel Craven, her Vice-Chamberlain, who was also a keen member of the Fancy. The Queen and Lord Hood left their carriages and walked up to the great doors. 'I present to you your Queen. Surely it is not necessary for her to have a ticket,' Lord Hood said. The gatekeeper and guards would not admit her. She did need a ticket. He tried again. 'This is your Queen. She is entitled to admission without such a form.' Still no admittance. 'Yes, I am your Queen,' she said. 'Will you not admit me?' They would not, and Queen Caroline got back into her carriage and drove away. That night she was ill, and she died the following month having overdosed on laudanum, opium and castor oil.[65] As far as crowd-control and law and order were concerned, the event had been a great success. Lord Gwydyr sent all the prize-fighters a letter of appreciation and gave them a thank-you dinner at his own expense at which he presented them with a gold coronation medal donated by the King. They raffled it among themselves and Tom Belcher won it.[66]

In the years since Waterloo, the social order – the gentlemen on one side and the lower order on the other – was undergoing great change. Fewer young gentlemen with money to burn were joining the Fancy, and a new commercially driven middle class was becoming important. The lower order now came from the new towns, and were part of an emerging working class motivated by money, not honour or the demonstration of manliness. A correspondent in *The Sporting Magazine* could see the writing on the wall: when 'the spirit of manly combat' gives way to greed, and 'the art of boxing is made a trade of', then deceit and trickery are not far behind.[67] He had a point. Some of the biggest fights were suspect, and had been for years. On April Fools' Day in 1818, for example, there were so many questions about Ned Painter giving up a fight after an hour and 29 minutes and 31 rounds of fighting that the dispute over it lasted for over a year and a half. Eventually, to clear his name, Ned Painter had to get a certificate from Mr Cline, an eminent surgeon, to the effect that his shoulder blade was so badly injured by a blow from the corner post that he could not use his arm. A committee of the Pugilistic Club considered the case and decided in his favour.[68] On 4 May 1819, and while this dispute still raged, a fight took place on Crawley Downs between Jack Randall and Jack Martin. Randall won, but it was commonly believed that on the morning of the fight he had been hocussed with a glass of red wine. Fortunately for Randall it did not have the soporific effect that was intended, but acted as a purgative and went straight through him.[69]

Despite all the evidence that their sport was on the slippery slope of corruption and greed, the ever hopeful Fancy still held their dinners, still sang their songs afterwards and still gave, listened to and applauded speeches about the importance of boxing to the nation. After the 'excellent dinner' following the Randall – Turner fight, for example, 'an amateur of distinction' eulogised the virtues of 'scientific pugilism' from a 'national point of view'. He spoke about it 'flooring Dandyism, and levelling that sort of effeminacy that is making such rapid progress at the present time, in degenerating the true character of Englishmen'. He went back to the victories of the war, victories that 'had decided the fate of Europe, overthrown tyranny and oppression'. It was all down to one thing the 'pluck of Englishmen'. 'To increase the breed – to promote true courage upon all occasions – and to perpetuate the honour of his country was his only aim, and the aim of all the admirers of English boxing'. Thunderous applause followed.[70] The Fancy loved it, but they were increasingly out of step with what was happening around them.

In May 1823 Tom Cribb had now been the Champion for over ten years without once having to defend his title in the ring and things could not go on like this for much longer. Tom Cribb was given the title of Honorary Champion for life, a sort of Champion Emeritus, and was presented with a belt decorated with silver fists. He formally announced his retirement – it was the end of an era.[71]

An even more significant event was the dispute involving Gentleman Jackson and one of the new fighters, John Martin, and his backer, a Mr Elliott. It was clear that the new men did not have the same values or code of honour, and Gentleman Jackson believed that dealing with them would tarnish his reputation. He immediately declared he would never again act as stakeholder and gave up his rooms on Bond Street.[72] Pierce Egan's description of him as 'the LINK that keeps the whole CHAIN together', was absolutely correct.[73] The Prize Ring and the Fancy began a steady downward decline from which they never fully recovered. Indeed, looking back in 1823, Daniel Mendoza claimed that 'there have not been ten honest fights within the last ten years'. The rot had already set in.[74]

The gentlemen of the Fancy were now less numerous and less influential. At Tom Cribb's farewell do, after he thanked the gentlemen of the Fancy who had supported him, he concluded by saying 'may your purses never fail you', precisely because there was every sign that they would.[75] There had been an influx of men from the other end of the social scale. Men who were streetwise and tricky, and some from the darker, grimier, criminal classes. Men like John Thurtell, who followed sport because it provided a cloak for the shadiest of activities.[76] Captain Barclay retreated from the Fancy to the smaller core of old-fashioned gentlemen sportsmen who were his friends. They were something of an anachronism, but perhaps with their influence sport could be returned to its old ways.

# CHAPTER TWELVE

# *The Blood of the Murdered*

*I certainly felt much distressed, that I should in any way, have been instrumental, in hurrying a fellow creature into eternity.*

ROBERT BARCLAY ALLARDICE, 1830

*The men of rank and fortune who assisted in the brutal exhibition ought not to be allowed to escape. The claims of justice, the blood of the murdered, and the well being of the country alike all call for an example.*

THE TIMES, 17 JUNE 1830

*The Captain had to get into a Dundee smack, and then hide for some time in Forfarshire till the Government tired and dropped the prosecution.*

FIELD AND FERN
THE DRUID, 1865

*I*t was in 1822 that Captain Barclay decided to create a new life for himself based at Ury. The 'serious' side of his life would be taken up with farming, and he would rely on a circle of local friends for his sport and entertainment. Lord Panmure and the Marquis of Huntly were part of his old set. Then there was John Wilson, who was appointed Professor of Moral Philosophy at Edinburgh University in 1820 because of his strong Tory sympathies, and was one of the oddest professorial appointments imaginable. He was six years younger than Captain Barclay, energetic, flamboyant and unpredictable, and knew more than most about boxing, pedestrianism and cock-fighting. Thomas de Quincey said of him that 'no man was a better judge upon questions of bodily prowess; and no man, at least no gentleman, was better acquainted with the records of the Fancy'.[1] He and Captain Barclay had a lot in common. Under the nom-de-plume 'Christopher North' he was a hugely successful journalist and in 1817 joined the editorial staff of *Blackwood's Magazine*. He was also a very popular Professor of Moral Philosophy, drawing large, enthusiastic audiences to his theatrical lectures, which was all the more remarkable because he knew less than he should about what he lectured so successfully on and relied heavily on notes provided by his friend Alexander Blair. Professor Wilson invariably clutched a handful of Blair's notes as he made his way into the lecture theatre, spread them out on the table in front of him and proceeded to give an eccentric tour de force that had his credulous audience eating out of his hand and cheering him as he came to a dramatic close.[2] John Wilson was a showman.

Perhaps we can get a hint of his style from the end of a review he did for *Blackwood's* in 1826 of the book *An Elementary Course of Gymnastic Exercises* by Captain Clias, a Swiss writer. A review, incidentally, in which he questions the author's knowledge and refers to his friend Captain Barclay to correct at least one of his facts. He winds up with a flourish:

Captain Clias, we wish you good morning. Gentle readers! remember that all the gymnastic exercises in the world are not worth a bam, without regular, sober, active habits of life. All kinds of debauchery and dissipation incapacitate equally for lying, standing, walking, running, leaping, wrestling, skating, swimming, and a thousand things else beside. O what a charm in moderation! How strong the heart beats and the lungs play! The eye, how it sparkles! And the mantling blood on the clear cheek, how beautiful! But your fat, pursy, purfled son of a witch, who, from morn to night, guzzles and gurgles like a town-drake in a gutter, and from night to morn snorts and snores to the disturbance of other two tenements, no system of gymnastics will keep that man alive till Christmas . . .[3]

What wonderful stuff! No wonder they queued up to hear him and hung on his every word, even if neither they nor he knew precisely what he was talking about.

Less eccentric friends were Deacon Williams, a rich and exuberant butcher from Aberdeen;[4] William Weatherell, a livestock auctioneer;[5] and Keillor Watson, the cattle farmer from Coupar Angus.[6] In Captain Barclay's group there were also young sportsmen who were the continuation of the Daft Laird tradition: Archibald Farquarson, who had been involved with Captain Barclay in the infamous Sturt affair, and Lord William Kennedy, a close neighbour. Like the Daft Laird, Lord Kennedy was a committed gambler who lost heavily at Crockford's and elsewhere.[7] On one occasion he wagered £500 a hole in a three-hole golf match at Montrose that was finally decided in the dark at 10.30 at night.[8] Unlike the Daft Laird, he was also a truly talented all-rounder, an excellent horseman, an outstanding shot, an enthusiastic and able driver of a coach and four, and a skilful fisherman. In August 1822, for a wager, Lord Kennedy shot 40 brace of grouse and rode 140 miles, all within 24 hours. Captain Barclay, who was the umpire, thought it was one of the best physical feats ever recorded.[9] Lord Kennedy also wagered that Captain Barclay could not find a man to throw a cricket ball 100 yards 'both ways' (that is out and back). The event eventually came off in December

1822 in Hyde Park.[10] Captain Barclay was not a particularly good judge of throwers and he and his thrower lost the wager.

He was not a particularly good judge of cattle either, which was a particular drawback for a man who had decided to become a cattle farmer. Fortunately, his trio of friends, Williamson, Weatherell and Watson, were free with their advice which he was happy to take, and this brought him results. He tended to overdo everything. He kept his cattle up to their knees in grass, and grazed only half the number he could on his fields. They were certainly well fed. So well, they were far too fat at calving.[11] Indeed, he was so extravagant with feed he outstripped his ability to provide it locally and had to import hay from Rotterdam.[12] Nevertheless, he bought well at the sales, and he bred from his own herd and held his own sales. He probably over-catered too. One visitor thought the catering was the most notable feature of his cattle sales.[13] Even his plates and glass tumblers were the largest anyone had seen.[14] He also kept flocks of Leicester and Southdown sheep and grew wheat, oats and barley, but although his results were often good, he overspent on almost everything to achieve them. He had one other major fault. He was very good at the hands-on side of management at Ury and enjoyed going from place to place giving instructions, but the office seldom attracted him. Paper accumulated on his desk and on the floor around it.[15] His records were incomplete, his accounts were sketchy and he couldn't find the papers he needed. His success in building a new herd was hampered by not always remembering to record which bull went to which cow and often failing to enter his animals in the Herd Book.[16]

In comparison to his earlier years, the pattern of his life had completely changed. Now that he had the girls at home, Ury was his base, and he ventured south on relatively rare occasions. He went to church regularly and he took more interest in local affairs than ever before. To create a market for his and other local barley, he built a whisky distillery at Glenury[17] and contributed to the building of a steeple with a clock and bell for the County Buildings in Stonehaven.[18] He even attempted to provide a practical example of moral leadership by bringing a case before the local Justices of the Peace against Bill Findlay, one of his ploughmen, for mistreating a horse. The JPs fined Findlay 2 guineas for the use of the poor of the parish, and they took his wages of 7 guineas from him and gave them to Captain Barclay.[19] Captain Barclay might not have had the same qualms if the 'mistreatment' had been of another man, as Mr Sturt would have testified. Captain Barclay, himself had the reputation for being able to 'knock down an insolent bully as easily as a butcher fells an ox', and people learned not to cross him. Little wonder that they also said of him that 'when any company he formed a part of was annoyed by rudeness or puppyism, a very quick hint from him that the room had a door generally produced an effect of causing the offender to take the outside'.[20]

His style of discipline, however, was either the strong-arm variety or none at all. He let his girls go their own way. They did as they pleased and had the free run of Ury playing wherever they liked. It was a shattering blow to Captain Barclay on 14 October 1823, when Mary, who was four years old, died of scarlet fever.[21]

With Ury as his permanent base it was rarely feasible to spend several weeks training an athlete for an event, so, for some years he took on no new training challenges, but as the preeminent expert on pedestrianism he was much in demand as an official. In September 1824 he went to Kent to act as the deciding referee for Mr West's match to go the 66 miles from London to Maidstone and back.[22] In December he was at Hadley Park in Buckinghamshire as the umpire and recorder for the 20-mile match between Captain Methwin and Mr Nicholson.[23] In 1825 he actually accompanied Ralph Abernethy, a Scottish pedestrian, on his 285-mile, four-day wager, which started in Chelsea and went through Egham, Bath, Cheltenham, Oxford and Winchester.[24] In February 1826 he was umpire for Captain Fairburn's match to go 93 miles in 20 hours[25] and in April he was at Stockbridge Stour race course as umpire for the 24-hour match between Young Beddoe, Captain Fairburn and R.W. Paulett.[26]

Captain Barclay also kept his connections in the boxing world.

In May 1823 he travelled to Hinckley Down, near Andover, to see Tom Spring defeat Bill Neat in 37 minutes and formally become the first Champion of the Prize Ring since Tom Cribb, whose protégé he was.[27] In 1824 he was the deciding referee for the title fight at Chichester between Tom Spring and Jack Langan, an Irishman. Gentleman Jackson was called out of retirement to make the arrangements for it and more than 16,000 turned out to watch it. This was the second time Captain Barclay had refereed a fight for the Championship, but it was described as 'one of fairest battles ever witnessed' and, as referee, he had little to do. Spring won it after 1 hour and 49 minutes.[28]

Such highlights could not disguise the decline of both prize-fighting and pedestrianism, neither of which the Fancy controlled in any real sense any more. The growing number of working class athletes were creating their own version of sport. In 1823, for example, *The London Packet* reported 'the great Foot Race' between Defoe and James on Walsall race course in the Black Country. There were no free-spending gentlemen of the Fancy at Walsall. The crowd consisted entirely of '400 coal men and women', and the ground had to be roped to 'prevent jostling'.[29] At the same time at Kendal, Bernard McMullen withdrew from his attempt to walk 18 miles in three hours because the spectators were chiefly of the lower orders and managed to raise only 4 shillings as prize money. Bernard McMullen's mother, Mary, was a more famous pedestrian than he was. When she was in her 60s her speciality was 92 miles in 24 hours, and she travelled the country barefoot competing on market days and collecting money during her long efforts. But there was often very little in the collection tins.[30] Driven by want, even little girls were part of the action. Emma Matilda Freeman was only eight, yet in 1823 she competed in four events in nine weeks, none shorter than 30 miles. Her mother and father seem to have been her managers.[31] Many pedestrian matches were now squalid affairs, riddled with fraud and drugs, and no one could trust that the competitions were fair. Boxing's decline continued too, with disputes without number about the stake money and boxers withdrawn before their fights, or simply failing to turn up if their backers couldn't get the right odds. Pedestrianism and the Prize Ring had become a sordid business. Matches were fixed and fighters were hocussed. A cloud of dishonesty, deceit and mistrust hung over it all.

The Pugilistic Club was wound up in 1825.[32] But something was needed, and a Fair Play Club was formed in 1828.[33] The downward trend seemed irreversible, however, and in 1829 it slithered to its lowest point on the cricket ground at Leicester. The Champion of the Prize Ring was Jem Ward, following Tom Spring's retirement in 1825. He was the oldest of seven children born of Irish parents, and his father had a butcher's shop off Ratcliffe Highway in London's East End. In March 1829 Jem Ward dubiously declared himself unfit on the morning of a scheduled title fight against Simon Byrne, and left 14,000 fight fans waiting in vain at the ringside. Most were convinced that the only thing unfit was the odds he and his backers could get. This incident became known as 'the Leicester Hoax' and months of arguments followed.[34]

Captain Barclay decided that the Prize Ring needed a new start. Central to his plan was a powerful Scottish fighter named Alexander, or 'Sandy', McKay, who came originally from Badenoch, a sparsely populated area of Invernesshire, but had moved to Glasgow where he worked as a porter. His mother was said to be an illegitimate daughter of a Highland gentleman who carried in his veins the blood of Black Lochiel who had supported the Stuart cause so conspicuously at Culloden in 1745. Captain Barclay's grandmother was a daughter of Black Lochiel, and so, if the story is true, Sandy McKay and Captain Barclay were related, albeit on Sandy McKay's side, from the wrong side of the blanket.[35]

Sandy McKay was a very unusual build. He was 5'9" tall and weighed 14 stone. Squire Osbaldeston described him as:

> . . . the most powerful man for his inches I ever saw; his legs were so large, but at the same time so muscular that they were quite a curiosity. I should think he could lift any weight any man ever

did. . . . He was slow and devoid of science and trusted to his herculean strength.[36]

Huge arms completed the picture with the name '*Alex McKay*' tattooed in gunpowder on his right, rock-hard bicep.[37] His appearance conveyed a sense of menace and The Druid described him as an 'ugly, slouching, round-shouldered man'.[38] Behind the mask however, he was a mild and peaceful man with a gentle personality.

Sandy McKay had only ever fought once. It was in Dunoon on the River Clyde where he fought Simon Byrne. In the fifth round and after 47 minutes, McKay's second protested that Byrne 'went down unfairly'. The umpires disagreed and his supporters withdrew McKay in protest, and he consequently lost his £50 share of the stake money.[39] For over two and a half years McKay stayed out of the ring and showed no inclination ever to go back into it. Those who knew him said he had too gentle a nature to fight anyway, and so in normal circumstances Sandy McKay would have been destined for pugilistic obscurity. However, his reputation for prodigious strength and the accident of their blood bond attracted Captain Barclay. He thought that under his supervision McKay could win the Championship, and the Prize Ring could be given a new lease of life. First, McKay would need to win a rematch against Simon Byrne.

Captain Barclay orchestrated a series of letters from Sandy McKay to *Bell's Life in London*, Britain's top sporting newspaper, that stung Byrne into accepting the challenge.[40] Jubilant at his success, Captain Barclay left Ury for London to sign the Articles of Agreement. The fight was to be in June for £200 a side, and at an undisclosed location 150 miles from London.[41] Although Simon Byrne had been lured into the fight, he didn't really want it. He had set his heart on fighting Jem Ward next. Sandy McKay was even less keen to fight and became so down about his prospects that it affected his training. Even worse, he developed 'a gloomy foreboding' that he would not come out of the fight alive.[42]

Captain Barclay trained Sandy McKay at Ury throughout April

and May and reassured him that he had been watching fights all his life and had never seen anyone seriously hurt. In August 1824 *The Fancy Gazette* robustly dismissed the idea put about by the press that there had been many deaths in the ring. Of the 33 deaths quoted over the previous ten years, at least 29 could be dismissed as the result of 'accidental meetings, turn-ups, or quarrels'. In eight cases drink may have been a major factor and three were muggings.[43] Captain Barclay did everything he knew to lift McKay's mood, control his diet and improve his wind, speed and technique, but with limited success. McKay remained slow and his technique barely improved. Worst of all his confidence and self-belief were at rock bottom. He was unshakeable in his depressing view that he would not survive the fight. Captain Barclay worked out a fight strategy in which McKay would use his strength either against the ropes or in wrestling.

Captain Barclay approached Gentleman Jackson to come out of retirement to 'superintend' the fight and invited Squire Osbaldeston to be the deciding referee. They both agreed. The venue was arranged between Salcey Forest and the village of Hanslope, near the boundary between Northamptonshire and Buckinghamshire. Tom Cribb and George Cooper were appointed as second and bottle-holder for Sandy McKay. This would be a fight under the Fancy's old management. Simon Byrne appointed Tom Reynolds and Ruben Martin, two well-known Irish ex-fighters as his second and bottle-holder.[44]

On the morning of the fight, 2 June 1830, Gentleman Jackson oversaw the arrangements while Captain Barclay double-checked that everything for his fighter was in order. It was like old times. Around dawn the ring was built and the fighters went through their early-morning rituals and had a light breakfast. Richard Monday, the village barber, cut Sandy McKay's hair.[45] Squire Osbaldeston arrived from London with Sir Harry and Francis Holyoake and many gentlemen of the Fancy, while a large band of Irish fight fans arrived to support Simon Byrne. Later in the morning when Simon Byrne and Sandy McKay stepped into the ring followed by their seconds and bottle-holders there were thousands of fans at the ringside. The Irish put their money on Byrne of course, but McKay had many backers too. Most of the money, however, came from Captain Barclay and John Harrison from Buckinghamshire.[46]

It turned out to be the hottest day many could remember, but the fight went without great incident. The rounds were short as Byrne moved in quickly to deliver one, two, three blows and then went down to avoid retaliation. There was only one chance for McKay to employ his fight strategy, but as he was about to subdue Byrne with a wrestling hold, either his second or his bottle-holder pulled Byrne away by the 'band of his drawers'. The officials conferred, but the fight went on. Apart from this one opportunity there was nothing for Sandy McKay's fans to cheer. He took some terrible punishment with many blows on and around the left temple. One eyewitness said he was 'frightfully cut and disfigured' and a 'confused mass of gore and bruises'. After 53 minutes he was felled by a left-handed blow to the throat that ended the fight.[47]

Tom Cribb and George Cooper carried him back to his corner where Captain Barclay and Gentleman Jackson confirmed at a glance that he was unconscious. This was most unusual. The knock-out punch was not a regular part of prize-fighting. Boxers were worn down by their opponents with a mixture of blows and throws in what was essentially a trial of endurance. They finished their fights black and blue from bruising but seldom unconscious, except if their heads struck a corner post. Without gloves or taping on their fists, a big blow was as likely to break or damage a fighter's own hands as to knock out his opponent. Jem Belcher was a prime example. He could strike with greater speed and power than his own fists could stand and a fighter with a broken hand has little future. An unconscious boxer in the ring, therefore, was unexpected and alarming. A local surgeon, Joseph Heygate and a doctor friend hastened to McKay's corner. They bled him for half an hour but to no avail. It was obvious he had to be moved to receive better treatment elsewhere. Captain Barclay arranged for 'a kind of break', or wagon, to take McKay to the local inn, the Wat's Arms, while Dr Heygate kept his fingers in McKay's mouth to prevent him swallowing his own tongue. It was a subdued, anxious group that accompanied the motionless McKay.[48]

On arrival at the Wat's Arms there were so many people anxious to help they got in each other's way. There was total confusion. They tried to take the unconscious McKay upstairs on a makeshift stretcher but made the mistake of taking him feet first. The doctors protested that he should be carried with his head up, but the stairs were too narrow to turn him round.

The Fancy usually left the scene of a fight as soon as it was over but on this occasion they waited for news about McKay. There was a gloomy feeling in the air because they knew of his belief that he would die in the ring. Anxiety grew throughout the night and all the next day as Sandy McKay lay unconscious for about 30 hours. He died in the arms of the usually jovial Jack Carter, the Lancastrian fighter, at nine o'clock in the evening of 3 June.[49]

How did he know he was going to die in the fight? Had his foreboding been a premonition? Was his death predestined? An element of the supernatural insinuated itself eerily into the atmosphere of shock that hung over Captain Barclay and the others in the Wat's Arms on that June evening. Somewhat fatalistically Captain Barclay put it all down to 'unforeseen circumstances' that 'poor frail human foresight, never contemplated'. The fates were to blame, and 'I have nothing to upbraid myself for', he said.[50] Nevertheless they all took advantage of the long summer daylight hours to put as many miles between themselves and the Wat's Arms as possible.

Simon Byrne, Tom Reynolds and Ruben Martin left hurriedly for Ireland. Tom Cribb and George Cooper went into hiding somewhere in England.[51] Gentleman Jackson returned to London and stayed at home waiting to be called to give his evidence. Squire Osbaldeston also went home and waited. Precisely what Captain Barclay did has always been a mystery. The story went round that he rode at speed back to Scotland, probably travelling by minor roads, and then went into hiding, first in a fishing boat off the coast at Dundee, and later, somewhere in Forfarshire.[52]

Simon Byrne, Tom Reynolds and Ruben Martin were arrested at Liverpool on the Dublin steamer, but no other arrests were made. At the coroner's court under the Rev. Prettyman, a verdict of manslaughter was upheld against Simon Byrne, who was committed to jail pending the hearing at the Buckinghamshire County Assizes on 22 July, six weeks later. Reynolds, Martin, Cribb and Cooper were also charged with manslaughter, but whereas Reynolds and Martin were instructed to appear at the County Assizes, Cribb and Cooper could still not be found. In summing up, the Rev. Prettyman did not go as far as to name Captain Barclay personally, but there is no doubt that he was referring specifically to Captain Barclay when he said that there were 'persons more highly placed in society who ought also to be in the dock'.[53] Both the other officials, Gentlemen Jackson and Squire Osbaldeston, were at the fight because Captain Barclay had invited them, and the fighters, seconds and bottle-holders would not have been there had Captain Barclay not set the fight up. It was he who was the instigator and prime mover, and so he carried the major responsibility. He and Squire Osbaldeston were lucky not to be charged. Perhaps it wasn't merely luck. Squire Osbaldeston later complained that the episode 'cost me £200 or £300 to get out of it ... Prettyman the cause'.[54] It must have cost Captain Barclay at least as much.

Over the next few weeks leading up to the County Assizes, the press both reflected and led the public mood and demanded that the wealthy men behind the scenes be arrested. Perhaps there was a time when a gentleman might have been able to escape such public outcry but the gentlemen no longer had it all their own way. William Cobbett and the radicals were changing the rules. *The Times* wrote about the public indignation and alarm, and spoke of McKay's death as murder. Only Simon Byrne was in jail, '. . . the men of rank and fortune who assisted in the brutal exhibition ought not to be allowed to escape. The claims of justice, the blood of the murdered, and the well being of the country alike all call for an example.'[55]

Captain Barclay stayed in hiding. One week later, *The Times* continued with its campaign: '. . . we have not heard of the apprehension of any of the wealthy abettors . . .'[56] Even one month later no arrests had been made and the repeated appeals by the press that the men who were guilty of this 'murder' should meet justice, had all come to nothing. With the help of loyal friends, Captain Barclay, Tom Cribb and George Cooper kept out of reach.

While they were in hiding news came through of the death of George III, the former Prince Regent. This had the immediate effect of sending Sir Henry Halford and Sir Waller to Bushey at 6 a.m. on 26 June to wake the Duke of Clarence with the news. He was now King William IV. The wags passed on the story that he shook their hands and went back to bed because he had always wanted to sleep with a Queen. He had stopped sleeping with Mrs Jordan years before. After 20 years and after giving her ten children, he left her and she died in 1816 almost penniless. The Queen who was in bed at Bushey was Adelaide.[57] She was 27 years younger than the new King.

Captain Barclay knew the King well from their days following the Fancy. When he was still the Duke of Clarence, he had been at many fights with Captain Barclay but now he was 65 and he could have no influence on the fate of the Fancy or the Prize Ring. Other forces were now at work.

The trial at Buckingham County Assizes was the focus of great public interest and excitement and the court itself was 'crowded to excess'. The first hour was taken up with legal manoeuvrings, as Simon Byrne's counsel challenged no fewer than 20 potential jurors. Justice Littledale, who presided, announced that he would hear the indictments against the two seconds and two bottle-holders last, to give Tom Cribb and George Cooper the opportunity to surrender.[58]

If the court upheld the charge of manslaughter, it was virtually certain that warrants would go out for the apprehension and arrest of Captain Barclay, Cribb and Cooper. Perhaps John Harrison and others who had put up money for the fight might also be indicted. Captain Barclay could not hide for ever and he secretly made his way to Buckingham and waited there ready to surrender if the verdict went against Simon Byrne.[59]

In the trial, the defence was well organised and unscrupulous, even claiming under oath that Byrne and McKay were not fighting for money. The central issue however, turned out to be Dr Heygate's medical evidence. He described how at the autopsy he found 'a considerable effusion of blood, three or four tablespoons full' in McKay's brain. Such a rupture he believed, could have been caused by strong excitement, a blow to the head, a fall or strong bodily exertion. Most critical to Simon Byrne and Captain Barclay was his next conclusion: 'I think it most probable that what I saw arose from a fall than a blow; a fall from a man missing a blow might produce it.'[60] If this was the case, McKay might be responsible for his own death! The defence was then able to produce a witness, George Pacey, a local baker, who gave the following crucial evidence: 'I saw a man get over a gate about an hour before the fight. This was two miles from the fighting place. He fell over the gate onto the rough stones; the gate sprung from him, and he fell over it. His head was downwards. He got up and went on.'[61] The man was identified as Sandy McKay by his tattoo.

The jury reached their decision with almost indecent haste, deliberating for only two minutes. They announced their verdict – Simon Byrne was 'not guilty'. Captain Barclay came out of hiding and joined Simon Byrne and his supporters in their celebrations.[62] But for Captain Barclay, Gentleman Jackson, Tom Cribb and the rest of the ageing Fancy, it had been a close thing, and they were now associated in the public's mind with the worst excesses of a disreputable sport. How times had changed.

The extended Barclay family was horrified. Those that had been won over against their natural prejudices by his sporting successes, quickly reverted. Samuel Galton, the brother-in-law who had led the rest of the family in confronting Captain Barclay when he was a teenager, with his 'rather a disgrace' comment, was now old and infirm. Joseph John Gurney, a distant cousin, took his place. He was nearly ten years younger than Captain Barclay but universally loved and respected in the extended family for his kindness, good nature and generosity and had been known since childhood as the 'bright shining star'. He was a Quaker and a banker with a 'charming and benevolent countenance' and with an even more charming and benevolent disposition. He dressed so plainly that even his fellow Quakers made gentle jokes about it. He had long since given up sport and even thought fishing cruel.[63] After the trial Joseph John Gurney wrote to Captain Barclay to rebuke him on behalf of the family and to try to lead him to a better way. Captain Barclay defended himself, of course. Yes, he had been 'a patron and an encourager' of boxing and yes, he did have a 'staunch partiality' for 'general athletic exercises', but he had never done it out of 'any feeling of ferocity or *desire*, to make strife amongst men'. On the contrary, his motives were honourable ones, a conviction 'that I was encouraging a science, which tended to create, generosity of feeling amongst the lower orders, particularly to a foe, &c ... do away with rancorous feelings of revenge for real or supposed injuries'.[64]

He continued:

> If all mankind possessed your well constituted & pious mind there would be no necessity for public pugilistic exhibitions to impress the lower orders with a feeling of mercy & fair-play to a fallen foe – neither would there be occasion for soldiers, muskets, swords, &c – &c ... but, I am afraid, as long as human nature remains constituted as it is ... particularly amongst the lower orders, my idea on that subject has always been – that it was far better to encourage them to settle their disputes by fair and open combat, than harbour malice & ill will in the mind.

He should be judged, he said, by 'the intentions of the heart'. In short, his sport had always been prompted by gentlemanly motives – to be a good example to the lower classes. It was a private letter and none of his drinking partners in the Fancy taverns nor the Fancy themselves could make any comment.

The Prize Ring's reputation and that of the Fancy had sunk virtually without trace. No amount of denial on Captain Barclay's part could change the facts. Intentions were all very well but Sandy McKay, who would otherwise have been alive, was dead. It was another defining moment in Captain Barclay's life and he continued his letter to the 'bright shining star' with the following solemn words, 'I have . . . promised my friends, & made up my own mind, never again to take part in such like sports.' And to complete his humiliation, he concluded by thanking Joseph John contritely, 'I beg to assure you that I trust your kind advice will not be lost upon me.' He was 51 and his life would never be the same again.

## CHAPTER THIRTEEN

# *Barefoot in St James's*

*Self willed & imperious, no one attempted to control her
[Margaret] ... The child ran wild at Ury, barefoot as the
children of the poor.*

MARIA BARCLAY, 1917

*The 'Captain's Daughter' had always a welcome quite eloquent
in its warmth.*

STONEHAVEN JOURNAL, 20 AUGUST 1903

*None ... will forget ... the brilliance of her [Margaret's]
conversation, and her powers of description.*

ABERDEEN FREE PRESS, 28 AUGUST 1903

*S*evering his life-long links with pugilism meant doing the same with the Fancy. It was made easier by James Scott, a stagecoach proprietor in Edinburgh, who was starting a coach service between Edinburgh and Aberdeen and was looking for a local celebrity to drive the new coach, called *Defiance*, on its inaugural run. Scott approached Captain Barclay.[1] He was the obvious candidate. For nearly 30 years he had travelled the 500 miles from Aberdeen to London by coach and had seen at first hand the revolution on the roads. Travelling time had been cut in half as Thomas Telford, John McAdam and their like transformed the roads. In October 1824 *The Times* announced that workmen had erected temporary fencing in London and begun to macadamise 'the wide roadway' from Charing Cross to Parliament Street.[2] Two years later the same paper reported that macadamisation was progressing rapidly through the West End.[3] All over the country the volume and efficiency of road traffic grew quickly and by 1828 there were at least 600 long-distance coach services based in London alone.[4]

Throughout the country the effect was the same. The new competition forced proprietors to increase the speed of coaches and keep to tight, new timetables. They were now less able to tolerate the gentleman who for fun might ask to take the reins for a stage or two. Those with skill however, were still able to bribe the coachman. Captain Barclay was certainly one of those. Twenty years earlier he had driven the Royal Mail from London to Perth, reputedly without rest,[5] and in the intervening years had matched that drive several times. Or so he claimed. Once he drove every stage from Edinburgh to London, a distance of 397 miles in 45½ hours.[6] On another occasion he drove the reverse journey, again reputedly without a rest, though he must have left the box to obey the call of nature. On arrival in Edinburgh he was met by his own horse and gig which he drove home to Ury, a further 116 miles.[7] Many thought these unauthenticated claims were exaggerated, and Lord Kennedy wagered 'a large sum' that Captain Barclay could not drive the Royal Mail from London to Aberdeen (526 miles) under full scrutiny by an umpire, without any breaks, other than those normal ones allowed the passengers for their refreshment. Captain Barclay accepted the wager. The drive must have taken at least 58 hours, but on arrival in Aberdeen he 'was so little exhausted' he offered to immediately drive the return journey under the same conditions. Lord Kennedy conceded defeat.[8] As an endurance athlete, Captain Barclay was still indestructible, inexhaustible and unbeatable.

On 1 July 1829 it was, therefore, a well-qualified Captain Barclay who sat on the box seat of the richly beribboned, shiny, new *Defiance* as it left the Star Hotel on Princes Street in Edinburgh to the cheers of the crowds and a fine tune on the horn. As the coach made its way north, excited crowds greeted Captain Barclay and the *Defiance*, and it arrived in Aberdeen 15 hours later amidst scenes of wild enthusiasm. In the memory of many locals the journey would have taken three or four days. To those who lined the road to see it the *Defiance* was a magnificent sight. It had a blue body with red wheels picked out with pale yellow and carried 15 passengers. On its normal run it had two coachmen and a guard, all wearing crimson jackets, grey breeches and top hats.[9] The *Defiance* revolutionised travel on the east coast of Scotland and Captain Barclay took a turn with the reins whenever he could.

In his 50s Captain Barclay was still a strong and imposing man, with a receding hairline. He continued to walk as many miles each day as a rural postman, and the hours he spent out of doors winter and summer gave him a weather-beaten look. Over the years his dress had become somewhat unusual and shabby, but stylishly so. On hot summer days he wore a linen jacket, knee breeches, top boots and coarse, white worsted stockings, often with a patch on the knee. At Ury, however, it was seldom warm enough for that and he wore a green coat with large gilt buttons. Around his neck he wore either a blue or yellow Belcher handkerchief, named after the late Jem Belcher, who tied wonderfully flamboyant knots in them. In the cold, dark winters he put on a long, yellow cashmere waistcoat, and to keep his head warm, a black beaver hat. The Druid said of him: 'His dress was curious, but still it never concealed the high bred gentleman of primitive tastes . . . he always had a little quid of tobacco in his mouth, to which he gave one or two rolls before his long measured speech began.'[10] As he walked by, people stopped and stared, regarding him, with some justification, as a great curiosity. He was moving inexorably from individuality to eccentricity.

The signs were to be found at Ury too. It was a Spartan sportsman's house, full of mementoes. In the entrance hall hung a sketch by one of the Alken family of Tom Cribb's first fight with Tom Molineux;[11] the one at East Grinstead that Captain Barclay didn't go to. In the dining room were pictures of Tom Cribb, John Gully and the Game Chicken over the sideboard, all 'in attitude', and one of himself as he appeared at Newmarket in the 1,000-mile match, wearing a cock and pinch hat and a yellow handkerchief. Elsewhere in the house was another portrait of Tom Cribb, not in attitude this time, and another one, nearly life-size, of himself in hunting costume, wearing Jackson's breeches. There were pictures of Lord Camelford's and Jem Belcher's old dog *Trusty*, one of *Snowball*, the famous greyhound, and one of his own dog *Billy*. In the porch there were many other portraits. No concessions were made to comfort or effeminacy, however. Nimrod wrote:

> I do not recollect seeing even an arm chair in the house. For those in the dining room, if the seats of them were made of hearts of oak itself they could not be much harder than they are, and the backs of them are as straight, and nearly as high, as a poplar tree. I believe there is a sofa in the drawing-room, but as for ottomans and footstools, and such like, you might as well look for an Elephant at Ury.[12]

Rodney had got used to it over the years and Margaret seems to have accepted it too, largely perhaps because she spent most of her time outside, at least in the summer.

Captain Barclay adopted a very free-and-easy attitude to Margaret from the very start. But after her mother and then her little sister died he never stopped her doing anything. She grew up bright, intelligent and totally free. Like her father, she liked being out of doors and wandered, always barefoot, around the farms at Ury and around Megray Hill and the River Cowie, as she pleased. She was always certain of a welcome at the various farms because she had an engaging personality and 'the tenants and retainers adored her'. They kept an eye on her and she often ate and drank with them and sometimes even slept at a farm or cottage when she was tired.[13]

Members of the family who saw how Margaret was growing up, became concerned and insisted with Captain Barclay that he should impose some discipline on her. He should send her to school. It was probably too late. Margaret's free spirit would not be broken. At the girls' boarding school she was sent to in Edinburgh she refused to wear shoes. She pined for the freedom of Ury. One day when her father's old regiment went marching by, she rushed out 'imploring their protection', and threw her arms around the neck of one of the soldiers. She was lifted on to his shoulders and, to the horror of the schoolmistress in charge of her, was taken back to barracks, and next day a detachment marched to Ury with her. In a belated effort to control her Captain Barclay gave her a good hiding and took her back, but it didn't make her any more manageable or any less miserable.[14]

The rest of the Barclay family decided that Ury was unsuitable for Margaret and they pressured Captain Barclay to send her away for someone else to look after her. The plan was that she should spend half a year with Charles Barclay, who had two girls of about her age, at Bury Hill in Surrey, and the other half with her Aunt Mag and Uncle Hudson Gurney, who lived part of the year at Keswick in Norfolk, and part in St James's Square in London, and had no children of their own. It never really worked out that way. Margaret didn't get on with the girls at Bury Hill, and she spent her time largely with the Gurneys. Hudson Gurney was a very wealthy banker, a slim, attractive and energetic man with blue eyes and the panache to wear pink waistcoats. His sister called him 'dashing smart'. His wife, Captain Barclay's sister Mag, was a little grand and haughty but brimmed with benevolence. They lived in a fashionable house at Number 9 St James's Square and Hudson had bought himself a parliamentary seat in the Isle of Wight, on the understanding, or so it was said, that he never set foot in it – a restriction that hardly bothered him at all. He ran his Norfolk banking business and his Isle of Wight parliamentary concerns largely from St James's Square, where he also entertained the great and the good of London society.[15] St James's Square was very close to Captain Barclay's old territory, where he once met and drank with the Fancy and where so many of his wagers were made. William Pitt had once lived at Number 10, and Lord Castlereagh, the Tory Foreign Secretary and Leader of the House of Commons, was living at Number 14 when he slashed the carotid artery in his neck, thus becoming the third member of the Cabinet to commit suicide in almost as many years. Neighbours in St James's Square were able to see at close quarters the grand funeral-party gather outside the house at 8.30 a.m. on Tuesday 20 August 1822 before moving off to Westminster Abbey. The High Constable of Westminster, carrying his silver staff of office and wearing a mourning cloak and cocked hat, led the way with several constables. The eight pallbearers, all members of the Cabinet – Lord Liverpool, Lord Eldon, Lord Sidmouth, Lord Stowell, the Duke of Wellington, the Duke of Marlborough, Frederick Robinson and Nicholas Vansittart – followed in mourning coaches. A man on horseback carried Lord Castlereagh's coronet, and immediately behind him came the hearse, drawn by six horses, each dressed with plumes of black ostrich feathers and led by a page. Another ten carriages followed carrying the main mourners, his doctor, his solicitor and Sir Thomas Lawrence, who had painted his portrait four times.[16]

Just before his suicide Lord Castlereagh had told the King that he had been accused of 'the same crime as the Bishop of Clogher' and that police officers were searching for him.[17] The Bishop of Clogher had been caught engaging in homosexual sex in the White Hart in St Alban's Place, Westminster. Charles Greville said that he would have escaped 'if his breeches had not been down'. But they were, and he was arrested, then released on bail. Later he jumped his bail, went to Edinburgh under the assumed name of Thomas Wilson and worked there as a butler. Lord Castlereagh was less fortunate. He was already hated by the radicals and was blamed for almost every unpopular piece of legislation for years. After his death he was the subject of one of Byron's most cruel, and pithy quatrains:

Posterity will ne'er survey
A nobler grave than this:
Here lie the bones of Castlereagh
Stop, traveller, and ////![18]

St James's Square did not always see such drama but an MP's house that was open to the leading names in finance, politics and literature was always a buzz of topical excitement. Everyone there soon learned that Margaret's determination was as strong as her father's. She 'refused to conform to any civilisation' at Bury Hill, Norfolk or in St James's Square. She still refused to wear shoes. After a protracted battle of wills, the Gurneys were forced to concede. Margaret too, had become remarkable for her heels. Eventually, when it was no longer an issue, she gave up her bare feet, voluntarily.[19]

Although Margaret was forced to give up the freedom of Ury, she gained a lot from the Gurneys. They were so fabulously wealthy and so well connected they gave Margaret an excellent life. Under the watchful eye of her Aunt Mag, she was given a governess and involved fully in all the family activities. When she was old enough she was allowed a 'personal attendant', Sarah Scarnell.[20] Margaret responded by entrancing the Gurneys and their fashionable friends with 'her wonderful cleverness of intellect, (and) the brilliance of her conversation, and her powers of description'.[21] She returned to Ury only when her governess had her annual holiday.[22]

When Captain Barclay came out of hiding after the Simon Byrne trial, it was a very quiet Ury he returned to. Margaret, who was 14, was living with the Gurneys; David, his youngest brother, had died at Otranto in Italy; and there were only Rodney, a few servants and memories to fill Ury. He went out and got himself a young puppy, whom he named 'Dan' and who would be his favourite dog and faithful companion for the next 16 years.[23]

Visitors to Ury now found it difficult to escape. A gentleman farmer who attended one of the cattle sales at Ury described how he and the other purchasers were entertained once the sale was over:

The Captain sat at one end of the table behind a huge round of beef, and after the company had done justice to the more solid viands, whisky punch was introduced. My friend, mindful of the long Scots miles that lay between him and his home, said to his companion, 'We'll just take one tumbler of toddy, and then we'll start'. But, on making for the door, they found, to their dismay, that it was securely locked, and had to resume their seats. They remarked, however, that a fresh supply of hot water would soon be wanted, and they resolved that, as soon as the servant opened the door, they would take the opportunity and bolt immediately. But, behold, when the call was made for more water, instead of the door being opened, a little boy emerged through a hole in the wall with the necessary supplies, and no mode of exit was to be found! After the night was well spent, and some of the guests had well nigh succumbed to the influence of their potations, the doors were flung open, and the Captain said, 'Well, gentlemen, look about and see if you can find beds for yourselves. I don't know that we have got rooms for you all, but those who are unable to find accommodation, can just sit here with me, and I will keep you company till morning.'[24]

An all-night session of drinking and socialising did not dull his appetite for exercise. He still breakfasted at 6 a.m. and walked a dozen or so miles in the morning, covering as much as 70 miles on foot and horseback before 3 p.m., when he had dinner. With his herd of Shorthorn cattle, his flock of purebred Leicester sheep and about 20 horses, he provided work for at least 80 men and women at Ury at this time, but there was little there to replace the buzz that surrounded the Fancy. Captain Barclay got together with Keillor Watson to buy out John Scott, and took over the ownership of the *Defiance*.[25]

He poured money into the new venture. Two new *Defiance* coaches were bought from Wallace, the coachbuilder in Perth, one for each end of the Aberdeen to Edinburgh route. They were sprung and padded and a safety rail was added to the top so that 12 passengers could now be carried on top. For the benefit of the inside passengers, candles were fitted so they could read. Every last detail was considered.[26] The organisational structure was changed and some of the stages were sub-let. The proprietors of The Royal Hotel at Aberdeen, The Ship at North Queensferry and the Waterloo Hotel at Edinburgh, all sub-leased their stages, and Captain Skelton and the three guards sub-leased the unprofitable 'middle ground', but at a preferential rate. To signal the new management, the colour of the coaches was changed to primrose yellow with red doors and wheels, and yellow lapels and silver buttons were added to the crimson jackets of the two coachmen. The Edinburgh–Aberdeen *Defiance* cut over two and a half hours off its time and became the model for speed, punctuality, efficiency, smartness, courtesy and service. None could match it in Scotland, and perhaps none in the whole of Britain. Such improvements came at a cost however, and the economic return did not match the effort that was put into it.[27] Perhaps the profits would come later.

Under the new arrangements *Defiance* now left the Waterloo Hotel in Edinburgh on the up run at 6.55 a.m. and arrived at the Royal Hotel in Aberdeen at 7.10 p.m. One hundred and twenty miles in 12¼ hours which included the ferry crossing and 20-minute breakfast stop at the Ship, the 10-minute lunch stop at the Castleton Inn, and 14 changes of horses at an average of one and a half minutes per change, some taking as little as a minute. They could, and did, set the church clock by the *Defiance*. The whole route up and down required 60 good horses. They worked a six-day week because the horses, as well as coachmen, innkeepers and proprietors, needed a day of rest. Nimrod was extravagant with his praise:

> This coach [the *Defiance*] reflects great credit on the Captain and all others concerned with it. So complete, however, are its arrangements; so respectable and civil are the servants employed upon it; so well does it keep to time – in addition to the honour of very often being driven by the Captain himself – that the first people in the country are, or were, found in and about it.[28]

The colourful, shiny coaches that sped along Britain's new road network with exemplary punctuality were not only a thrilling sight, they were also a symbol of a new, more egalitarian age. Anyone could travel now and there were more strangers and visitors in the towns than ever before. In June 1832 the 3rd Reform Bill passed through the Lords and into law, and Parliament for the first time became more responsive to the wishes of the people, rather than to those of the landed classes and gentlemen alone. Such changes cannot come without some tumult. The radicals had been talking of revolution and anarchy for years and no one was sure what lay ahead. Some feared the radical riffraff would see the elections of 1832 as an opportunity to settle old scores, and so the elections became nervous, boisterous and tense affairs.

While the elections were going on in Stonehaven, Captain Barclay was upstairs at the Mill Inn with a powerfully built farm overseer from Ury, Admiral Duff and Johnny Murray, a well-known local figure who, in the absence of universal access to banks, had developed a business as a bill-discounter. A small man with a 'parchment-looking face', he was also working as an agent for the Tories at the election. Outside, a crowd described as 'weavers and other radicals' gathered, shouted and 'howled'. Little Johnny Murray went downstairs to send them away, telling them that he knew who they were and that they would pay later for their disturbance. But those were the old social rules of master and servant. The new Bill would change all that. A woman in the crowd was in no mood to be intimidated and came forward telling him gleefully that he didn't know who *she* was, and 'struck him a wallop' with a corn sack across the eyes, momentarily blinding him. Johnny Murray retreated into the Mill Inn, shut the door, wiped his eyes and went back upstairs to report to Captain Barclay and Admiral Duff. Enraged, Captain Barclay grabbed his walking stick and, calling to the farm overseer to join him, rushed downstairs to confront the mob. The handle of his walking stick was filled with lead and he used it to ferociously lay into anyone within reach. The crowd judiciously backed off and Captain Barclay and everyone in the Mill Inn got away safely.[29] The 'siege' of the Mill Inn was over, and Captain Barclay's reputation as the local hard man was reinforced. Those in the Mill Inn felt indebted to him for being so solid and unflinching when they needed him, and they told wonderfully supportive stories of his bravery and quick action. It was inevitable, however, that such episodes alienated him from others and reinforced their view that he was a bully who actually liked throwing his weight about. There was no middle way. People liked and admired him or they hated and despised him. When the new Reform Parliament met in Westminster, John Gully, ex-Champion of the Prize Ring and Captain Barclay's training partner, was there as MP for Pontefract.[30] John Gully would have approved.

In November 1833 Captain Barclay's mother died, which opened up the possibility of him petitioning his old friend, the King, for the title of Earl of Airth and Menteith. But the *Defiance* filled a big part in Captain Barclay's life. What would people think of an Earl driving a coach? Surely he wouldn't have to give up coach-driving as he had pedestrian contests and pugilism? Would he rather give up coaching or the title? He asked his friends. Lord Panmure wrote back unambiguously:

> Dear Barclay,
> — I see no objections to your driving the *Defiance* when

you are the Earl of Menteith and Airth, and I will be your guard.

Panmure.[31]

Another friend, the Duke of Gordon, pointed out that a Marquis often drove the Brighton *Defiance*, so he saw no reason why an Earl should not drive the Edinburgh to Aberdeen *Defiance* – '. . . at all events, if you think it infradig to be the coachman, you may undoubtedly be the guard'.[32] That settled it, he would continue with the *Defiance* and petition the King for his new title.

His legal team began to prepare the application in 1833. Earldoms seldom come cheaply. The legal cost alone would be huge and his financial resources were modest. True, he owned the 3,800 acres at Ury, which brought in £7,000 in a good year, but he had no cash assets. His winnings at Newmarket and Thistleton Gap had gone on innumerable other wagers that were less successful and on living life with the Fancy to the full. The *Defiance* was famous for its efficiency but it never made any real money and his farming was more spectacular than commercially successful. Meeting the legal bills to secure the Earldom would be an enormous commitment and would rank with anything he had ever done. He couldn't sell Ury to raise the money because if his petition was successful, and he expected it would be, he would need a suitable country seat. So he decided instead to borrow against it, and in April 1834 he contacted his factors to raise a loan of £80,000.[33]

At five percent, it would take more than half his entire income just to keep up with the interest payments, and there would be little chance of ever paying back the capital. It is not surprising that the application wasn't successful. Nevertheless he did manage to raise £70,000, and so his petition began. One of the first things his legal team advised was that he should petition for the Earldom of Airth only. This was duly submitted to the King, and in June 1834 it was referred to the House of Lords.[34] Within twelve months Captain Barclay was negotiating the loan of a further £10,000.[35]

Years went by as the various legal knots were unravelled. Bills followed. Lots of bills. Nevertheless, this was one of the most contented periods of his life. He visited and entertained friends, hunted, improved his cattle, ran his fishery and whisky distillery, and above all he had the *Defiance*. He pursued excellence in coach-driving with the vigour and single-mindedness that was almost uniquely his and he travelled the country learning as much as he could. On one occasion on the Brighton Road, he and Philip Carter, a young coachman, were on the box seat of the *Red Rover*, overloaded with passengers, when its axle broke. They struggled together to bring it under control as it dropped down from Thornton Heath into Streatham and approached an awkward turn. Left to himself Captain Barclay would have tried to use his strength to pull the horses up, but Philip Carter, the professional, stopped him, and allowed the disabled coach to continue down the hill and then pulled it up safely at the Pied Bull at the top of the next hill.[36] The professional coachmen's skills were almost legendary, and they became well-known public personalities. Captain Barclay went to Cambridge to get lessons from one of the most famous, Joe Walton, who drove *The Star* from London in the morning, and then back again in the afternoon. Eventually Captain Barclay could handle even the worst setbacks, even turning the *Defiance* over: 'She fell as easy as if she had fallen on a feather bed, and looking out for a soft place, I alighted comfortably on my feet.' No mention of the safety of the passengers! It was part of the learning process and you could not claim to be qualified to drive a coach until you had 'floored it'. So successful did he become as a coach driver that Lord Kintore described him as 'Joe Walton secundus'.[37] Praise indeed.

Nimrod visited Ury for the New Year celebrations of 1835 and stayed in the neighbourhood for a couple of months. He gives us a glimpse of life there. On one day Captain Barclay entertained Deacon Williamson, the butcher, to dinner – a mixture of business and pleasure. On another, he entertained three captains from the 14th

Light Dragoons and the Marquess of Carmarthen, who was the local expert on hawking. Captain Barclay took Nimrod to Edinburgh to see his friend Professor Wilson. On other days Captain Barclay was found hunting at Gordon near Kelso, at Keith Hall near Inverey and at Gask near Turriff. These hunting days were each followed by a 'jovial night' of singing and drinking to excess. On one such, Nimrod admitted to drinking 'four fox's heads of claret . . . besides the general allowance', and on another night Captain Barclay and Lord Kintore led the singing 'in the very best style' and with 'great force'.[38] The fact that he was up to his eyes in debt did not seem to worry him at all. There were many distractions to keep him occupied.

In 1835 he approached the King who agreed to Captain Barclay adding the word 'Royal' to the name of his whisky distillery, which consequently was renamed, rather grandly, The Royal Glenury Distillery. Things were going well. Judged by every criterion except that of income, the *Defiance*, was also a great success. So great that Lord Kintore organised a dinner for Captain Barclay and Keillor Watson at Forfar on 1 July 1835 'as a testimonial of esteem and mark of approbation for their exertions in the establishment and continuance of the *Defiance Coach*'. Lord Arbuthnot was in the chair and after the dinner Captain Barclay and Keillor Watson were each presented with a silver bowl with 'an appropriate coaching device, beautifully executed in frosted work' made in London by Garrards and valued at £50.[39]

Captain Barclay was now an important and influential member of the local community. He attended the county meetings and was even appointed a Justice of the Peace. Ever popular among his circle – Nimrod described him as 'a cheerful friend' – he was a good conversationalist and full of humour when he chose. To those who weren't his friends, he continued to be brusque to the point of rudeness. Before the dinner in 1835 at Forfar he wrote to Captain Skelton, who sub-leased the middle ground from Captain Barclay and Keillor Watson and so was an important man in the running of the *Defiance*, as he might to a junior employee:

Ury June 25th

Dear Sir,
   Don't omit being at the dinner at Forfar on the 1st.
   I am
   truly yours
   Barclay Allardice
   Have the party all delivered *in time* to the door men.[40]

In 1830 John Robertson brought a libel action against him for comments he had made about a poaching charge,[41] and in 1837 he was again accused of assaulting someone. This time it was Thomas Ryder of the Theatre Royal, Aberdeen, at the Royal Hotel.[42] Captain Barclay found it very hard to be polite to someone who did not show him the respect he thought his athletic achievements and social rank had earned him. He was as comfortable with gentleman landowners and aristocrats as with prize-fighters. What he had difficulty with was those in between – the social climbers. In particular he didn't like baronets, and said he always knew when there was one in the room.[43]

In 1837 Margaret was 21 and had been living with the Gurneys in London for several years. She had thrived and emerged as a captivating and vivacious young woman, who received more than her fair share of admiring attention. She met and charmed some of the most fashionable men in London, including some of the leading artists and writers such as David Wilkie, the King's Painter-In-Ordinary, and a young novelist named Benjamin Disraeli, and she was presented at the court of King William and Queen Adelaide.[44] If Captain Barclay's petition for the Earldom of Airth were successful Margaret would become Countess of Airth on his death. Three years had passed however, and Captain Barclay's petition was still bogged down in legal red tape and bureaucracy. Only the legal bills showed it was still alive. Now that Margaret's education was over, there was the inevitable talk of finding a suitable man for her to marry. Hudson Gurney thought that Arthur Kett Barclay, a cousin ten years older, was a possibility.[45] Her marriage to Arthur would keep the title within the family, but it came to nothing. He was not Margaret's choice, nor indeed were any of the other hopefuls that were paraded past her at innumerable at-homes and parties in St James's. Eventually they gave up; it was time for Margaret to go home to Ury.

After entrancing London society the girl who had run barefoot at Ury, and whose mother had been a young servant there, returned with her own lady's maid, to live with her father and Aunt Rodney. At Ury as the laird's daughter and heir, she took full charge of the house, servants and 'everything'. In keeping with her status Margaret also 'presided' at the dinner table, which was not just a nominal task. The social life at Ury may not have been as high powered as in St James's Square, but it was busy enough. She visited all the genteel families around Kincardineshire and in Forfarshire and 'up beyond' Inverness, calling on the Duchess of Gordon, Lord Arbuthnott, Lord James Hay of Seaton, Sir Francis McKenzie of Connaugh House near Inverness, the Duffs of Fetteresso, the Inneses of Raemoir, the Inneses of Cowie, and many more.[46] They all went to Ury to see her too, although Margaret was never very impressed by them.

While Captain Barclay waited to hear about the outcome of his petition, recognition of another kind appeared. He was asked if he would consider the post of Governor of an 'infant agricultural colony' of 300,000 acres in Australia in which 'neither slave labour nor convict labour was allowed'.[47] Captain Hindmarsh of the Royal Navy had originally been approached but the offer was withdrawn for some reason. Full of enthusiasm for the challenge and the honour, Captain Barclay asked his friends to write him references. The Duke of Richmond, the Earl of Aberdeen, the Viscount of Arbuthnott and the Earl of Leicester duly obliged. The Earl of Leicester, alias Thomas Coke of Holkham, was 86 and had been a great friend of Captain Barclay's father. He wrote of Captain Barclay that he 'could hardly conceive any person so eminently qualified to take charge' of the undertaking – a reference to be prized. Captain Barclay travelled down to London for the interviews and concluded virtually all the arrangements. All seemed plain sailing. At the last minute however, 'an invisible hand suddenly checked the whole concern'. The commissioners, with whom Captain Barclay had been in discussions, found that they did not have the authority to appoint after all, only the Colonial Secretary did. Despite his glowing referees, Captain Barclay had no real political power, and had managed in his life to insult, offend or shock too many people.

Locally, however, his friends continued to praise him, and in 1838 a second, larger public dinner was thrown in his honour. Two hundred 'gentry and farmers' were invited, and to provide a big enough venue the organisers had to take over the large granary at the Royal Glenury Distillery. The dinner was an all-male affair, but after dinner the ladies entered to a round of applause. They were Rodney, Margaret Innes, Captain Barclay's niece, and her stepmother. Margaret, his daughter, was not present.

The granary was decorated with evergreens, flowers, the Royal Coat of Arms and those of Captain Barclay – a shield containing references to the Barclays, Allardices, Grahams and Stuarts that made up the family blood, supported on the right by a lion and on the left by a wreathed savage with a club over his shoulder. Beneath were the mottoes: *In cruce spero*, for the Barclays, and *Right and Reason* for the Allardices. John Carnegie of Redhall was in the chair and proposed the toast to Captain Barclay's patriotic character, his 'kindness' as a landlord, his 'valuable services' to the community and 'his genuine goodness of heart', each of which was cheered loudly. There were several speeches, well over 30 toasts, nearly 30 bouts of cheering and not a little laughter. Everyone complimented everyone else. Everyone basked in the warm glow of mutual thanks and congratulations and at 10.00 p.m., with much rosier faces than when they began, 'the company broke up'.[48]

A few weeks before the dinner, there was an unexpected development regarding the Earldom of Airth. Sir William Scott from Ancrum also petitioned for the title and for the Earldom of Menteith.[49] As a matter of routine this was referred to the House of Lords and served to draw their Lordships' attention to Captain Barclay's earlier claim. Once again at considerable cost, his legal counsel was called on to prepare his case – this time for presentation to the Lords' Committee for Privileges. To raise the money, Captain Barclay was forced to sell his shorthorn herd. The sale of eighty head of cattle brought in about £3,000.[50] The sale was luckily timed – it saved him from having to face the tribulations of the outbreak of foot and mouth disease the following year.[51] The Lords' Committee for Privileges met on 9 July 1839 but came to no conclusion. Sir John Campbell, the Attorney General, believed that more evidence was needed.[52] As it was the custom to print the evidence before it was summed up, there was still a chance to get the evidence they wanted. The committee was adjourned *sine die*. Within a matter of days however, the picture was complicated further, and from an unexpected source. Mrs Mary Bishop from Twickenham also claimed the title, Earl of Airth, for her grandson who was still an infant.[53] So the Lords' Committee was reconvened twice in August 1839.[54] The general consensus was that Captain Barclay and his expensive legal team had seen off the challenges from Sir William Scott and Mrs Bishop, but the Committee decided that his petition for the Earldom of Airth alone did not give them scope to resolve some of the tricky legal points. They advised that Captain Barclay should also claim the earldoms of Strathern and Menteith. More intense activity from his legal counsel followed and a year later Captain Barclay petitioned the young Queen Victoria for the 'titles, honours and dignities' of the additional two earldoms.[55] Time had moved on. He had been born a Georgian, had flourished in the Regency and matured in the reign of William IV. Now Captain Barclay was a Victorian.

One day in April 1840 in Stonehaven Captain Barclay came upon

Margaret, who was now 23, talking rather too eagerly to a handsome, 'superior' looking sergeant of his old regiment. Captain Barclay strode across and in his brusque, direct way, spoke disapprovingly to him. To Captain Barclay's astonishment the sergeant's response was to put his arm around Margaret and announce that they were going to be married. His name was Samuel Ritchie, a local man from Aberdeen, but he was not superior enough for Captain Barclay, who was furious.[56] When Margaret confirmed the story to be true, his anger turned to intractable hostility and so Margaret promptly ran away with Samuel Ritchie and they married in London, in St Mary's Church, Kensington.[57] Her Aunt Mag and Uncle Hudson Gurney gave her wedding presents of linen, furniture, china and silver plate to set up her new home.[58] Captain Barclay, however, remained implacably opposed and to escape his wrath, Margaret and her new husband left their wedding presents behind and sailed to Upper Canada to start a new life. Margaret was delighted to go and she was full of optimism. Not only was she escaping her angry father, she was also escaping Scotland with its 'cutting atmosphere' and 'chill foggy blasts'. Even better, she said, she was escaping from its 'miserable inhabitants' and the 'tardy denizens of a cold climate'.[59] And so Margaret cut all her ties with Ury and with Scotland, emotional as well as physical.

There was plenty of time in the winter of 1840–41 for Captain Barclay to ponder the future of his daughter 3,000 miles away, and the point of spending more money and time pursuing the Earldoms of Airth, Strathern and Menteith. He certainly had no intention that Samuel Ritchie should benefit from it. After his death what title would Samuel Ritchie acquire?

Eventually he decided to drop his claim, but, like a run-away coach, his application to Queen Victoria had a momentum of its own and it was automatically referred to the House of Lords on 4 March 1841 when they again called for the evidence to be printed.[60] This however, was the end. Captain Barclay progressed no further and he was content to remain Robert Barclay Allardice and to be known publicly for the rest of his life as 'Captain Barclay'.

# CHAPTER FOURTEEN

# *Always in Condition*

*... a great eater, in fine simple faith and always in condition.*

JAMES SINCLAIR, 1907

*When upwards of seventy years old, ... he asked ... a man of more than 12 stone in weight, to stand on his hand ... [and] thereupon lifted and landed him on the table.*

FRANCIS GALTON, 1908

*A*s he was pondering his final decision to abandon the pursuit of the earldom, Captain Barclay turned once again to the world of pugilism. Even those still intimately involved in the Prize Ring recognised that in comparison to the days of Belcher, Gully and Cribb, it was in 'its sere and yellow leaf'. Vincent Dowling, editor of *Bell's Life in London*, wrote quite bluntly, 'the history of the Ring, we fear, is drawing to a close'.[1] It was Tom Cribb's benefit that tempted Captain Barclay back. It was held in November 1840 at the National Baths on Westminster Road in London. Tom Cribb had given up the Union Arms, had suffered 'domestic troubles', and fallen on hard times.[2] This was to be his last public appearance as a sparrer. He was only a few months away from his 60th birthday, time even for Tom Cribb to give up. Captain Barclay was 61.

Boxing shows at the National Baths were a new development. Originally the indoor showcase for the sport was the Fives Court in Little St Martin's Street but this was demolished in 1826. This left the Royal Tennis Court on Great Windmill Street, Haymarket as the only large venue, but it too went into decline through bad management and the general decay of pugilism. Men who were scheduled to fight did not turn up and others were badly matched, and eventually the gentlemen withdrew their patronage and the proprietor let out the Tennis Court for other purposes. Fourteen boxers got together to form a new association to put on boxing shows at the National Baths and agreed penalties with each other if any failed to turn up, thus guaranteeing a good show every time.[3] And a good show was needed to warrant the cost of draining the pool and building an elevated stage over it. If it was successful, it would be an outstanding venue, as the Baths could hold a crowd of 5,000, paying one or two shillings each, larger than any previous indoor arena. The new association, however, was led by the old brigade. Five were 40 or over — a tribute to the durability of the old-style pugilists. They were:

| | | | |
|---|---|---|---|
| Tom Cribb | 59 | Tom Oliver | 51 |
| Tom Spring | 45 | Jack Tisdale | 44 |

| | | | |
|---|---|---|---|
| Barney Aaron | 40 | Peter Crawley | 39 |
| Dick Curtis | 38 | Alex Reid | 38 |
| Ned Neal | 35 | Deaf Burke | 30 |
| Owen Swift | 26 | John Hannan | 23 |
| Tom Maley | 22 | Johnny Walker | 21 |

Their shows fed the nostalgia for a sport they all recognised was fading away but could do little to rescue. After an experimental small event the 14 planned eight major shows over the winter, and Captain Barclay was a regular VIP among the crowd. Gentleman Jackson was also seen there. He was now 71. Two to three thousand turned up each time but they never had a full house, or even a half-full one.

While Captain Barclay was in London, Margaret wrote to him from Canada. In an attempt to heal the wounds between them she asked his advice about the relative merits of buying land for a farm in either Canada or the United States of America.[4] Captain Barclay jumped at the opportunity. He put Ury into the hands of managers, suspended plans for a new herd of shorthorn cattle,[5] sold his interest in the *Defiance*,[6] put the Royal Glenury Distillery on the market,[7] filled his pockets with letters of introduction to influential people on the other side of the Atlantic, and booked a ticket on *Britannia* to sail from Liverpool at 11 a.m. on Tuesday 20 April 1841.

*Britannia* was one of four wooden mail steamers on the route from Liverpool to Halifax, Nova Scotia, run by the Royal Mail Steam Packet Company that had been set up by Samuel Cunard. Apart from Her Majesty's Mail there were 90 'select' passengers on board paying the full £41 one-way fare.[8] They turned out to be 'agreeable and anxious to make things mutually pleasant'. No steerage passengers were on board. The cabins however, were tiny. Nine months later when Charles Dickens made the same journey in the same boat, he complained that the cabins were too small and that his bed was like 'a muffin, beaten flat' and his pillows were 'no thicker than crumpets'.[9] The ship's captain, Captain Cleland, welcomed Captain Barclay on board and asked if he was 'the celebrated Captain Barclay'. Word soon got round. 'Everybody knew me,' he said.

After two days sailing, the *Britannia* steamed into strong winds and heavy seas. 'On Sunday . . . we encountered a gale truly tremendous — the sea running mountains high, and frequently sweeping us from stern to stern'.[10] One of the crew broke his leg and the select passengers' main memory of the voyage turned out to be the 'constant crashing of plates and other movable objects'. The wretched, cramped journey took 14 days and when they got to Nova Scotia they were allowed only eight hours on shore. Halifax turned out to be a miserable, dirty town with narrow streets, a foot deep in mud. Back on board there was another day and a half's sailing to Boston. The unhappiness about the journey was lessened however, by the knowledge that had they gone by sail it might have taken six weeks.

Captain Barclay disembarked at Boston at 6 a.m. on Thursday 4 May 1841 and settled into the very comfortable Albion Hotel, where he took a cold bath and had a good breakfast before setting out to walk through the town. It was 'much to be admired', he decided, with 'everything . . . proclaiming Boston to be a place of importance'.[11]

The next three weeks in the United States were packed with travel by rail, stage-coach and steamer as he used his various letters of introduction and visited farms from Boston, south to Connecticut and New York, and north-west to Albany, Auburn, Canandaigua, Geneso, Caledonia, Batavia, Lockport and Niagara. Then across the Canadian border and up to Toronto, which he left by steamer on Friday 28 May to sail down Lake Ontario to Hamilton, where Margaret and her husband lived. Hamilton was a town of about 6,000 people still suffering from the after-effects of a political uprising three years before. The memories of military action, deaths and hangings remained vivid and the town was still full of 'conflict and rancour'. The hopes of many who had speculated on land had 'withered . . . having received little or no return for their money', and a mood of 'universal gloom' hung over the town.[12]

Captain Barclay kept a diary which he later wrote up and

published under the title *An Agricultural Tour in the United States and Canada*. In that account he mentions meeting many members of the local Scottish community in and around Hamilton – Adam Ferguson ('an old friend'), the Chief of Macnab, Sir Allan Macnab and Lady Macnab, and their respective families. He was particularly pleased to find Margaret in good health, but makes no mention whatsoever of meeting Samuel Ritchie, his son-in-law, nor that Margaret only nine days prior to his arrival, had given birth to a son, Captain Barclay's first grandson.

The christening was arranged for Sunday 6 June at St Andrew's Presbyterian Church, a small, wooden-framed building on James Street South, in the heart of Hamilton. In an attempt to further cement the reconciliation the baby was christened Robert after his grandfather and all the other Roberts in the Barclay family tree. The Rev. Alexander Gale conducted the service, which was attended by Margaret, Captain Barclay and other guests, but not by the baby's father.[13] When he left Hamilton two days later, Captain Barclay wrote that he 'took leave' of his daughter and returned by steamer to Toronto, but made no mention of leaving his grandson or Samuel Ritchie, who seems to have kept away during the whole of Captain Barclay's visit.[14] The reconciliation was clearly not complete. Nevertheless, Captain Barclay had done his job. He had been there and given his advice. She should leave Canada, he concluded, and settle in the United States.

Captain Barclay stayed eleven days in Hamilton but when he left he was in no hurry to go home and spent nearly six weeks as a tourist, visiting friends and acquaintances. He went sightseeing, visited a college, a theatre, a prison and the Chinese Museum. He was in holiday mood. From Toronto he crossed the United States' border at Buffalo and then went on to Pittsburgh, Washington DC, Richmond, Baltimore, Philadelphia, New York and Boston. He visited the Allegheny Mountains and George Washington's tomb. He enjoyed the Independence Day celebrations in New York and was struck by the fact that no one was drunk. He relaxed and let his guard down in his diary sufficiently to write of Mrs Sheaff's four 'very agreeable' daughters and to extol the virtues of Mrs Hamilton, a Scottish lady and her daughter, 'a very interesting young lady', with whom he boarded on Pennsylvania Avenue in Washington. Captain Barclay was enjoying himself. The pinnacle of the American leg of his trip came the following day when Mr Greig took him to Capitol Hill and introduced him to John Tyler, President of the United States, who received Captain Barclay 'very graciously'.[15]

It had been a strange year for the Presidency. It had opened with Martin Van Buren in office, but he was defeated in an election by William Henry Harrison, who died of pneumonia only one month after his inauguration. John Tyler, his Vice-President took over and so became the third President in almost as many months.

From Washington DC Captain Barclay went to Richmond, Virginia, and came face to face with slavery. 'I found slavery here possesses none of the horrors I had at home been accustomed to hear connected with it,' he wrote.

> There may be masters who are tyrannical and cruel to their slaves, but unhappily tyranny and cruelty to dependants are not peculiar to slave owners. I believe it might be easy to address authenticated instances of the treatment of parish apprentices in free England, the atrocity and horribleness of which would draw tears from the eyes of any slave owner in Virginia . . . the condition of the slave is not peculiarly subject to the inflictions of inhumanity, or liable to any of the atrocious barbarities which in my own country are unsparingly imputed to slave owners, often, I believe, by persons whose zeal is greater than their knowledge.[16]

He may have been right about the atrocities and horribleness inflicted on the apprentices in England but his attack on the anti-slave campaigners for having more zeal than knowledge was guaranteed to offend members of his own family unnecessarily. The Quakers' attitude to slavery was well known. It was almost as if he was again driven to prove his strength and independence by showing that he didn't need their approval. With comments like this, he certainly wasn't going to get it.

He returned to Boston, exactly ten weeks after he had left, and on Saturday 17 July set sail again on *Britannia*. They retraced their outward route to Halifax from where they sailed two days later for Liverpool. The midsummer return crossing turned out to be as easy as the outward journey in April had been turbulent and the *Britannia* docked at Liverpool at 7 p.m. on Thursday 29 July – a crossing of nine days and 20 hours. As he left, Captain Cleland turned to Captain Barclay and said: 'You have now crossed the Atlantic in shorter time than ever it was crossed since the Atlantic was the Atlantic, – and you may tack that to the rest of your feats.'[17]

Back at Ury, Captain Barclay settled down to write the account of his 'agricultural tour' and dedicated it to Lord Panmure, one of his oldest friends and a link back to his youthful days with Fletcher Reid and the Daft Laird. He settled again into the annual cycle of life at Ury. In October the annual sheep and cattle sale was 'as usual, numerously and respectably attended'.[18] But, having cut so many of the threads of his old life before he left for the United States of America, he was now free to decide which ones he wanted to reinstate. the *Defiance* was not one of them. When he had sold out earlier in the year, the stagecoach business had already passed its commercial peak. the *Defiance* may have been the finest coach service ever seen in Scotland but its costs were high and its profit margins small. It was however, not business efficiency that threatened its future, and the future of every other stagecoach in the country. It was the railways.

Modern engineering had brought the roads and the coaches to a new, and previously unthought of, peak of perfection. But it also ensured that their end would come swiftly and completely. In 1838, during a House of Commons Select Committee debate on the railways, the chairman asked a simple question of Benjamin Horne, one of England's leading coaching proprietors, and received the following stark reply:

CHAIRMAN: As the railway system expands, you calculate upon the probability of a great diminution of the business of coach proprietors?

HORNE: Annihilation is the best word to apply.[19]

Although Aberdeen is a long way north and the railways would take some time to reach there, it was obviously not the time to buy back the *Defiance*.

Nevertheless, every year, on Midsummer Day he joined in the *Defiance*'s annual birthday celebrations. The long day began very early when the coach, decorated with greenery and the horses hung with flowers and streamers, took to the road.[20] Alec Cook's horn roused the laggards from their sleep, and Captain Barclay, dressed proudly in his red coat, took the reins. The drive was more ceremony than business and was no more than an overture to the long anniversary dinner at Forfar that went on long into the night as singer after singer, Captain Barclay included, did their party piece. He was well lubricated by the time he made his uncertain way upstairs to bed, blew out the candle and went to sleep. He woke almost gassed. The candle he had blown out was one of those new-fangled gaslights. The Druid describes how Captain Barclay's natural instinct saved the day: 'Awakening nearly suffocated, he at once relieved himself in his crude, emphatic fashion, not by groping for the door, but by delivering, one, two straight from the shoulder, through the window panes.'[21]

He also decided not to get involved again in the declining Prize Ring. With time on his hands, Captain Barclay socialised, spent time travelling and indulged himself. He visited the various branches of the family and continued going out with the local hunt wherever he happened to be. It kept him active and fit. In the summer he went to the races, and even bought a racehorse called Fancy Girl, which he put into training with William I'Anson at Gullane, just east of Edinburgh.[22]

Now in his mid 60s, Captain Barclay was as proud of his physical prowess as ever. When he went to dinner with his old friend Lord

Panmure at Brechin Castle, 26 miles away, he still sent his man ahead with his dress clothes and then followed himself, on foot.[23] His return journey the next day was also completed on foot – a fairly regular round trip of 52 miles. One of his friends described him still, as 'a great eater, of fine, simple faith and always in condition'.[24] One night a tailor met him walking back home to Ury from Edinburgh, a distance of 116 miles. He had just crossed the River Forth, probably by ferry from Leith to Burntisland. The camaraderie of the road took them together across Fife, and they crossed the River Tay and continued north along the east coast. Captain Barclay settled into a steady five-miles-an-hour gait, hour after hour, refreshing himself only with oat-cakes at each tollgate, even though his companion offered him whisky. In the 40 or so miles from Burntisland to Arbroath the tailor tried over and over again to tempt him. Captain Barclay always resisted, but the tailor managed to drink 15 glasses. When they parted Captain Barclay was still fit and strong and continued on his way to Ury.[25] The tailor probably slept by the side of the road.

His enjoyment of his trip to the United States and his freedom from other responsibilities tempted Captain Barclay to continue travelling. This time he went to Europe, visiting Paris and Rome. In Rome lived a Scottish sculptor named Lawrence Macdonald, who originally had come from Gask, near Perth, where Captain Barclay had spent so much of his time with the Turriff Hunt.[26] Macdonald was in his 40s, twenty years younger than Captain Barclay. In 1823, when he was only 24, he had, somewhat precociously, been one of the founders of the British Academy of Art in Rome. He had an unusual talent for capturing a flattering likeness in marble and so became highly popular among the moneyed patrons of the arts as a portrait sculptor and eventually came under the patronage of Prince Albert. After going back to Scotland and developing his talents and reputation in Edinburgh, Macdonald returned to Rome in 1833 and became the eternal city's most popular portrait sculptor. His studio was described as being full of 'the peerage done into marble, a plaster galaxy of rank and fashion'.[27] Lawrence Macdonald was a sculptor in the late neoclassical mould and his speciality was to capture his sitters in the Roman style, but with a measured elegance and with the costume and accessories of current fashion. Captain Barclay paid him a visit. In the past, Big Bob Gregson had posed naked alongside the Elgin Marbles and Gentleman Jackson and John Gully's portraits had been painted with their fine, manly physiques shown off alongside statues from classical antiquity. It gave them status and a sort of timeless power. In conversation with Macdonald, Captain Barclay decided to go one better. He commissioned Macdonald to sculpt a full-length figure of him, in marble, as Hercules. When it was finished, it was described as 'colossal'. Captain Barclay shipped it to Scotland where it stood in the entrance hall at Ury to greet all the visitors. One such, Frederick Locker-Lampton, described it:

> . . . without a stitch of clothing, except a baby lion's skin fastened athwart his shoulders — a garment barely wider than the garment of our first parents. However to make up for this startling nudity, he was armed with a tremendous club . . . The first object that greeted the coy visitor on entering . . . was his lordship erect in the hall, in a decidedly threatening attitude.[28]

He also arranged for a new engraving of himself to be published locally by Andrew Anderson. It was a head and shoulders portrait showing him dressed comfortably in a patterned waistcoat, with a large Belcher handkerchief elaborately tied round his neck and carrying his walking stick. The background showed Ury, his shorthorn cattle and the old Quaker Meeting House.[29] Printed underneath in his own handwriting, were the words '*Yours Truly, Robert Barclay Allardice*'. It was ideal to send to admirers.

One admirer was Ann Angus. She had been given the most rudimentary education and was young enough to be his daughter. He always liked young girls from the lower social classes. Ann Angus was a heavy drinker with such a liking for whisky and brandy that it was thought unwise to let her have more than £2 at a time, as she would blow the lot on drink.[30] She was also a Roman Catholic. The Barclay family was bound to disapprove. Captain Barclay and Ann Angus's admiration was obviously mutual as she bore him a son, who was christened *Robert* on 11 March 1845.[31] So by the time Captain Barclay was 65 he had a son and a grandson both named after him, with only three years' difference in their ages. Ann and baby Robert did not move in to Ury. Rodney drew the line at that, and they stayed in Aberdeen.

Ury looked much the same as before. The Apologists study was still there, so were the pictures of Cribb, the Game Chicken, Gully, and the huge naked figure in marble in the entrance hall, but now Captain Barclay was merely a tenant. His trips to the United States, Canada and Europe were expensive, and when he could not meet the repayments on his huge earlier loans, he was forced in June 1844 to transfer Ury to his creditors.[32] For the first time in his life he had little or no money at his disposal and very few ways of raising any.

In the years since Captain Barclay had been to Canada to see his daughter, she had two more sons and a daughter by Samuel Ritchie, but Captain Barclay had not seen any of them. His relationship with Margaret did not improve after the attempted reconciliation in Canada, and it remained strained and tense. In 1845 Samuel Ritchie died, giving father and daughter an opportunity to start afresh.[33] She was 29 and thought that she and her sons would inherit Ury, but Captain Barclay knew differently, and said nothing. His new son and his relationship with Ann Angus, and his guilt over losing Ury, were obstacles too big to negotiate, and his relationship with Margaret hardened.

Financial necessity now forced him back to the *Defiance*, this time managing it for the new owners and attempting to restore its old standards and reputation for punctuality.[34] Everyone knew, of course, that once the railways reached Aberdeen its days would be over. For the time being, however, it enabled him to carry on more or less normally. He managed and drove the *Defiance* and still lived at Ury where he enjoyed playing the role of laird, though no longer owning it. He ate well, went to church, and, of course, walked many miles every day.

Everyone in the neighbourhood knew his routine. He was famous for it. Winter and summer, breakfast was early, and then, regardless of the weather, he walked for at least a couple of hours. One Monday, after breakfast, as he was leaving the house at Ury he met a group of needy locals outside his door and gave sixpences to them. There were many needy locals, and soon it became a tradition. Every Monday he filled his waistcoat pocket with sixpenny pieces, knowing that 20 to 30 hard-up people would be there, waiting for him after breakfast.[35] We know what they didn't, that the sixpences he gave out weren't his own and that, in his way, he was as needy as they were.

The vast legal bills to pave the way to his aborted attempt to be recognised as an Earl, the large marble statue of himself, huge platters of food to entertain his guests, his cows pampered up to their knees in long grass. All might have been sustainable if he had been a tight manager. He was not. His skills as a manager were the products of his authoritarianism, not his thoroughness. When Arthur and Robert Kett had visited Ury 20 years earlier, they had been shocked to see heaps of waste paper in the study.[36] Years of poor record-keeping magnified the effect of years of extravagance. Now with no windfall income from any sporting wagers Captain Barclay was in deepening financial trouble. Ury was in the hands of his creditors but his debts and the costs of his new family continued to climb. In 1847 he cashed in some of his last assets and held his final cattle sale. It raised £2,826 and 12 shillings.[37]

Captain Barclay decided from the very beginning not to marry Ann Angus, so their son remained illegitimate. The chapter of his life which included Margaret, his daughter, and her children, remained stubbornly closed. Ury now seemed to taunt him. Why did he stay there? It was an expensive place to live. Margaret and her children were in the United States and estranged from him. There was no future for them at Ury. Ann's son had no future there either. The Barclay family's links to Ury were broken, so Captain Barclay decided to leave and allow it to go on the market. Perhaps that would pay off the debts and produce some surplus cash. In May 1848 the particulars were drawn up:

Celebrated Scotch Estate ... For sale, by Private Treaty ...
This fine Estate ... in productive cultivation and apt embel-
lishment ... equalled by very few Estates, and surpassed by
none ... valuable salmon fishery ... The Mansion House,
an ancient Baronial Building of massive structure, picturesquely
situated ... The Offices ... The Garden ... seven foot wall of
solid masonry, several miles in circuit ... 3,800 acres ... further
information from the Proprietor at Ury; Johnston, Farquar,
and Leech, solicitors, London; Walter Duthie, Edinburgh, or
Blaikie and Smith, advocates, Aberdeen, who have the Title
Deeds ... Kinnear and Munro, writers and local factors in
Stonehaven will give directions for shewing the Lands.[38]

The particulars were printed and all the parties were ready, waiting
only for Captain Barclay to deliver the title deeds to Blaikie and
Smith in Aberdeen. The waiting went on long enough to become
a major embarrassment. Captain Barclay couldn't find them and the
sale was called off.

The world of the Fancy, of which he had been a star, had slipped
quietly away. Gentleman Jackson died at his home in London in
October 1845,[39] and in May 1848 Tom Cribb died,[40] thus severing
Captain Barclay's last ties to his sporting past. Even William Cross
had retired and was living in Galashiels. Every New Year's Day he
had his friends to dinner at Ury and they all had to make a speech
giving their own resumé of the year. His was described as 'quite an
oration' and he always concluded with a special eulogy to those who
had died during the year. Often he killed one or two off before their
time, but said 'it didn't much matter'.[41] What mattered more was the
death of Dan, his dog, that had been his favourite for 17 years. He had
a plaque inscribed in his memory and placed in the Barclay family
burial vault where the Great Master and his other ancestors lay.[42]

By the time of his 70th birthday in August 1849, many of
the younger generation knew vaguely that he had done something

remarkable, but not exactly what he had done. Only six days after his birthday, *Bell's Life in London*, London's leading sporting newspaper, printed a reply to a sporting question: 'G.M. – Captain Barclay walked 1,000 miles in 1,000 hours at Newmarket. Finished July 10, 1809.'[43] More than forty years had passed since that great day, and a new generation of sportsmen had to be told about it all over again. The passage of forty years had stripped away most, if not all, of the details of what he had done. What was left in the public's collective memory was the image of an almost superhuman man who had performed prodigious feats of strength and endurance, and had stretched the limits of human effort and persistence to the limit. Edgar Allan Poe and Charles Dickens gave him walk-on parts in their stories – 'Loss of Breath' and 'The Lazy Tour of Two Idle Apprentices' respectively. Poe used Captain Barclay as a symbol of tough, uncompromising competitiveness; but for Dickens, Captain Barclay was an example of how extremism could be pursued almost to the point of lunacy. Nevertheless, Dickens recognised that extremism in himself. When he was working on the last chapters of *Great Expectations* he wrote – I work here like a Steam Engine, and walk like Captain Barclay.'[44]

On the other hand, for George Borrow, who was six when Captain Barclay completed his famous 1,000-mile wager, Captain Barclay remained the personification of manly athleticism. Borrow knew, even in 1862, 53 years after Captain Barclay's wager, that when he wrote in *Wild Wales* that he was putting out his legs in 'genuine Barclay fashion' his readers would know exactly what he meant.[45]

In October 1849, just two months after his 70th birthday, Linley Murray Hoag, an American Quaker who was visiting families with Quaker roots in Aberdeen, asked if he could visit Ury. He arrived on a cold afternoon and Captain Barclay invited him to stay the night, saying that it would make his onward journey to England easier and also allow him to see Ury by candlelight. Linley Hoag was already tired and chilled and asked if he could go straight to bed with a basin of gruel.

Next morning at breakfast he, Captain Barclay and Rodney were standing in front of the fire, looking at an old portrait of Colonel David

Barclay, when the following conversation took place:

HOAG: Ah, there is my friend of last night.

RODNEY: Not quite, that is an ancestor of ours who has been dead nearly 200 years.

HOAG: Oh, he looks like the old gentleman who came into my room last night. (*breakfast was served*)

CAPTAIN B: Will you please tell me, Mr Hoag, who it was who came into your room last night and what he was doing there?

HOAG: Well, I was just going off to sleep when there was a knock on the door and a sweet old gentleman very like that portrait came into the room. He had a candle in his hand which he shaded with his other hand, and apologised for disturbing me. He then went round the foot of the bed and opened a cupboard in the wall at the other side, taking out some old papers which looked like parchment.

When breakfast was over:

CAPTAIN B: Did you ever hear the like of that!

RODNEY: Why there is no cupboard there.

CAPTAIN B: Mr Hoag, will you please do me the favour of showing me exactly where the old gentleman found the papers?[46]

To oblige his hosts, Linley Hoag led the way upstairs to the bedroom. Rodney was right, she knew every inch of Ury; there was no cupboard there. On tapping the wall however, it sounded hollow, so Captain Barclay tore away a corner of wallpaper and found some wooden boards underneath. He prised them away with a poker and revealed an iron door behind. The poker made no impression on the iron door and so a blacksmith was called. After much effort he opened the iron door of a safe and revealed the lost deeds of Ury inside.

When Linley Hoag left Ury later that day to travel south, he took the *Defiance*, one of the last people to do so, for the railway line that had been creeping up from Edinburgh for months finally arrived and was open to passengers from 1 November 1849.[47] At first it went only as far as Limpet Hill, three miles from Stonehaven, but the days of the *Defiance* were finally over. On the very day that the first railway passengers paid their fares, *Defiance* set out on its final journey. Captain Barclay, who had taken it out on its inaugural trip over 20 years before climbed for the last time, resplendent in his red coat, into the box seat of the *Defiance* at Montrose, took in his hands, the ribbons of the four horses, especially and lovingly groomed for the occasion, and set out on the coach's farewell journey to Aberdeen. Black crêpe hung over the shop doorways, as the locals mourned the loss of their famed and favoured *Defiance*. Young and old lined the route to mark its passing.[48]

Captain Barclay was 70 years old but had the bearing, physique and stature of a much younger man. Active he certainly was, as Ann Angus could testify, for as she looked up at him as he set the horses in motion, she was in the final stages of pregnancy with another of his sons. The baptism took place on 7 January 1850 at the Roman Catholic Church of the Assumption in Aberdeen. The baby was baptised David Stewart Barclay.[49] Captain Barclay's strength and virility were a continuing source of comment and amazement. His irritability never seemed to mellow, however, even in church where he could throw quite a tantrum if anyone took over his favourite pew and relegated him to the gallery. 'I can't say my prayers in a gallery pew,' he said.[50] Nevertheless, he was always willing to oblige when it came to talking about his past feats, or even demonstrating them. On one occasion while he was sitting round the dinner table having dessert with the Galtons in Leamington, he was asked if he still performed any feats of strength. Old habits die hard, and to Captain Barclay the words sounded more like a challenge than a question. By 'slightly bending his body' he placed his right hand on the floor, palm up, and asked Darwin Galton, 'a fully adult man of more than 12 stone in weight', to stand on it. Then, asking Darwin to steady himself by laying one finger on his shoulder, Captain Barclay promptly 'lifted and landed him on the table'.[51] More than 45 years had gone by since he had similarly lifted the 18-stone Captain Keith. It was an impressive party trick, but sad to relate, he strained his shoulder doing it and there is no record of him ever doing it again.

In 1853 Rodney died,[52] leaving Captain Barclay alone at Ury, and he promptly moved in Ann Angus and the two boys, Robert Jnr who was eight, and David, three. Ann and the boys seemed to rekindle the sporting fire in him and in April, when after the long cold winter the weather began to improve, he bought the boys two cricket bats and two balls from David Walker's in Aberdeen.[53] They were about to be initiated into the mysteries of sport by one of its greatest practitioners. Within a couple of weeks however, he suffered a couple of mild strokes, which left him partly paralysed.[54] He responded in the only way he knew; he got out as soon as he could and pushed himself to his physical limit doing the various chores that were always there to be done on the farm. This therapy seemed to serve him well and he recovered quickly, but at the end of April, when he was out in one of the fields at Ury trying to break in a pony, it kicked him in the head. He was nearly 75. For a while he seemed none the worse.

Early on 1 May 1854 he was suddenly taken ill. So ill that Dr Thomson was immediately called for, but arrived a few minutes too late. Captain Barclay died at 9.15 on May Day morning,[55] the day on which, for centuries, young men and women celebrated the coming of spring with games and sporting contests. Not many of those who ran and frolicked that day knew that the world had just lost one of its most celebrated sportsmen, and one who stayed true to his athletic temperament right to the very end.

# Notes and References

## Chapter 1

1. Walter Thom, *Pedestrianism*, Aberdeen, D. Chalmers and Co., 1813, pp. 127–8. The last three days of the event coincided with the first three days of the four-day 'July Meeting' at Newmarket. The crowds were said to be 'unprecedented' (Thom, *Pedestrianism*, p. 127). Even three weeks before, however, the numbers attending were described as 'immense' (*The Edinburgh Evening Courant*, 26 June 1809).
2. Wages varied from county to county and from year to year. Fifty guineas (£52.50) a year, or about £1 per week, may be an optimistic figure as an 'average' wage. The average wage at the start of the twenty-first century was £400. Thus, we need to multiply by 400 to get an approximate modern equivalent. However, what people in 1809 could, or needed to, buy with their wages was quite different from now. But to calculate the present purchasing power of their wages we need to multiply by only 40. For a general review of these topics, see Robert Twigger, *Inflation: The Value of the Pound, 1750–1998*, Research Paper 99/20, London, House of Commons Library, 23 February 1999; Venetia Murray, *High Society in the Regency Period*, London, Penguin Books, pp. 66–88; and G.D.H. Cole and Raymond Postgate, *The Common People, 1746–1946*, London, Methuen & Co., 1971.
3. *The Times*, 14 July 1809.
4. Anthony Burgess, *Historical Commentary*, in *Coaching Days of England*, London, Paul Elek, 1966, p. 14.
5. Plutarch, *Fame of the Athenians*, *Opera Moralia*, 347C.
6. Lucian, *A Slip of the Tongue*, 3.
7. For a review of the texts of Plutarch and Lucian, see Waldo E. Sweet, *Sport and Recreation in Ancient Greece*, Oxford University Press, 1987, and H.M. Lee, 'Modern Ultra-Long Distance Running and Philippedes' Run from Athens to Sparta', in *Ancient World*, 9, 1984.
8. Plutarch, *Life of Aristedes*, 20.5.
9. The wager was made with James Wedderburn Webster in October 1808 and reported by *The Times*, 6 December 1808.
10. Thom, p. 202.
11. *The Edinburgh Advertiser*, 18 July 1809.
12. *The Examiner*, 17 July 1809.
13. *The Times*, 14 July 1809.
14. The event started on 1 June on a course starting from the house of Francis Buckle, the jockey. The course was changed on 16 June, and from then on he started from a house adjoining Mr Parkinson's and near the Horse and Jockey. He moved to escape the smell of cooking and to have more room (Thom, pp. 123–4 and 133). He may also have moved because he thought he would be safer on the open heath (*The Edinburgh Advertiser*, 23 June 1809).
15. *The Sporting Magazine*, vol. 19, p. 96, November 1801.
16. He weighed 13 stone 4 pounds at the start and 11 stone on the day he finished, a weight loss of 32 pounds (Thom, p. 125).
17. *The St James's Chronicle*, 11–13 July 1809.

18. Thom, *Pedestrianism*, states that 'in his arms particularly, he possesses uncommon strength' (p. 208), and 'the deltoid muscle of his arm is uncommonly large' (p. 209).

19. From the twelfth day Thom reports that Captain Barclay 'felt a little pain in his legs'. This developed to 'some pain', 'pain increasing', 'worse', 'much worse', 'still worse', 'great pain', 'excessive pain' to 'very ill' on the fortieth day. Authenticity to these claims is given by Thom, who wrote that he had copied 'with perfect fidelity' the manuscript given him by 'a gentleman who had attended him [Captain Barclay] from the commencement' (Thom, *Pedestrianism*, p. 128).

20. William Cross was involved throughout the event. See *Say's Sunday Reporter*, 25 June 1809; Thom, p. 154–5; and Druid, *Field and Fern*, London, Rogerson and Tuxford, 1865, pp. 199–200.

21. William Will, *The Kincardineshire Volunteers: A History of the Volunteer Movement in Kincardineshire from 1798 to 1816*, Aberdeen, *The Aberdeen Weekly Journal Press*, 1919, p. 104.

22. *The Sporting Magazine*, vol. 34, p. 160, June 1809.

23. Thom, p. 202.

24. Ibid., pp. 211–12.

25. *The London Chronicle*, 10–12 June 1809; *The St James's Chronicle*, 15–17 June 1809.

26. John Ashton, *The Dawn of the XIXth Century in England*, London, T. Fisher Unwin, 1906, pp. 201–7.

27. *The St James's Chronicle*, 13–15 June 1809; *The Edinburgh Evening Courant*, 6 July 1809.

28. *Say's Sunday Reporter*, 25 June 1809.

29. *The Edinburgh Advertiser*, 23 June 1809.

30. Druid, *Field and Fern*, pp. 199–200.

31. Thom, *Pedestrianism*: ligaments, p. 147; toothache, p. 130; rain, pp.142 and 148.

32. Ibid., pp. 172–90.

33. Ibid., p. 137.

34. Ibid., pp. 138–41.

35. Thom, pp. 123–4 and 133, and *The St James's Chronicle*, 15–17 June 1809.

36. Verily Anderson, personal communication, 11 September 1982.

37. *The Times*, 26 June 1809; Anderson, personal communication, 11 September 1982.

38. *The Edinburgh Advertiser*, 4 July 1809.

39. *The London Chronicle*, 27–28 June 1809.

40. Pierce Egan, *Sporting Anecdotes, Original and Selected – A New Edition Considerably Enlarged and Improved*, London, Sherwood, Jones and Co., 1825, p. 9.

41. Leslie A. Marchand, *Lord Byron: Letters and Journals, volume 3, 'Alas the Love of Women'*, London, John Murray, 1974, p. 133.

42. Ibid., pp. 123 and 133.

43. T.A.J. Burnett, *The Rise and Fall of a Regency Dandy*, London, John Murray, 1981, pp. 231–2.

44. Thom, p. 202.

45. Ibid., p. 154.

46. *The Edinburgh Advertiser*, 18 July 1809.

47. *The Times*, 14 July 1809; *The Examiner*, 17 July 1809.

48. Thom, p. 125.

49. Thom, p. 155.

50. *The St James's Chronicle*, 29 June–1 July 1809.

51. J.W. Fortescue, *A History of the British Army, vol. VII, 1809–1810*, London, Macmillan, 1910, p. 56.

52. Arthur Bryant, *Years of Victory: 1802–1812*, London, Collins, 1975, pp. 325–6.

53. Thom, p. 213; Nimrod, *Nimrod's Northern Tour*, London, Walter Spiers, 1838, p. 298; Druid, *Field and Fern*, p. 208.

54. *The St James's Chronicle*, 22–25 October 1808; *The Times*, 24 October 1808.

55. Amanda Foreman, *Georgiana, Duchess of Devonshire*, London, HarperCollins, 2000, pp. 219–26.

56. Thom, p. 122.

57. For a discussion of the events around Wagram see Bryant, pp. 295–339, and James Trager, *The People's Chronology*, London, Aurum Press, 1992, pp. 370–1.

58. *The Edinburgh Evening Courant*, 22 July 1809.

59. Thom, p. 214.

60. Bryant, p. 326.

61. Thom, p. 214.

62. Ellangowan, *Sporting Anecdotes*, London, Hamilton, Adams, 1889, p. 56.

63. Druid, p. 200.

# Chapter 2

1. Walter Thom gives August 1794 and 1796 as the date for this event. See Thom, *Pedestrianism*, pp. 101 and 156. 1794 is almost certainly an error. See also Pierce Egan, *Sporting Anecdotes, Original and Selected – A New Edition Considerably Enlarged and Improved*, London, Sherwood, Jones and Co., 1825, p. 4.

2. See Thom, p. 205, and F.H.W. Sheppard (ed.), *Survey of London, vol. XXVI, The Parish of St Mary Lambeth, Part II, Southern Area*, London, The Athlone Press, 1956, pp. 109–10 and 139.

3. Letter from RBA to his father, 23 September 1794. QL, Temp MSS 285, Box VIII, 495.

4. Thom, p. 205. Also letter from RBA to his father, 17 October 1791. NAS/GD49/581.

5. Letter from David Barclay of Youngsbury to Samuel Galton, 8 October 1798. QL, Temp MSS 285, Box VII, 458.

6. For a review of the energy-cost of walking and running, see J. Amar, *The Human Motor*, New York, E.P. Dutton and Co., 1920, and L.E. Morehouse and J.M. Cooper, *Kinesiology*, St Louis, C.V. Mosby Co., 1950. For the betting on such a task, see Christopher North, 'Gymnastics', in *Blackwood's Magazine*, August 1826, and Professor Wilson, *Essays – Critical and Imaginative, vol. I*, Edinburgh, William Blackwood and Sons, 1856, pp. 94–127.

7. Christopher Hibbert, *George IV, Prince of Wales, 1762–1811*, London, Longman, 1972, p.176.

8. Ibid.

9. Archibald Watt, *Highways and Byways Around Stonehaven*, Aberdeen, Waverley Press, 1976, p. 174.

10. Thom, pp. 282–5.

11. Verily Anderson, *Friends and Relations*, London, Hodder & Stoughton, 1980, pp. 170–1.

12. Hubert F. Barclay and Alice Wilson-Fox, *A History of the Barclay Family, Part III*, London, St Catherine's Press, 1934, p. 215.

13. Thom, p. 283.

14. Thomas Dick Lauder, *Highland Rambles and Long Legends to Shorten the Way, vol. 1*, Edinburgh, Adam and Charles Black, 1837, pp. 162–5, and Ellangowan, *Sporting Anecdotes*, London, Hamilton, Adams & Co., 1889, pp. 167–9.

15. Verily Anderson, *Friends and Relations*, London, Hodder & Stoughton, 1980, pp. 170–1.

16. Nimrod, *Nimrod's Northern Tour*, p. 338.
17. Leslie George de Rune Barclay, *History of the Scottish Barclays*, Folkstone, Bewley, 1915, p. 38.
18. Alexander Gordon, 'The Great Laird of Ury', in *The Theological Review*, October 1874, pp. 524–555.
19. David MacGregor Peter, *The Baronage of Angus and Mearns,* Edinburgh, Oliver & Boyd, 1856, p. 19.
20. Barclay and Wilson-Fox, *A History of the Barclay Family, Part III*, pp. 210–214.
21. NAS/GD49/521/3.
22. H. Nicolas, *History of the Earldoms of Strathern, Menteith and Airth*, London, William Pickering, Stevens and Norton, 1842, pp. xix and 119.
23. Peter, *The Baronage of Angus and Mearns*, pp. 4–5.
24. Barclay and Wilson-Fox, *A History of the Barclay Family, Part III*, p. 218.
25. Ibid., p. 217.
26. Robert Scott Fittes, *Sports and Pastimes of Scotland*, Paisley, Alexander Gardner, 1891, p. 181.
27. Peter, *The Baronage of Angus and Mearns*, pp. 100–101.
28. Letter from RBA to John Joseph Gurney, 17 September 1830. BP, Box 31, No. 8, 802–866.
29. House of Commons, *Return of Members Parliament, vol. 2, 1357–1874*, London, 1878.
30. For a review of this illness see Hibbert, *George IV, Prince of Wales, 1762–1811*, pp. 71–81.
31. Daniel Mendoza, *Memoirs of the Life of Daniel Mendoza*, London, G. Hayden, 1816.
32. A mug commemorating the fight between Mendoza and Humphreys in 1788 was issued, showing each of the fighters, seconds and bottle-holders. See Paul Magriel (ed.), *The Memoirs of the Life of Daniel Mendoza*, London, B.T. Batsford, 1951, p. 65 (facing).
33. Pierce Egan refers to Richard Humphries as 'the gentleman boxer!' because of his 'genteel appearance and behaviour'. See One of the Fancy, *Boxiana, or Sketches of Ancient and Modern Pugilism*, London, G. Smeeton, p. 102. Vincent Dowling refers to John Jackson's 'well-deserved cognomen of "Gentleman Jackson"' because of his 'universal good conduct in and out of the ring'. See The Editor of Bell's Life in London, *Fights for the Championship; and Celebrated Prize Battles*, London, Bell's Life, 1855, p. 15. Vincent George Dowling founded *Bell's Life in London* and edited it for nearly 30 years. He also began *Fistiana*. When he died in 1852 these titles were taken over by his son, Francis Dowling.
34. One of the Fancy, *Boxiana, or Sketches of Ancient and Modern Pugilism*, pp. 297–300.
35. George Borrow's father also read the Bible to him as he was dying. See George Borrow, *Lavengro, the Scholar – the Gypsy – the Priest*, London, Collins, 1851, pp. 10–11.
36. The Editor of Bell's Life in London, *Fights for the Championship; and Celebrated Prize Battles*, p. 10.
37. Magriel (ed.), *The Memoirs of the Life of Daniel Mendoza*, pp. 31–2.
38. For a brief overview of the Barrymore family see Saul David, *Prince of Pleasure – The Prince of Wales and the Making of the Regency*, London, Little, Brown, 1998, pp. 130–3.
39. This pamphlet was probably by Charles Pigott. See David, *Prince of Pleasure – The Prince of Wales and the Making of the Regency*, pp. 132–3.
40. Fred Henning, *Fights for the Championship – The Men and Their Times, vol. 1*, London, The Licensed Victuallers' Gazette, 1902, pp. 114–18.
41. One of the Fancy, *Boxiana, or Sketches of Ancient and Modern Pugilism*, pp. 291–2 and 219–20.
42. *The Edinburgh Evening Courant*, 11 December 1773, and An Amateur Sportsman, *Sporting Anecdotes; Original and Select,* London, Thomas Hurst, 1804, pp. 322–4.
43. *The Morning Post and Daily Advertiser*, 9 July 1792.

44. John Mayhall, *The Annals of York, Leeds, Bradford, Halifax, Doncaster, Barnsley, Wakefield, Dewsbury, Huddersfield, Keighley, and Other Places in the County of York*, Leeds, Joseph Johnson, 1860, p. 175.

45. Johnson wore 'rose shoe-strings' in his fight against Perrins. Perrins, who was from Birmingham, wore 'large Artois buckles'. *The Morning Post and Daily Advertiser*, 28 October 1789.

46. *The Caledonian Mercury*, 24 August 1793.

47. Ibid.

48. Including *Morning Post*, 17 April 1793.

49. *The London Chronicle*, 20–23 April 1793.

50. Although it was reported that 'the faculty attributed his death to over-exertion' (S. Baring-Gould, *Yorkshire Oddities, Incidents and Strange Events*, London, John Hodges, 1877, p. 22), other contemporary reports suggest that prior to his death he had received inexpert surgery on a lump in his neck. See *The Sporting Magazine*, April 1793, p. 48.

51. *The Morning Post and Daily Advertiser*, 29 January 1788.

52. For an overview of the Duke of York and the military establishment of the time see Philip Haythornthwaite, *The Armies of Wellington*, London, Brockhampton Press, 1998, pp. 15–17.

53. Hibbert, *George IV, Prince of Wales, 1762–1811*, p. 100.

54. David, *Prince of Pleasure – The Prince of Wales and the Making of the Regency*, pp. 136–7.

55. Hibbert, *George IV, Prince of Wales, 1762–1811*, pp. 14–28.

56. John Ford, *Prizefighting – The Age of Regency Boximania*, South Brunswick, Great Albion Books, 1971, pp. 74–5.

57. One of the Fancy, *Boxiana, or Sketches of Ancient and Modern Pugilism*, pp. 97–100.

58. Ibid., p. 245.

59. *Jackson's Oxford Journal*, 16 October 1790.

60. *The Edinburgh Advertiser*, 16–20 October 1789.

61. *The Caledonian Mercury*, 14 October 1790.

62. *Jackson's Oxford Journal*, 16 October 1790.

63. Allen Guttmann, *Women's Sport – A History*, New York, Columbia University Press, 1991, p. 73.

64. Leslie P. Wenham, personal communication, September 1983.

65. *The London Chronicle*, 30 August–2 September 1788.

66. *The Sporting Magazine*, May 1793, p. 121.

67. *The Sporting Magazine*, March 1793, p. 370.

68. See Peter Radford, 'Women's Foot-Races in Britain in the 18th and 19th Centuries: A Popular and Widespread Practice', *Canadian Journal of History of Sport*, vol. XXV, No. 1, May 1994, pp. 50–61.

69. *The Sportsman's Magazine or Chronicle of Games and Pastimes*, March 1824, pp. 51–2.

70. *Lincoln, Rutland and Stamford Mercury*, 5 November 1790.

71. *The Sporting Magazine*, March 1793, p. 370.

72. *The Sporting Magazine*, November 1792, p. 103.

73. *The Sporting Magazine*, March 1794, p. 118.

74. *The Sporting Magazine*, March 1793, p. 369.

75. Thom, *Pedestrianism*, p. 283.

76. John Nyren, *The Young Cricketer's Tutor, and The Cricketers of My Time*, London, Effingham Wilson, 1833, pp. 55–61.

77. John Marshall, *The Duke Who Was Cricket*, London, Frederick Muller, 1961, pp. 90–98.

78. David Underdown, *Start of Play, Cricket and Culture in the Eighteenth Century*, London, The Penguin Press, 2000, p. 63.

79. R.L. Arrowsmith, *A History of County Cricket – Kent*, Newton Abbot, Sportsman's Book Club, 1972, p. 19.
80. John Stevens, *Knavesmire – York's Great Racecourse and Its Stories*, London, Pelham Books, 1984, pp. 50–8.
81. *The Sporting Magazine*, October 1807, pp. 6–7.
82. NAS/GD49/521/3.

# Chapter 3

1. Hubert F. Barclay and Alice Wilson-Fox, *A History of the Barclay Family, Part III*, London, 1934, p. 219.
2. Letter from John Durno to Samuel Galton, 11 June 1797. QL, Temp MSS 285, Box VI, 402.
3. For a general overview of these events, see Arthur Bryant, *The Years of Endurance 1793–1802*, London, Collins, 1944, pp. 192–6.
4. Ibid., pp. 201–21.
5. Ibid., p. 195.
6. Letter from RBA to Samuel Galton, 3 May 1797. QL, Temp MSS 285, Box VI, 399.
7. Letter From J.H. Tritton to Samuel Galton, 24 August 1798. QL, Temp MSS 285, Box VII, 443.
8. Letter from RBA to Samuel Galton, 9 July 1797. QL, Temp MSS 285, Box VI, 406.
9. Letter from Lucy Galton to RBA, 27 February 1798. QL, Temp MSS 285, Box VI, 414.
10. Anderson, *Friends and Relations*, pp. 178–9 and 220.
11. Report from William Paul re RBA's education, June 1798. QL, Temp MSS 285, Box VI, 423.
12. Letter from Samuel Galton to William Paul, 26 August 1798. QL, Temp MSS 285, Box VII, 447.
13. Hubert F. Barclay and Alice Wilson-Fox, *A History of the Barclay Family, Part III*, p. 221, and letter from Alexander Crombie to Samuel Galton, 16 May 1798. QL, Temp MSS 285, Box VI, 420.
14. Will, *The Kincardineshire Volunteers*, pp. 14–15.
15. Ibid., p. 17.
16. Ibid., p. 23.
17. Letter from RBA to Samuel Galton, 1 July 1798. QL, Temp MSS 285, Box VI, 432.
18. Letter from David Barclay to Samuel Galton at Birmingham, 8 October 1798. QL, Temp MSS 285, Box VII, 458.
19. NAS/GD51/901/2.
20. Extract of letter from RBA, 24 August 1798, and letter from John. H. Tritton to Samuel Galton, 24 August 1798. QL, Temp MSS 285, Box VI, 444 and 443.
21. Letter from Samuel Galton to William Paul, 26 August 1798. QL, Temp MSS 285, Box VII, 447.
22. Thom, pp. 101–2 and 156.
23. One of the Fancy, *Boxiana, or Sketches of Ancient and Modern Pugilism*, p. 258.
24. See Douglas Goldring, *Regency Portrait Painter: The Life of Sir Thomas Lawrence*, London, Macdonald & Co., 1951, p. 55.
25. Ibid., p. 54.

26. One of the Fancy, *Boxiana, or Sketches of Ancient and Modern Pugilism*, p. 295.

27. Henry Downes Miles, *Pugilistica, A History of British Boxing, vol. 1*, Edinburgh, John Grant, 1906, pp. 93–4.

28. Goldring, *Regency Portrait Painter: The Life of Sir Thomas Lawrence*, p. 74.

29. Ibid., pp. 77–8.

30. Ibid., p. 75, and Kenneth Garlick, *Sir Thomas Lawrence: A Complete Catalogue of the Oil Paintings*, Oxford, Phaidon, 1989, p. 295.

31. Goldring, *Regency Portrait Painter: The Life of Sir Thomas Lawrence*, p. 110.

32. Naomi Royde-Smith, *The Private Life of Mrs Siddons*, London, Gollancz, 1933, p. 239.

33. Goldring, *Regency Portrait Painter: The Life of Sir Thomas Lawrence*, pp. 117–45.

34. Ibid., p. 111.

35. Ibid., p. 194.

36. Ibid., pp. 337–8.

37. Ibid., pp. 122–3.

38. Letter from Samuel Galton to RBA, 25 August 1798. QL, Temp MSS 285, Box VII, 445.

39. Letter from RBA to Lucy Galton, 7 September 1798. QL, Temp MSS 285, Box VII, 453.

40. Letter from David Barclay to Samuel Galton, 8 October 1798. QL, Temp MSS 285, Box VII, 458.

41. Will, *The Kincardineshire Volunteers: A History of the Volunteer Movement in Kincardineshire from 1798 to 1816*, p. 24.

42. Letter from RBA to Samuel Galton, 24 October 1798, and letter from David Jones to Samuel Galton, 8 November 1798. QL, Temp MSS 285, Box VII, 464 and 467.

43. George Pryme, *Autobiographic Recollections of George Pryme Esq. MA*, London, Deighton, Bell and Co., 1870.

44. Letter from RBA to Samuel Galton, 11 November 1798. QL, Temp MSS 285, Box VII, 468.

45. See J.A. Venn (*Alumni Cantabrigiensis, Part II, vol. 1*, Cambridge, The University Press, 1940, p. 2), who has the identity of RBA confused, and letter from RBA to Samuel Galton. QL, Temp MSS 285, Box VII, 468.

46. Sylvanus Urban, *The Gentleman's Magazine and Historical Chronicle, vol. LXXIX, Part 2*, London, John Nichols and Son, 1809, p. 1,125.

47. Letter from RBA to Samuel Galton, 11 November 1798. QL, Temp MSS 285, Box VII, 468.

48. Pryme, *Autobiographic Recollections of George Pryme Esq. MA*, p. 43.

49. Barclay and Wilson-Fox, *A History of the Barclay Family, Part III*, p. 221.

# Chapter 4

1. See letter from John Durno to Samuel Galton, 11 June 1797 (QL, Temp MSS 285, Box VI, 402) and *The English Chronicle*, 5 November 1801.

2. NAS/GD49/521/3.

3. NAS/GD51/901/3.

4. Letter from RBA to Henry Dundas, 17 September 1800. NAS/GD51/903/3.

5. *The Sporting Magazine*, September 1801, p. 93.

6. John Ashton, *The Dawn of the XIXth Century*, London, T. Fisher Unwin, 1906, pp. 16–18.

7. Andrew Service, *The History and Traditions of the Lindsays in Angus and Mearns*, Edinburgh, David Douglas, 1882, pp. 348–9.

8. Alexander Elliot, *Lochee As It Was and As It Is*, Dundee, J.P. Mathew, 1911, pp. 109–14.

9. Thom, *Pedestrianism*, pp. 102 and 156.

10. *Paterson's 'Roads'* was essential equipment for anyone who travelled at the time. It gave information on all the roads and distances between every town and village in England, and the names of all the coaching inns. Its full title was *A New and Accurate Description of the Direct and Principal Roads in England and Wales and Part of the Roads of Scotland: With Correct Routes of the Mail Coaches and a Great Variety of New Measurements*. Its author was Lieutenant-Colonel Daniel Paterson. See Daniel Paterson, *Direct and Principal Roads in England*, London, Longman and Rees, 1803.

11. An Amateur Sportsman, *Sporting Anecdotes: Original and Select*, pp. 236–41.

12. See John Robert Robinson, *Old Q: A Memoir of William Douglas, Fourth Duke of Queensberry Kt.*, London, Sampson Low, Marston and Co., 1895, pp.16–24, and An Amateur Sportsman, *Sporting Anecdotes: Original and Select*, p. 238.

13. Robinson, *Old Q: A Memoir of William Douglas, Fourth Duke of Queensberry Kt.*, pp. 39–40.

14. For the full story of the Hambledon Club see Ashley Mote, *The Glory Days of Cricket – The Extraordinary Story of Broadhalfpenny Down*, London, Robson Books, 1997, p. 63.

15. Ibid., pp. 27–82.

16. *The Sun*, 13 November 1801.

17. *The Times*, 14 November 1801, and *Jackson's Oxford Journal*, 21 November 1801.

18. Henning, *Fights for the Championships – The Men and Their Times*, pp. 176–7.

19. *The Sun*, 13 November 1801.

20. For a description of Broughton's Rules and a discussion of their significance see Dennis Brailsford, *Bareknuckles – A Social History of Prize-Fighting*, Cambridge, Lutterworth Press, 1988, pp. 8–11.

21. Ford, *Prizefighting – The Age of Regency Boximania*, pp. 138–9.

22. J.D. Aylward, *The House of Angelo – A Dynasty of Swordsmen*, London, The Batchworth Press, 1953, p. 157.

23. Pierce Egan, *Boxiana, or Sketches of Ancient and Modern Pugilism, vol. II*, London, Sherwood, Neely and Jones, 1818, pp. 11–12.

24. Ibid.; *The Sporting Repository*, January 1822, p. 47; The Editor of Bell's Life in London, *Fights for the Championship; and Celebrated Prize Battles*, p.17; and Miles, *Pugilistica, A History of British Boxing, vol. 1*, p. 97. There were rooms of various sizes on the ground and first floor. The largest was a single-storey building at the back. The rooms also had a basement and extended to the second floor but were probably not for exercise.

25. Miles, *Pugilistica, A History of British Boxing, vol. I*, p. 98.

26. Ibid., p. 96.

27. Henning, *Fights for the Championships – The Men and Their Times, vol. 1*, p. 166.

28. Hubert Cole, *Beau Brummell*, London, Granada Publishing, 1977.

29. Goldring, *Regency Portrait Painter: The Life of Sir Thomas Lawrence*, p. 196, and Garlick, *Sir Thomas Lawrence: A Complete Catalogue of the Oil Paintings*, p. 216.

30. Nimrod, *Nimrod's Northern Tour*, London, Walter Spiers, 1838, p. 379.

31. *The Sporting Magazine*, June 1799, p. 129.

32. Nimrod, *Nimrod's Northern Tour*, pp. 379–80.

33. Miles, *Pugilistica, A History of British Boxing*, pp. 92–3.

34. Thom, p. 102.

35. Wilson, *Essays – Critical and Imaginative, vol. I*, 1856, pp. 103–4.

36. Thom, pp. 102 and 156.

37. Sir John Sinclair, *A Collection of Papers on the Subject of Athletic Exercises, etc.*, London, privately printed and distributed, 1806.

38. Sir John Sinclair, *The Code of Health and Longevity, vol. II*, Edinburgh, Arch. Constable & Co., 1807, p. 135.

39. Thom, p. 102.

40. William Norrie, *Dundee Celebrities of the Nineteenth Century*, Dundee, published by the author, 1873, pp. 136–9.

41. Elliot, *Lochee As It Was and As It Is*, p. 114.

42. The Editor of Bell's Life in London, *Fistiana; or The Oracle of the Ring*, London, Bell's Life in London, 1868, p. 40.

43. Magriel, *The Memoirs of the Life of Daniel Mendoza*, p. 104.

44. Ibid., p. 87.

45. Ibid., pp. 103–4.

46. Ibid., pp. 80–93.

47. Ibid., pp. 34, 85, 101, 106 and 108.

48. Letter, 8 November 1798, from L. Windham to Count Bruhl agreeing that Mendoza should not be sent out of the country on a mere suspicion. NAS/GD157/3444/2.

49. Miles, *Pugilistica, A History of British Boxing*, p. 122.

50. Henning, *Fights for the Championships – The Men and Their Times*, pp. 176–7.

51. One of the Fancy, *Boxiana, or Sketches of Ancient and Modern Pugilism*, pp. 120.

52. Ibid., p. 121.

53. Ibid., p. 144; Henning, *Fights for the Championships – The Men and Their Times*, pp. 170 and 131–2; and Denzil Batchelor, *British Boxing*, London, Collins, 1948, pp. 12–15.

54. One of the Fancy, *Boxiana, or Sketches of Ancient and Modern Pugilism*, p. 128, and The Editor of Bell's Life in London, *Fistiana; or The Oracle of the Ring*, p. 8.

55. Ibid., pp. 128–9 and p. 8 respectively.

56. One of the Fancy, *Boxiana, or Sketches of Ancient and Modern Pugilism*, pp. 131–2.

57. Henning, *Fights for the Championships – The Men and Their Times*, pp. 189–90.

58. Ibid., p. 196.

59. One of the Fancy, *Boxiana, or Sketches of Ancient and Modern Pugilism*, pp. 132–4, and The Editor of Bell's Life in London, *Fistiana; or The Oracle of the Ring*, p. 8.

60. William Norrie, *Dundee Celebrities of the Nineteenth Century*, Dundee, published by the author, 1873, pp. 136–9.

61. Ibid., p. 137.

62. J. Fairfax-Blakeborough, *Northern Turf History, vol. IV; History of Horse Racing in Scotland*, Westerdale, published by the author, 1973, pp. 6 and 265–6.

63. *The Edinburgh Advertiser*, 6–10 March 1801, and Thom, p. 103.

64. *The Sporting Magazine*, December 1798, pp. 165–6.

65. *The Sporting Magazine*, January 1799, p. 235.

66. *The Edinburgh Advertiser*, 6–10 March 1801.

67. *The Sporting Magazine*, March 1801, p. 301.

68. *The Edinburgh Advertiser*, 6–10 March 1801, and *The Times*, 9 March 1801.

69. Quoted by Fairfax-Blakeborough, *Northern Turf History, vol. IV; History of Horse Racing in Scotland*, p. 4.

70. Ibid.

71. *The Sporting Magazine*, March 1801, p. 303.

72. *The Sporting Magazine*, May 1801, p. 106.

## Chapter 5

1. Captain Barclay, *Agricultural Tour in the United States and Canada*, Edinburgh, William Blackwood & Sons, 1842, pp. v–vi.

2. J. Fairfax-Blakeborough, *Northern Turf History, vol. I; Hambleton & Richmond*, London, J.A. Allen, 1949, p. 61, and *The Sporting Magazine*, November 1801, p. 94.
3. *The Sporting Magazine*, December 1798.
4. Thom, *Pedestrianism*, pp. 103 and 156.
5. *The Edinburgh Advertiser*, 13–17 November 1801.
6. *The Edinburgh Evening Courant*, 3 September 1801.
7. Ibid.
8. *The Edinburgh Advertiser*, 28 August–1 September 1801.
9. See Kenneth Garlick and Angus Macintyre (eds.), *The Diary of Joseph Farington, vol. V*, Yale, New Haven, Yale University Press, 1979, p. 1,587.
10. Sir John Sinclair, *The Code of Health and Longevity, vol. II*, Edinburgh, Arch. Constable & Co., 1807, p. 281.
11. *The Sporting Magazine*, December 1798, pp. 165–6.
12. Thom, p. 227.
13. *The Edinburgh Advertiser*, 13–17 November 1801.
14. *The Times*, 14 November 1801.
15. *The Edinburgh Advertiser*, 24–27 November 1901.
16. *The Sporting Magazine*, December 1798, pp. 165–6.
17. J. Fairfax-Blakeborough, *Northern Turf History, vol. III; York & Doncaster Races*, London, J.A. Allen, 1950, p. 267.
18. Nikolai Tolstoy, *The Half-Mad Lord*, London, Jonathan Cape, 1978, pp. 111–12.
19. *The Sporting Magazine*, June 1799, p. 88.
19. Magriel, *The Memoirs of the Life of Daniel Mendoza*, pp. 106–7.
20. Henning, *Fights for the Championships – The Men and Their Times, vol. 1*, pp. 205–6.
21. Tolstoy, *The Half-Mad Lord*, pp. 107–9.
22. Miles, *Pugilistica, A History of British Boxing, vol. 1*, pp. 136–7, and Henning, *Fights for the Championships – The Men and Their Times, vol. 1*, pp. 206–9.
23. Quoted by Henning, p. 209.
24. One of the Fancy, *Boxiana, or Sketches of Ancient and Modern Pugilism*, p. 132, and Tolstoy, *The Half-Mad Lord*, pp. 109–10.
25. *The Sporting Magazine*, October 1801.
26. *The Times*, 8 January 1802. The correspondent's diet for athletes was flesh of lion or bear for strength, legs of fine jack hare for speed, fox's brains for cunning, and so on.
27. Henning, pp. 209–10.
28. Tolstoy, *The Half-Mad Lord*, pp. 113–16.
29. Ibid., p. 141.
30. One of the Fancy, *Boxiana, or Sketches of Ancient and Modern Pugilism*, pp. 440–1.
31. For a review of the status of black fighters in the prize ring see Ford, *Prizefighting – The Age of Regency Boximania*, pp. 38–9, and Brailsford, *Bareknuckles – A Social History of Prize-Fighting*, pp. 53–65.
32. Tolstoy, *The Half-Mad Lord*, p. 116.
33. Ibid., pp. 117–18.
34. See *Cobbett's Annual Register, vol. I, January to June 1802*, London, Cox and Baylis, 1802, p. xii.
35. Tolstoy, *The Half-Mad Lord*, p. 118.
36. Ibid., pp. 119–33.
37. Sinclair, *The Code of Health and Longevity, vol. II*, p. 106.
38. Foster Powell, *The Craftsman; or Say's Weekly Journal*, 19 July 1788; A Jewish Peddler, *The Sporting Magazine*, January 1797, p. 203; Waite, *Aris's Birmingham Gazette*, 13 December 1773; Wills, *The Sporting Magazine*, January 1794, pp. 205–6.
39. Thom, pp. 104, 156 and 255.

40. Ibid., p. 104.
41. *The English Chronicle*, 12–14 November 1801.
42. *The Edinburgh Advertiser*, 10–13 November 1801.
43. Thom, p. 105.
44. *The Edinburgh Advertiser*, 13–17 November 1801.
45. *The English Chronicle*, 10–12 November 1801.
46. *The Edinburgh Advertiser*, 13–17 November 1801.
47. *The Sun*, 13 November 1801.
48. *The English Chronicle*, 14–17 November 1801.
49. *The Edinburgh Advertiser*, 13–17 November 1801.
50. Ibid.
51. *The Edinburgh Advertiser*, 24–27 November 1801.
52. *The Edinburgh Advertiser*, 17–20 November 1801.
53. Stanley Harris, *The Coaching Age*, London, Richard Bentley and Son, 1885, p. 279.
54. Henning, p. 217.
55. *The English Chronicle*, 24–26 November 1801.

# Chapter 6

1. Thom, *Pedestrianism*, pp. 108, 156 and 211.
2. See Peter H. Clias, *An Elementary Course of Gymnastic Exercises, Intended to Develop and Improve the Powers of Man*, London, Sherwood, Jones, 1823, and Wilson, *Essays – Critical and Imaginative, vol. I*, p. 104.
3. See, for example, Richard Holmes, *Coleridge – Early Visions*, London, Hodder & Stoughton, 1989, pp. 194 and 292.
4. See, for example, 25 February and 12 March 1798; William Knight (ed.), *Journals of Dorothy Wordsworth, vol. 1*, London, Macmillan and Co., 1904, pp. 11 and 13.
5. William Hazlitt, *On My First Acquaintance with Poets*, 1823. See Ronald Blythe, (ed.), *William Hazlitt: Selected Writings*, London, Penguin Classics, 1987.
6. One of the Fancy, *Boxiana, or Sketches of Ancient and Modern Pugilism*, p. 138.
7. Henning, *Fights for the Championships – The Men and Their Times, vol. 1*, p. 230.
8. *The Sporting Magazine*, October 1803.
9. Although most of the sporting writers were reticent about this, not all were. See *The Sporting Magazine*, October 1792, and for a discussion of the topic see Stephen Deuchar, *Sporting Art in Eighteenth-Century England*, New Haven, Yale University Press, 1988, pp. 93–133.
10. *The St James's Chronicle, or British Evening Post*, 22–25 September 1804.
11. George Gater and F.R. Hiorns, *Survey of London, vol. XX, Trafalgar Square and Neighbourhood (Parish of St Martin-in-the-Fields), Part III*, London, London County Council, 1940, pp. 6 and 90–1.
12. Henning, pp. 224–5.
13. Thom, pp. 108 and 158.
14. Ibid., pp. 108 and 156.
15. Ibid., pp. 109 and 158.
16. Ibid., p. 209.
17. One of the Fancy, *Boxiana, or Sketches of Ancient and Modern Pugilism*, p. 141.
18. See *The Sporting Magazine*, October 1803, p. 43, and December 1806, p.103.
19. Druid, *Silk and Scarlet*, London, Vinton & Co., 1859, p. 53.
20. Henning, pp. 240–1.
21. NAS/GD49/330; *The Army List*, 1804. Alterations while printing, unpaginated, and Norman Holme, personal communication, 23 May 1985.

22. *The Times*, 14 February 1804.
23. *The Times*, 15 February 1804.
24. *The English Chronicle*, 25 November 1804.
25. Thomas Geering, 'Our Parish – Tales and Sketches of Old Sussex', *Sussex County Herald*, 25 October 1919.
26. Holmes, *Coleridge – Early Visions*, p. 354.
27. *The Edinburgh Evening Courant*, 23 August 1804.
28. *The Sporting Magazine*, September 1804, pp. 313–14.
29. Thom, pp. 111 and 158.
30. Geering, 'Our Parish – Tales and Sketches of Old Sussex'.
31. *The Army List*, 1805, and Holme, personal communication, 1985.
32. *The St James's Chronicle, or British Evening Post*, 10–12 April 1804.
33. Aubrey Noakes, *The World of Henry Alken*, London, Witherby, 1952, pp. 86–7, and Murray, *High Society in the Regency Period, 1788–1830*, pp. 110–11.
34. Tolstoy, *The Half-Mad Lord*, pp. 96–7.
35. *The St James's Chronicle, or British Evening Post*, 2–5 June 1804.
36. There was more than one version of the story. See also Tolstoy, *The Half-Mad Lord*, pp. 101–2.
37. *The St James's Chronicle, or British Evening Post*, 8–10 March 1804.
38. The newspapers covered the event and the coroner's inquest in detail. See, for example, *The English Chronicle, or Whitehall Evening Post*, 10–13 March 1804, and *The Sun*, 13 March 1804.
39. *The St James's Chronicle, or British Evening Post*, 8–10 March 1804.
40. Barclay and Wilson-Fox, *A History of the Barclay Family, Part III*, p. 227.
41. Druid, *Silk and Scarlet*, p. 53.
42. Thom, pp. 112 and 157.
43. *The Evening Mail*, 5–7 June 1805; *The Edinburgh Evening Courant*, 20 June 1805, and *The Sporting Magazine*, June 1805, p. 166.
44. Thom, pp. 113 and 156.
45. One of the Fancy, *Boxiana, or Sketches of Ancient and Modern Pugilism*, pp. 160–6.
46. Thom, p. 213, and R. Cannon, *Historical Record of the 23rd Regiment, or Royal Welch Fusiliers, Containing an Account of the Formation of the Regiment in 1689 and of Its Subsequent Services to 1850*, London, Parker, Furnival and Parker, 1850, p. 129.
47. Ibid., and Fortescue, *A History of the British Army, vol. V, 1803–1807*, pp. 285–300.
48. *The Sporting Magazine*, October 1807, pp. 7–8.
49. Ibid., and Thom, p. 208.
50. *The Edinburgh Advertiser*, 27 June 1809.
51. For a brief overview of Colonel The Hon. Charles Lennox (afterwards 4th Duke of Richmond) see David Rayvern Allen, *Cricket – An Illustrated History*, Oxford, Phaidon, 1990, pp. 33–6, and Sir Pelham Warner, *Lord's – 1787–1945*, London, George G. Harrap & Co., 1946, p. 22.
52. Robert Southey, *A Journal of a Tour in Scotland in 1819*, Edinburgh, James Thin, 1972, pp. 64–5.

## Chapter 7

1. *The Army List*, 1807.
2. Thom, *Pedestrianism*, pp. 112 and 157.
3. Holme, personal communication.
4. *The Sporting Magazine*, July 1806, pp. 186–7.

5. *The Edinburgh Evening Courant*, 21 July 1806.
6. *Bell's Weekly Messenger*, 11 October 1807.
7. *The Sporting Magazine*, August 1806, p. 242.
8. Haythornthwaite, *The Armies of Wellington*, pp. 38–9.
9. Warner, *Lord's – 1787–1945*, p. 18.
10. *The Sporting Magazine*, August 1806, p. 242.
11. Ibid.
12. *The Sporting Magazine*, September 1806, pp. 276–7.
13. One of the Fancy, *Boxiana, or Sketches of Ancient and Modern Pugilism*, p. 151.
14. Thom, p. 91.
15. Nimrod, *Nimrod's Northern Tour*, pp. 335–6, and Nimrod, *The Life of a Sportsman*, London, John Lehmann, 1842, p. 226.
16. An Old Boy, *Tom Brown's Schooldays*, London, Blackie and Son, 1857, pp. 58–9.
17. Nimrod, *Nimrod's Northern Tour*, pp. 335–6.
18. *The Sporting Magazine*, December 1806, p. 103.
19. Thom, pp. 113–14 and 157.
20. *The Sporting Magazine*, February 1807, p. 219.
21. Service, *The History and Traditions of the Lindsays in Angus and Mearns*, p. 349.
22. One of the Fancy, *Boxiana, or Sketches of Ancient and Modern Pugilism*, pp. 387–92, and *The Fancy*, vol. I, No. I, April 1821, pp. 7–12.
23. *The Fancy*, vol. I, No. V, June 1821, p. 112.
24. One of the Fancy, *Boxiana, or Sketches of Ancient and Modern Pugilism*, p. 392, and Henning, *Fights for the Championships – The Men and Their Times, vol. 1*, pp. 302–4.
25. *The Sporting Magazine*, July 1807, pp. 193–5, and Henning, p.304.
26. See Philip Ziegler, *King William IV*, London, Collins, 1971, and Claire Tomalin, *Mrs Jordan's Profession*, London, Viking, 1994, p. 198.
27. One of the Fancy, *Boxiana, or Sketches of Ancient and Modern Pugilism*, pp. 392–5.
28. *Bell's Weekly Messenger*, 27 July 1807.
29. *The Sporting Magazine*, July 1807, pp. 193–5.
30. *The Sporting Magazine*, August 1807, pp. 224–5.
31. *The Morning Herald*, 12 August 1807.
32. *The Times*, 17 August 1807, and *The Sporting Magazine*, August 1807, p. 245.
33. *The Sporting Magazine*, September 1807, p. 288.
34. Henning, p. 312.
35. Miles, *Pugilistica, A History of British Boxing, vol. 1*, pp. 263–4.
36. *The Sporting Magazine*, October 1807, p. 6.
37. *Bell's Weekly Messenger*, 11 October 1807.
38. *The Morning Herald*, 15 September 1807.
39. *The Sporting Magazine*, October 1807, p. 7.
40. *The News*, 11 October 1807.
41. *The Times*, 13 October 1807.
42. *The Morning Herald*, 13 October 1807.
43. Aylward, *The House of Angelo – A Dynasty of Swordsmen*, pp. 164–5.
44. *The Morning Herald*, 14 October 1807.
45. *The Times*, 13 October 1807.
46. *The Sporting Magazine*, September 1807, p. 288.
47. *The Morning Herald*, 14 October 1807.
48. There are two detailed accounts of this event. Both were printed in *The Morning Herald* on 14 October 1807.
49. *The Times*, 16 October 1807.
50. *The News*, 18 October 1807.

51. *The Sporting Magazine*, October 1807, p. 7.
52. *Bell's Weekly Messenger*, 19 October 1807; One of the Fancy, *Boxiana, or Sketches of Ancient and Modern Pugilism*, pp. 176–180; and Henning, pp. 312–15.
53. William St Clair, *Lord Elgin and His Marbles*, Oxford, Oxford University Press, 1998.
54. *The Times*, 16 October 1807.
55. For a description of Tattersall's and the way it worked see Pierce Egan, *Pierce Egan's Book of Sports, and Mirror of Life*, London, Thomas Tegg, 1844, pp. 177–85.
56. To 'Hocus' or 'Hocus Pocus' a man was 'to put something into his drink, *on the sly*, of a sleepy or stupefying quality, that renders him unfit for action' (Pierce Egan, *Boxiana, or Sketches of Ancient and Modern Pugilism, vol. III*, London, Sherwood, Neely and Jones, 1821, p. 196. See also *The Fancy*, October 1821, p. 336; Miles, *Pugilistica, A History of British Boxing, vol. 1*, p. 350; and *The Sporting Magazine*, October 1807, p. 6.
57. *The Sporting Magazine*, October 1807, pp. 6–7.
58. *The St James's Chronicle*, 24–7 and 29–31 October 1807; *The Morning Herald*, 30 October 1807; and *The Sporting Magazine*, December 1807, p. 149.
59. *The Sporting Magazine*, January 1808, p. 163.
60. Ibid., pp. 162–3.
61. Ibid., p. 163.
62. *The St James's Chronicle*, 2–5 January 1808; *The Selector, or Say's Sunday Reporter*, 31 January 1808; and *The Sporting Magazine*, January 1808, pp. 163–4.
63. Thom, p. 212.
64. Ibid., pp. 121–2 and 157.

# Chapter 8

1. Haythornthwaite, *The Armies of Wellington*, pp. 236–7.
2. W. Fortescue, *A History of the British Army, vol. VII, 1809–1810*, pp. 88–9; Bryant, *Years of Victory: 1802–1812*, pp. 326–33.
3. Thom, *Pedestrianism*, p. 214.
4. *The Edinburgh Advertiser*, 28 July 1809.
5. The Revd William B. Daniel, *Rural Sports*, London, B. & R. Crosby & Co., 1813, p. 489.
6. The Sportsman (ed.), *British Sports and Sportsmen – Sportsmen of the Past, Part 1*, London, Sport & Sportsmen, undated, p. x.
7. *The Sunday Reporter*, 19 November 1809.
8. *The Gentleman's Magazine,* November 1809, p. 885.
9. The Highland Society, *Prize Essays and Transactions of Scotland, New Series, vol. I*, Edinburgh, William Blackwood, 1829, p. 410.
10. NAS/GD49/330, and Will, *The Kincardineshire Volunteers: A History of the Volunteer Movement in Kincardineshire from 1798 to 1816*, pp. 119 and 128–9.
11. Henning, *Fights for the Championships – The Men and Their Times, vol. II*, pp.16–19.
12. C. A. Wheeler (ed.), *Sportascrapiana, 2nd Edition*, London, Simpkin, Marshall & Co., 1868, pp. 184–5, and Captain L. Fitz-Barnard, *Fighting Sports*, London, Odhams Press, 1921, p. 223.
13. Henning, p. 22.
14. One of the Fancy, *Boxiana, or Sketches of Ancient and Modern Pugilism*, pp. 362–3.
15. Henning, p. 22.
16. Fitz-Barnard, *Fighting Sports*, p. 240.
17. Miles, *Pugilistica, A History of British Boxing, vol. 1*, p. 253.
18. Thom, p. 215, and Nimrod, *Nimrod's Northern Tour*, pp. 298–300.

19. One of the Fancy, *Boxiana, or Sketches of Ancient and Modern Pugilism*, pp. 401–2.
20. One of the Fancy, *Boxiana, or Sketches of Ancient and Modern Pugilism*, p. 402, and Dowling, *Fights for the Championship; and Celebrated Prize Battles*, p. 42.
21. One of the Fancy, *Boxiana, or Sketches of Ancient and Modern Pugilism*, pp. 405–6. For a discussion of this episode see also Carl B. Cone, *The Molineaux–Cribb Fight, 1810: Wuz Tom Molineaux Robbed?*, *Journal of Sport History*, vol. 9, No. 3, 1982, pp. 83–91.
22. One of the Fancy, *Boxiana, or Sketches of Ancient and Modern Pugilism*, p. 364.
23. *The Sportsman's Magazine*, February 1824, p. 28.
24. Henning, p. 49.
25. One of the Fancy, *Boxiana, or Sketches of Ancient and Modern Pugilism*, p. 364–6, and Henning, p. 36.
26. One of the Fancy, *Boxiana, or Sketches of Ancient and Modern Pugilism*, p. 366.
27. Louis Simond, *An American in Regency England – The Journal of a Tour in 1810–11*, London, Pergamon Press, 1968, p. 142.
28. Ibid., p. 141.
29. Henning, p. 37.
30. Ibid., and Dennis Prestige, *Tom Cribb at Thistleton Gap*, Melton Mowbray, The Brewhouse Press, 1971, p. 30.
31. *The Sporting Magazine*, June 1811, p. 146, and Henning, p. 38.
32. Will, *The Kincardineshire Volunteers: A History of the Volunteer Movement in Kincardineshire from 1798 to 1816*, pp. 112 and 130.
33. Thom, p. 244.
34. Ibid., p. 228.
35. Ibid., p. 245.
36. One of the Fancy, *Boxiana, or Sketches of Ancient and Modern Pugilism*, pp. 416–17.
37. Ibid., p. 417.
38. Ibid., pp. 417–18.
39. Thom, p. 234.
40. George Thomas, Earl of Albemarle, *Fifty Years of My Life, vol. I*, London, Macmillan and Co., 1876, p. 321.
41. Thom, pp. 225–48, and Sinclair, *The Code of Health and Longevity, vol. II*, pp. 82–111.
42. Thom, p. 247.
43. Simond, *An American in Regency England – The Journal of a Tour in 1810–11*, p. 49.
44. One of the Fancy, *Boxiana, or Sketches of Ancient and Modern Pugilism*, pp. 151–2.
45. Burnett, *The Rise and Fall of a Regency Dandy*, p. 108.
46. There are several versions of this story. See Thom, pp. 247–8, and Ellangowan, *Sporting Anecdotes*, London, Hamilton, Adams & Co., 1889, p. 105.
47. *The St James's Chronicle*, 29 July 1811.
48. One of the Fancy, *Boxiana, or Sketches of Ancient and Modern Pugilism*, pp. 141–3.
49. Thom, p. 246, and Druid, *Field and Fern*, p. 207.
50. Thom, p. 230.
51. Thom, pp. 244–8, and G. Maret, 'Remarks on Training', *Blackwood's Magazine*, vol. IV, No. XXI, December 1818, pp. 313–18.
52. *The Times*, 16, 18 and 21 September 1811.
53. Prestige, *Tom Cribb at Thistleton Gap*, pp. 29–36.
54. Henning, p. 41.
55. For a brief review of this see Prestige, *Tom Cribb at Thistleton Gap*, p. 38.
56. Druid, *Silk and Scarlet*, pp. 52–3, and Henning, p. 41.
57. Henning, pp. 41–2.
58. One of the Fancy, *Boxiana, or Sketches of Ancient and Modern Pugilism*, p. 410.
59. Henning, p. 42.

60. A detailed account of the first eight rounds appeared in *The Times*, 30 September 1811. Pierce Egan's account in *Boxiana* is very similar but gives details of a further three rounds. See One of the Fancy, *Boxiana, or Sketches of Ancient and Modern Pugilism*, pp. 412–13.

61. One of the Fancy, *Boxiana, or Sketches of Ancient and Modern Pugilism*, p. 412.

62. Prestige, *Tom Cribb at Thistleton Gap*, p. 43.

63. One of the Fancy, *Boxiana, or Sketches of Ancient and Modern Pugilism*, p. 413.

64. *The Times*, 30 September 1811.

65. *The St James's Chronicle*, 4–8 October 1811.

66. Henning, p. 46.

67. *The St James's Chronicle*, 19–21 September 1811.

68. *The St James's Chronicle*, 7–10 September 1811.

69. Ashton, *Social England under the Regency*, p.73.

70. *The Times*, 30 September 1811.

71. Henning, p. 46.

72. *The St James's Chronicle*, 28 September–1 October 1811, and One of the Fancy, *Boxiana, or Sketches of Ancient and Modern Pugilism*, pp. 414–15.

73. One of the Fancy, *Boxiana, or Sketches of Ancient and Modern Pugilism*, pp. 477–9.

74. Published 15 October 1811 by Thomas Tegg, Cheapside, London, price one shilling, coloured.

75. Published 16 October 1811, also by Thomas Tegg, as 73 above.

## Chapter 9

1. Thomas, *Fifty Years of My Life*, vol. I, pp. 321–2.

2. One of the Fancy, *Boxiana, or Sketches of Ancient and Modern Pugilism*, pp. 481–2.

3. Bryant, *Years of Victory: 1802–1812*, pp. 447–52, and Haythornthwaite, *The Armies of Wellington*, pp. 168 and 246.

4. Haythornthwaite, *The Armies of Wellington*, p. 49.

5. Egan, *Boxiana, or Sketches of Ancient and Modern Pugilism*, vol. II, p. 39.

6. Egan, *Boxiana, or Sketches of Ancient and Modern Pugilism*, vol. II, pp. 39 and 378, and Miles, *Pugilistica, A History of British Boxing*, vol. 1, pp. 164 and 442.

7. Pierce Egan, *New Series of Boxiana, Being the Only Original and Complete Lives of the Boxers*, London, George Virtue, 1828, p. 28.

8. Egan, *Boxiana, or Sketches of Ancient and Modern Pugilism*, vol. II, pp. 379–81.

9. *The St James's Chronicle*, 28–30 November 1811.

10. *The St James's Chronicle*, 7–10 December 1811, and P.D. James and T.A. Critchley, *The Maul and the Pear Tree, The Ratcliffe Highway Murders, 1811*, London, Sphere Books, 1971.

11. James and Critchley, *The Maul and the Pear Tree, The Ratcliffe Highway Murders, 1811*, p. 181.

12. Ibid., p. 180.

13. Thom, *Pedestrianism*, pp. 218–19.

14. James Leslie, 'The Parish of Fordoun', in *The New Statistical Account of Scotland*, vol. XI, *Forfar and Kincardine*, Edinburgh, William Blackwood and Sons, 1845, pp. (Kincardine) 88–9.

15. David MacGregor Peter, *The Baronage of Angus and Mearns*, Edinburgh, Oliver & Boyd, 1856, p. 76, and House of Commons, *Return of Members Parliament*, vol. 2, *1357–1874*, London, 1878.

16. Carolly Erickson, *Our Tempestuous Day, A History of Regency England*, London, Robson

Books, 1986, p. 70, and Richard Holmes, *Coleridge – Darker Reflections*, London, HarperCollins, 1998, pp. 307–9.

17. *The St James's Chronicle*, 16–19 May 1812.
18. Erickson, *Our Tempestuous Day, A History of Regency England*, p. 71.
19. *The St James's Chronicle*, 16–19 May 1812.
20. *The Times*, 22 July 1812.
21. *The Edinburgh Advertiser*, 17 July 1812.
22. Wheeler, *Sportascrapiana, 2nd Edition*, pp. 184–5.
23. For a review of the various editions of *Boxiana* and its imitators see J.C. Reid, *Bucks and Bruisers, Pierce Egan and Regency England*, London, Routledge & Kegan Paul, 1971, pp. 12–49 and 232–4.
24. See Reid, *Bucks and Bruisers, Pierce Egan and Regency England*, pp. 17–18.
25. Thom, pp. iv–v.
26. Ibid., p. vi.
27. Ibid., pp. 247–8.
28. Ibid., p. 248.
29. Ibid., p. 206.
30. Ibid., pp. 206–7.
31. Ibid., p. 218.
32. Ibid., p. 219.
33. Ibid., p. 213.
34. *The Sporting Magazine*, April 1813, p. 42.
35. One of the Fancy, *Boxiana, or Sketches of Ancient and Modern Pugilism*, pp. 452–6.
36. *The Star*, 21 April 1813, and *The Edinburgh Advertiser*, 28 May 1813.
37. *The Courier*, 24 and 25 May 1813, and *The Sporting Magazine*, May 1813, pp. 84–6.
38. *The News*, 30 May 1813.
39. *Edinburgh Advertiser*, 22 June 1813.
40. *The St James's Chronicle*, 12–15 June 1813.
41. *The Sporting Magazine*, June 1813, p. 139.
42. Ibid., and *The Edinburgh Advertiser*, 22 June 1813.
43. Peter Hawker, *The Diary of Colonel Peter Hawker, 1802–1853, vol. I*, London, Greenhill Books, 1988, p. 77.
44. Erickson, *Our Tempestuous Day, A History of Regency England*, pp. 100–1, and T.H. McGuffie (ed.), *Peninsular Cavalry General (1811–13), The Correspondence of Lieutenant-General Robert Long*, London, George G. Harrap & Co., 1951, pp. 268–76.
45. Haythornthwaite, *The Armies of Wellington*, pp. 250–1.
46. Erickson, *Our Tempestuous Day, A History of Regency England*, pp. 1,001–2.
47. Ashton, *Social England under the Regency*, pp. 173–5, and Erickson, *Our Tempestuous Day, A History of Regency England*, pp. 1,001–2.
48. Erickson, *Our Tempestuous Day, A History of Regency England*, pp. 1,001–2.
49. Barclay and Wilson-Fox, *A History of the Barclay Family, vol. III*, p. 227.
50. The Injured Party, *Letters from Captain Barclay; Mr Farquarson, General Burnett, and Mr Sturt, With a Statement of Facts Addressed to the Impartial*, Leith, James Burnet, 1814, p. 6.
51. Ibid., p. 7.
52. NAS/GD105/718. Letter from RBA to Mr Sturt, 9 October 1813.
53. The Injured Party, *Letters from Captain Barclay; Mr Farquarson, General Burnett, and Mr Sturt, With a Statement of Facts Addressed to the Impartial*, pp. 11–12.
54. Ashton, John, *Social England under the Regency*, London, Ward and Downey, 1890, pp. 185–6.
55. Ibid., pp. 187–8, and The Injured Party, *Letters From Captain Barclay; Mr Farquarson,*

General Burnett, and Mr Sturt, With a Statement of Facts Addressed to the Impartial, p. 27.

# Chapter 10

1. *The Sporting Magazine*, October 1813, pp. 57–8.
2. Egan, *New Series of Boxiana, Being the Only Original and Complete Lives of the Boxers*, p. 28.
3. Ibid.
4. See *The Sporting Magazine*, October 1813, p. 42.
5. One of the Fancy, *Boxiana, or Sketches of Ancient and Modern Pugilism*, pp. 473–4, and Egan, *Boxiana, or Sketches of Modern Pugilism, vol. II*, pp. 470–1.
6. Egan, *New Series of Boxiana, Being the Only Original and Complete Lives of the Boxers*, p. 22.
7. *The Sporting Magazine*, October 1813, p. 57.
8. Miles, *Pugilistica, A History of British Boxing, vol. 1*, p. 262.
9. Wheeler, *Sportascrapiana, 2nd Edition*, pp. 184–5.
10. *The Sporting Magazine*, October 1813, p. 57.
11. Ibid.
12. Erickson, *Our Tempestuous Day, A History of Regency England*, pp. 106–7.
13. Henning, Fred, *Fights for the Championships – The Men and Their Times, vol. II*, p. 86.
14. Egan, *Boxiana, or Sketches of Modern Pugilism, vol. II*, p. 106.
15. *The St James's Chronicle*, 18–20 July 1814.
16. Peter Quennell, *Byron – Selected Verse and Prose Works*, London, Collins, 1959, p. 595.
17. Ibid., p. 597.
18. Ibid., p. 598.
19. Ibid., p. 600.
20. Egan, *Boxiana, or Sketches of Modern Pugilism, vol. II*, p. 496.
21. The Sporting Magazine, May 1814, p. 91, and Egan, *Boxiana, or Sketches of Modern Pugilism, vol. II*, pp. 24–8.
22. Peter Hawker, *The Diary of Colonel Peter Hawker, 1802–1853, vol. I*, London, Greenhill Books, 1988, p. 95.
23. For general accounts of these festivities see Erickson, *Our Tempestuous Day, A History of Regency England*, pp. 114–18, and Murray, *High Society in the Regency Period – 1788–1830*, pp. 212–18.
24. J.B. Priestley, *The Prince of Pleasure and His Regency, 1811–20*, London, Sphere Books, 1969, p. 122.
25. Murray, *High Society in the Regency Period – 1788–1830*, p. 215.
26. Egan, *Boxiana, or Sketches of Modern Pugilism, vol. II*, pp. 12–14.
27. Ibid., pp. 13–14.

# Chapter 11

1. Anon, *Genealogical Account of the Barclays of Urie*, London, John Herbert, 1812.
2. As John Moore points out in his introduction to Nimrod's *The Life of a Sportsman*, this was a world in which 'a man could be almost pitied for possessing such a "comparatively limited" income as ten thousand a year!' See Nimrod, *The Life of a Sportsman*, London, John Lehmann, 1948, p. 8.

3. NAS/GD49/528/1 (Memorial and queries from RBA relating to the legitimacy of his elder daughter, 1820).

4. M.D. Lobel, (ed.), *The Victoria History of the Counties of England – A History of the County of Oxford, vol. VI, Ploughley Hundred*, Oxford, Oxford University Press, 1959, p. 136.

5. NAS/GD49/528/9 (Disposition from Hannah Rogers, 7 September 1871).

6. NAS/GD49/528/9 (Disposition from Mary Reeves, 7 September 1871).

7. Nimrod, *Nimrod's Northern Tour*, p. 324, and Cuming, *Squire Osbaldeston: His Autobiography*, London, John Lane, The Bodley Head, 1927.

8. Druid, *Silk and Scarlet*, p. 53.

9. Cole, Hubert, *Beau Brummell*, London, Granada Publishing, 1977, pp. 89–121.

10. NAS/GD49/528/8 (Note of entries made by RBA on title page of family Bible, 30 August 1820) and NAS/GD49/528/4 (Copy of Margaret's certificate of baptism, 12 October 1816).

11. NAS/GD49/528/9 (Disposition from William Jennings, 7 September 1871).

12. *The Courier*, 27 December 1815.

13. *The Sporting Magazine*, September 1811, p. 190.

14. Thom, *Pedestrianism*, pp. 51–2.

15. *The Times*, 20 August 1811.

16. *The Liverpool Mercury*, 5 June 1812.

17. *The Liverpool Mercury*, 26 July 1816.

18. *The Liverpool Mercury*, 25 October 1816.

19. An unnamed pamphleteer claimed that Wilson had his fifty-fifth birthday on 11 September 1815. See Anon, *Memoirs of the Life and Exploits of George Wilson*, London, Dean & Munday, undated (internal evidence suggests that it was printed in 1815), p. 7.

20. Ibid., pp. 14–17.

21. George Wilson, *A Sketch of the Life of George Wilson, the Blackheath Pedestrian*, London, Hay and Turner, 1815, p. 50.

22. *The Maidstone Journal*, 17 June 1817.

23. *The Edinburgh Evening Courant*, 23 March 1818.

24. The Sporting Magazine, New Series, April 1818, p. 296.

25. Egan, *Boxiana, or Sketches of Modern Pugilism, vol. II*, p. 318.

26. Miles, *Pugilistica, A History of British Boxing, vol. 2*, pp. 170–2.

27. Egan, *Boxiana, or Sketches of Modern Pugilism, vol. II*, p. 241.

28. Miles, *Pugilistica, A History of British Boxing, vol. 1*, p. 332.

29. Ibid.

30. Henning, *Fights for the Championships – The Men and Their Times, vol. II*, p. 60.

31. Miles, *Pugilistica, A History of British Boxing, vol. 2*, p. 2.

32. Egan, *Boxiana, or Sketches of Modern Pugilism, vol. III*, London, Sherwood, Neely and Jones, 1821, p. 274.

32. Egan, *Boxiana, or Sketches of Modern Pugilism, vol. II*, p. 241.

33. Ibid.

34. Ibid, p. 318.

35. BP, Box 31, 976 (Letter from Margaret Ritchie to A.W. Kinnear, 23 June 1854).

36. NAS/GD49/528/1.

37. Henning, *Fights for the Championships – The Men and Their Times, vol. II*, p. 60.

38. For a general overview of this period see E.L. Woodward, *The Age of Reform, 1815–1870*, Oxford, Oxford University Press, 1954, pp. 1–83, and Erickson, *Our Tempestuous Day, A History of Regency England*, pp. 227–223.

39. NAS/GD49/528/1.

40. *The Edinburgh Advertiser,* 6 February 1819.

41. Nimrod, *Remarks on the Condition of Hunters*, London, M.A. Pittman, 1837,

p. 82; Nimrod, *Nimrod's Northern Tour*, p. 327; and Nimrod, *The Life of a Sportsman*, p. 225.

42. *The Sporting Magazine*, New Series, April 1818, p. 296.

43. Egan, *Boxiana, or Sketches of Modern Pugilism, vol. III*, p. 274.

44. Miles, *Pugilistica, A History of British Boxing*, p. 302.

45. NAS/GD49/528/1.

46. NAS/GD49/528/5 (Certificate of marriage between RBA and Mary Dalgarno, 19 July 1819).

47. William Maynard Atkins, *The Parish Church of St George, Hanover Square*, London, Dix (Charlmont Press) Ltd., 1976, p. 17.

48. NAS/GD49/528/8.

49. NAS/GD49/528/1.

50. Ibid.

51. Ibid.

52. NAS/GD49/521/5 (Note by Margaret Allardice Innes, RBA's niece, and Une Cameron Barclay's daughter, undated, c. 1840). See also notice of death in *The St James's Chronicle*, 5–7 September 1820.

53. NAS/GD49/528/8.

54. NAS/GD49/528/7 (Certificate of burial of Mary Barclay Allardice, 5 September 1820) and BP, Box 31, 1074 (Minutes of Evidence for the Claim to the Earldom of Airth, 5 August 1870, pp. 9–14).

55. Paul Johnson, *The Birth of the Modern – World Society 1815–1830*, London, Weidenfeld & Nicolson, 1991, pp. 421–3.

56. For a brief review of Jeffrey and his views see R.W. Harris, *Romanticism and the Social Order, 1780–1830*, London, Blandford Press, 1969, pp. 48–53.

57. NAS/GD49/528/1.

58. NAS/GD49/528/3 (Memorial and queries from RBA, plus answers from Francis Jeffrey, 9 November 1820, and George Cranstoun, 28 November 1820).

59. Ibid.

60. *The Fancy*, July 1821, pp. 166–7.

61. J. Brady, *Strange Encounters, Tales of Famous Fights and Famous Fighters*, London, Hutchinson, 1946, pp. 90–1.

62. Egan, *Boxiana, or Sketches of Modern Pugilism, vol. III*, pp. 597–8.

63. Egan, *New Series of Boxiana, Being the Only Original and Complete Lives of the Boxers*, pp. 623–4.

64. Ibid., pp. 10–13.

65. Christopher Hibbert, *George IV, Regent and King, 1811–1830*, London, Allen Lane, 1973, pp. 202–5.

66. Egan, *New Series of Boxiana, Being the Only Original and Complete Lives of the Boxers*, p. 13.

67. The Sporting Magazine, New Series, February 1822, p. 246.

68. Egan, *Boxiana, or Sketches of Modern Pugilism, vol. III*, pp. 136–7.

69. Ibid, pp. 193–8.

70. Ibid., pp. 187–9.

71. Egan, *New Series of Boxiana, Being the Only Original and Complete Lives of the Boxers*, pp. 13–15.

72. Ibid., p. 119.

73. Egan, *Boxiana, or Sketches of Modern Pugilism, vol. III*, p. 14.

74. *The Sportsman's Magazine, or Chronicle of Games and Pastimes*, February 1824, p. 26.

75. Egan, *New Series of Boxiana, Being the Only Original and Complete Lives of the Boxers*, p.14.

76. J.C. Reid, *Bucks and Bruisers, Pierce Egan and Regency England*, pp. 93–116, and Ford, *Prizefighting – The Age of Regency Boximania*, pp. 163–5.

# Chapter 12

1. David Masson, *The Collected Writings of Thomas de Quincey, vol. VIII*, Edinburgh, Adam and Charles Black, 1890, p. 71.
2. David Daiches, *Literary Essays*, Edinburgh, Oliver & Boyd, 1956, pp. 122–31.
3. Christopher North, *Essays – Critical and Imaginative, vol. I*, pp. 126–7.
4. Nimrod, *Nimrod's Northern Tour*, pp. 376–7, and Druid, *Field and Fern*, pp. 157–8.
5. Druid, *Saddle and Sirloin*, London, Frederick Warne & Co., 1870, pp. 165–72.
6. Nimrod, *Nimrod's Northern Tour*, pp. 329–30, and Druid, *Field and Fern*, pp. 183–5.
7. Wheeler, *Sportascrapiana, 2nd Edition*, pp. 71 and 106.
8. Ibid., p. 94.
9. Egan, Pierce, *Anecdotes, Original and Selected, of the Turf, the Chace, the Ring, and the Stage*, London, Knight and Lacey, 1827, pp. 172–3.
10. *Annals of Sporting*, February 1823, p. 141.
11. Druid, *Field and Fern*, p. 198.
12. The records of his hay imports from Rotterdam are found in QL, Box XII, 571.
13. Nimrod, *Nimrod's Northern Tour*, pp. 336–7, and Druid, *Field and Fern*, pp. 200–1.
14. Druid, *Field and Fern*, p. 200.
15. J. Barclay, *Diary of Alexander Jaffray*, London, Harvey and Darton, 1833, pp. iii–iv.
16. James Sinclair, *History of Shorthorn Cattle*, London, Vinton & Company, 1907, p. 401.
17. G. Thomson, 'The Parish of Fetteresso', in *The New Statistical Account of Scotland, vol. XI, Forfar and Kincardine*, Edinburgh, William Blackwood and Sons, 1845, p. (Kincardine) 261, and Barclay Allardice, *Agricultural Tour in the United States and Canada*, p. 179.
18. Watt, *Highways and Byways Around Stonehaven*, p. 59.
19. *Annals of Sporting*, February 1823, p. 142.
20. *The Times*, 16 May 1854.
21. Additions to entry on title page of diary, NAS/GD49/528/8, and BP, Box 31, 1074, p. 9.
22. *The London Packet and Chronicle*, 13–15 September 1824.
23. *The London Packet and Chronicle*, 31 December–3 January 1825.
24. *The Fancy*, February 1825, p. 625.
25. *Annals of Sporting*, March 1826, p. 178.
26. *The Sporting Magazine*, New Series, June 1826, p. 185.
27. Henning, *Fights for the Championships – The Men and Their Times, vol. II*, pp. 110–11.
28. *The Sportsman's Magazine, or Chronicle of Games and Pastimes*, 1824, pp. 205–16.
29. *The London Packet and Chronicle*, 29 September–1 October 1823.
30. *Annals of Sporting*, November 1826, pp. 305–6; January 1827, pp. 45 and 49; and *The London Packet and Chronicle*, 5–7 November 1827.
31. *Annals of Sporting*, July 1823, p. 123; September 1823, p. 277; and *The Fancy*, August 1823, p. 355.
32. Reid, *Bucks and Bruisers, Pierce Egan and Regency England*, pp. 136–8.
33. Brailsford, *Bareknuckles – A Social History of Prize-Fighting*, p. 98.
34. Ibid., pp. 88–9.
35. Druid, *Field and Fern*, pp. 206–7, and *The Times*, 23 June 1830.
36. Cuming, *Squire Osbaldeston: His Autobiography*, p. 174.
37. *The Times*, 24 July 1830.

38. Druid, *Field and Fern*, p. 206.

39. Henning, *Fights for the Championships – The Men and Their Times, vol. II*, p. 178.

40. See Tom Spring's testimony, *The Times*, 24 July 1830.

41. Cuming, *Squire Osbaldeston: His Autobiography*, p. 261.

42. Druid, *Field and Fern*, p. 207.

43. *The Fancy Gazette* was printed as a regular part of the monthly *Annals of Sporting*. See *Annals of Sporting*, September 1824, p. 179.

44. *Bell's Weekly Messenger*, 6 June 1830.

45. *The Times*, 24 July 1830.

46. The Times, 5 June 1830.

47. The Times, 5 June 1830; *Bell's Weekly Messenger*, 6 June 1830; and *The Sporting Magazine*, New Series, July 1830, pp. 254–5.

48. *The Times*, 5 July 1830.

49. *Bell's Weekly Messenger*, 6 June 1830.

50. BP, Box 31, 8.

51. *The Times*, 5 June 1830.

52. Druid, *Field and Fern*, p. 207.

53. *The Times*, 5 July 1830, and Cuming, *Squire Osbaldeston: His Autobiography*, p. 262.

54. Cuming, *Squire Osbaldeston: His Autobiography*, pp. 261–3.

55. *The Times*, 5 July 1830.

56. *The Times*, 17 July 1830.

57. Ziegler, *King William IV*, p. 144.

58. Cuming, *Squire Osbaldeston: His Autobiography*, p. 262.

59. *The Sporting Magazine*, July 1830, pp. 272–6.

60. *The Times*, 24 July 1830.

61. Ibid.

62. *The Sporting Magazine*, July 1830, p. 276, and Cuming, *Squire Osbaldeston: His Autobiography*, pp. 262–3.

63. Verily Anderson, *The Northrepps Grandchildren*, London, Hodder & Stoughton, 1968, pp. 114–16.

64. BP, Box 31, 8.

## Chapter 13

1. S. Harris, *The Coaching Age*, London, Richard Bentley and Son, 1885, p. 380, and Leslie Gardiner, *Stage-Coach to John O'Groats*, London, Hollis & Carter, 1961, p. 125.

2. *The Times*, 8 October 1824.

3. John Copeland, *Roads and Their Traffic, 1750–1850*, Newton Abbot, David & Charles, 1968, p. 32.

4. John, P.G. Ransom, *The Archaeology of the Transport Revolution 1750–1850*, Tadworth, Surrey, World's Books, 1984, p. 107.

5. *The Sunday Reporter*, 19 November 1809.

6. Harris, *The Coaching Age*, p. 383.

7. Frank Siltzer, *The Story of British Sporting Prints*, London, Peter Loveday Prints, 1979, p. 207, and N.W. Webster, *The Great North Road*, Bath, Adams and Dart, 1974, pp. 12–13.

8. Nimrod, *Nimrod's Northern Tour*, p. 335.

9. Druid, *Silk and Scarlet*, p. 202, and Gardiner, *Stage-Coach to John O'Groats*, p. 115.

10. Druid, *Silk and Scarlet*, p. 208.

11. Now hanging in Brodick Castle, Isle of Arran.

12. Nimrod, *Nimrod's Northern Tour*, pp. 334–5.

13. Note on Margaret by Harriet Maria Barclay, 1917, in BP, Box 31, unnumbered (802–866).

14. Ibid.

15. Anderson, *The Northrepps Grandchildren*, p. 112.

16. H. Montgomery Hyde, *The Strange Death of Lord Castlereagh*, London, Heinemann, 1959, pp. 30–1.

17. Ibid., pp. 50–3.

18. Ibid., p. 35.

19. BP, Box 31, unnumbered (802–866).

20. NAS/GD49/528/6 (Disposition from Sarah Scarnell, 28 December 1869).

21. *Aberdeen Free Press*, 28 August 1903.

22. BP, Box 31, 1074.

23. NAS/GD49/536.

24. Sinclair, *History of Shorthorn Cattle*, p. 391.

25. Nimrod, *Nimrod's Northern Tour*, pp. 325–6 and 337; Gardiner, *Stage-Coach to John O'Groats*, p. 113; and A.R. Haldane, *Three Centuries of Scottish Posts*, Edinburgh, The University Press, 1971, p. 82.

26. Druid, *Field and Fern*, p. 202, and Gardiner, *Stage-Coach to John O'Groats*, p. 115–16.

27. Nimrod, *Nimrod's Northern Tour*, p. 328.

28. Ibid., p. 272–3.

29. Charles A. Mollyson, *The Parish of Fordoun; Chapters in Its History*, Aberdeen, John Rae Smith, 1893, pp. 301–2.

30. Bernard Darwin, *John Gully and His Times*, London, Cassell & Co., 1935, pp. 123–32.

31. Nimrod, *Nimrod's Northern Tour*, p. 328.

32. Ibid.

33. QL, Box VIII, 499 (Request from RBA to Alexander Burness requesting a contract for a loan of £80,000, 9 April 1834). The loan papers are extensive and run into several boxes. See QL, Box XVII to XX1, 587/1 – to 587/338, 12 February 1832–29 April 1854.

34. *House of Lords Journal*, 1834, pp. 66 and 533, and Nicolas, *History of the Earldoms of Strathern, Menteith and Airth*, pp. 134–8 and 242.

35. See QL, Box XVII.

36. Duke of Beaufort, *Driving*, London, Longman, Green & Co., 1894, pp. 199–201.

37. Nimrod, *Nimrod's Northern Tour*, p. 329.

38. Ibid., pp. 334–90.

39. Ibid., pp. 330–3.

40. NAS/GD1/675/118/29, 25 June 1835.

41. QL, Box XVI, 578 (Libel action against RBA by John Robertson, 1830).

42. QL, Box XVI, 581 (Details of RBA's assault on Thomas Nicholas Ryder).

43. Locker-Lampson, Frederick, *My Confidences – An Autobiographical Sketch Addressed to My Descendants*, London, Thomas Nelson and Sons, 1896, p. 174.

44. *Aberdeen Free Press*, 28 August 1903.

45. BP, Box 31, unnumbered (802–866).

46. BP, Box 31, 1074 (Evidence of Sarah Officer, pp. 6–7).

47. Barclay Allardice, *Agricultural Tour in the United States and Canada*, pp. 168–70.

48. Ibid., pp. 161–81.

49. Nicolas, *History of the Earldoms of Strathern, Menteith and Airth*, pp. 139–42.

50. Druid, *Field and Fern*, p.199.

51. Ibid., p. 121.

52. *House of Lords Journal*, 1839, pp. 71, 462–3 and 476; NAS/GD22/4/49 (Evidence

of RBA's claim to the Earldom of Airth), 1839; and Nicolas, *History of the Earldoms of Strathern, Menteith and Airth*, pp. 143–77.

53. Nicolas, *History of the Earldoms of Strathern, Menteith and Airth*, pp. 177–84.
54. *House of Lords Journal*, 1839, pp. 71, 524 and 540, and Nicolas, *History of The Earldoms of Strathern, Menteith, and Airth*, pp. 180–241.
55. *House of Lords Journal*, 1840, pp. 72 and 615–16, and Nicolas, *History of the Earldoms of Strathern, Menteith and Airth*, pp. 241–8.
56. BP, Box 31, unnumbered (802–866), and Barclay and Wilson–Fox, *A History of the Barclay Family, Vol. III*, p. 229.
57. Margaret married Samuel Ritchie on 2 April 1840. See note in NAS/GD49/549, and Nicolas, *History of the Earldoms of Strathern, Menteith and Airth*, p. xix. Later, although she wrote of her 'excellent worthy husband', she admitted 'my marriage was an imprudent deed' (BP, Box 31, 979).
58. BP, Box 31, 976(c) (Letter from Margaret Ritchie to A.W. Kinnear, 23 June 1854).
59. BP, Box 31, 976(b) (Letter from Margaret Ritchie to A.W. Kinnear, 5 June 1854).
60. *House of Lords Journal*, 1841, pp. 73 and 65.

# Chapter 14

1. See Reid, *Bucks and Bruisers, Pierce Egan and Regency England*, pp. 117–38, and Brailsford, *Bareknuckles – A Social History of Prize–Fighting*, pp. 93–103.
2. Miles, *Pugilistica, A History of British Boxing, vol. 1*, p. 274.
3. Francis Dowling, *Fistiana; or The Oracle of the Ring*, London, William Clement Jnr, 1841, pp. 68, 259 and 272.
4. Barclay Allardice, *Agricultural Tour In The United States and Canada*, p. vii.
5. Thomson, *The Parish of Fetteresso*, in *The New Statistical Account of Scotland, Vol. XI, Forfar and Kincardine*, p. 258, and Druid, *Field and Fern*, pp. 109–10.
6. Barclay Allardice, *Agricultural Tour in the United States and Canada*, p. vii.
7. Thomson, 'The Parish of Fetteresso', in *The New Statistical Account of Scotland, vol. XI, Forfar and Kincardine*, p. 261.
8. Barclay Allardice, *Agricultural Tour in the United States and Canada*, pp. 1–4.
9. Peter Ackroyd, *Dickens*, London, Sinclair–Stevenson, 1990, p. 338.
10. Barclay Allardice, *Agricultural Tour in the United States and Canada*, p. 2.
11. Ibid., pp. 7–8.
12. Marjorie Freeman Campbell, *A Mountain and a City – The Story of Hamilton*, Toronto, McClelland & Stewart, 1966, pp. 88–99.
13. BP, Box 31, 1077 (Extract from old parochial registers recording baptism of Robert Ritchie and giving his date of birth as 19 May 1841) and Nicolas, *History of the Earldoms of Strathern, Menteith and Airth*, p. xix.
14. Barclay Allardice, *Agricultural Tour in the United States and Canada*, pp. 72–3.
15. Ibid., pp. 73–104.
16. Ibid., pp. 92–5.
17. Ibid., p. 158.
18. Ibid., p. 27.
19. Ransom, *The Archaeology of the Transport Revolution 1750–1850*, pp. 193–4.
20. Druid, *Field and Fern*, p. 205.
21. Ibid., pp. 205–6.
22. Ibid., p. 166.
23. Ibid., p. 200.
24. Ibid., p. 207.

25. *The Sketch*, 24 August 1898, p. 198.
26. Locker-Lampson, *My Confidences – An Autobiographical Sketch Addressed to My Descendants*, pp. 173–4.
27. J. Turner, *Dictionary of Art*, London, Grove, 1996, p. 878.
28. Locker-Lampson, *My Confidences – An Autobiographical Sketch Addressed to My Descendants*, pp. 173–4.
29. Engraving by R.M. Hodgetts, published in January 1843 by Andrew Anderson, Queen Street, Aberdeen, from a painting by James Giles RSA.
30. See letter from A.W. Kinnear to Hudson Gurney re advisability of giving Ann Angus more than £2 at a time (QL, Box XXX, 768, 29 May 1854) and letter from B. Thompson to A.W. Kinnear describing how, after Captain Barclay's death, Ann Angus drank a bottle of whisky and one of brandy on alternating days for eight days (BP, Box 31, 1113(b), 24 February 1855).
31. NAS/GD49/540 (List of documents detailing birth, baptism and later careers of RBA and Ann Angus's sons, dated 1845–71).
32. QL, Box XVII, 587/1–587/79 (RBA loan papers, 1832–54).
33. Barclay, *History of the Scottish Barclays*, p. 39.
34. Gardiner, *Stage-Coach to John O'Groats*, p. 125.
35. Druid, *Field and Fern*, p. 209.
36. Barclay, *Diary of Alexander Jaffray*, pp. iii–iv.
37. Sinclair, *History of Shorthorn Cattle*, pp. 390–1.
38. BP, Box 31, unnumbered (Printed details of Ury, headed 'The Celebrated Scotch Estate – Ury – For Sale, by Private Contract', May 1848).
39. Editor of Bell's Life in London, *Fistiana; or The Oracle of the Ring*, pp. 64–5.
40. Ibid., p. 28.
41. Druid, *Field and Fern*, p. 209.
42. NAS/GD49/536 (Inscription taken from the Barclay howff, undated).
43. *Bell's Life in London*, 19 August 1849.
44. Peter Ackroyd, *Dickens*, London, Sinclair-Stevenson, 1990, p. 901.
45. George Borrow, *Wild Wales, Its People, Language and Scenery*, London, T. Nelson & Sons, 1862, p. 146.
46. J.W. Richardson, *Memoirs of John Wigham Richardson, 1837–1908*, Glasgow, Hugh Hopkins, 1911, pp. 37–8.
47. Druid, *Field and Fern*, pp. 164 and 207.
48. Gardiner, *Stage-Coach to John O'Groats*, p. 125.
49. NAS/GD49/540.
50. Locker-Lampson, *My Confidences – An Autobiographical Sketch Addressed to My Descendants*, p. 174.
51. Francis Galton, *Memories of My Life*, London, Methuen & Co., 1911, pp. 5–6.
52. NAS/GD49/549 (Genealogy details of the Barclays of Ury, 1757–1883).
53. BP, Box 33, 1192 (Account from David Walker, 135 Union Street, Aberdeen, 1 April 1854: 2 Cricket Balls – 1/-; 8 April 1854: 2 Bats – 2/-).
54. *The Gentleman's Magazine*, July–December 1854, pp. 80–2.
55. *The Times*, 16 May 1854; *The Gentleman's Magazine*, July–December 1854, pp. 80–2; and *The Dictionary of National Biography, vol. I* (Leslie Stephen, ed.), Oxford, Oxford University Press, 1885, p. 299.

# SELECT BIBLIOGRAPHY

## Documents

*NAS = National Archives of Scotland, Princes Street, Edinburgh*

NAS/GD1/675/118/29 (Letter from RBA to Captain Skelton, 25 June 1835).

NAS/GD22/4/49 (Evidence of RBA's claim to the Earldom of Airth, 1839).

NAS/GD49/330 (Dispositions from RBA and John Innes re property, 1819).

NAS/GD49/521/3 (Unsigned, handwritten note on genealogy, probably pre-1810).

NAS/GD49/521/5 (Note by Margaret Allardice Innes, RBA's niece, and Une Cameron Barclay's daughter, undated, c. 1840).

NAS/GD49/528/1 (Memorial and queries from RBA relating to the legitimacy of his elder daughter, 1820).

NAS/GD49/528/3 (Memorial and queries from RBA, plus answers from Francis Jeffrey, 9 November 1820, and George Cranstoun, 28 November 1820).

NAS/GD49/528/4 (Copy of Margaret's certificate of baptism, 12 October 1816).

NAS/GD49/528/5 (Certificate of marriage between RBA and Mary Dalgarno, 19 July 1819).

NAS/GD49/528/6 (Disposition from Sarah Scarnell, 28 December 1869).

NAS/GD49/528/7 (Certificate of burial of Mary Barclay Allardice, 5 September 1820).

NAS/GD49/528/8 (Note of entries made by RBA on title page of family Bible, 30 August 1820).

NAS/GD49/528/9 (Disposition from Hannah Rogers, 7 September 1871).

NAS/GD49/536 (Inscription taken from the Barclay howff, undated).

NAS/GD49/540 (List of documents detailing birth, baptism and later careers of RBA and Ann Angus's sons, dated 1845–71).

NAS/GD49/549 (Genealogy details of the Barclays of Ury, 1757–1883).

NAS/GD49/581 (Letter from RBA to his father, 17 October 1791).

NAS/GD51/901/2 (Letter from David Barclay to the Rt. Hon. Henry Dundas, 26–7 July 1800).

NAS/GD51/901/3 (Letter from RBA to the Rt. Hon. Henry Dundas, 17 September 1800).

NAS/GD105/718 (Letter from RBA to Mr Sturt, 9 October 1813).

NAS/GD157/3444/2 (Letter from L. Windham to Count Bruhl, 8 November 1798).


*QL = Quakers' Library, Friends' House, London.*
*All from Temp MSS 285*

QL, Box VI, 399 (Letter from RBA to Samuel Galton, 3 May 1797).

QL, Box VI, 402 (Letter from John Durno to Samuel Galton, 11 June 1797).

QL, Box VI, 406 (Letter from RBA to Samuel Galton, 9 July 1797).

QL, Box VI, 414 (Letter from Lucy Galton to RBA, 27 February 1798).

QL, Box VI, 420 (Letter from Alexander Crombie to Samuel Galton, 16 May 1798).

QL, Box VI, 423 (Report from William Paul re RBA's education, June 1798).

QL, Box VI, 432 (Letter from RBA to Samuel Galton, 1 July 1798).

QL, Box VI, 443 (Letter from J.H. Tritton to Samuel Galton, 24 August 1798).

QL, Box VI, 444 (Extract of letter from RBA, 24 August 1798).

QL, Box VII, 445 (Letter from Samuel Galton to RBA, 25 August 1798).

QL, Box VII, 447 (Letter from Samuel Galton to William Paul, 26 August 1798).

QL, Box VII, 453 (Letter from RBA to Lucy Galton, 7 September 1798).

QL, Box VII, 458 (Letter from David Barclay to Samuel Galton, 8 October 1798).

QL, Box VII, 464 (Letter from RBA to Samuel Galton, 24 October 1798).

QL, Box VII, 467 (Letter from David Jones to Samuel Galton, 8 November 1798).

QL, Box VII, 468 (Letter from RBA to Samuel Galton, 11 November 1798).

QL, Box VIII, 495 (Letter from RBA to his father, 23 September 1794).

QL, Box VIII, 499 (Request from RBA to Alexander Burness requesting a contract for a loan of £80,000, 9 April 1834).

QL, Box XIII, 571 (Records of RBA's hay imports from Rotterdam).

QL, Box XVI, 578 (Libel action against RBA by John Robertson, 1830).

QL, Box XVI, 581 (Details of RBA's assault on Thomas Nicholas Ryder).

QL, Box XVII, 587/1–587/79 (RBA loan papers).

QL, Box XVIII, 587/80–587/147 (RBA loan papers).

QL, Box XIX, 587/148–587/218 (RBA loan papers).

QL, Box XX, 587/219–587/338 (RBA loan papers).

QL, Box XXX, 768 (Letter from A.W. Kinnear to Hudson Gurney, 29 May 1854).


*BP = Barclay family papers*

BP, Box 31, 8 (Letter from RBA to John Joseph Gurney, 17 September 1830).

BP, Box 31, 976(b) (Letter from Margaret Ritchie to A.W. Kinnear, 5 June 1854).

BP, Box 31, 976(c) (Letter from Margaret Ritchie to A.W. Kinnear, 23 June 1854).

BP, Box 31, 979 (Letter from Margaret Ritchie to A.W. Kinnear, 16 July 1854).

BP, Box 31, 1074 (Minutes of evidence for the claim to the Earldom of Airth, 5 August 1870).

BP, Box 31, 1077 (Extract from Old Parochial Registers recording baptism of Robert Ritchie and giving his date of birth as 19 May 1841).

BP, Box 31, 1113(b) (Letter from B. Thompson to A.W. Kinnear, 24 February 1855).

BP, Box 31, unnumbered, 802–866 (Note on Margaret Barclay Allardice by Harriet Maria Barclay, 1917).

BP, Box 31, unnumbered (Printed details of Ury, headed 'The Celebrated Scotch Estate – Ury – For Sale, by Private Contract', May 1848).

BP, Box 33, 1192 (Account from David Walker, Aberdeen, 1–8 April 1854).

# Newspapers and Magazines

*Aberdeen Free Press*, 1903.

*Annals of Sporting*, 1823, 1824, 1826, 1827.

*Aris's Birmingham Gazette*, 1773.

*Bell's Life in London*, 1849.

*Bell's Weekly Messenger*, 1807, 1830.

*The Caledonian Mercury*, 1790, 1793.

*The Craftsman, or Say's Weekly Journal*, 1788.

*The Courier*, 1813, 1815.

*The Edinburgh Advertiser*, 1789, 1801, 1809, 1812, 1813, 1819.

*The Edinburgh Evening Courant*, 1773, 1801, 1804, 1805, 1806, 1809, 1818.

*The English Chronicle*, or *Whitehall Evening Post*, 1801, 1804.

*The Evening Mail*, 1805.

The Examiner, 1809.
The Fancy, 1821, 1823, 1825.
The Gentleman's Magazine, 1809, 1854.
Jackson's Oxford Journal, 1790.
Lincoln, Rutland and Stamford Mercury, 1790
The Liverpool Mercury, 1812, 1816.
The London Chronicle, 1788, 1793, 1809.
The London Packet and Chronicle, 1824, 1825, 1827.
Maidstone Journal, 1817.
The Morning Herald, 1807.
The Morning Post and Daily Advertiser, 1788, 1789, 1792.
The Morning Post, 1793.
The News, 1807, 1813.
The St James's Chronicle, or British Evening Post, 1804, 1808, 1809, 1811, 1812, 1813, 1820.
The Selector, or Say's Sunday Reporter, 1808, 1809.
The Sporting Magazine, 1792, 1793, 1794, 1797, 1798, 1799, 1801, 1803, 1804, 1805, 1806, 1807, 1808, 1809, 1811, 1813, 1818, 1826, 1830.
The Sporting Repository, 1822.
The Sportsman's Magazine, or Chronicle of Games and Pastimes, 1824.
The Star, 1813.
The Sun, 1801, 1804.
The Sunday Reporter, 1809.
The Times, 1802, 1807, 1808, 1809, 1811, 1812, 1824, 1830, 1854.

## Personal Communications

Anderson, Verily, 11 September 1982.
Holme, Norman, 23 May 1985.
Wenham, Leslie P., September 1983.

## Government Publications

The Army List, 1804, 1805.
Return of Members Parliament, Vol. 2, 1357–1874, 1878.
House of Lords Journal, 1834, 1839, 1840, 1841.
Robert Tigger, Inflation: The Value of the Pound, 1750–1998, Research Paper 99/20, London, House of Commons Library, 23 February 1999.

## Books and Journals

Ackroyd, Peter, Dickens, London, Sinclair-Stevenson, 1990
Allen, David Rayvern, Cricket – An Illustrated History, Oxford, Phaidon, 1990
Amar, J., The Human Motor, New York, E.P. Dutton and Co., 1920
Amateur Sportsman, An, Sporting Anecdotes; Original and Select, London, Thomas Hurst, 1804
Anderson, Verily, The Northrepps Grandchildren, London, Hodder & Stoughton, 1968
Anderson, Verily, Friends and Relations, London, Hodder & Stoughton, 1980
Anon, The Jockey Club, or a Sketch of the Manners of the Age, Part 1, London, 1792

Anon, *Genealogical Account of the Barclays of Urie*, London, John Herbert, 1812

Anon, *Memoirs of the Life and Exploits of George Wilson*, London, Dean & Munday, 1815

Apperley, Charles James, *Remarks on the Condition of Hunters*, London, M.A. Pittman, 1837

Apperley, Charles James, *Nimrod's Northern Tour*, London, Walter Spiers, 1838

Apperley, Charles James, *The Life of a Sportsman*, London, John Lehmann, 1842

Arrowsmith, R.L., *A History of County Cricket – Kent*, Newton Abbot, Sportsman's Book Club, 1972

Ashton, John, *The Dawn of the XIXth Century in England*, London, T. Fisher Unwin, 1906

Ashton, John, *Social England under the Regency*, London, Ward and Downey, 1890

Atkins, William Maynard, *The Parish Church of St George, Hanover Square*, London, Dix (Charlmont Press), 1976

Aylward, J.D., *The House of Angelo – A Dynasty of Swordsmen*, London, The Batchworth Press, 1953

Barclay, Captain, *see* Barclay Allardice, Robert

Barclay, J., *Diary of Alexander Jaffray*, London, Harvey and Darton, 1833

Barclay, Leslie George de Rune, *History of the Scottish Barclays*, Folkstone, Bewley, 1915

Barclay, Hubert F., and Wilson-Fox, Alice, *A History of the Barclay Family, Part III*, London, St Catherine's Press, 1934

Barclay Allardice, Robert, *Agricultural Tour in the United States and Canada*, Edinburgh, William Blackwood & Sons, 1842

Baring-Gould, S. *Yorkshire Oddities, Incidents and Strange Events, vol. I*, London, John Hodges, 1877

Batchelor, Denzil, *British Boxing*, London, Collins, 1948

Beaufort, Duke of, *Driving*, London, Longman, Green & Co., 1894

Bertram, James Glass, *Sporting Anecdotes*, London, Hamilton, Adams & Co., 1889

Blythe, Ronald (ed.), *William Hazlitt: Selected Writings*, London, Penguin Classics, 1987

Borrow, George, *Lavengro, the Scholar – the Gypsy – the Priest*, London, Collins, 1851

Borrow, George, *Wild Wales, Its People, Language and Scenery*, London, T. Nelson & Sons, 1862

Brady, J., *Strange Encounters, Tales of Famous Fights and Famous Fighters*, London, Hutchinson, 1946

Brailsford, Dennis, *Bareknuckles – A Social History of Prize-Fighting*, Cambridge, Lutterworth Press, 1988

Bryant, Arthur, *Years of Victory: 1802–1812*, London, Collins, 1975

Burgess, Anthony, *Historical Commentary*, in *Coaching Days of England*, London, Paul Elek, 1966

Burnett, T.A.J., *The Rise and Fall of a Regency Dandy*, London, John Murray, 1981

Campbell, Marjorie Freeman, *A Mountain and a City – The Story of Hamilton*, Toronto, McClelland & Stewart, 1966

Cannon, R., *Historical Record of the 23rd Regiment, or Royal Welch Fusiliers*, Containing an Account of the Formation of the Regiment in 1689 and of Its Subsequent Services to 1850, London, Parker, Furnival and Parker, 1850

Clias, Peter H., *An Elementary Course of Gymnastic Exercises, Intended to Develop and Improve the Powers of Man*, London, Sherwood, Jones, 1823

Cobbett, William, *Cobbett's Annual Register, vol. I, January to June 1802*, London, Cox and Baylis, 1802

Cole, G.D.H., and Postgate, Raymond, *The Common People 1746–1946*, London, Methuen & Co., 1971

Cole, Hubert, *Beau Brummell*, London, Granada Publishing, 1977

Coleridge, Ernest Hartley (ed.), *Letters of Samuel Taylor Coleridge, vol. II*, London, Heinemann, 1895

Cone, Carl B., 'The Molineaux–Cribb Fight, 1810: Wuz Tom Molineaux Robbed?', *Journal of Sport History*, vol. 9, No. 3, 1982, pp. 83–91

Copeland, John, *Roads and Their Traffic, 1750–1850*, Newton Abbot, David & Charles, 1968

Cuming, E.D., (ed.), *Squire Osbaldeston: His Autobiography*, London, John Lane, The Bodley Head, 1927

Daiches, David, *Literary Essays*, Edinburgh, Oliver & Boyd, 1956

Daniel, William B., *Rural Sports*, London, B.&R. Crosby & Co., 1813

Darwin, Bernard, *John Gully and His Times*, London, Cassell & Co., 1935

David, Saul, *Prince of Pleasure – The Prince of Wales and the Making of the Regency*, London, Little, Brown, 1998

Deuchar, Stephen, *Sporting Art in Eighteenth-Century England*, New Haven, Yale University Press, 1988

Dixon, Henry Hall, *Silk and Scarlet*, London, Vinton & Co., 1859

Dixon, Henry Hall, *Field and Fern*, London, Rogerson and Tuxford, 1865

Dixon, Henry Hall, *Saddle and Sirloin*, London, Frederick Warne & Co., 1870

Dowling, Francis, *Fights for the Championship; and Celebrated Prize Battles*, London, Bell's Life in London, 1855

Dowling, Francis, *Fistiana; or The Oracle of the Ring*, London, Bell's Life in London, 1868

Druid, *see* Dixon, Henry Hall

Editor of Bell's Life in London, The, *see* Dowling, Frances

Egan, Pierce, *Boxiana, or Sketches of Ancient and Modern Pugilism*, London, G. Smeeton, 1812

Egan, Pierce, *Boxiana, or Sketches of Modern Pugilism, vol. II*, London, Sherwood, Neely and Jones, 1818

Egan, Pierce, *Sporting Anecdotes, Original and Selected*, London, Sherwood, Jones and Co., 1820

Egan, Pierce, *Boxiana, or Sketches of Modern Pugilism, vol. III*, London, Sherwood, Neely and Jones, 1821

Egan, Pierce, *Sporting Anecdotes, Original and Selected – A New Edition Considerably Enlarged and Improved*, London, Sherwood, Jones and Co., 1825

Egan, Pierce, *Anecdotes, Original and Selected, of the Turf, the Chace, the Ring, and the Stage*, London, Knight and Lacey, 1827

Egan, Pierce, *New Series of Boxiana, Being the Only Original and Complete Lives of the Boxers*, London, George Virtue, 1828

Egan, Pierce, *Pierce Egan's Book of Sports, and Mirror of Life*, London, Thomas Tegg, 1844

Ellangowan, *see* Bertram, James Glass

Elliot, Alexander, *Lochee As It Was and As It Is*, Dundee, J.P. Mathew, 1911

Erickson, Carolly, *Our Tempestuous Day, A History of Regency England*, London, Robson Books, 1986

Fairfax-Blakeborough, J., *Northern Turf History, vol. I; Hambleton & Richmond*, London, J.A. Allen, 1949, and *The Sporting Magazine*, November 1801

Fairfax-Blakeborough, J., *Northern Turf History, vol. III; York and Doncaster Races*, London, J.A. Allen, 1950

Fairfax-Blakeborough, J., *Northern Turf History, vol. IV; History of Horse Racing in Scotland*, Westerdale, published by the author, 1973

Fittes, Robert Scott, *Sports and Pastimes of Scotland*, Paisley, Alexander Gardner, 1891

Fitz-Barnard, Lawrence, *Fighting Sports*, London, Odhams Press, 1921

Ford, John, *Prizefighting – The Age of Regency Boximania*, South Brunswick, Great Albion Books, 1971

Foreman, Amanda, *Georgiana, Duchess of Devonshire*, London, HarperCollins, 2000

Fortescue, W., *A History of the British Army, vol. V, 1803–1807*, and *Vol. VII, 1809–1810*, London, Macmillan, 1910

Galton, Francis, *Memories of My Life*, London, Methuen & Co., 1911

Gardiner, Leslie, *Stage-Coach to John O'Groats*, London, Hollis & Carter, 1961

Garlick, Kenneth, *Sir Thomas Lawrence: A Complete Catalogue of the Oil Paintings*, Oxford, Phaidon, 1989

Garlick, Kenneth, and Macintyre, Angus (eds.), *The Diary of Joseph Farington, vol. V*, Yale, New Haven, Yale University Press, 1979

Gater, George, and Hiorns, F.R., *Survey of London, vol. XX, Trafalgar Square and Neighbourhood (Parish of St Martin-in-the-Fields), Part III*, London, London County Council, 1940

Geering, Thomas, 'Our Parish – Tales and Sketches of Old Sussex', *Sussex County Herald*, 25 October 1919

Goldring, Douglas, *Regency Portrait Painter: The Life of Sir Thomas Lawrence*, London, Macdonald & Co., 1951

Gordon, Alexander, 'The Great Laird of Ury', in *The Theological Review*, October 1874

Guttmann, Allen, *Women's Sport – A History*, New York, Columbia University Press, 1991

Haldane, A.R., *Three Centuries of Scottish Posts*, Edinburgh, The University Press, 1971

Harris, R.W., *Romanticism and the Social Order, 1780–1830*, London, Blandford Press, 1969

Harris, S., *The Coaching Age*, London, Richard Bentley and Son, 1885

Hawker, Peter, *The Diary of Colonel Peter Hawker, 1802–1853, vol. I*, London, Greenhill Books, 1988

Haythornthwaite, Philip, J., *The Armies of Wellington*, London, Brockhampton Press, 1994

Henning, Fred, *Fights for the Championships – The Men and Their Times, vol. I and Vol. II*, London, The Licensed Victuallers' Gazette, 1902

Hibbert, Christopher, *George IV, Regent and King, 1811–1830*, London, Allen Lane, 1973

Highland Society, The, *Prize Essays and Transactions of Scotland, New Series, vol. I*, Edinburgh, William Blackwood, 1829

Holmes, Richard, *Coleridge – Early Visions*, London, Hodder & Stoughton, 1989

Holmes, Richard, *Coleridge – Darker Reflections*, London, HarperCollins, 1998

Hughes, Thomas, *Tom Brown's Schooldays*, London, Blackie and Son, 1857

Hyde, H. Montgomery, *The Strange Death of Lord Castlereagh*, London, Heinemann, 1959

Injured Party, The, *see* Sturt, H.

James, P.D., and Critchley, T.A., *The Maul and the Pear Tree, The Ratcliffe Highway Murders, 1811*, London, Sphere Books, 1971

Johnson, Paul, *The Birth of the Modern – World Society 1815–1830*, London, Weidenfeld & Nicolson, 1991

Knight, William (ed.), *Journals of Dorothy Wordsworth, vol. 1*, London, Macmillan and Co., 1904

Lauder, Thomas Dick, *Highland Rambles, and Long Legends to Shorten the Way, vol. 1*, Edinburgh, Adam and Charles Black, 1837

Lee, H.M., 'Modern Ultra-Long Distance Running and Philippedes' Run from Athens to Sparta', in *Ancient World*, 9, 1984

Leslie, James, 'The Parish of Fordoun', in *The New Statistical Account of Scotland, vol. XI, Forfar and Kincardine*, Edinburgh, William Blackwood and Sons, 1845

Lobel, M.D. (ed.), *The Victoria History of the Counties of England – A History of the County of Oxford, vol. VI, Ploughley Hundred*, Oxford, Oxford University Press, 1959

Locker-Lampson, Frederick, *My Confidences – An Autobiographical Sketch Addressed to My Descendants*, London, Smith, Elder & Co., 1896

Lucian, *A Slip of the Tongue*, 3

Magriel, Paul (ed.), *The Memoirs of the Life of Daniel Mendoza*, London, B.T. Batsford, 1951

Marchand, Leslie A., *Lord Byron: Letters and Journals, vol. 3, 'Alas The Love of Women'*, London, John Murray, 1974

Maret, G., 'Remarks on Training', *Blackwood's Magazine*, vol. IV, No. XXI, December 1818, pp. 313–18

Marshall, John, *The Duke Who Was Cricket*, London, Frederick Muller, 1961

Masson, David, *The Collected Writings of Thomas de Quincey, vol. VIII*, Edinburgh, Adam and Charles Black, 1890

Mayhall, John, *The Annals of York, Leeds, Bradford, Halifax, Doncaster, Barnsley, Wakefield, Dewsbury, Huddersfield, Keighley, and Other Places in the County of York*, Leeds, Joseph Johnson, 1860

McGuffie, T.H. (ed.), *Peninsular Cavalry General (1811–13), The Correspondence of Lieutenant-General Robert Long*, London, George G. Harrap & Co., 1951

Mendoza, Daniel, *Memoirs of the Life of Daniel Mendoza*, London, G. Hayden, 1816

Miles, Henry D., *Pugilistica, A History of British Boxing, vol. 1 and vol. 2*, Edinburgh, John Grant, 1906

Mollyson, Charles A., *The Parish of Fordoun; Chapters in Its History*, Aberdeen, John Rae Smith, 1893

Morehouse, L.E., and Cooper, J.M., *Kinesiology*, St Louis, C.V. Mosby Co., 1950

Mote, Ashley, *The Glory Days of Cricket, The Extraordinary Story of Broadhalfpenny Down*, London, Robson Books, 1997

Murray, Venetia, *High Society in the Regency Period – 1788–1830*, London, Penguin Books, 1998

Napier, James, *Stonehaven and Its Historical Associations*, Stonehaven, J. Taylor, 1870

Nicolas, H., *History of the Earldoms of Strathern, Menteith and Airth*, London, William Pickering, Stevens and Norton, 1842

Nimrod, *see* Apperley, Charles James

Noakes, Aubrey, *The World of Henry Alken*, London, Witherby, 1952

Norrie, William, *Dundee Celebrities of the Nineteenth Century*, Dundee, published by the author, 1873

North, Christopher, *see* Wilson, John

Nyren, John, *The Young Cricketer's Tutor, and The Cricketers of My Time*, London, Effingham Wilson, 1833

Old Boy, An, *see* Hughes, Thomas

One of the Fancy, *see* Egan, Pierce

Peterson, Daniel, *Direct and Principal Roads in England and Wales*, London, Longman and Rees, 1803

Peter, David MacGregor, *The Baronage of Angus and Mearns*, Edinburgh, Oliver & Boyd, 1856

Plutarch, *Fame of the Athenians*, Opera Moralia, 347C

Plutarch, *Life of Aristedes*, 20.5

Prestige, Dennis, *Tom Cribb at Thistleton Gap*, Melton Mowbray, The Brewhouse Press, 1971

Priestley, J.B., *The Prince of Pleasure and His Regency, 1811–20*, London, Sphere Books, 1969

Pryme, George, *Autobiographic Recollections of George Pryme Esq. MA*, London, Deighton, Bell, and Co., 1870

Quennell, Peter, *Byron – Selected Verse and Prose Works*, London, Collins, 1959

Radford, Peter, 'Women's Foot-Races in Britain in the 18th and 19th Centuries: A Popular and Widespread Practice', *Canadian Journal of History of Sport*, vol. XXV, No. 1, May 1994, pp. 50–61

Ransom, John P.G., *The Archaeology of the Transport Revolution 1750–1850*, Tadworth, Surrey, World's Books, 1984

Richardson, J.W., *Memoirs of John Wigham Richardson, 1837–1908*, Glasgow, Hugh Hopkins, 1911

Reid, J.C., *Bucks and Bruisers, Pierce Egan and Regency England*, London, Routledge & Kegan Paul, 1971

Robinson, John Robert, *Old Q; A Memoir of William Douglas, Fourth Duke of Queensberry Kt.*, London, Sampson Low, Marston and Company, 1895

Royde-Smith, Naomi, *The Private life of Mrs Siddons*, London, Gollancz, 1933

Service, Andrew, *The History and Traditions of the Lindsays in Angus and Mearns*, Edinburgh, David Douglas, 1882

St Clair, William, *Lord Elgin and His Marbles*, Oxford, Oxford University Press, 1998

Sheppard, F.H.W. (ed.), *Survey of London, vol. XXVI, The Parish of St Mary, Lambeth, Part II, Southern Area*, London, The Athlone Press, 1956.

Siltzer, Frank, *The Story of British Sporting Prints*, London, Peter Loveday Prints, 1979

Simond, Louis, *An American in Regency England – The Journal of a Tour in 1810–11*, London, Pergamon Press, 1968

Sinclair, James, *History of Shorthorn Cattle*, London, Vinton & Company, 1907

Sinclair, Sir John, *The Code of Health and Longevity, vol. II*, Edinburgh, Arch. Constable & Co., 1807

Southey, Robert, *A Journal of a Tour in Scotland in 1819*, Edinburgh, James Thin, 1972

Sportsman, The (ed.), *British Sports and Sportsmen – Sportsmen of the Past, Part 1*, London, Sport & Sportsmen Ltd., undated

Stephen, Leslie (ed.), *The Dictionary of National Biography, Vol. I*, Oxford, Oxford University Press, 1885

Stevens, John, *Knavesmire – York's Great Racecourse and Its Stories*, London, Pelham Books, 1984

Sturt, H., *Letters From Captain Barclay; Mr Farquarson, General Burnett, and Mr Sturt, With a Statement of Facts Addressed to the Impartial*, Leith, James Burnet, 1814

Sweet, Waldo E., *Sport and Recreation in Ancient Greece*, Oxford, Oxford University Press, 1987

Thom, Walter, *Pedestrianism*, Aberdeen, D. Chalmers and Company, 1813

Thomson, G., 'The Parish of Fetteresso', in *The New Statistical Account of Scotland, vol. XI, Forfar and Kincardine*, Edinburgh, William Blackwood and Sons, 1845

Thomas, George, *Fifty Years of My Life, vol. I*, London, Macmillan and Co., 1876

Tolstoy, Nikolai, *The Half-Mad Lord*, London, Jonathan Cape, 1978

Tomalin, Claire, *Mrs Jordan's Profession*, London, Viking, 1994

Trager, James, *The People's Chronology*, London, Aurum Press, 1992

Turner, J., *Dictionary of Art*, London, Grove, 1996

Underdown, David, *Start of Play, Cricket and Culture in the Eighteenth Century*, London, The Penguin Press, 2000

Urban, Sylvanus, *The Gentleman's Magazine and Historical Chronicle, vol. LXXIX, Part 2*, London, John Nichols and Son, 1809

Venn, J.A., *Alumni Cantabrigiensis, Part II, vol 1*, Cambridge, The University Press, 1940

Warner, Sir Pelham, *Lord's – 1787–1945*, London, George G. Harrap & Co., 1946

Watt, Archibald, *Highways and Byways Around Stonehaven*, Aberdeen, Waverley Press, 1976

Webster, N.W., *The Great North Road*, Bath, Adams and Dart, 1974

Wheeler, C.A. (ed.), *Sportascrapiana, 2nd Edition*, London, Simpkin, Marshall & Co., 1868

Will, William, *The Kincardineshire Volunteers: A History of the Volunteer Movement in Kincardineshire from 1798 to 1816*, Aberdeen, The Aberdeen Weekly Journal Press, 1919

Wilson, George, *A Sketch of the Life of George Wilson, the Blackheath Pedestrian*, London, Hay and Turner, 1815

Wilson, John, *Essays – Critical and Imaginative, vol. I*, Edinburgh, William Blackwood and Sons, 1856

Woodward, E.L., *The Age of Reform, 1815–1870*, Oxford, Oxford University Press, 1954

Ziegler, Philip, *King William IV*, London, Collins, 1971

# Index